D1451942

FRANK SOBEY

Frank Sobey bringing in a load of lambs purchased from local farmers to his father's meat market.

THE MAN AND THE EMPIRE

FRANK SOBEY

Harry Bruce

Macmillan of Canada
A Division of Canada Publishing Corporation
Toronto, Ontario, Canada

Canadian Cataloguing in Publication Data

Bruce, Harry, date.
Frank Sobey

Bibliography: p.
Includes index.
ISBN 0-7715-9835-1 (deluxe ed:).
ISBN 0-7715-9834-3 (regular ed.).

1. Sobey, Frank, 1902- 2. Businessmen — Canada — Biography. 3. Capitalists and financiers — Canada — Biography. 4. Sobeys Supermarkets - History. 5. Empire Limited — History. I. Title.

HF5469.23.C34S62 1984 381'.4'0924 C84-099712-4

Macmillan of Canada
A Division of Canada Publishing Corporation
Toronto, Ontario, Canada

Design by Don Fernley

Edited by Anne Holloway

Printed and bound in Canada

CONTENTS

ACKNOWLEDGEMENTS

I AM GRATEFUL to the *Financial Post* library, Toronto, for granting me access to its files. Without them, I'd never have been able to tell the full story of the Sobeys' extraordinary acquisition of Provigo Inc. stock in 1977-78. When I began the book, Shirley Elliott was still running the Legislative Library, Province House, Halifax, and she helped me (as she had done so often before) by suggesting assorted reading on the history of Pictou County. The scrapbooks and correspondence of Robert Manuge, then of Halifax, amounted to private archives on Industrial Estates Limited during Frank Sobey's term as president there; and Mr. Manuge not only opened these records to me but let me take them home by the boxload. Furber Marshall, custodian of the Maritime Tel & Tel archives in Middleton, N.S., was kind enough to send me photocopies of the New Glasgow, N.S., telephone directories for various years from before the First World War to after the Second World War. A. C. Dunlop of the Public Archives, Nova Scotia, uncovered a file of newspaper clippings on the Sobey family for me, and the archives' microfilms of Pictou County newspapers not only helped me confirm dates but also gave me a flavour of the East River towns in bygone times. Frank Sobey himself, as well as his sons, offered both business records and family documents and photographs.

If I am grateful to these individuals and institutions for the kinds of information one finds only on paper, I am grateful to many more people for kinds that come only from memory. Frank Sobey used a tape recorder to preserve memories about all periods of his life, and sent me transcripts. Moreover, in Halifax, in Pictou County, at his modest riverside retreat in Guysborough County and his condominium in Florida, he endured long interviews even when it seemed to me there were other things he'd rather have been doing. He rarely let me escape without a drink and an excellent meal, and that was as typical of the man as it was of his beloved county.

In Pictou County, I interviewed not only several members of the Sobey family, but also pioneer employees of Sobeys Stores, men and women who'd known Frank for six decades, local politicians, businessmen who'd long admired his smarts and long remembered good times with him at service-club dances, on fishing trips, at weekend parties on the Eastern Shore, on beaches from Chance Harbour, N.S., to the Gulf Coast of Florida. In Halifax, Montreal, and Toronto, I interviewed bankers, brokers, corporation lawyers, and corporation presidents. Once, I found myself bobbing chest-deep in the ocean near West Palm Beach while trading Frank Sobey stories with a Toronto stockbroker and a construction magnate.

Whether I was in a widow's home in Tatamagouche, the St. James's Club in Montreal, or a sumptuous office in the clouds over Toronto, I found that those who'd known Frank wanted to extol him. He had a lot of friends in a lot of places, and this alone suggested he practised what he believed: "If you can't get along with people, you can't do anything." Only a few hedged their admiration with the odd critical observation, and I'm thankful to them, too, for providing perspective. Even fewer, upon hearing I wanted to discuss Frank Sobey, decided they had no time for me. To them, of course, I owe nothing.

The list of those to whom I am indebted follows. It includes none of Frank's relatives because their contribution to my research is obvious in the text. The list reveals no one by title, occupation, or address because, again, such identification is clear in the text.

Nor have I ranked people according to the value of what they told me. Nor have I named the few who've died since I saw them. I simply wanted to acknowledge, here, all those non-Sobeys who freely gave time to my effort to write about Frank Sobey. If there are those I've failed to mention, I hope they'll accept both my apology and my thanks; and I imagine they'll find themselves somewhere in the pages that follow.

The list, in alphabetical order: A. Gordon Archibald, Donald Archibald, Edna Brenan, A. Garnet Brown, Charles F. W. Burns, James M. Cameron, R. B. Cameron, Roy F. Chisholm, Thomas L. Coffin, John N. Cole, Frank M. Covert, Gordon Stewart Cowan, Lois Creighton, Arthur Crockett, H. Larry Doane, George P. Destounis, Mrs. Howard Elliot, H. Garfield Emerson, Jim Ferguson, Alice Flemming, Brian Flemming, J. Gregor Fraser, Richard C. Giles, James W. Gogan, G. Eric Golding, Lance Hale, David R. Hayman, Jean-Claude Hébert, David Hennigar, Charles Higgins, George C. Hitchman, Alan H. Holman, Bill Jamieson, John J. Jodrey, S. W. Kenney, Edward F. King, Walter Klinkhoff, Allen T. Lambert, Bertram Loeb, Robert F. McAlpine, N. Douglas Macdonald, R. B. MacDonald, Alexander J. MacIntosh, Ian M. MacKeigan, Jessie MacKnight, Cecil MacLaren, H. L. P. McNeil, Edward A. Manson, R. W. Manuge, Walter C. Miller, J. William E. Mingo, Helen and Willard Monteith, Robert Munroe, H. R. "Mike" Murphy, Sam T. Paton, C. Arnold Patterson, Ronald H. Perowne, Gerald A. Regan, Harold A. Renouf, Henry B. Rhude, J. William Ritchie, John Roach, Les Sharp, Robert Stanfield, Harry Sutherland, Bob Tibbetts, Frank McLeod Warnock, Donald G. Willmot, Davies Wilson.

Finally, I am grateful to Anne Holloway, editorial director at Macmillan of Canada, for the skilful way she cut certain fatty sections from the manuscript; to Marilyn MacDonald, former editor of *Atlantic Insight*, for tolerating my playing hookey from my duties at the magazine while I worked on the book; and to Harry Flemming of Halifax, a friend for thirty-odd years, who volunteered to read the galleys and corrected a horde of typos and stylistic inconsistencies. My wife Penny accompanied me during interviews with Frank Sobey, dug out research, offered editing advice, typed the entire manuscript, retyped it, typed some of it yet again. My debt to her is measureless.

HARRY BRUCE
January 1985

FRANK SOBEY

PROLOGUE

IT WAS October 19, 1981, and Frank Hoyse Sobey, age seventy-nine, sat under his Krieghoffs in his rangy brick house in Pictou County, Nova Scotia, fiddled with his pipe, watched a National League baseball game on one of his three elderly Clairtone television sets, and made stabs at explaining to a visitor why it was that, without ever having left this unpromising corner of Canada, he was now the patriarch of a family that ran a vast and voracious business empire. He was five-foot-nine, 160 pounds, trim enough to indicate he looked after himself. He'd been bald for forty years. His small blue eyes were shifty, not with evasiveness but with impatience. He could not quite hide his feeling that watching baseball and talking about himself were profitless.

His problem, if you could call it that, was that he wanted to get into his blue Mercedes-Benz with his black Lab, drive six miles up the East River to Stellarton, and, with the Lab, report to the converted warehouse that had been headquarters for his multifarious business concerns for thirty-three years. There, he could once again check up on the family business. There, he could put heat on his three sons, on a couple of grandsons, on a nephew, on assorted senior executives, and indeed on anyone, high or low, he thought required correction.

"He goes into the office in the morning and gets them all steamed up," a Halifax stockbroker said. "Then he goes home for lunch and a nap, and comes back at four to see what they've done. He's a pusher." Local newspaper editor Harry Sutherland, a Sobey-watcher for half a century, said, "You know, Frank could be pretty rough on his boys. I've seen him with Bill [the first of Frank's sons]. It made my hair curl." Monday was the most pressure-ridden day at Sobey headquarters, and friends invited Frank to play golf on so many Mondays that he once asked, only half joking, if his partners weren't part of a plot with the "the boys" to keep him out of their hair. Assessing his father's clout in the family companies, youngest son Donald Sobey said, "He knows all about what each of us is doing, and that means he knows more than any one of us." Montreal businessman Jean-Claude Hébert said, "If Frank Sobey lives to be ninety, he'll know what's going on at every company in which he's got money."

"What sort of man was your father?" the visitor asked during the seventh-inning stretch.

"He was a lovely fellow," Frank said, "a real hard worker. Go ask Bill Jamieson [a pioneer employee in the Sobey grocery-store chain]." So much for the subject of J. W. Sobey, Stellarton meat merchant of the Edwardian age.

Frank could be articulate when denouncing government-fuelled inflation or laying down the principles of sound investment, but getting him to talk entertainingly about his own uncommon life during the sixty-odd years since he'd served his father as a boy butcher was like shucking oysters with a butter knife. He wasn't modest, but he refused to presume that he was interesting. Moreover, answering questions was not his style. Lawyers had often irritated him with useless questions. If you were talking, you weren't learning. He was a notorious brain-picker, and had always preferred to do the asking, not the answering. "If you're vague with your replies," Halifax developer William B. Hardman said, "he'll put you through the grill like there's no tomorrow. If you're emphatic, he'll leave you alone."

Frank was also congenitally restless, and sitting before a TV screen for three hours wasn't easy for him. Still, this was no ordinary ball game. It was the fifth in a tied-up series between the

Montreal Expos and the Los Angeles Dodgers. It was the Expos' last chance of the year to make the World Series, and fans across Canada hung on every pitch. When Stellarton was still a booming coal-mining and railway town, Frank recalled, he'd played street baseball there and cricket, too, but that was an awful long time ago and kids in those days made their own balls by wrapping string around rocks and, if they were lucky, smaller rubber balls. Trouble was, he said, he couldn't learn to throw a curve. Old men had told the visitor that Frank never really gave a damn about sports anyway. At an age when other Stellarton boys rhymed off statistics about Tinkers, Evers, and Chance, he preferred the numbers in the *Financial Post*.

"I don't think I could throw a ball too good today," he confessed. "I'd probably throw my arm out." His tone, however, suggested no one should think it unusual for a seventy-nine-year-old to pitch hardball. After all, he still played golf, and trudged through wilderness to find good fishing.

Empire Company Ltd., at 115 King Street – that's the warehouse beside the railway tracks in Stellarton – is both the major Sobey investment company and the umbrella for myriad Sobey operating companies. In April 1982, six months after the baseball game, Empire issued $3 million worth of non-voting shares at $8 each (in July 1983, incidentally, they were trading at $16). The prospectus revealed what Frank, with help from his sons, had built in a part of Canada that the national business community had largely ignored or, worse, regarded as an investment sinkhole.

Between 1976 and 1982, Empire's assets rose from $28 million to $268 million. This massive increase was due to shrewd investment decisions by Frank and "the boys", and to the fact that Empire, to make its new shares attractive, had acquired voting control of the family's flagship, Sobeys Stores, Ltd. The creation of Frank, more than anyone else, the supermarket chain sold food throughout the Atlantic provinces, along the Gaspé coast, and in Ontario. It had seventy-five supermarkets, eleven "Lofood" stores, and wholesaling subsidiaries in Nova Scotia, New Brunswick,

Newfoundland, and southern Ontario. In 1977, annual sales totalled $237 million. By 1982 they'd more than doubled, and nudged half a billion. This was the business that, seventy-five years earlier, Frank's father had started with a Stellarton butcher shop that peddled meat door-to-door in a horse-drawn, canvas-covered wagon.

In 1982, Empire subsidiaries also owned forty-three drugstores in the Atlantic provinces, and eight movie theatres with seventeen screens. Moreover, Empire and Famous Players Canadian Corporation Ltd. each owned half of Maritime Theatres Ltd., which ran seventeen theatres with thirty-two screens. Frank had owned Stellarton's only theatre during the Depression, put it on its feet financially, abandoned the movie business in 1946, wished he hadn't, plunged back into theatre ownership more than two decades later. "When I found out about his vast interests in other holdings," George Destounis said in 1982, "I was amazed by his enthusiasm for this business. He was enamoured of the industry." A hulking, soft-spoken Canadian of Greek ancestry, Destounis was president of Famous Players Canadian Corporation. To satisfy Frank's sentimental desire to possess his own copy of the musical *Alexander's Ragtime Band* (1938), Destounis pulled strings, wrote letters, haggled with studio lawyers. "It took me six years, maybe more," he said, "but I got it for him." Frank was grateful, but did not own a movie projector.

Empire owned bowling alleys and an insurance company. It held the Avis Rent-A-Car franchise for seven Maritime cities, with a fleet of more than five hundred vehicles. Its subsidiaries owned shopping malls, warehouses, office towers. Empire also owned more than a third of Halifax Developments Ltd. and, along with allies in the powerful Jodrey family of Nova Scotia, controlled it. HDL's chief asset was the seventeen-acre Scotia Square complex, which, in the heart of Halifax, boasted more than a million square feet of office and retail space, 466 apartments, and C. P. Hotels' 312-room Château Halifax. HDL held half of Durham Leaseholds, which owned the following neighbours of Scotia Square: Royal Bank Tower, Bank of Commerce Tower, and Barrington Place,including

Empire Company Limited offices in Stellarton, Nova Scotia.

the posh 203-room Delta Barrington hotel. All in all, Empire companies owned roughly 3.5 million square feet of leasable space and, along with others, a further 1.5 million. The total was equivalent to ninety-two Canadian football fields.

Frank's associates and rivals credit him with always having had an uncanny ability to sniff out potentially valuable land. But not only did he spot it before others, and buy it; he also kept it. Dominion Stores, his fiercest competitor, would buy a mall location, sell it to a developer, and rent back the most choice site for a supermarket. Dominion wanted to concentrate its money and talent on the business it knew best, selling food. Frank wanted everything: the food business, control of the rent his supermarket would pay, the flow of that rent into another Sobey company, rent from other shops, and the financing muscle that arose from ownership of land and buildings. He figured out how to get it all, and that's one reason that in 1982 real estate accounted for almost forty per cent of Empire's assets. The company was a massive landlord.

Money moved directly and ceaselessly into Empire subsidiaries from movie fans, bowlers, car-renters, cigarette-smokers, from those who went to drugstores for everything from penicillin to shampoo, and from hundreds of thousands of people who simply wanted to glom down a hotdog or put food on the table twenty-one times a week. But that was not the whole story of Empire's regular income. Since shopkeepers in Sobey-owned malls paid rent, Empire indirectly reaped money from the sale of books, jewellery, furniture, clothing, video games, stereo sets, and, indeed, the whole extravagant range of goods that attracts millions of people to modern shopping centres. Then, of course, there was the rental individuals paid for apartments and businesses paid for offices.

What was Empire doing with its money? The answer lay in the three convictions that have ruled Frank's business life:

1) To keep any business healthy, even a small farm, you must always put more back into it than you take out of it.
2) The moment a business stops expanding, it starts to stagnate. It cannot flourish while staying still.
3) Whether you're running a business or investing in it, your success depends on the quality of its management.

Empire companies therefore put money into servicing debt, upgrading buildings, replacing equipment, hiring or promoting the right managers, and generally humming along as competitively as they could. Since stagnation was fatal, they also financed relentless programs of acquisition and expansion. "We opened twenty-two [food stores] in 1980 and 1981," said Frank's son David, who'd been president of Sobeys Stores, Ltd., at the time. "It took tremendous effort by management but it enabled our stores to move into the dominant position in Atlantic Canada, and we did it while carrying on an aggressive remodelling program. All this had a negative effect on our earnings at the time, but now [in 1983] it's paying off." In 1980, Sobey-owned drugstores increased from thirty-two to forty-three. In 1981, Atlantic Shopping Centres Ltd., an Empire subsidiary, opened three new shopping malls, bought a fourth, expanded and renovated four more, acquired a seventy-per-cent interest in a ten-storey office building under construction in St. John's, and bought an office building in downtown Halifax. And so it went, pretty well throughout the empire of Empire.

But alongside these operating companies, a separate fruit of their revenue was growing. Empire had 25 per cent of a company that sought the right to distribute natural gas throughout Nova Scotia. It was a partner in an outfit developing oil and gas wells in Alberta, and owned stocks that on January 31, 1981 - four months after the struggle between the Expos and the Dodgers - had a market value of $124 million. Empire's portfolio included banks, utilities, and oil, steel, mine, and manufacturing companies, but the key to the Sobeys' investment strategy lay in the five outfits in which they'd taken major positions. Sobeys Stores, Ltd., owned more than 20 per cent (worth $50,252,055) of Provigo Inc., a Montreal-based giant of the Canadian food industry. Empire held 10 per cent ($19,606,314) of Dominion Textile, the biggest textile-maker in Canada, with factories and salesmen around the world; 17 per cent of the common ($13,000,475) and 27.2 per cent of the convertible preferred ($2,618,850) shares of Wajax, Ltd., suppliers of equipment for the mining, oil, gas, transportation, manufacturing, and construction industries; 8 per cent ($11,847,200) of Jannock Ltd., which, in addition to making electrical components, and steel, brick, and cement products, had an interest in a sugar refinery; and 22 per cent ($4,461,641) of Hannaford Brothers company, a supermarket chain in northern New England.

Frank had first bought shares of Hannaford in 1974, after an article in the U.S. business periodical *Barron's* had touted its growth and management; but by 1981 the Sobeys had quietly corralled so many shares that some of the chain's American owners feared a takeover. The jittery Hannaford crowd launched legal action to restrain the Sobeys, and, to the immense irritation of Frank, this ate up not only Sobey time but also hundreds of thousands of dollars in lawyers' fees. During a grilling by a Hannaford lawyer in a Halifax hotel room, Frank's replies were sometimes cryptic and occasionally revealing. In the latter vein, he said, "It's always our policy to forward our proxies [to management]. We always have. . . . That's right, we've never voted against management in our lives, that I know of." The Sobeys had set up ECL Investments "to hold Hannaford shares so that we saved taxes"; and "ECL votes stock the same as all our companies do, for management."

A Frank Sobey principle of investment: find a company that's run by smart, loyal, hard-working men who know not only what's going on in their industry but also how to get along with people. Invest enough in their firm that you have a right to visit them in their offices. If your confidence in them continues, keep buying shares till the company appoints you a director. Keep right on buying till you have a big enough chunk to help protect the management team – upon whom you've been betting all along – from a takeover by a greedy, insensitive corporate giant. You prove your loyalty to management. Management, by performing well, proves its loyalty to you. Make sure aging managers train the younger guys who must inevitably replace them. Consider yourself in the game for keeps, or until you see an irreversible deterioration in the quality of the bosses. Remember, all industries rest on capital, labour, and management, but the greatest of these is management. If you've got that, you can always get the other two.

Back to the ball game. "Expos fired their manager [Dick Williams] with one month to play in the regular season," Terry Scott of Canadian Press would later report, "and replaced him with a man [Jim Fanning] who hadn't made out a lineup card in over twenty years." Fanning, however, seemed to be doing all right during that cold, spitting October afternoon in Montreal. The Dodgers' ace pitcher, the chubby Fernando Valenzuela, did have the Expo batters stymied; but Montreal's Ray Burris, a 225-pound junk-food addict, a journeyman pitcher who looked like a star that day, was baffling the Dodgers. He had a five-hitter going for him in the eighth inning, and the score was one-all. Fanning pulled him for a pinch-hitter, but the Expos failed to score. Frank was not a knowledgeable baseball fan. A couple of times he asked the visitor, "Was that a double play?" But there was one thing he knew: when a man's performing well, you do not send him to the showers.

The construction of the Sobey empire was neither flashy nor swift. Frank was never in on the discovery of a gold mine, the founding of a Xerox corporation, the drilling of an Imperial Leduc No. 1, or the quick bucks of a Vancouver real estate boom. If he reaped the occasional windfall, he'd either caused it himself or seen it coming in time to get to the tree first. Once he'd decided to do something, he could move like a mongoose attacking a cobra, but before making the move he often sweated for weeks, using his cronies and particularly his wife, Irene, as sounding-boards. While courting her in 1924, when he was twenty-two, he already knew he wanted to turn his father's grocery shop into a chain and, with that base, build a business dynasty for Sobeys for generations to come. He proceeded to do it the only way he could in the torpid economy of the Maritimes, the way beavers built dams, Egyptians built the pyramids, and his forebears carved out farms in the county he chose never to leave. He built his business one step at a time, decade after decade; and, like those same forebears, he recruited his boys into the enterprise just as soon as they were old enough to knock the sprouts off potatoes.

Every businessman is a gambler. Entrepreneurs acknowledge this when they argue that they deserve rewards for taking risks. Frank, however, resented any suggestion he'd ever gambled on anything. "I always felt I couldn't afford to lose money," he said, "and I couldn't afford to take money from my friends. They couldn't afford to lose it, either." Gamblers blew money at racetracks and Las Vegas, or on tips from brokers and "insiders" who didn't know the management of the company they were touting. "I never bought a lottery ticket in my life," he told the visitor. When he bought a business, he *knew* he could make it work. When he opened a new supermarket, he *knew* that if it ran into trouble he was smart enough, and willing enough to work his butt off, to get it straightened out. When he invested heavily in a certain stock, he *knew* its management would guarantee its long-term future, but "I never bought a stock with the idea that I was going to sell it tomorrow and make a profit." He was not a gambler, he insisted, he was an investor who took "calculated risks".

That, of course, is how gamblers talk, about calculated risks. The real difference between them and Frank lay in motives. To him, it was boring to get money simply for its own sake. "Hell, I always knew I could go out and make a buck," he said, as though making a buck was so easy anyone could do it. Business wreckages in his own beloved county suggested otherwise, but in any event "I learned that money did not make me very happy. A good, healthy business did." He had sold his theatres in New Glasgow and Stellarton thirty-five years before, "and I got a cheque for $75,000, and there wasn't much pleasure in looking at that. The pleasure was always in developing and strengthening a *business*, and creating jobs, and getting good people around you to help." Indeed, the pleasure of building businesses had inspired him to work for a dozen years, while Robert Stanfield was premier, as the unpaid president of Nova Scotia's high-flying, high-profile Industrial Estates Limited; and he'd once calculated that the time he devoted to this Crown corporation, rather than to his own affairs, "cost me at least a million."

"Frank Sobey never went crazy," George C. Hitchman said. "It was all steady, steady growth. A store here, a supermarket there, a mall here." A cordial, heavy-set man with gentle eyes, Hitchman exuded the authority one expected from a former deputy chairman of the Bank of Nova Scotia. "Frank has a very good native ability in investments," Hitchman continued, "but he never tried to go out and buy the world. I never saw him ask for too much [while borrowing]. He wouldn't go over the hill, as it were. And he never came to the bank asking only to be taken off the hot seat. Practically everyone else has been in the hot seat recently." But not the Sobeys. "In the last two months in particular," Hitchman said in February 1982, "a lot of others have gone to the bottom." But not the Sobeys. Some companies had borrowed too heavily, to invest too heavily, and when the recession and killer interest rates struck they collapsed like card houses. But not Empire. "I have never seen Frank Sobey get caught by changes in history," Hitchman concluded.

Frank feared a change in September 1981. During his interrogation by a U.S. lawyer about Sobey designs on Hannaford Brothers, he said, "I've been after the boys to liquidate some stuff. We've got good stocks, but you know the old saying in Wall Street: when the paddywagon comes around, the good girls are picked up with the bad. That's a common saying, you know. The good stocks go down with the bad, that's right. Never hear that?" Within a few months, the Sobeys would do some dramatic liquidating.

Halifax rumours suggested in March 1982 that the Bank of Nova Scotia had forced them to sell almost $16 million worth of Provigo holdings in order to pay bank loans. The rumours were wrong. Sobeys Stores had indeed sold $15,888,697 worth of Provigo to Caisse de Dépôt et Placement du Québec, and thereby reaped an $8,247,678 capital gain, but not because anyone forced it to do so. "You just have to look at the mathematics," Donald Sobey explained. "Provigo was paying dividends of forty cents a share, and with four million shares [the Sobeys' total holdings before the sale] you therefore got $1.6 million. At $11 a share the stock was worth $44 million, and if you put $44 million in the bank, at seventeen per cent, you'd collect nearly $7.5 million in interest." Interest rates were so high in March 1982 that it made no sense *not* to sell some Provigo; and Caisse de Dépôt, with its enormous resources, was an obvious potential buyer.

There was another good reason for the sale. Sobeys Stores, Ltd., Donald continued, "were going through a tough time. They'd suffered a slight loss, and a very serious strike in their distribution system had hurt them. It was a time to be a bit more liquid, so we took an $8 million capital gain." Sobeys Stores, Ltd., were the main cash-generating engine for all of Empire's enterprises, and a short explanation of why the Sobeys suddenly reduced their Provigo holdings from 20.6 to 13 per cent is that they wanted to reduce debt, make the chain more liquid, and generally look after the shop. "There's always something you can do if your business is healthy," Donald said, sounding like his father.

"We never like to owe the banks too much money," Frank said.

"Heavy borrowing is fine in good times," Halifax business journalist Lyndon Watkins explained, "but look at outfits like Dome Petroleum. They borrowed and borrowed, and bought and bought. They did it for political reasons that had nothing to do with business logic. Now they're in huge debt. They're in terrible trouble. . . . A lot of what was going wrong with the economy wouldn't be seen in Ontario. Accountants run everything up there by sitting in glass towers and looking at numbers. But the Sobeys run a business that keeps them down among the people where they can see what's happening and, as Maritimers, they know it's possible to go broke and go hungry. They stay in Stellarton. Their offices are unpretentious. Their assets are *real* assets, not overblown paper ones. They use common sense.

"They were smart enough to foresee that the economy was going to pot, and they were specially vulnerable to high interest rates. A lot of their loans were on real estate leased to other businesses. They couldn't increase their rents too much and, if the shops weren't getting much trade, they wouldn't get their usual cut on the gross.

"You could say they ate humble pie by not pretending the declining economy wasn't going to hurt them," Watkins continued, "but paying off bank loans was a very sensible thing to do. They recognize that, in the long term, you always have to pay your debts, and they've shown that conservatism is a very good business policy. I think it all comes from that native Presbyterian Scottish canniness of theirs."

Frank's canniness was evident in prescient advice he gave to his sons on September 11, 1975. He told them to avoid "any long-term pay-out projects, like real estate, without permanent long-term financing arranged and committed." Moreover, he said, "I do not consider trust company money, where they can change the rates in five years, as being in the long-term category. This also applies to term bank loans." He knew in his gut that interest rates would soon zoom.

"The government has continually reduced its reserves to the point where, in order to make money available, it'll be pretty hard to reduce them any further," he wrote in a memo to senior executives.

"There is also a strong push on to force money into the housing market. Canada is running an all-time-high deficit in our trade balance, in interest payments on foreign debt, and in government deficits, both federal and provincial. To finance these deficits, the Bank of Canada has increased its lending rate by ¾ of a point, an abnormal increase that shows an urgency to attract U.S. dollars. These are short-term dollars. What will happen in the next round, if American rates increase?"

He had the answer: "*Canada will have to shove rates up abnormally high to keep on attracting this short-term money. The signs all point to higher rates* . . . and to tighter credit conditions at the banks." To the dismay of the entire country, events would soon prove that the Stellarton grade-school drop-out, then seventy-three, was no slouch at economic forecasting. Since "we are being urged in Canada to increase our costs and price ourselves out of world markets," he concluded, "we will have to borrow more money to cover deficit spending. When rates are forced so high we cannot pay them, we will have to reduce our standard of living and our cost of product to get back in the ball game."

Jim Fanning fingered Steve Rogers to replace Ray Burris in the ninth inning. "Rogers is our best and I wanted to go with him," he later explained. "I have absolutely no second guesses about any phase of the game today." Rogers was indeed one of the finest pitchers in baseball, but he was not a relief pitcher. He was a starter, and it usually took him an inning or two to hit his stride. Not since July 1978 had any manager asked him to pitch in relief. Moreover, he'd pitched nine innings against the Dodgers only a couple of nights before. With two out in the ninth, seasoned pro Rick Monday came to bat for the Dodgers. The count went to three balls and one strike, and then Rogers fired an inside fastball. Monday snapped it over the fence in right centrefield, and Canada's darlings kissed goodbye to the World Series.

Frank Sobey turned to the visitor. "You know what lost that game?" he asked. "Bad management, that's what. Just bad management."

1

A PICTOU COUNTY BOY

THE GRANDMOTHER told the boy that the family had ancient connections with the royal family of Poland. If she said it was so, surely it was so. For she was a pioneer Nova Scotia Scot, a Christian of such purity that when she died in 1920 (the boy would be eighteen by then) the *Pictou Advocate* eulogized, "Although a great sufferer, she bore her suffering with a Christian fortitude that was beautiful, and living evidence of her trust in Him who doeth all things well."

But it wasn't her own Scottish forebears the grandmother was discussing. It was her husband's people, the boy's grandfather's people, the people from whom he took his odd name: Sobey. She herself was born Janet MacIntosh. Still, she would not tell him Sobeys had once been connected with Polish royalty if she did not believe it, and surely he had reason to believe her. She had more than six decades on him. She had gone to school in this very county when the textbook was the Bible and the writing paper was birch-bark.

She had crossed the seas, and come home again. In England, Bermuda, and here in the tannery town of Lyons Brook, N.S., she had done her bit for the Empire by bearing no fewer than ten children. She was forty-six when she bore the last of them. His name was Frank and, like most of his brothers and sisters, he joined the westward drift that drained Pictou County of people. When he died near Brandon, Manitoba, in 1901, he was only eighteen.

"I guess Grandmother took a special interest in me," the boy recalled a long time later, "because except for Father and my Uncle Charlie and Aunt Mary, all the rest of her children had moved away. I was named after her youngest son, Frank, the one who died in the West."

So the grandmother told stories to the new Frank Sobey:

Once upon a time, a man named Sobieski was King of Poland. But during a revolution in Poland certain Sobieskis fell out of favour, crossed the English Channel, and secretly came ashore on the intricate coast of southwestern England. There they put down roots and became "Sobeys". William Sobey, husband of Janet MacIntosh, descended from these same outcasts, and therefore so did their grandson, the boy Frank.

Was there any truth in this romantic, word-of-mouth genealogy? It's doubtful. But William Sobey *was* born at Crediton, a market town in Devonshire, in southwestern England; and church records from Cornwall, the adjacent county in the west, prove Sobeys were in the neighbourhood at least as early as the 1720s. Moreover, John III, a famous Polish king, was indeed a Sobieski. He ruled from 1674 to 1696, and died miserable. But none of his three known sons ended up either on the Polish throne or, alas, in southwestern England. If those English Sobeys shared John III's blood, their connection to his ancient family either pre-dated his reign or arose from a bastard line that never made the history books.

Janet MacIntosh Sobey doubtless treasured the Sobieski legend in her husband's family because, by way of Highland history, it linked her own heritage to his. A quarter-century after John III died, his beautiful granddaughter, Princess Clementina Sobieski, married James Francis Edward Stuart, The Old Pretender to the throne of Great Britain. Clementina preferred life in a convent to life with The Old Pretender, but their marriage did spawn The Young Pretender: Bonnie Prince Charlie, the half-Polish darling of the Jacobite movement. It would be a MacIntosh – indeed, a *Lady* Mackintosh – who, on one notable occasion during the doomed Jacobite rising of the 1740s, rallied clansmen to fight for Prince Charlie.

Then came Culloden. On April 16, 1746, William, Duke of Cumberland, son of King George II, unleashed overwhelmingly superior firepower on the prince's Highland warriors, and wiped them away. Gore followed gore. The crushing of the clan system, crop failures, a local population surge, cruelty to Catholics, the expulsion of unprofitable tenants in favour of profitable sheep, misery at home, and enticements abroad inspired hordes of Scots to sail away forever. "Then up amang the lakes and seas," Robert Burns wrote, "they'll mak what rules an' laws they please." They did. But they also remembered Charlie so well that the spirit of the Jacobite Cause became a racial inheritance. Like him, they were exiles. They remembered the villain, too. In 1912, when Frank Sobey was nine and Janet MacIntosh Sobey was seventy-four, Pictou County politician Adam Bell complained in the Senate about a cattle-killing weed. Bell called it "Stinking Willie", after William, Duke of Cumberland, "the butcher of Culloden". The weed was so obnoxious the government put a bounty on it. "I helped pull it out in the fields," Frank recalled. "You'd make bundles out of it with binder twine, and then they'd burn it. You got a dime a bundle. A man could do about ten bundles a day, and in those days that was a decent wage."

The Scottish emigrants remembered faces on the shore, the hills of home. Their heartbreak inspired a plaintive branch of literature, a poetry of homesickness that so mourned a lost land of gloom that it struck those from sunnier cultures as perverse, like the love of haggis. Janet MacIntosh, born in 1837 at West Branch River John, Pictou County, was a child of an exiled people. The boy would grow up with memories of his grandfather's house and his grandmother's stories, but he would never suffer homesickness. He stayed in Pictou County, and became its king of business.

When Janet MacIntosh was born, Scots had been arriving in eastern Nova Scotia for more than half a century. Tens of thousands had disembarked at Pictou Harbour, and as early as 1817 a county census showed twenty-eight heads of families named McIntosh. Names of the census-takers revealed almost as much about Pictou

Frank Sobey's grandfather, Staff Sergeant William Sobey, in the uniform of the Royal Engineers, circa 1865.

County as the census itself did: Peter Grant, Robert Lowden, and Alex, John, Duncan, and Angus McDonald. In 1805 (the year Nelson died at Trafalgar) certain McKenzies and other Highland Scots settled at West Branch River John. McDonalds, McKays, Marshalls, Murrays, and more McKenzies soon followed. They built a schoolhouse in 1825, and in 1837, when Janet was born, a kirk.

She was a Nova Scotia Scot who, in the time of the U.S. Civil War, emerged from the backwoods to entrance a mature English soldier. She was raised a Presbyterian. William Sobey, a sapper with the Royal Engineers, was an Anglican. While she was a farmer's daughter from a raw land of ice, rum, moose, bear, caribou, coal, clashing clergy, and bloody election riots, he was a silversmith's son from a garden place of thatched cottages, deep lanes, tall hedges, arching boughs, sweet cider, clotted cream, and country vicars.

A carpenter, he'd joined up in 1855, and was soon shipped to Halifax for seven years. He was short, erect, blue-eyed. His hair was a thick and wavy light-brown, and, in a photograph taken after he became a sergeant, he sported a full mustache. In dress uniform, he wore a scarlet tunic with dark-blue collar and cuffs. The piping, the band on his cap, the knots on his sleeves were yellow. He boasted a badge for musketry proficiency, and even as a mere sapper (private), he doubtless cut a bright figure in grey mist. One legend in the Sobey family was that when Janet MacIntosh first saw him on the streets of Halifax, she announced, "That's the man I'm going to marry."

What he saw in her may have been exactly what a New Brunswick newspaper correspondent saw in the farm girls of Pictou County in 1863: "I heard Rev. Mr. Pollock preach at West River to the plainest, neatest congregation ever I saw. No crinoline rising over the top of the pew doors when ladies were entering. If any New Brunswick boy wants a wife, not ashamed to work, let him go to West River, and there he will find the red-cheeked Scotch lassie. The piano they play at this time of year is the hay rake, which goes far to make them so healthy and hearty."

But what was the red-cheeked Janet MacIntosh doing in Halifax? "She and her sister went to Halifax for a while," Frank said. "I think she took a job down there." It's tempting to assume that as early as 1860 she was among the throng that welcomed the Prince of Wales to the garrison port. No member of the royal family had ever before made a state visit to North America, and Halifax greeted the Prince with insane joy. N. R. Woods, an Englishman, wrote that everyone's mind was concentrated "on one darling purpose, that of giving the Prince a grand and hearty welcome. . . . The great street was soon entered – one long vista of flags, arches, flowers, and wreaths, with the roadway densely crowded, and all the windows, roofs and balconies thronged with hundreds of ladies waving handkerchiefs and throwing down bouquets till the whole place seemed fluttering in the wind. . . . The people seemed actually as if they were taking leave of their senses."

The Royal Engineers paraded for the Prince, and Sobey was

probably among them, crisp in the garb of the thin, red line. And Janet MacIntosh? No one knows, but nothing in her upbringing would have discouraged loyalty to Crown and Empire. Nova Scotia Scots were not merely loyal, they were loyal as a matter of racial inheritance. Loyalty had been the glue of the clan system and, though that died, the habit of mind endured. "The loyalty formerly given to the chiefs," D. Campbell and R. A. MacLean asserted in *Beyond the Atlantic Road* (1974), "was transferred elsewhere, to military units, to business houses, to ships, to universities, to the church, the monarchy and political parties." So far as loyalty to Queen Victoria went, Pictou County Scots were like most English-speaking people in British North America. They were, as N. R. Woods put it, "as sterlingly English as any yeoman from Land's End to John o'Groats."

Janet MacIntosh was twenty-five and William Sobey twenty-nine when they married on Sunday, September 21, 1862, ten weeks after Britain had approved the idea of union among the British colonies of North America. The church they chose was St. Matthew's, a major ornament of New World Presbyterianism, not in Pictou County but in Halifax. The pastor was the Reverend John Scott, who, according to the Reverend Alexander Maclean in the *Pictou Advocate* (1911), was a "worthy specimen of the Christian scholar and gentleman". In Scott's church, we may be sure, the Sobeys were well and truly wed. St. Matthew's had (and still has) a high pulpit, box pews, and a towering spire, which the couple could see from out on the masted harbour the very next day, when they were already outward bound for the mother country. Fourteen years and six children later they'd be back to stay.

Dover Castle stood 375 feet above sea level and glowered at France. "Grandmother told me a lot of stories about Dover and her experiences there," Frank recalled. "She talked about Kent, where the great hop-fields were. She said the hops grew higher than your head. They lived in barracks in Dover Castle and some of the houses were cut out of the chalk cliffs." Dover was "the Key to England". It was "like the Straits of Gibraltar, the Isthmus of

Suez, Hong Kong or Manhattan, through which mankind has funnelled ideas, memories and aspirations from one civilisation to another," Jan Morris wrote. "What the English knew of Europe, they mostly knew through the medium of this port, and by the instruments of their trade, language and empire, they distributed it across half the world." Dover's attitude toward Europe once expressed itself in a newspaper headline: "THICK FOG OVER CHANNEL: CONTINENT ISOLATED." It was no mean thing to have served the Empire at Dover Castle.

In 1869, however, the army moved Sobey - a corporal by now, and the father of two - to Camp Aldershot in Hampshire. Aldershot would become England's biggest army training centre, with forty thousand troops there at once, but when the Sobeys arrived it was a few wooden huts on a fir-dotted heath. It was here that John William Sobey, father of Frank, was born in 1869. Charles Sobey followed in 1871, and, shortly after that, the growing Sobey brood sailed back across the Atlantic to Bermuda. This posting was William Sobey's last with the British Army, and for him and his family the voyage was very nearly the last adventure of their lives.

"I remember her talking about it," Frank said. "They were blown almost up to Greenland, and they lost their rudder. The men tried to steer the ship with a log. The women and children were battened down on a lower deck for a week, and she told me no one down there knew whether the men were washed overboard or not. There were children and sick women, and the stench was terrible. It took them six weeks to get from Liverpool to Halifax, and the British Admiralty reported the ship lost." From Halifax, Sergeant Sobey - he had his final promotion by then - Mrs. Sobey, and the four little Sobeys sailed for Bermuda, which lay nearly nine hundred miles south in the ocean that had come so close to killing them.

American tourists had already discovered the balmy delights and eternal greenery of Bermuda. After Aldershot, it may have struck the Sobeys as paradise. Janet gave birth to Sara there in 1873, and to Mary in 1875. Now Sergeant Sobey had six children, the oldest of whom, Margaret, was eleven. Half his life was gone, and he made his most important decision since his marriage. He quit soldiering for farming, and in 1876, when he turned forty-three, the Sobeys boarded a seagoing vessel for the last time. Inbound in Halifax harbour, William and Janet would see St. Matthew's spire once again. Though the wanderings of their children had just begun, they themselves were on their way home for good. To her home, Pictou County. Nine decades later, their grandson Frank bought a house in Bermuda. He called it "Nova Haven".

Sergeant William Sobey of the Royal Engineers served for twenty-one years and fifty-nine days, and in all that time his name never once appeared in the Regimental Defaulters' Book. He earned four good-conduct badges, and his discharge papers said, "it appears that his conduct has been very good." The papers also revealed that, although he never saw action, he had "lost top joint of second finger of Right hand." By the time he got his discharge, on Boxing Day, 1876, he had already not only found his farm but paid twelve hundred dollars for it. He had bought it in August from some McKenzies in Truro, N.S.

The property, 120 acres in all and surrounded by McKenzies and McDonalds, was at Lyons Brook, fifteen miles from Janet's birthplace. It looked south across the widening of West River as it flowed toward Pictou Harbour and the sea. The neighbourhood suffered no shortage of farm expertise. Indeed, it had been at West River in 1817 that Scottish farmers had formed the first agricultural society in Nova Scotia. Their motto went like this: "Let this be held the farmers' creed. For stock, seek out the finest breed. In peace and plenty, let them feed. Your land sow with the best of seed. Let it not dung nor dressing want. And then provisions won't be scant."

"When they built the place it was all woods just back of the barn," Frank said. "They cleared it out for a full mile." With the help of Janet's brother George, a miserly bachelor, William Sobey built a house. It sat on a slope overlooking the sparkling harbour,

Frank Sobey's birthplace, his grandfather's farm at Lyons Brook.

and boasted both enough gingerbread to prove its owner's pride and enough hedges to remind him of Devon.

Lyons Brook had one county bigshot, John Logan. His tannery employed thirty-five men in the 1880s, turned out 275 tanned hides a day, survived financial collapse and fires, and gave up the ghost in 1921. Then there was the railway. While the Sobeys were clearing their land, the Great American and European Short Line Railway laid track for a route that Pictou County sensibly abbreviated to "The Short Line". It linked the Stellarton-New Glasgow area with Oxford Junction, and included a spur to Pugwash. Using the fashionable hyperbole of the day, a newspaper called it "the greatest work and the most important for the province", and also classified the construction equipment and crew at a sod-turning ceremony: "twenty-four axemen, twelve carts, forty pickmen, one hundred and seventy shovellers, thirty double wagons, and twenty-five scrapers". As the tracks approached Lyons Brook, the Sobeys took in railway workmen as boarders and, since they also had nine children by the early 1880s, they had their hands full.

The children were like those of countless other Maritime parents: they grew up on a farm, looked around, succumbed to the pull of the far West. In the last decades of the nineteenth century and in the early twentieth century, Maritimers went west by the carload, sometimes earning themselves an unpleasant reputation, as recalled by one Pictou County woman who made the long trip:

> Carloads in other years had done desperate things, like tying a cow to the train . . . and at some Ontario stops the excursioners would descend from the cars and loot the shops. I don't know that the Maritimers were always responsible, but they were certainly always *blamed*, and the villagers along the line dreaded the arrival of the Harvest Excursion trains. . . . At a stop in Northern Ontario where a store had been looted in previous excursions, someone knocked on our windows and warned us about the angry townspeople. "Don't get out! They've got guns and they're ready to shoot." So we stayed where we were.

Out they went, all of Frank's uncles and aunts on the Sobey side. Margaret and James died in Seattle, Frederick in San Francisco, Henry in Edmonton, Charles, Sara, and Mary in British Columbia. The youngest, the one after whom Frank was named, went west on a Harvest Excursion, fell ill, and died in the blue hills of Brandon at the farm of a Pictou County couple. They were Charles and Anna Stewart, and Anna was a sister of the woman who would shortly give birth to the later Frank Sobey. The few Sobeys who stayed behind became a tightly knit, independent bunch. They looked after one another.

William Sobey was a careful farmer. Right after using equipment, he cleaned it, oiled it, sharpened it, put it indoors. To this day, Frank hates to see even a hand rake lying in the grass. William's only weakness, apparently, was a fear of horses; he let his boys look after them. When the old soldier died in 1910, the *Pictou Advocate* said Lyons Brook had lost "a good citizen". Throughout his life, "the soldierly bearing and promptitude of his early calling was characteristic of him. In his later years, he took the avocation of farming, which he carried on successfully."

The last of his sons to go west was Charles, a stonemason and notable marksman. Charles was forty-two when he left in 1913 and, before going, he sold the family farm at Lyons Brook and auctioned off just about everything on it. Today all that's left of the outbuildings is stone foundations, drowning in foliage. The big white house is deserted and shabby. It has five roomy bedrooms and ten windows upstairs, thirteen windows and four outside doors on the ground floor, and along the front, three narrow porches, all facing the water. The windows are tall, with low sills. The sunny room downstairs in the southwest corner has a fireplace and an ornate pattern on the ceiling, a framed necklace of green leaves, pink and gold flowers, heavenly curlicues, and a single robin. The bird is leaving the nest and westward bound. The terraces on the lawn that was once William Sobey's manicured pride are a clotted mass of weeds, and the property appears to have been deteriorating ever since he died and then Charlie went west. Negligence and overgrowth are swallowing it whole. It was here that Frank Sobey was born, and spent such perfect summers that he'd remember them all his life.

John William Sobey, the English-born second son of the old soldier, was seven when the Sobeys quit military life in Bermuda for farming life at Lyons Brook. He would stay in Pictou County, learn carpentry from his father, help build the family farm, remain single till he was thirty-two. When he did marry, he brought his bride to live at the house his father had constructed and he himself had never left. She was Eliza Bessie Creighton, a Nova Scotia Scot and solid Presbyterian. Her father, Daniel Creighton, had been the tinsmith at Durham, a few miles upriver from the Sobey homestead; and just to assure the Scottishness of her blood her mother was a MacLellan.

Eliza was the youngest of four children, all girls. When she was a 24-year-old schoolteacher, earning two hundred dollars a year, an inspector wrote, "Her work has been uniformly satisfactory. . . . I consider her a capable, pains-taking and faithful teacher and have no hesitation in recommending her as such." When she agreed

John William and Eliza Sobey, circa 1945.

to marry J. W. Sobey, she was twenty-nine, a tall, angular, self-willed woman with reddish-brown hair. The wedding was at the home of a sister in Sydney, N.S., and John William's brother Charles was a witness. The couple's life together began at the dawn of the century: they married on New Year's Day in the morning, 1901.

Sydney was as good a place as any to get married and greet a century. Speechifiers marvelled over the miracles foreign capital was already achieving for its coal and steel industries; predicted the coal beds would provide three million tons a year for a thousand years; bragged that, in only eighteen months, Sydney's population had boomed from three thousand to ten thousand; gloated that when the great German steel syndicates pondered the potential rivalry of Sydney they "trembled with misgivings". The year 1901 was a dramatic launching for a turbulent century. Wall Street panicked. The Boer War raged. Vice-President Theodore Roosevelt urged the United States to "Speak softly and carry a big stick." An anarchist assassinated President William McKinley with a small pistol. Guglielmo Marconi, flying a kite antenna from Signal Hill, St. John's, Nfld., received the first transatlantic wireless message. Prime Minister Wilfrid Laurier said, "Let us keep in our heart this thought: Canada first, Canada for ever, nothing but Canada." King C. Gillette set up a factory above a Boston fish store to make safety razors, the Sylvania Electric Company started to make light bulbs, and three weeks after the Sobey wedding Queen Victoria died.

By the fall of 1901 the Sobeys of Lyons Brook knew that, for the first time in nineteen years, there'd be a newborn babe in their house. Eliza gave birth to Frank Hoyse Sobey at the farm on the late queen's birthday, May 24, 1902. Frank spent his first three years on the farm with his grandfather and his grandmother, whose stern faith did not prevent her doting on him, with his loving parents, who were both in their thirties, with his Aunt Mary Sobey and Uncle Charlie Sobey, who had not yet gone west, and with whatever other Sobeys and Creightons cared to drop round. He was not a neglected infant.

Scottish attitudes toward God, business, neighbours, and land flowed at Frank Sobey not only from the women in his life - grandmothers, mother, maternal aunts, and, later, wife and in-laws - but also from all the hills, river valleys, and towns of Pictou County. As the tourist booklet *Nova Scotia for Beauty and Business* (1923) said, it was "The Home of the Scotch Race in Canada". Most of his school chums, teachers, and preachers were of Scottish descent. So were hundreds of Stellarton coal miners and railway workers, whose appetite for meat was crucial to his father's butcher shop. Local farmers were almost exclusively Nova Scotia Scots, and as a teen-aged drop-out from school Frank bought animals from these grizzled, hard-bargaining, bluenose Highlanders.

"I learned more about sound business practices from Pictou County farmers then I could have learned any other place," he said in his old age. "I learned you had to know all the costs that went into a product, and then price it a little higher so you'd have seed for next year, and the year after. You had to buy feed and fertilizer, and you had to know the right time to sell animals. Those fellows were shrewd, sharp. They *had* to be, just to stay in business. They were as smart as any people I ever did business with."

The county shaped Frank Sobey and the county was New World Scottish. It was the most Presbyterian corner of Canada. In Pictou County, Presbyterians outnumbered all others two to one. "The [pioneer] community was mostly Presbyterian of the most rigid and uncompromising form," the Reverend Alexander Maclean told readers of the *Pictou Advocate* in 1912. "Any departure from Presbyterian tenets was heresy, a deadly error, and the man suspected of a leaning in that direction lost caste, and was looked upon as lost, in the most serious and extreme sense of the word. . . . For every pin in the Tabernacle and for every syllable in the Shorter Catechism and Confession of Faith, they were firm as the rock and in its defence would, like their fathers, sacrifice their lives."

The old religion *was* sturdy, and, like his neighbours, Frank's father, J. W. Sobey, was deeply religious. A hefty, amiable, quiet butcher, he had a fresh-faced, innocent look about him, and rarely raised his voice. "I worked for him for eight years," Billy Jamieson said, "and in all that time the only thing he ever said to me was, 'Billy, I wish you'd try to get in here a little earlier in the morning.' " Jamieson, who worked for J.W. alongside Frank more than sixty years ago, also recalled, "He wasted no money on over-paying his staff." Still, Jamieson remembered him as "a lovely man, a mild man, a fine, fine man".

J.W. never cursed and, like his father, never drank ale, wine, or liquor. He was not pious about his teetotalling. Indeed, when J.W. joined friends on trips to see the Stellarton Albions play baseball against, say, the Springhill Fencebusters, the others entrusted their liquor to him because, as an old ball fan recalled, "J.W. was the only one you could trust." If you couldn't trust an elder of Sharon St. John Church, whom could you trust?

"Father went to church twice every Sunday and also to prayer meetings on Wednesday night," Frank said. "I sometimes went to the prayer meetings with him, and I went to Sunday school, too. We had a good Sunday-school paper and, when I got home, Father would always read me the stories from the paper. He was quite a temperance man, and he took me to temperance meetings. There'd be someone preaching about the evils of drink, and they'd always sing 'Onward Christian Soldiers'."

Eliza Creighton Sobey possessed a faith that was not as deep as her husband's, but her belief in the church as an institution was unshakeable. She went to church because all decent people went to church, and she hurled herself into the good works of its Afternoon Auxiliary. Moreover, although J.W. was community-minded, Eliza was a community leader. In 1931, she became the first president of Stellarton's Local Council of Women, and she later earned a life membership in the National Council of Women.

The Creighton side of the family, younger Sobeys averred, included "some real characters", all of them Presbyterian women. Eliza "was an iron-willed woman," said her grandson, Bill Sinclair. "She told me that J.W. once injured his hand so badly with a saw that the doctors discussed amputating a couple of his fingers. She said no. She put her foot down. She made a poultice for him out of a patent medicine called Zam-Buk. The wound healed, and you should have heard her denounce those 'darn doctors'. Yes, she had a will of iron."

In Pictou County God was stern and Sundays were as grim as the winter mists that swirled above the Northumberland Strait. "We were never allowed to shine our shoes on Sunday morning," Frank said. "We had to do it on Saturday night so we'd be ready for Sunday school and church. I couldn't read anything on Sunday, except Bible books, but sometimes I'd sneak up to my room to read." And music? "On Sunday, it was all hymns." When he grew up, he had Sunday rules of his own. Rather than drive to church, he insisted the family walk. His sons envied Catholic kids because the Catholics were allowed to use their toboggans on Sunday afternoon. Little Bill Sobey sometimes fought Sunday boredom in the thirties by crossing the railway tracks in Stellarton to visit the "hobo jungle", where drifters from across the continent heated tins of beans over bonfires, and, if they could get it, drank wine.

This preservation of the Sabbath was a principle J.W. lived by right until his last years on earth. One Sunday in August 1947 he was leaving church when someone told him that Sobeys Stores employees were *working* on the Sabbath. The family's first modern supermarket was set to open in New Glasgow and a few men were rushing to complete last-minute jobs. J.W., at seventy-eight, hustled over to New Glasgow and kicked everyone out. Thirty-four years later, when his son Frank was seventy-nine, cash registers at one Sobey supermarket were actually jingling on Sunday, but only because a rival supermarket had been violating the Sabbath for two years. Here, Frank's lifelong habit of never giving an inch in business competition clashed head-on with his conscience. He solved the dilemma in a typically practical way. He urged his sons to get government to pass legislation to outlaw Sunday openings for both stores.

"I came from a very good Presbyterian family," he has said.

Pictou County Presbyterianism had once been the most quarrelsome religion in Canada. It imported doctrinal differences from Scotland which, however meaningful there, served no purpose in Pictou but to split the faith into bitter factions. These were the Kirks and the Antiburghers, and their religious conflicts were also political conflicts. "Almost every Kirkman was a Conservative and every Antiburgher a Liberal," the Reverend Alexander Maclean said in the *Pictou Advocate* in 1911. After one winter election in the town of Pictou, Maclean recalled, "The streets were covered with snow [but] the snow was not all white. The red was there and not sparingly. Patches of blood were here and there along the street. Savage Indians could not surpass the brutal violence of that day in the Presbyterian town of Pictou. This served the purpose of the enemy as effectually [as] car loads of heresy could do. The two parties . . . trampled under their feet all kind and neighbourly feelings and all reverence for God and his laws."

"The night before voting time in Pictou," Roland H. Sherwood wrote in *Pictou Pioneers* (1973), "the opposing parties gathered their followers under their banners, and armed with sticks, stones, pitchforks and broken bottles, prepared for the polling on the following day. . . . It was said that, in those days, a man made his will before he cast his vote."

When Frank was a boy, the most bitter strife in Presbyterianism had died and, though blind loyalty, blatant patronage, and election-day rum still characterized the county's political life, bloodshed at the polls was gone. It was not so long gone, however, that J.W. couldn't remember it. He told Frank that Lyons Brook voters had always crossed a bridge to vote in Pictou, and that he'd once heard a Tory neighbour shout, "There's a bunch of Grits at the Gut Bridge with sticks! We'll have to fight our way to the polls."

If Pictou County Scots were lions in war, they were also "lambkins in peace". They failed at loving all their neighbours, but considering some had been so impoverished as pioneers that it shocked them all their lives to see anyone discard even a potato peel, they were miraculously open-handed with the neighbours they did love. The Reverend Alexander Maclean wrote in 1911, "Hospitality in its most generous and largest form then prevailed over the whole county. . . . Neighbours lived in the bonds of sincere and honest affection. After the day's work was over, they visited, and when work too heavy had to be done they did not need to be asked. It was a favour to be allowed to help. This condition of mind and circumstances secured a larger measure of real enjoyment than wealth and luxury ever could confer. . . ."

Hardship and isolation spawned helpfulness, but so did Christianity. Those stern, nosy deacons were also the first to comfort the ill with bedside prayer and Bible readings. Frank's father-in-law was such a man even in the mid-twentieth century, and hoboes of the Depression knew that his mother would never close the door in a hungry man's face. At Christmas, when Micmac women came to peddle hand-crafted wreaths, she invited them into her house. Frank himself, a true son of Pictou County, grew up both frugal and generous. He preferred to share another man's newspaper, rather than buy his own, yet the stranger who visited his mansion to talk business was unlikely to escape without being offered whisky and a hearty meal.

Finally, it was the settlers' faith, more than anything else, that made their terribly hard lives tolerable. An old local poem said that the first Scottish settlers "met the saffron morn upon their knees", and as late as the Second World War it was customary for Frank, his wife, and his children to pray on their knees during Sunday visits to his father-in-law's house in New Glasgow. On the day Frank was born, the *Presbyterian Witness* of Halifax, the masthead slogan of which was "The Bible is our great church directory and statute book," published President Theodore Roosevelt's florid tribute to Presbyterian Home Missions in the United States. It applied, too, to the tough old clergy of Pictou County. "It is such missionary work which prevents the pioneers from sinking perilously near the level of the savagery against which they contend," Roosevelt said. "Without it the pioneers' fierce and rude virtues and sombre faults would have been left unlit by the flame of pure and loving aspirations. Without it the life of this country would have been a life of inconceivably hard and barren materialism. . . . [The missionaries] bore the burden and heat of the day. They toiled obscurely and died unknown that we might come into a glorious heritage."

The same issue of the *Witness* boasted a classic expression of Presbyterian disapproval of ostentation. Noting that those at "the grand ceremonial of King Edward's coronation" would doubtless spend "enormous amounts of money" on "gorgeous apparel", the paper said, "The study of ornamental clothing, the man-millinery business, is not particularly elevating or edifying. . . . We always see with regret any tendency towards display in ecclesiastical, scholastic, social, or political or civic demonstrations. The beauty and grandeur of simplicity ought to be recognized and cherished. The pomp and circumstance of court functions and of warlike celebrations and demonstrations are not born of the highest civilization."

The *Witness*, on Frank's day of birth, also worried that, among businessmen, " 'Put money in thy purse honestly if thou canst, but put money in thy purse,' has supplanted the gospel of our Lord and Saviour." It chose as its "Golden Text" that day, "Thou therefore endure hardness, as a good soldier of Jesus Christ."

New Glasgow, Nova Scotia, at the turn of the century.

Frank was born in a county that never suffered from an underdeveloped sense of its own importance. As far back as 1828, Joseph Howe noted the irritating pride of Pictou. He wrote, "We knew that we might almost as safely run our head into a hornets' nest, as attempt to show, that in the midst of many very intelligent and well-disposed folk, there were some very great simpletons in Pictou, and that a man might, while endeavouring to prove himself a Patriot, prove himself a fool. A few folks in that quarter who (forgetting that there is a fine flourishing County called Sydney, one highly cultivated called Kings, another remarkable for its mines and scenery called Annapolis, to say nothing of half a dozen others, with a corresponding proportion of wealth and population) have for some time past been anxious to prove that the Province of Nova Scotia was only another name for the District of Pictou. We know if we disputed this, we should be assailed by a score of newly fledged students and unemployed Attornies. . . ."

In Pictou County, Pictou County felt, a superior people lived in a superior territory. "Merely as a piece of Mother Earth, it is deserving of the most enthusiastic admiration and ardent attachment," the Reverend J. P. MacPhie wrote in 1914. "Its beautiful elm-studded valleys, its clear, winding streams, its sunlit hills with their fertile fields gently sloping toward the sea, its bonnie, happy homes, its thriving towns, its peaceful villages, its infinitely varied forests and even its rugged glens present charms which never pall." Love of the Pictou countryside inspired one local author to compare West River, which is pretty but puny, to the Rhine; and to describe nearby hilltops "as sentinels of scenes unequalled", as though they rivalled the Alps. The Pictou Highlands soar to roughly nine hundred feet.

But more important than the environmental charms of the place that local tourist bumf has called "The County Air-Conditioned by Nature" was the character of its residents. In MacPhie's unhumble opinion, "No spot in our wide Dominion of equal size and population, has contributed so much that is best in our national life. Nowhere else have religion and education so effectually joined hands for the uplift of the people and the promotion of good. Nowhere have righteousness and truth been more genuinely wedded, or produced finer fruitage."

The fruitage in Stellarton, a Stellarton pamphlet boasted in 1964, included "some of the best racial groups in the world", while back in MacPhie's time other boosterism in print had noted the "intelligence, persistence and thrift . . . of the Scottish race [in Pictou County] . . . from among whom have come some of the brightest minds of the Dominion." Not surprisingly, a people with so generous a portion of self-respect also had legendary forebears. In Frank's boyhood, old men still yarned about such ancient local heroes as Farquhar Falconer, who gripped a huge bear by the ears while his father dispatched the brute with a pitchfork; and the noble Alex McKay, who could run so fast he caught caribou on foot, and, when charged by a berserk cow, hurled her to the ground and promptly butchered her.

"Yes, they were indeed giants in those days," A. MacGregor wrote in 1920, "mighty men of renown." MacGregor, however, was talking not about bear-stabbers and caribou-grapplers but about the industrial pioneers of Pictou County. "No section of Nova Scotia has made such marvelous industrial progress as the district of which the towns of New Glasgow, Stellarton, Westville and Trenton are the civic centres," a local promotional booklet exulted when Frank was thirteen. The progress had "a more than national importance". The booklet defined all four towns, with their 20,000-odd residents, as "The Birthplace of Steel in Canada", though Trenton (named after Trenton, N.J.) liked to reserve that title exclusively to itself. Stellarton was content to be "The Birthplace of Heavy Industry in Canada", while New Glasgow settled for "The Sheffield of Nova Scotia".

Few counties anywhere have suffered worse attacks of "firstitis". As A. MacGregor said in 1920, "Here we made the first steel axles forged in Canada; the first Acid Open Hearth Steel made in Canada; the first Basic Open Hearth Steel made in Canada. Here was operated the first Cogging or Blooming Mill in Canada; the first Fluid Compression Plant and the first Hydraulic Forging Plant in Canada. Here, too, was produced the first and only Steel from native Pig Iron, smelted from native ores. Here was built the first steel steamer in the Maritime Provinces, the first steel sailing vessel and the first steel merchant freighter on the Atlantic Coast. And here, too, the making of Shells for the Great War was begun, and carried on to a greater extent and with greater success than in any other part of Canada." Is it any wonder MacGregor saw Pictou as "The banner county of Canada"?

But Pictonians have ferreted out much earlier provincial, regional, national, and even continental firsts with respect to both the use of steam to drive local engines, locomotives, and vessels, and Presbyterian initiative. The passion to corral firsts has inspired historical sleuths to slide from the sublime to the obscure. Thus, we find not only that the first Presbyterian college in Canada was in Durham, Eliza Sobey's home town; not only that the world's first Christian Sunday school was in Lyons Brook, Frank Sobey's birthplace; not only that Canada's first Presbyterian seminary was in

Pictou; and not only that Pictou Presbyterians were the first in the British colonies to send a missionary overseas. As if those firsts were not sufficient, "The first cash contribution from outside Britain received by the British and Foreign Bible Society in London came from Pictou in 1807."

Moreover, it's understandable to declare that the *Royal William*, the first ship ever to cross the Atlantic under steam power (1833), started the voyage to England in Pictou Harbour, and burned Pictou County coal; but the fact that a Pictou shoe shop "installed the first x-ray foot machine in the Province of Nova Scotia, outside Halifax" falls somewhat short of being a watershed in commercial history. If such facts failed to impress the visitor, a knowledgeable Pictonian might trot out the news that prominent among the county's many ancestors of distinguished men was "the grandmother of Bonar Law".

County pride was so strong that being born in Pictou conferred on any child lifelong membership in a kind of clan. The clan was not peaceful. Trenton, New Glasgow, Stellarton, and Westville, sometimes known as "the four towns", are cheek-by-jowl. Strangers cannot tell when they've left one and entered another, but all campaigns to unite the towns as a city have been swallowed up in canyons of village pride as deep as the schisms that once divided Presbyterians. Bloody-minded rivalry among the industrial towns expressed itself in baseball, hockey, curling, and dance-hall brawls that recalled the thudding fists, spurting noses, and cracked skulls of the bad old elections. "That's what goes on *inside* the county," Lance Hale, a Stellartonian who now works in Halifax, explained. "Once you get outside, it's a whole different ball game. Right now, I know just about everyone in Halifax of my generation who came from any one of the four towns. I know their names, the number of their children, and who they married. Outside the county, we're like one big, loyal family, with our own jokes and inside references, and an attitude that says it's us against the world."

Still, it was not only Pictou people who thought highly of Pictou people. "I had, I discovered, an exalted opinion of Pictou - brought about no doubt by the fact that all my life I had heard Pictou referred to as a place somewhat apart from the ordinary place, with a people somehow above the ordinary folk," Clara Dennis wrote in *More About Nova Scotia* (1937). "It would be impossible for me to translate into writing the tone in which I had always heard it said, *'He's from Pictou County.'* "

Such a man would respect loyalty, hard work, self-reliance, plain talk, and plain food. Such a man would be leery of pretentiousness. He would avoid behaviour that suggested he thought he was better than his neighbours. Such a man would be argumentative but secretive, frugal but generous, slow to forgive but quick to offer food and drink. He would have an undying interest in buying land, and if his rights to property were challenged, he'd defend them as stubbornly as he defended his opinions. He would believe in the value of his church, the virtue of free enterprise, his God-given right to be a shrewd businessman, and the splendour of his stamping grounds. Frank Sobey is such a man, a chip off old Pictou County, if ever there was one.

2

A BOY BUTCHER ON THE RISE

J. W. SOBEY was thirty-six when, in 1905, he quit the family farm and, with his wife and three-year-old boy, moved up the East River to settle among the miners and railway workers of Stellarton. There, it seemed, steam whistles would hoot night and day forever. Local promoters soon boasted that the Nova Scotia Steel and Coal Company in nearby Trenton had "an unequalled railway car axle manufacturing shop, which produces a greater output monthly than any similar works in the British Empire"; and that Stellarton was queen of "an almost inexhaustible supply of coal which, mined at the rate of 1,000,000 tons annually, will be active for hundreds of years to come." (How could anyone know that in truth the mines would be active for merely tens of years to come?) What lured J.W. to this hotbed of industry was a job with the Acadia Coal Company, Ltd., which was sinking the Allan Shaft. Known as "The Million-Dollar Mine", the Allan actually cost about $1,250,000. It was "one of the most up-to-date and best equipped shafts on the continent," the *Pictou Advocate* (January 25, 1918) reported, "and at the time of its construction was the deepest in America." Its Number One shaft plummeted almost a third of a mile.

"None of the coal operations in the County of Pictou so epitomized the hopes, achievements, disappointments and tragedies as the Allan Shaft," James M. Cameron said in *The Pictonian Colliers* (1974). "Its surface plant and adjoining power house, topped with a 165-foot smoke stack . . . dominated the landscape for miles around. . . . Its danger potential, so frequently realized, created in the public mind a love-hate relationship. The Allan Shaft was a part of life, a living legend in Pictou County for forty-six years."

During its construction, Aubrey Dorrington said in *Stellarton*, "Work was carried on continuously from midnight Sunday to midnight Saturday, with three eight-hour shifts, the same shifts doing the drilling, mucking and timbering." J.W.'s job was to help timber the shaft with Georgia yellow pine and install tongue-and-groove lagging. Since the seam exuded murdering methane faster than any other mine in the world, the work was decidedly less pleasant than helping out at the family farm, but J.W. did get danger pay. Frank said, "Potatoes had gone down to only sixty cents a bushel, and Father left the farm. He got a job as a carpenter in the Allan Shaft at a dollar a day. Carpenters normally earned ninety cents, but he got ten cents extra for working inside the shaft. They used to go up and down on a bucket, and the bucket swung from one side of the shaft to the other. One time, the stage had Father and a couple of other men on it, and the bucket was coming up and struck them. Father grabbed onto a compressed-air pipe going down, and another man grabbed the bucket. So for that extra dime I guess it was pretty dangerous work."

By 1907, the Allan Shaft was hoisting a thousand tons a day. J.W.'s job was done, but he liked Stellarton. He'd already built a frame house on Allan Avenue, and he lived there with his wife and Frank, who was five and just starting his inglorious career in school; with two-year-old Donald Creighton Sobey, who would live only till 1908; and with baby Edith Sobey. J.W. thought there might be a future for all of them in Stellarton.

Rich Belgians bought control of Acadia Coal that year, and European miners streamed into town. The county's first automobile, a one-cylinder Reo, raised eyebrows and terrified horses. Folks talked about the birth of transatlantic wire telegraphy, the maiden voyage of the S.S. *Lusitania*, the Chicago Cubs' marvellous infielders, and the proper fact that Boston police had arrested a woman for wearing a one-piece, skirtless bathing suit. And in the bare, gritty, clanking, whistle-blowing town of Stellarton – where a dozen passenger trains stopped every twenty-four hours, where mine managers lived in white mansions on manicured lawns and miners lived in weather-mottled, dun-coloured wooden copies of the tiny, sooty row-houses of British coal towns, where the inky passageways of old mines, some active and some sealed by tragedy, snaked like the trails of gargantuan termites under the very streets – it came to J. W. Sobey, at the age of thirty-eight, that he could sell meat.

He bought a meat business from a Stellarton man named Angus Rankin, became a butcher, and hired drivers of horse-drawn wagons to peddle meat door-to-door. This was the modest beginning of the whole Sobey business empire. J.W.'s sons, his grandsons, and some of his great-grandsons would all contribute to the relentless expansion of this tiny operation; and seventy-six years later, in 1983, sales of Sobeys Stores, Ltd., would surpass half a billion dollars a year.

By 1912, J.W.'s younger brother Charles had joined him in the business, and together, smack in the middle of Stellarton, they erected the two-storey shop that, among future Sobeys, would always be known simply as "Number One". To build it, Charles cut logs on the family farm at Lyons Brook in the winter, hauled them to a sawmill, and took the lumber in to Stellarton. J.W. sold his house on Allan Avenue and moved his brood onto the second floor of the new building, but in 1913 Charles succumbed to the song of the West and joined his brother James in the sawmill business on the Pacific coast. Meanwhile, Eliza gave birth to Harold in 1911 after J.W.'s second son had died. In the Sobey scheme of things, Harold would one day be second only to his older brother, Frank.

The moment school ended every June, Frank moved back to his grandparents' farm, where the glory of his summers compensated for the tedium and stinging palms of the classroom. Pictou Harbour, in Edwardian summers, was a paradise for boys. He and a youngster from New Glasgow played among sighing pines on a beach near the fascinating wreckage of an abandoned railway pier. "We mostly lived in our bathing suits," Frank said. "We'd swim, and we'd dig clams with sticks, and then take a few stones and put them around with a flat rock on top and a fire underneath. We would cook the most beautiful clams on those stones. . . . Sometimes, on a real hot day, we'd go up to a stone house, which was handy to Gramma's place and owned by a Mrs. O'Brien. This house was lovely and cool. Her husband was a Captain O'Brien who had died quite a few years before, and she told us stories about him and showed us all the relics that he'd brought back from China. She also had a fine library of boys' books, a lot of *Boy's Own Annuals*, which were great books, and we used to look through these and read them. . . . This went on for quite a few summers."

In the bosom of a large, loving family, Frank took his turn at the farm chores. "I was certainly very happy there," he said. "You can understand how I had great affection for my grandmother and grandfather." His grandmother was specially protective. Once, while showing off in the barn, Frank fell into a morass of cow manure. Pigs had made it exceptionally vile. "Well, they got me out of that," he recalled, "but Uncle Charlie and Aunt Mary were laughing, and Gramma gave them a talking-to for laughing at 'that poor child'. She took my clothes off, put me under the pump, and pumped water all over me. I was that much of a mess."

Frank visited his Sobey grandparents not only in summer but also at Christmas, and, as a tot, he once persuaded his Uncle Charles to take him along on a horse-drawn sleigh while Charles cut firewood. "I was standing around and started to cry with the cold," Frank said, "but Uncle Charlie told me I'd just have to wait till he got his load. I was getting colder and colder, but all at once I saw Grandmother coming through the woods with a big shawl. She wrapped me in the shawl and carried me all the way back to the farmhouse. She set me on her knee in front of the stove with the oven door open and held me until I got warm."

Then, in September 1910, William Sobey died and for his grandson summers at Lyons Brook would never again be quite the same. Under the heading "Lyon's Brook", the *Pictou Advocate* reported,

"The death took place here on Sunday evening, 18th inst., at about 8 o'clock, of Mr. William Sobey, in the 77th year of his age. Mr. Sobey had been in ill health since February last, and suffered greatly from an affection of the heart, which ultimately caused his death." Frank said, "They'd moved a bed downstairs to the dining room for him, and just before he died they called me in. He gave me his watch." Frank was eighty in 1982. He still had the watch.

Without television, radio, electronic games, or, indeed, spare cash, Frank and his boyhood friends in Stellarton were as self-reliant at play as their pioneer forebears had been at survival. They made their own baseball and cricket bats, and since there were few motor vehicles to disrupt an inning, they set up their diamonds and wickets on the dirt streets. With boards and two sleighs he made a bobsled, "and we also skated on a pond handy to where I lived. We'd build a fire on the shore where we could warm our feet." In line with Canada's hoariest hockey tradition, "We used a piece of frozen horse manure for a puck. It worked just about as good." On summer days he could join other boys at swimming-holes on the East River. Boys wore sneakers, straw hats, and khaki cotton pants.

"We learned to do everything with a bicycle," he said. "We could take it apart, put new parts in, replace spokes, do our own tires, and everything like that." With a boy named Lloyd Munro, he collected stamps, and "made telegraph keys out of the magnets on doorbells we got, using a dry-cell battery. Lloyd had a battery that he made by buying some acid at the drugstore and putting it in a jar with a piece of carbon and a piece of zinc."

Frank was still in short pants when he first yearned to be a businessman, as other boys yearned to be sports heroes, and the business he had in mind was construction. One day he really would own construction companies, but meanwhile, "The best thing I ever got for Christmas was a Meccano set. . . . You could make cranes and bridges and buildings and, since you could get an electric motor, you could even make things that moved on wheels. If you had a dry-cell battery, you could spend days putting things together." Christmas after Christmas, Frank's parents enlarged his Meccano set.

Even more engrossing, however, were the electrical intestines of the Jubilee movie theatre. The Jubilee and the Sobeys' Number One store both rose on Stellarton's dusty, treeless main street shortly before the First World War, and they stood side by side. The theatre was thus an accidental tribute to the idea that man could not live by Sobey meat alone, and it gripped the boy so strongly that, for the rest of his long life, he could never shake his passion for the movie business. In time, he'd buy and sell the Jubilee, and other movie houses as well. As a man, he'd haunt movie sets in Hollywood and Sarasota, ingratiate himself with actresses, come home with glossy photos they'd signed for him. As a boy, however, what intrigued him about the Jubilee was simply its wiring.

The projectionist was a fellow named Mert McRae. His responsibilities included the wiring, and "After school I could hardly wait to get down there. I used to work with him, and crawl around. In those days the wires they put in were copper, covered with black stuff. Each pair of wires was stretched and held on porcelain knobs. You twisted the joints together with pliers and wrapped them with electric tape. I did a lot of that when I was a kid. You'd be surprised, the number of wires in that building, because they had a stage for live shows, too. I guess when I was fifteen or sixteen I was awful anxious to get out of school and get to work."

"Frank wasn't a good student," Billy Jamieson said, "and neither was I. In fact, we were the two dumbest kids in the class." A miner's son, Jamieson was a month older than Frank. He went to work at Number One in 1917 at fifteen. "I was just the flunky boy," he said. "I was a clerk but I also ran orders with a basket, mostly on foot, but if Frank's bike was available, on wheels." Jamieson, at eighty, lived up to his ancient reputation as a natty bachelor. Still working, as a salesman for a Stellarton car-lot, he had a pink, baby-smooth face, white hair as trim as a toothbrush, a chocolate suit as sharp as his memory. No one had known Frank Sobey longer. As a schoolboy, he said, Frank was so lazy that a despairing teacher named Martha Savage warned him a more studi-

The Sobey meat wagon is drawn by oxen in a parade in front of the Jubilee theatre during the First World War.

ous boy would become mayor of Stellarton, " and you, Frank Sobey, will be digging ditches for him." (Sobey, in 1937, became the youngest mayor in the town's history, and the smart kid dug ditches for him.)

School was tough. Alex MacIntosh, a poor boy from Stellarton who became a corporation lawyer in Toronto and then a luminary in Canadian business life, said that during his youth students at the town high school consistently led all Nova Scotia in provincial exams. "The whole town was proud of that record," he said, "and one reason it was so good was that the grade school was a farm system for the high school. If you weren't prepared to study, you had trouble graduating from grade eight. You just weren't allowed to fool around." Frank, however, was not prepared to study. He had trouble graduating from grade eight. He fooled around.

"I wouldn't say my school years were happy," he reminisced.

"They were just years I had to go through. I always day-dreamed I'd be in some type of business. I was quite a day-dreamer, and the result was, my marks were poor. Anyway, young men started earlier in those days." Sylvia Keith, a notorious martinet among local schoolmarms, regularly strapped him with thick strips of industrial belting from the Stellarton shell-making factory. "What I wouldn't study or absorb," he said, "she used to strap into me. That strap would almost bring the blood to your hands." But it rarely altered his refusal to study, his playing hookey, his dipping pigtails in inkwells. He was sixteen in grade eight, and it was time for him to leave school and never darken Sylvia Keith's door again. But he'd remember her with gratitude rather than rancour: "She was the old type of schoolteacher who'd really correct you, and she was a hard worker. She was the best teacher I ever had. I loved Sylvia Keith and I appreciate all she did for me, including the strappings, which I deserved." (He believed in restoring the noose to the justice system and the strap to the school system. The strap taught discipline, he said.)

Nothing about young Frank distressed his mother more than his school record. She'd been a competent teacher herself, she had the Scottish Presbyterian reverence for education, and he was her firstling. "She always expected the best of you at school," her grandson, Bill Sinclair, said. "She said a man who was educated was a man to be respected, because of what he knew." She reviewed Bill's report cards, urged him to work harder, do better. She had done these same things with Frank forty or more years before, but the advice had not taken. "His performance at school," his sister, Edith Sinclair, said, "really used to provoke her." Eliza hired a tutor for him but after a while the tutor quit, saying Frank was "a most heedless student".

Why? Well, an ex-teacher in her nineties – a woman who had made Frank memorize multiplication tables forwards and backwards in grade three, and had read in a magazine article in 1981 about his troubles in grade eight in 1918 – wrote to him when he was seventy-nine to blame Sylvia Keith: "She should have found out early that your difficulty was *why* you didn't study, or why you didn't *like* to study, instead of increasing your 'stubborn streak' by forcing you to do the impossible. You were lucky your father was in a business you could understand."

But the "why" of his classroom indolence lay in the fact that, for him, earning even a little money was overwhelmingly more intriguing than answering "What do you know about any four of the following: 'The Gael'; Lady Alice; Captain Hardy; Excalibur; Valhalla; King Francis?" While still in grade school, the *Financial Post* interested him more than, say, the name of the English king at the time of the Treaty of Aix-La-Chapelle. He pored over the *Post* every Monday night. Rather than draw "two views of a hexagonal nut", rather than calculate "the number of yards required to build a fence five wires high around a 12-acre field which is 60 rods long", he preferred to go out and get his hands dirty, buying and killing animals for cash.

"One day I persuaded Father to give me an excuse to get out at three," he said. "Usually, I was kept in. I took the truck and went down to Merigomish. I was able to buy six lambs [from farmers]. They were a fairly good weight. I bootchered them on the farm. We always bootchered our lambs on the farms, and hung them up in the barn. All farm barns had facilities for that in those days. Father had made me a little collapsible stool to sit the lambs on while I took the pelts off. I made a profit of sixty dollars on those six lambs for Father's business, and that looked a lot better to me than going to school." So did the stock market. In grade eight he bought ten shares of Canada Cement on margin and within two weeks pocketed a one-hundred-dollar profit.

The *Financial Post* gave him the education he craved: "I learned about money, how it was created, how it was related to the gold standard, how the price of money was related to productivity, how money was related to a country's balance of trade. If you read business papers and trade magazines, you get to know about the political and financial situation of a country, and its trade and commerce, and that's what I did. I never stopped reading trade magazines and good financial papers, not to this day. You have to be educating yourself all your life." Even as a teenager, he also studied financial statements. "I learned to watch out for good-will and written-up assets and so forth that might show up on the bottom line," he explained. "I didn't consider them to be worth much, and that's what you have to watch for in financial statements. Also, the most important parts are the notes at the back."

His mother's sister, Mary, fanned his interest in the business world. He had another Aunt Mary, his father's sister, whom he knew at Lyons Brook, but this business-minded Aunt Mary, a prime "character" among the Creighton characters, had more influence on him. She was nine years older than Eliza, and her background was enough to intrigue any young nephew. She had first married a Pictou County sea captain, Henry Matheson. "She went round the Horn with him twice," Frank said. "Once they were blown right back into the Atlantic Ocean, and it took them a month to get back to where they'd been." Later, for the sake of Captain Matheson's health, they camped for a while in Arizona, and to prevent snakes from slithering into their bedding they surrounded their tent each night with tarred rope.

Matheson, after quitting the sea, studied dentistry in San Francisco, and then the couple went home to Durham, where he set up a practice. His drill, Frank said, had "one of those sewing-machine treadles". Ever the grocer, Frank remembered Matheson "as a great one for eating dry cereals like Grape Nuts and Force Wheat Flakes. They were just coming along in those days." When Matheson expired he left his money to Mary, on the understanding that when she died the inheritance would go to a Bible society. Meanwhile she could use it, and since God helps those who help themselves she played the stock market. "I think there was some friction with the Bible society," Frank said, "but she was a smart investor."

She was in her fifties when she married J. E. MacBride - "I got tired of living alone," she explained - and moved with him to Ontario. This decision, however, weakened her interest in neither the market nor Pictou County. Indeed, she was back in her sister's house in Stellarton almost as often as when she'd lived in Durham, and sometimes for months on end. "She once got Harold [Frank's younger brother] and me to invest in a couple of penny mining stocks," Edith Sinclair said. "One was called Big Missouri. We used to sit around listening to stock-market quotations on the radio and getting excited." Before that, however, it had been Mary who'd inspired Frank, as a teenager, to subscribe to the *Financial Post*. "This," Frank said, "was the aunt who got me interested in the market. She encouraged me to read about business, about what made trade in other countries, and what made the standard of living, and that's why I was eager to go to business college."

Anyone unfamiliar with industrial history in Nova Scotia might think of Pictou County in 1910-20 as a place in which only a rooster's crow or a calf's bawling broke the silence. An early photo of central Stellarton confirms the notion. A deserted tram track disappears up a dirt road. Wooden shops brood in the low sun of late afternoon. Some have awnings. A man with a straw hat leans against a tilting telephone pole, and a barrel sits on the sidewalk. Five boys loiter in the distance. The only vehicle in sight is a horse-drawn buggy, and the sky yawns.

Nor do county statistics suggest urban vigour. About 36,000 people shared 1,118 square miles, much of which they had not tamed. The county stretched beside salt water for fifty miles, and at its deepest point penetrated inland thirty-four miles. Nine little rivers tumbled from the lakes, bogs, and gorges of the modest hills, then slid north on an undulating plain and out to sea. Merely 20,000 people lived in Trenton, New Glasgow, Stellarton, and Westville – "the East River towns", or simply "the four towns" – and therefore, even if you lumped them as one city, you scarcely had a New York, or for that matter a Halifax. Outside New Glasgow and Stellarton there wasn't a paved road in the county.

If the four towns were a city, they were a hick city. Families kept cows and hens. Boys earned a quarter per animal by rounding up stray cattle and horses and taking them to a pound. Though Stellarton alone had four shoe-repair shops and several barbers, some fathers in the East River towns fixed their own shoes and cut their children's hair. Some bought enough food and fuel in autumn to last till spring. They stocked up on staples from the Prince Edward Island schooners that tied up each fall in New Glasgow. Townsfolk bought butter, fruit, vegetables, and fresh chicken from farmers who delivered door to door.

The wilderness was within smelling distance, and it occasionally swallowed a child forever. Game laws, as late as the 1890s, allowed any hunter to take two moose per season, and five caribou. You could kill a bear, wolf, wildcat, shunk, or raccoon whenever you saw one; and in Frank's youth there was no shortage of pheasant, partridge, ducks, geese, or trout. When strikes, disasters, or closures threw miners out of work, some went up the East River a way and, using nets (which were illegal), caught hefty salmon for their families. "The poor buggers," said New Glasgow newspaperman Harry Sutherland, "they had to eat fresh salmon day after day." In this "city", every boy knew a fishing hole within a coal-lump's throw of his back door or schoolyard and, on summer nights, drifted to sleep to the resonant lullaby of a thousand whistling frogs.

During the day, however, the less peaceful music of steam whistles shrilly punctuated the rural quiet, for Pictou was booming industrially as it never had before.

Small-city industry is more noticeable than big-city industry, more vivid in the landscape of memory. Its relationship to everyone's well-being is inescapable. The slumps and hot streaks of a major-league industry in a minor-league town are as recognizable as those of any baseball team; and when Frank was young, industries all around him were on the hottest streak of their lives. If he grew up in a rural city, he also grew up among riverside enterprises where the aroma of profit was as strong as the stink of smoke. (Businessmen liked both smells, but Babe Ruth, during a batting exhibition in Westville, was supposedly so overcome by sooty air that he coughed "I'm going to die from all this dust in my throat.")

By 1914, the tannery at Lyons Brook was making two million pounds of shoe leather a year. Other manufacturers made bottles, jewellery, underwear, cigars, candy, bread, soap, mine and farm equipment, motorboats and marine engines, firebrick and drain-

Harold, Edith, and Frank Sobey, circa 1915.

pipe, doors and windows, cradles and coffins. So many lobster canneries were sprinkled along the coast that Pictou thought of itself as the lobster capital of the world. The Francis Drake Aerated Water plant sold its famous "stone ginger" as far away as the Magdalen Islands. Local men imported American tobacco, processed it, called it "Pictou Twist", sold it locally, in France, and on the Pacific coast. Whether smoked or chewed, it was not for the effeminate.

Stellarton was "The Railway Centre of Northern Nova Scotia", and a local brochure marvelled in 1916 that "Thirteen passenger trains leave Stellarton every twenty-four hours, and 800 engines are dispatched from the yards monthly." New houses, shops, theatres, schools, a new bakery and a new dairy . . . all these rose along the nine-mile route of the blue-and-cream electric trams that noisily sewed together the four towns. Two Americans, the Flaherty brothers, had created the street railway in 1904 because, to them, the East River towns looked like the next Pittsburgh.

The brochure *Nova Scotia's Industrial Centre* boasted that stamp sales at the New Glasgow Post Office jumped from $7,000 in 1900 to $27,000 in 1915, and ran a full-page photograph of the seven-storey Maritime Building, "New Glasgow's Sky Scraper". More thrilling news, however, was that a 638-foot-long lock was under construction near Trenton, and "it would give the district of which these towns are the life and centre, ocean connections with all parts of the world." The four towns, the booklet concluded, "are on the eve of a great real-estate and building revival."

At the heart of all this optimism lay the Nova Scotia Steel and Coal Company Ltd.

"Such a splendid, humming thing as this factory," a character said in the movie *The Magnificent Ambersons*, and that is exactly how Pictou County felt about Nova Scotia Steel and Coal. By 1914, local leadership, labour, and capital had turned it into a $14-million colossus, the producer of half the steel purchased in Canada, the employer of seven thousand men at mines, quarries, furnaces, ovens, mills, and shipping wharves not only at home but also in Cape Breton and Newfoundland. Its vessels carried coal and iron across the seas. Its aggressive and gigantic new subsidiary, Eastern Car Company, Ltd., Trenton, began to build two thousand cars for the Grand Trunk Railway in 1913, and during the First World War it filled fat orders for France and Russia.

For Pictou County, there were respects in which the war itself was a splendid, humming thing. "Seventeen weeks after the British Empire went to war against Germany on August 14, 1914," James M. Cameron said in *Pictou County's History* (1972), "there was forged in Trenton – ironically on the German-made Big Chief press – an eighteen-pounder shell block, the first of fourteen million shells forged in Trenton until the Armistice in 1918. . . . No plant in the Empire outside of Great Britain equalled Trenton's production of forged shells, some of which were machined in the steel works, the car works, other Pictou County plants . . . ."

Trenton made armour-plate for tanks, and, to replace vessels sunk by U-boats, the first ocean-going steamships ever built in the Maritimes or Newfoundland. By 1915, eight local plants had war contracts - mostly to forge or finish shells in the imperial and profitable effort to halt what the provincial department of education called "a cancer of Hohenzollern absolutism which is endeavouring to envelop the earth and forestall the federation of a free world and the Parliament of man." Every Canadian soldier who aimed a Ross rifle at one of the abominable Boches lined him up in a rifle sight from Canada Tool and Specialty Company, New Glasgow. Stellarton's town rink, which was within sight and earshot of the school the young Sobeys attended, had been the jolly home of carnivals, moccasin dances, and moonlight skating to syrupy band music, but now it was the Albion Machine Company. It made 600 shells a day, employed 250 workers, and, every two weeks, paid $17,000 in wages. Some of the money doubtless bought meat from J. W. Sobey.

The Ora, boasting thirty rooms, was Stellarton's biggest hotel. Built in the boomlet that lured J. W. Sobey to town, it sat near the train station, south of what would one day be headquarters for the Sobey empire. The dwindling of the trains eventually killed the Ora, but when Frank was a boy it thrived, and the first errand he ever performed for his father was to walk to the hotel every day with a basketful of turnips and cabbage and a rump roast of beef.

J.W. rose at 6 a.m., fed his horses, ate breakfast, and cut meat for an hour. By 7.30, when his drivers arrived, he'd have his wagon loaded with beef, pork, lamb, veal, and fish, all set to go. When business was good, he'd send not one but two wagonloads of meat into the streets of Stellarton. Each wagon had a treated-canvas top, stretched over a frame and extending far enough forward to serve as a roof over the driver. The wheels and shafts were fire-engine red. Cream paint coated the canvas, and black letters declared, "J. W. Sobey Meats. Telephone 80." (By 1911, there were still only sixty-odd telephone numbers in Stellarton. Sobey's was a party line.)

Each wagon carried a hardwood butcher's block, weigh scales, a saw, knives, and a knife sharpener. In fine weather, the housewife came out to the street with a plate, chatted with the driver, and selected something from his meat display. Then he'd cut what she wanted. In foul weather, he'd go up to her door, describe that day's meaty goodies, take her order, fetch it from the wagon. It was as natural for the meat to go to the housewife as it would later be for the housewife to climb into a station wagon and go to the meat. Competing merchants each had their own line-up of regular customers, and service was highly personal. Sobey drivers, for instance, reserved the choice steaks that J.W. had cut at dawn for their best customers.

Though general stores still served hamlets in the hills, merchandising in the rural city was specialized. Housewives had no automatic washers and dryers, no refrigerators, vacuum cleaners, ovens that shut themselves off, or electric kettles, toasters, pressure cookers, or waffle-irons. They had neither oil-heated homes with thermostats nor automobiles exclusively for their own use; but they enjoyed delivery services that one day even their appliance-glutted granddaughters might envy. "You *dealt* with such-and-such a grocer," newspaperman Harry Sutherland reminisced. "You *dealt* with such-and-such a baker. You *dealt* with such-and-such a butcher." Competition was so fierce that not only did merchants deliver, but they delivered whenever the customer snapped her fingers. "The housewife really called the shots," Sutherland said. "She'd phone in an order at mid-morning, and she'd say, 'Now you get that over here by 12.30 or forget it.'" Charles Higgins, who joined the Sobeys in 1930, remembered women who would make a peremptory phone call to order one four-cent cake of yeast. "You had to deliver it," he said.

Customers had been no less demanding in 1912. When J.W. opened Number One, installed his marble meat-display slabs and a butcher's block, and first spread sawdust on the floor-boards cut from Lyons Brook trees, his chief competitor was the P. M. Hogan Meat Market, which also delivered by covered wagon. But at least eight other stores in Stellarton – most of them bearing such Scottish names as Fraser, MacDonald, MacKenzie, and McLeod – also sold either meat or groceries, or meat and groceries. Stellarton, when it came to food, was a buyer's market, and the buyers were

Number One, on Main Street, Stellarton, the first Sobeys store, was built in 1912 and from it J. W. Sobey's staff peddled meat door-to-door by horse-drawn wagon. Frank and Irene lived above the store after their marriage.

the wives of more than a thousand coal miners and hundreds of railway workers. To get and keep their trade, a butcher had to offer untiring friendliness, generous credit, prompt delivery.

Delivering meat in horse-drawn wagons, Billy Jamieson said, was "a job you did six days a week, even if there was a storm so bad you couldn't see the horse's ears for three days." In winter, Frank said, "we changed over to sleighs. You had to operate in all kinds of weather. Some days it was so cold the drivers had to blow on the bit so it wouldn't freeze to the horse's tongue. On icy days we'd have to replace the corks in the horse's shoes. We had a special wrench for that job."

J.W. owned at least one famous horse, not that famous horses were rare in Pictou County. Aubrey Dorrington, in *Stellarton*, described "King", a legendary beast who worked in the black Allan Shaft and, when offered food, got down on his knees. King could recite his age by pawing the ground, and "was trained to pull so many boxes, and whenever more were added would balk. He could always tell the number of boxes by the clicking of the couplings." But by comparison with J.W.'s "Prince", King was intellectually limited. Prince was from Prince Edward Island. He was a chestnut gelding with a splash of white on his face, and Jamieson remembered him with affectionate awe. "You could go into a yard, and get off the wagon," Jamieson said, "and all you had to say was 'Gee' and he'd go right or 'Haw' and he'd go left. You could go up to a freight shed, and it might have a dozen doors. You'd jump off the wagon and go inside, and when you come out, Prince would have the wagon backed up to the door you'd gone in . He was that smart.

"They used to leave him in a field next the storehouse. If his hooves got too long he'd just walk out on his own, and go down the street, and around the corner, and then around another corner and into the blacksmith's shop. That was Alec Fraser. Prince had his favourite spot in there, and if another horse was in it he'd just push his way inside and sort of squeeze the other one out. Well, after Alec had trimmed his hooves, old Prince would just walk back to the Sobey field on his own again. That's God's truth. Every word of it.

"He had one awful bad habit," Jamieson continued. "He'd lift his foot and jam it down fast on my foot. He give me an ingrown toenail." Frank agreed that Prince was sometimes "kind of a cranky old bugger. He'd bite you and step on your feet. But if I gave him a bit of oats, I could do anything with him, climb under him and on him, just like he was a dog. . . . That was quite a character, that horse. There was one house where he'd always stick his head right in the woman's back door."

Running meat wagons was Jamieson's job – he quit school in 1917, a year before Frank – but on days he was sick, J.W. let Frank play hookey to take over a route. Manpower was scarce while the shell-making factory was going full blast, and that, too, eased his escapes from the tyranny of Sylvia Keith to do a man's job on a covered wagon.

Frank Sobey's home county saw itself as neither remote nor insular. It had launched at least a thousand vessels in the nineteenth century, and bred hundreds of ocean-roaming captains. As a part of the county's heritage, international trade was almost as old as Presbyterianism. Moreover, by 1910 passenger trains were pulling in and out of the rural city almost hourly, and scheduled steamers sailed from the port of Pictou for Charlottetown, the Magdalen Islands, Quebec City, and Montreal. By rail, the return fare to Montreal was only $14. You could also take a train from New Glasgow to Windsor Junction, catch the Dominion Atlantic Railway's celebrated *Flying Bluenose* to Yarmouth, board the sumptuous *Prince Arthur* or *Prince George*, sail to Boston, and then come home again. All for $14.15.

But if the clang of industry, the fame of expatriates, and the brass, velvet, and grandeur of steamships and railways all suggested to a Stellarton boy that he'd lucked into a world in which anything was possible, so did the glittering amusements that those same vessels and trains dragged into his view from places he'd seen only on maps. Few knew in the 1980s that Empire Company Ltd., the supreme Sobey company, owed its name to New Glasgow's long-gone Empire Theatre, which, in Frank's childhood, featured such acts as "DR. MACDONALD, The Electrical Wonder of The Age, introducing the Lady that Defies the Death Chair". Dr. MacDonald, who had recently "mystified the leading electricians of the world", was at the Empire from Sept. 17 to Sept. 21, 1910, and that same week *The Old Homestead* and *The Alaskan* were at the Curlers' Theatre. Meanwhile, the *Pictou Advocate* celebrated upcoming performances by Hee Haw Maud, a performing donkey, and Jessie MacLachlan, "the prima donna of Scotland". *The Alaskan*, which was "Revised, Retuned, Fresh from Five Months Chicago Triumph", featured "the Prettiest, Sauciest, Daintiest Chorus of 'Girly Girls' ever organized". A decade later, American and British stock companies were still thrilling the East River towns. A typical import in 1920 was *Babe's in the Wood*: "Girls, Music and Gorgeousness. It Kidnaps your Admiration. . . . Twelve Big Scenes. Four Comedians. And A Bevy of British Beauties."

Just as industry hummed in the rural city, live entertainment rattled along at a pace that makes the television generation look sluggish, deprived. "Here played the stage elite of Canada," James M. Cameron wrote in *Pictou County's History*. "The Dumbells of First War Theatrical fame, and John Van Arnhem's Minstrels, who travelled in their own railway car. One of America's comic greats, Ed Wynn the Fire Chief, appeared in Pictou, Stellarton and New Glasgow in his youth. Few summers passed that did not see Uncle Tom's Cabin with boozy has-beens of the classic theatre emoting lines of black-face roles with Shakespearian declamations. There were phrenologists, ventriloquists, medicine men, astrologists, bell ringers, musicians who made music from water glasses, magicians, jugglers, tumblers and assorted athletic entertainers, soft shoe and tap dancers, and by no means least, lecturers. The latter varied from palpable humbugs . . . to such genuine celebrities as William Jennings Bryan, thrice Democratic candidate for the Presidency of the United States who spoke to an overflow New Glasgow audience at 50 cents a head, on the subject 'Science and Religion'."

Boredom was not a problem along the East River. Winter nights were a hectic round of professional and local theatre and music, of "amateur" hockey with paid players, of curling, skating, dances, lodge meetings, and silent flicks with feverish pit orchestras. Prize-fight films scandalized the pious. Summers were a time not only of gigantic rallies of the Orange Order - roughly ten thousand came to Westville by special trains on July 12, 1911 - but also of wave after wave of picnics, fairs, festivals, track meets, steamboat dances, motorboat races, beach excursions, baseball games, and band concerts. Coal miners, more than other men, loved the clean, windy freedom of baseball, and the way a brass band spread good news while the sun in the trees dappled the grass.

The band of the 78th Militia Regiment, Stellarton, was the finest in the county, and when war broke out it became the regimental band of the 85th Overseas Battalion, Nova Scotia Highlanders. It toured the United States, played for European royalty, and marched in the Victory Parade in London in 1919, but, before it became renowned internationally, Pictou County already knew how good it was. J. D. Logan - a local man who boasted an M.A. from Dalhousie University, a Ph.D. from Harvard, and the rank of private in the 85th - declared it "the Champion Military and Concert Band of Nova Scotia, and indeed of Canada". (Logan, incidentally, was so loudly critical of inferior bands in Toronto that, he said, if a Toronto bandsman "met me on the street, it would require a day's work with an ink eraser to gather up my bodily remains from the side-walk.") The leader, Stellarton's own Music Man, was Daniel Mooney. Frank, who'd gone to school with a son of Mooney, remembered Stellarton's chest-bursting pride in that band.

He also remembered the circuses.

For who could forget the kind of spectacle that the *Pictou Advocate* described in May 1920? Howe's Great London Circus was coming to town, and it boasted "a whole kindergarten of baby elephants, camels, lions and tigers. . . . In the mammoth main tent . . . a colossal coterie of exclusive, all-star features . . . thrilling, nerve-shattering aerialists, superbly astonishing equestrians, death-courting acrobats, lithe and sinuous contortionists, breath-taking wire-walkers and bicyclists, clever jugglers, phenomenally educated horses, ponies and wild beasts, and a myriad of other amazing and pleasing numbers. . . . [The street parade] will be two full scintillating miles of richly costumed lady and gentlemen riders, handsome chariots, tableaux vans, floats, open and closed dens of fierce wild beasts, brightly caparisoned horses and ponies, herds of elephants and camels and hosts of novelties." Ringling Brothers, Frank said, "came in two trainloads, and the parade was so big in New Glasgow that the front would be getting back to the grounds before the end of it had left." New Glasgow's biggest crowds were always circus crowds. People turned out even to watch a circus *leave* town. "Those elephants did a fair bit of work," Frank said, "specially when the circus broke camp. They'd pull out the big tent-pegs." A time came, long after his youth, when the elephants pulled up stakes for the last time.

"I was twelve when the war started," Frank said. "The men of Pictou County enlisted in great numbers, and boys just a few years older than myself were getting into the army. They were supposed to be eighteen but some of them, like Fred Blair, got their fathers' consent to get overseas when they were younger. The war years were very worrisome for a person my age." The recruitment campaign in Nova Scotia was so gung-ho it might well have made the war years worrisome for a person of any age. In a letter to schoolchildren on February 14, 1916, Lt.-Col. Allison H. Borden of the Nova Scotia Highlanders said, "Boys and girls of Nova Scotia, I am depending on your help to fill up the three Nova Scotia Highland Battalions."

He wanted 3,500 men to "go across the Atlantic with me to help beat the cruel Germans who are trying to destroy our Empire." He asked grade-school children to deliver recruitment pitches to "your fathers and big brothers, or any men who are strong and well in your section between the ages of eighteen and forty-five. . . . Now you will understand that it is very hard to persuade quiet people who chop in the woods, plow the fields, work in the mines, fish in the sea, or work in shops and offices, to leave the peaceful occupations . . . to fight the faithless Germans. But if the Nova Scotia men do not cross the sea to fight the Germans in France, the Germans may come to Nova Scotia and take or destroy our farms and houses. So you see I really need your help very badly. You must help me to raise these 3,500 men."

"Nova Scotia Schools Recruitment Day" occurred two weeks later, and the Department of Education circulated bulletins to tell all teachers, "Your effort that day will be a contribution to the saving of the Empire. . . . [Borden] expects every teacher to send him at least one recruit." The following autumn, the department preached dieting to "liberate full rations for our hard-working, weather-beaten, shell-pounded soldiers, who must always be ready to move at the 'double' with bayonet and bomb. . . . Children should be taught . . . that every particle of food wasted should be looked upon as withheld from starving men, women and children in Europe. . . . Waste in wartime is a crime. Your loyalty is measured by your saving."

Names of casualties in the local press, the clangour of war industries, and movies like the eight-reel *The Kaiser, The Beast of Berlin* kept the war at the front of everyone's mind for four years. *The Kaiser, The Beast of Berlin* came to Pictou County in June 1918, and its ads trumpeted, "Pronounced by Everyone Who Saw It The Greatest in Motion Pictures. . . . The Cast Includes Generals French, Haig, Joffre, Pétain, King George, King of the Belgians. Also The Kaiser, Hindenburg, and all the German Cut-Throats. This is The Picture That Will Make Your Blood Boil."

Not only the war but two other ghastly curses struck Stellarton in 1918. One was an epidemic, the other a mine disaster. The scourge of "Spanish influenza" - which killed 21,640,000 people around the world, and in some cities exhausted coffin supplies - spared the Sobeys but struck enough local folk to spread fear throughout the East River towns. Authorities outlawed gatherings of more than twenty people, and closed pool halls, dance halls, theatres, schools, even the churches. Stellarton's YMCA became an emergency hospital. "I was sixteen," Frank said. "If someone was talking to me in the street, I'd hold my breath. I didn't want to inhale his germs." He also walked on the upwind side of the streets so the germs of the infected would not blow his way.

The mine disaster, an explosion in the Allan Shaft, killed eighty-eight men, and paralysed Stellarton with grief. But it was merely the worst in a series of catastrophic convulsions and fires that cursed local mines for more than a century and, all told, took more than six hundred lives before their time. Though the mines eventually yielded seventy-five million tons, F. W. Gray said in the *Dalhousie Review* (April 1944) that the coal-bearing zone was "very small, roughly eleven miles long by three miles wide". After describing the number, thickness, and "extraordinary complexity" of the

The 1880 explosion at the Foord Pit in Stellarton killed fifty miners, entombing most of them a thousand feet below ground.

seams, Gray stated the fatal fact: "The whole stratigraphic column is carbonaceous, gaseous and prone to spontaneous combustion." Stellarton boosters bragged that the town sat atop the world's thickest coal seam, but, again and again, hideous events suggested it was the world's most perilous coal seam as well. The land and the East River exhaled gas.

Disaster had spawned the Allan Shaft. In the autumn of 1880, a flood and then a series of thunderous explosions in the county's biggest colliery, the Foord Pit, had killed fifty miners, entombing most of them a thousand feet down. (As late as 1943, another generation of miners was still finding their shrunken remains.) The Foord had never re-opened, but the thick coal, along with the corpses, was still underground. The Allan Shaft was just a quarter-mile south of the Foord tomb, and its purpose was to profit from that same fatal seam.

The cataclysm of 1918, when Frank was fifteen, began at 5.30 p.m. on Wednesday, January 23. The mine phone rang at the surface, and when employee D. C. MacDonald answered it, he heard a voice beg, "For God's sake, send the cage to the 1200." The caller hung up, rang back, said, "For Jesus' sake, send the cage to the 1200." Then, a puff of smoke blew from the main shaft. By Friday, the *Pictou Advocate* had the story: "The greatest mining disaster in the history of Pictou County occurred . . . when an explosion in the Allan Shaft on the Foord Pit seam entombed nearly one hundred miners. . . . It is believed . . . not more than a dozen will escape alive. . . . [The bodies recovered] were blackened and singed, and in such a condition to destroy hope for the safety of the other men." The *Eastern Chronicle*, New Glasgow, said, "It must have been hell in there. . . . It is stated that the bodies . . . were smashed in some cases almost beyond recognition." A week later, the paper reported that "the ghostly work" of bringing up the bodies continued. Forty-six had been recovered. Many were unrecognizable, "and that fact adds to the sadness of the affair." It took till May 27 to bring the last of them up.

"They had quite a crew of draegermen," Frank recalled, "men with breathing equipment they carried on their backs. Before they could go down to get the bodies, the company had to seal the mine to put out the fire. They'd cover the opening with a wooden platform, heap it with sand, and then put another layer on. When the fire was out, the draegermen went down. To get through the seal, they had to go through two doors. They had to open one and shut it before they could open the other. Then they started to work their way in, cleaning up levels and trying to get to the bodies. They'd strike a fall, and they'd have to dig away and clean it up, but after they'd crawled over it they might find five or six feet of water between that fall and the next one. If a man let his breathing equipment submerge, he'd lose his life. So they had a boat. They dragged it with them so they could get to the next fall and clean another path, and they worked like that for quite a while. . . . I have always thought the miners were a very courageous race."

Forty-eight days before what the *Eastern Chronicle* labelled "The

Holocaust at the Allan Shaft", the collision at Halifax of two vessels, one loaded with high explosives, had killed nearly two thousand people, blinded or maimed thousands more, flattened a huge tract of the city, and set blocks of wooden houses ablaze. "The whistles all blew in Stellarton," Frank remembered, "and the firemen came out, and they loaded their equipment on a flatcar and left for Halifax. We didn't go back to school that day. There was too much excitement. We were all watching the firemen getting ready to go." Moreover, not five months before that, a mine explosion in New Waterford, Cape Breton Island, had killed sixty-five men and boys.

It was with these horrors and the war in mind that, after the subterranean disaster in Stellarton, the *Eastern Chronicle* said Nova Scotia had been "in the path of the cyclone of death. Death from explosions at home and death from explosions abroad have given us a terrible punishment. What for?" The *Halifax Chronicle* added, "We are living in a dreadful and awful time." This was the time in which Frank, unlike the school drop-outs who became boy miners, set his sights on becoming a businessman. He enrolled for a year at a business college in New Glasgow, and with his friend Billy Jamieson continued to roam the nearby hills in search of lambs for the market.

To Frank, business college was everything public school had not been. It was totally practical. It taught him to typewrite, keep books, do basic accounting, and take mental-arithmetic shortcuts that, decades before the pocket calculator, helped him to think faster than the other fellow while negotiating, investing, borrowing, buying, selling, or running his chilly eyes over a balance sheet. "One thing you learned," he said, "was to figure percentages. Say you wanted to know 12 per cent of something. Well, you knew what 10 per cent was, and you knew what 1 per cent was. You just added 1 per cent, plus 1 per cent, plus 10 per cent, and you had the answer. That way you could work the percentages every time.

"We also learned to jump from percentages to fractions. We knew 12½ per cent was an eighth of a dollar, 33⅓ per cent was a third, 6¼ was a sixteenth, and right down the line like that. So you could turn percentages into fractions, and vice versa, to get quick answers. This was important, because in the grocery business we wanted to earn a certain percentage. Suppose you wanted to make 25 per cent on something that cost three dollars. You'd add a third. You'd add one dollar to make 25 per cent, because a dollar is 33⅓ per cent of three dollars, but it's 25 per cent of four dollars. It's the percentage of the selling price you worked on, not the cost."

Armed with his mental-arithmetic system, and a relish for haggling that would one day earn him enemies, Frank went out to buy animals. "Fresh lamb," he said, "was very expensive in the early spring, and hard to find. Anybody who had any early lamb could get a good price on the market in June. I'd go out in the country, sometimes as far as fifty miles away, to pick up a load of lambs, but it was hard work even to persuade the farmers to sell. If it was a good haying day, for instance, they didn't want to be bothered. You'd have to go out in the pasture and chase the sheep. Sometimes I ran so hard I'd have to lie down to get my breath."

"But the farmer, he had a tough life," Billy Jamieson said, "and he didn't get much. He wanted every cent he could. One time Frank dickered for two or three hours with a fellow over one lamb. Frank said it was a dwarf, and he only wanted to pay $3.50 instead of the regular $5. Well, finally the farmer gives in but he says, 'Sobey, you kill that goddamn lamb and get off this farm and never come back.'" For Frank, dickering with farmers was what a later generation might call "a learning experience". He won some bargaining sessions, and he lost some, but he won more than he lost. "He once bought small lambs for $5 each, sold the meat, and the next winter he sold the pelts alone for $3 each," his brother Harold once recalled. "I remember it very well because for most of that year I had to turn the pelts and salt them every week." If Frank brought in more meat than the family business could sell, he sold it to packers in Halifax.

It was the most famous flivver of them all, a Model T Ford, that launched him as a backwoods bargainer for animals and a teen-aged butcher. Henry Ford had introduced it in 1908. It had a wooden body on a steel frame, came only in black, was "stronger than a horse and easier to maintain". By 1915, when the Ford Company made 500,000 Model Ts and was clearly the lion of the North American automobile industry, Fords were on sale in New Glasgow for $590 (FOB Toronto). In July 1916, a Ford touring model, carrying two Americans and their Cape Breton-born wives, stopped at the showroom of a New Glasgow dealer during the last leg of a fifty-three-day, 4,766-mile trip from California to Cape Breton. Hundreds admired the car and caressed it, and all the East River towns buzzed about the astounding journey. Between then and Frank's quitting school in 1918, his father bought a Model T.

"We called it a half-ton truck," Frank said. "You see, you'd buy an old Model T, cut the back seat off, and build a box there. You'd put a leaf or two in the springs to carry the extra weight in the back." The driver and the passenger sat up front, out in the dusty open with no roof over their heads. "Tires were very poor quality," he said, "and you could expect a flat on every trip. We'd have to take it off, pull out the tube, and patch it with a piece of rubber and tire cement. Then we'd have to pump the tire up to eighty pounds' pressure by hand, and sometimes we had to patch three tires in one day."

Once, when potatoes looked more lucrative than lambs, he turned the nuisance of a flat into the joy of profit: "It must have been around 1920, in the spring. Potatoes got very scarce, and went up to $4 a bushel. Billy Jamieson and I went up past Eureka to Sunnybrae to pick up a few, but most of the farmers said they didn't have any left, that they'd used just about all of them up for seed. So we'd say, 'Well, can we go down and help you to pick some out of your cellar? We'll pay you $2 a bushel.' In that way we got some fourteen bushels, but on the way home, in Eureka, we had a flat tire. So while we were taking off the tire, and patching it, and pumping it up, a lot of people came along, and we just sold the fourteen bushels right off the truck. We got $4 a bushel. So after we got the tire fixed, we went up the country again and picked up another fourteen bushels. Of course, hours didn't mean anything in those days."

Since the Model T was too small to carry live lambs, Frank slaughtered them on the farmer's property. Often Jamieson was with him (and both, as old men, still pronounced "butcher" as "bootcher"). Within a couple of years, however, J.W. replaced the converted Model T with a real truck, which was big enough to bring thirty-five live lambs into the outskirts of Stellarton for slaughter. "This was what they called a ton truck," Frank said, "and Father built a top for it so we could carry the live lambs." Its front seat, like that of the Model T, had no roof. "All you had was the windshield," Jamieson said.

"Those Fords had three pedals," Frank recalled, "one for reverse, one for the low gear, and one for the brake. When you got her going fast enough in low, you let the pedal spring back and she'd jump into high. The trouble was, with a load coming back every so often, those pedals lasted only two or three days, and we'd always be replacing brakes. Many's the time I came home using the reverse gear for a brake, and I remember one day I wore out the reverse this way, and I was coming down a hill to this long bridge. I took her around the turn and onto the bridge by standing on the running board and holding on to the wheel. The lambs were no help at all. They all leaned over to the other side of the truck. I thought the truck would go over. I was ready to jump." Once, with twenty-eight lambs aboard, "I hit a soft spot on the road and turned the truck on its side. I spent the rest of the day chasing those lambs."

Killing animals has never been work for the squeamish. "I remember the first cow we killed," Jamieson said. "I hit her with the maul, and Frank had the knife. But she wasn't going down. You could hear that cow all the way to Stellarton." The two youths, however, soon became more skilful at the bloody work. "We bootchered together about twelve hundred lambs," Jamieson figured. "My average was maybe four an hour." Frank said, "When everything was going good, we could each bootcher up to six lambs an hour. Of course, you couldn't keep that up very long. You'd exhaust yourself." Jamieson agreed: "I've done one in ten minutes, but I was skinnin' a leg while he was still kickin'."

To kill the lambs, Jamieson said, "We just cut their throats. To get the pelt off, you cut down the belly, about an inch deep, and then you punched it off with your fists. That way, you got the whole pelt off." The scene of this activity, once they were bringing live animals down from the hills, was a shed that J.W. rented from a farmer in Plymouth, on the eastern edge of Stellarton. "I might get in at four in the afternoon with a load of lambs," Frank said, "and I'd pick up Billy. We'd go over to Plymouth and butcher these lambs, and then get them back to the store, and hang them up in the refrigerator. You'd be surprised how many lambs we could do in two or three hours. We were always anxious to get away early."

"I'd see Frank come in as late as six o'clock with thirty-five lambs," Jamieson said. "I knew I'd have to go over there [to the slaughter shed], and I wasn't getting any extra pay." Jamieson, at seventy-nine, beamed when he boasted he could "bootcher" lambs faster than Frank could. "One night," he said, "I was really hurrying. I had a date with a girl. I did my share, but Frank was way behind, and when I started to leave he says, 'Where do you think you're going?' So I says, 'I did my half, you do your half.' I always worked that way with him. Even if we were just sweeping a floor, I'd do just my half."

"We gradually got into the curing of ham and bacon," Frank said, "and we'd make up to eight hundred pounds of sausage a week." In winter the truck hibernated. Since no one ploughed the roads, horse-drawn sleighs replaced motor vehicles; and with a little time on his hands, Frank read books. They were not novels or poetry. "I got an English encyclopedia on curing meats, making sausage, and so forth," he said, "and started to cure hams and bacon in the basement.

"I put these hams down in barrels, and I took them out and turned them every few days. I'd wash them off and replace the pickle. We rigged up a smokehouse with molasses barrels and fired it with hardwood sawdust. It made a lovely smoke. These were mild-cured hams and not fast-cured, like the hams from the packing houses. The packing-house hams are injected with brine to get a fast cure. But I had a small operation. We just cured them in the slow, old-fashioned way and this made a much better-tasting, sweeter ham. We could sell all the hams we could possibly make."

Meat, all his life, would be both a business and a personal gustatory pleasure, but the experience of slaughtering one big hog put him off pork forever. The primitive abattoir that J.W. rented had two levels. Frank and Jamieson killed lambs on the upper level, and shoved the guts through a hole. The offal dropped to the pig below. This was a cheap way to fatten him, but, as Jamieson said, "You'd never get away with that today." You would also no longer get away with their method of slaughter.

"The one I bootchered with Frank," Jamieson said, "was so big he weighed 510 pounds. Dressed." First, they climbed down in "this foot-deep slime" of lamb offal, and got a chain around one leg of the mighty hog. With the chain hooked to the back of the truck, they dragged the screeching beast out into the open. To get at his throat, they had to hoist him with a block and tackle. He bellowed and fought to the last breath, and they fended him off with hay forks. "After a while," Jamieson said, "he looked like he had smallpox." They got him up, but he was "so fat and big" the knife they used on him had a blade a foot long. The creature's neck was so huge that after they'd cut it, Frank said, "You had to almost get your hand in the hole to reach the artery."

Jamieson threw away his rubber boots and overalls, and never helped slaughter another pig. "That was the last and only hog that Bill Jamieson and myself ever bootchered," Frank said. Jamieson went into the car business, and stayed with it for more than half a century. For the rest of Frank's long life, he avoided roast pork. He does not enter slaughterhouses. He's a keen angler and has shot wildfowl, but he does not hunt deer, or any other animals. He says simply, "I had enough of bootcherin' when I was young."

Janet MacIntosh Sobey was still alive in 1920, and as an exemplary Nova Scotia Scot and Presbyterian she doubtless agreed with the *Pictou Advocate* when it explained what was wrong with Canada: "Too many diamonds, not enough alarm clocks. Too many silk shirts, not enough flannel ones. Too many pointed-toe boots, not enough square-toed shoes. Too much décolleté and not enough aprons. Too many satin-upholstered limousines and not enough cows. Too much oil stocks and not enough savings accounts. Too much envy of the results of hard work, and too little desire to emulate it. Too many desiring the short cuts to wealth and too few willing to pay the price. Too much of the spirit of 'get while the getting is good', and not enough of the old-fashioned Christianity."

Janet, along with the rest of Lyons Brook, would have been happy to hear that the town's biggest industry had survived another crisis. The *Advocate*'s local stringer reported in May, "We celebrated right royally the news that the tannery had not been sold. About six thirty the residents assembled in front of the tannery and with bugles, horns, cowbells and red fire, they made merry until eight o'clock, when they formed a parade and marched to the big field in front of the hall where a huge bonfire was started. The way was illuminated with colored light giving a carnival effect. Never before has such a celebration been seen in Lyon's Brook." It was too bad the old soldier could not have enjoyed it, but he had been gone ten years.

The world had immeasurably changed, not only since Janet's girlhood, when the Prime Minister of Britain had been Robert Peel; not only since she'd returned to Pictou County from Bermuda, when Thomas Edison had first demonstrated a "phonograph or speaking machine"; but also, and most dramatically, just since her grandson Frank's birth, when no one in the county had yet seen an automobile. In 1919, an airplane actually circled above the East River towns. There were 400,000 automobiles in Canada in 1920, six times as many as in 1914. Janet's own son, J.W., had a motor vehicle, and her grandson drove it. Pictou County was even experiencing car accidents.

Sir James Alexander Grant, last member of the first Parliament of Canada, died in 1920, and so did the widow of Sir John A. Macdonald. If their deaths signalled the end of an era for the nation, Janet's was the end of an era for the Sobeys. "She had been in failing health for a number of years," the *Advocate* said on September 10, and "was lately confined to bed." She'd stayed in Lyons Brook with her daughter Mary, "who so faithfully cared for her all through her declining years." She died on September 1. She was eighty-three. "She had planned to join those of her family in the West," the *Advocate* said, "but the Good Lord who doeth all things well, willed it otherwise." Frank was one of nineteen grandchildren who mourned her passing.

3

A CHAIN IS BORN

A CHANGE OCCURRED in a Stellarton telephone listing in 1924: "Sobey, J. W., Butcher" became "Sobey, J. W., Meats & Groceries". It had been Frank, barely into his twenties, who had persuaded his 55-year-old father to deal not just in meat and fresh local vegetables but also in tea, coffee, spices, butter, cheese, tinned goods, etc. "In that first year in groceries," Jamieson said, "we did about $35,000. That was big business, but Frank, he says, 'Billy, do you think we'll ever get up to $50,000?' " In 1983, sales of Sobeys Stores, Ltd., rose to more than $500 million.

Groceries could be both profitable and, in some eyes, romantic. R. B. Seeton and Company Ltd., ancient Halifax wholesalers, once lovingly described their warehouse: "Lima beans from Madagascar, are piled side by side with split peas from Calcutta. Dates from Bagdad, figs from Egypt mingle their odours with the pungent smell of molasses from Barbados. Walnuts from Manchuria greet walnuts from France and California. Olives from Spain and Italy are neatly piled alongside caviar from Russia. Oranges from Spain and California salute their citrus cousin, the grapefruit from Florida and Trinidad. Rice from Burma and pineapples from Malay Straits, raisins from South Africa and Australia, nuts and tapioca from South America, all find their way to our warehouse." Now, in the early 1920s, the Sobeys, too, began to sell pungent molasses, saluting citrus, greeting walnuts.

But an attraction more romantic than Egyptian figs captivated Frank in 1924. Her name was Irene McDonald, second daughter of Mr. and Mrs. D. W. McDonald, New Glasgow. Her father, known as "Deacon Davey", was a Sunday-school teacher of such spectacular devotion he'd become a church elder at twenty-one. A lay preacher who spent much of each Sunday visiting the hospital, he insisted his dinner guests pray, while kneeling with their hands folded, both before and after eating. He'd helped found the successful New Glasgow corn mill Johnson and McDonald, Ltd., after moving from his birthplace, Durham. His father had run a flour-and-feed mill there. Durham was also the home town of Eliza Creighton Sobey, and by one of those coincidences that are too common to surprise anyone in a county as intimate as Pictou, Frank's mother had long known Irene's aunt.

Alice Fleming, widow of New Glasgow furniture merchant George Fleming, knew Frank and Irene before their courtship. Seventy-seven in 1981, Mrs. Fleming had snowy hair, smooth white skin, and bright dark eyes. She was fine evidence that Pictou County was a place in which people grow old gracefully and loyally. Frank said, "She was my first girlfriend," and she remembered him as "a very nice-looking young man with lots of light-brown hair. He wasn't a person who laughed a lot. He was a more serious type." Irene was "very attractive, a very pretty girl and a very nice person, and she still is. She had dark, curly hair. . . . Rene and I had a lot of fun together [in high school, and later]. We laughed at the same things.

"Frank brought me a piece of salmon he caught just this summer," Mrs. Fleming continued. "He hasn't changed in fifty years. He's the same as he was when he went to all the dances and didn't have fifteen cents in his pocket." She paused. "He'll never quit going to work, you know," she said. "He'll drop on the job."

Frank courted Irene McDonald in New Glasgow and rode home aboard the trams of the Pictou County Electric Company Ltd. The fleet of ten tram cars carried red and green oil lamps, cowcatchers, and, at bow and stern, billboards advertising upcoming events. On calm summer nights, the sound of the clanking

Frank and Irene Sobey, 1924.

cars drowned the noises of the crickets and frogs up and down the river. You could hear the trams from miles away, and long before one hove into view you'd see flashes from its pole and power line in the pale moonlight. The fare was a dime when Frank pursued Irene. The service covered nine miles and seventy-two stops in the four towns, and ceased each night at 11.30. "We called the last car 'The Lovers' Special'," Frank said. "If you missed that, you walked home." He told her of his dreams. His sister, Edith Sinclair, said, "Rene once told me that when he was first taking her out, he laid out all his plans, and told her everything he intended to do and build, step by step, and that he did it all, every bit of it."

Frank and Irene's wedding, a small family affair, occurred in the McDonald house on Nelson Street at 6 a.m., November 24, 1924. The young couple had a train to catch at 7.20. It would take them to a Halifax honeymoon in a wooden hotel that charged one dollar a night. Irene's friend Marguerite McDonald "presided at the piano and played the wedding march," the *Eastern Chronicle* reported. "The bride was given away by her father and the contracting parties were united under an arch of evergreens. After breakfast was served the young couple left on a wedding trip and on their return will make their home with Mr. and Mrs. McDonald for the winter months. Both Mr. and Mrs. Sobey are popular among the younger folk and have a host of friends in the two towns who will wish them happiness." The *Pictou Advocate*, under its standing head for weddings, "Hymeneal", described "a pretty wedding of interest to many friends".

The young couple moved in with Irene's parents, and Frank reported by rail to his father's store in Stellarton. "I'd catch the Sydney-to-Halifax train," he said. "It came through at 7.20 in the morning. I wasn't too good at getting up in those days, and I often came down the hill on the run, after she'd left the station. Just as she was passing the street I'd run down and jump on." The ride to Stellarton cost a dime, but that was all right. His father's wedding gift had been a raise, from $18 to $25 a week.

Frank, Irene, and her parents embarked on a major adventure in 1925: a trip by car to Boston. Half a century later, he'd remember little of his first trip to one of North America's most historic cities - except the grocery stores. While his wife and in-laws explored the cultural glories of "the Athens of America", Frank prowled food stores, sniffing for ideas. The habit would last all his life: "I never went anywhere without looking at grocery stores."

What fascinated him most in Boston wasn't the independent stores, like his father's, but the chains. "There was O'Keefe's, Ginter's, A & P, Mayflower, and so forth," he said. They bore little resemblance to the gleaming supermarkets of the future. "They only had what I call 'dump scales' in them," he continued. "That is, each scale had a weight on it. Also, all these stores had a cheese-cutter, a coffee-grinder, and a cash register." The cash register was significant. For, unlike Number One in Stellarton, which granted credit and let customers run charge accounts, the chains in Boston accepted only cash on the barrel-head. Frank liked that idea.

He went home, bought second-hand equipment for under $500, rented space in New Glasgow, and opened a small cash store: "The manager I hired was a young fellow named Fulton Jenkins. He eventually became vice-president of Metropolitan Life in New York. After work, I'd go down to New Glasgow, look things over, count up the change, and so forth. Anyway, we did $500 the first week. I thought that was pretty good." So, apparently, did J.W. He invited his first-born son to become his partner. Frank was twenty-four and Sobeys Stores were on their way to becoming a chain.

Frank was typical of the founders of every big retail chain in North America. They all began as single-store merchants, craved increases in sales volume, founded new outlets. Chain stores began in 1859 when George Huntington Hartford and George Gilman undercut other New York tea merchants by eliminating middlemen and buying tea direct from Asia. To do so, they founded what would one day be the world's biggest food retailer, A & P (The Great Atlantic & Pacific Tea Company, Inc.). Its birth was bizarre. "Their first shop," Tom Mahoney and Leonard Slane said in *The Great Merchants* (1966), "resembled something from the Arabian Nights. A gigantic capital T blazing with gas lights, illuminated the store's vermillion-red-and-gold front. Strings of red, white and blue globes festooned the windows. Inside, tea bins were painted red and gold, the cashiers' cages were built in the shape of Chinese pagodas and a green parrot stood on a stand in the centre of the main floor. A band played on Saturdays, often far into the night." Harbingers of sales gimmicks to come, "premiums were given away - dishpans, china, crockery, and coloured pictures of babies."

A & P had four hundred stores in 1912, and John Hartford, second son of the co-founder, had a brainwave. Why not wipe out the paperwork and credit risk of charge accounts, and also the cost of maintaining hundreds of horses and delivery wagons? Why not open one-man "economy" stores? They would neither deliver nor extend credit. Their fixtures would be modest, their profit margins low, their sales volumes high. The chain's growth was the most phenomenal merchandising adventure of its time. In 1924 it opened fifty outlets a week, and by 1930, when its sales shot above a billion dollars, it boasted no fewer than 15,737 stores. "We went so fast," John Hartford said, "that hoboes hopping off freight trains got hired as managers." Together, the American, First National, Kroger, Safeway, and National Tea grocery chains had another 14,716 stores.

Frank saw what was coming. A & P opened its Canadian division in 1927, soon had 160 stores in Montreal and Toronto, and announced plans to descend on the Maritimes. Dominion Stores, with 550 stores in Ontario and Quebec in 1930, also made ominous noises about moving east. The T. Eaton Company had 65 groceterias, and some were already in the Maritimes. Moreover, T. P. Loblaw of Toronto, exploiting an idea pioneered by the Piggly Wiggly chain in the United States, founded his own self-service stores in 1921, and by the end of the decade had 170 outlets in Ontario, Illinois, and northern New York. The giants were looking eastward, and sooner or later they'd wheel on a territory where the typical chain was small, weak, and local. Their imperative was, "Expand or die." In an economy crippled not only by the worldwide depression but also by the local mine shutdowns that disasters inspired, Frank now built his own battlement against chain-store invasion. By the early thirties, he and his father - who was increasingly preoccupied by baseball and curling - were running not only Number One in Stellarton, but also two stores in New Glasgow, another in Trenton, and yet another in Westville. They would soon open a sixth store in Antigonish.

Meanwhile, the chains had horrified their enemies across the continent. Their sin was brutal efficiency. Their might, in many eyes, was not right. Since they bought goods in huge quantities, they not only bypassed outraged wholesalers - cutting out middlemen just as the founders of A & P had done in 1859 - but also railroaded the food manufacturers into granting them cash discounts, volume rebates, advertising allowances, and other semi-secret concessions that the independents could not command.

The chains beat the independents in less scandalous ways as well. They could afford the best managers, and reap the benefits of widespread advertising. Their financial clout meant they paid lower interest rates than the independents, and their turnover was faster. "At a 5-per-cent figure," Frank explained, "it's costing you $250,000 a year to keep $5 million worth of goods in a warehouse or on the shelf. If money's worth 10 per cent, that's $500,000. So if you can double your turnover, and get along with $2.5 million worth of inventory, you're making yourself $125,000 or $250,000 right off the bat."

Moreover, the chains learned to save money by putting it out to work. Over the years these tactics became increasingly sophisticated, so that today, Frank said, "we never have money in the bank at night, not even on Fridays. With the banking service you get today, we can loan money in New York or Toronto on Friday, and get it back on Monday. We get estimates from all our stores of how much money will come in on Saturday, and we put that amount on deposit on Friday to collect interest over the weekend. When the Saturday money comes in from the stores on Monday morning, we take it back. That saves thousands and thousands because we're getting interest on any surplus money we have. Moreover, if we get ten days' or thirty days' credit from a manufacturer, and if we can turn the stock over that fast, we've got no money tied up in inventory. It's all out earning interest on deposit."

The chain stores had not yet mastered such money-handling techniques in the thirties, but in every respect except friendliness and personal service they whipped the little guy. Wherever they landed, they aroused hatred. The debate over "the chain-store menace" raged in newspapers, on radio, in the courts, at every level of government, even in schools. To hear the chains' enemies, chain stores were a filthy octopus. They were bloodsuckers, parasites. They drained money from towns, and destroyed their character. The chains supposedly crushed businessmen, trampled initiative, spawned an insidious caste system, bred a nation of clerks and servants. Their owners were "Wall-Streeters", evil, fat-cat strangers, hell-bent on dictating what whole nations could eat and drink. The cry went up: Soak the rich and powerful. Soak the chain stores with special taxes. Soak them to death.

Even English author G. K. Chesterton got in on the act. While he merely denounced the chain stores' "blatant advertising and stupid standardization", others saw the chains as a threat comparable to communism, as termites in the beams of democracy. The *Canadian Grocer* (July 8, 1927) called them "this sinister and antisocial development"; and one Frank Freericks told readers of the *Canadian Pharmaceutical Journal* (March 15, 1928) that chain-store owners "would be masters of all with whom and with what they come in touch." He called farmers and independent merchants "the very backbone of our national existence", and suggested their domination by chain stores would be "a menace to the public and our form of government". A report in the Montreal *Daily Star* (March 1, 1929) argued that chain-store expansion was "lowering the standard of Canadian citizenship, because it robs the individual of that sturdy independence of character which is an essential requirement in the building of a virile nation."

The most hysterical invective was often the work of wholesalers and independents with axes of their own to grind, but occasional convictions of chain-store employees on charges they'd monkeyed with weigh scales and cash registers to bilk customers did not help the chains' cause. Independents, of course, were also capable of trickery, but J. William Horsey, the boss of Dominion Stores, told *Maclean's* (Aug. 6, 1955) that when he took charge of Dominion in the mid-thirties, it was the chain-store situation that was "stinking". He said, "People regarded chains as chiselers." But rotten publicity could not defeat the fact that a housewife paid less for a tin of pork and beans at a chain store than she did at her friendly corner grocer's. Times were hard, and the price was right. Or at least better.

Meanwhile, Frank went about his business.

His chain was neither big, nor impersonal, and its ways of doing business now seem impossibly quaint. Most stores had a coal-burning stove to warm the gossiping shoppers. Number One boasted the only safe in the entire chain. At night, the Westville store hid the day's take in a bean bin. Charles Higgins – a calm, bespectacled man with silver hair who suffered three heart attacks during the last few of the forty years he worked for Sobeys Stores – remembered that "Every Saturday night, we just took the money from Westville to Stellarton and put it in the safe."

Molasses arrived at the stores in wooden casks, just as it had been arriving in Nova Scotia for more than a century. "In winter, it was one hell of a job to get it out of the puncheon," Higgins said. "You sometimes had to crank the pump a full hour." Frank had a similar memory: "When we delivered molasses to a house, we'd pour it from our can into the customer's container. It was some feat to pour molasses into a gallon jar on a cold day." Store employees pumped kerosene from basement tanks into five-gallon cans, delivered it, and poured it into the customer's vessel.

Though salt, coffee, chocolates, cereal, and soap were prepackaged, sugar and dried beans still came in 100-pound bags. "You dumped them into big bins out by the counter," Higgins said, "and the customers took them home in brown paper bags." Flour came in 24-pound and 98-pound bags, prunes in 50-pound boxes. Shortening, peanut butter, and tea came in bulk, and for "the candy room" that Frank installed at Number One, so did dates, jelly beans, Moirs Royal Mixture of creams and jellies, and certain goodies called "Hardhats and Honeymoons".

"There was no self-service," Frank said. "When you waited on a customer, or put up an order for delivery, you had to put up sugar, cereals, rice, potatoes, prunes, raisins, dates, or any kind of bulk goods, and weigh each one as required." His son Bill recalled that as late as the forties "we packaged and pumped and scooped and sliced and bagged everything." While the clerk packaged for one customer, the others waited their turn. So they talked. They had time for one another. The stores were social centres, hangouts for the exchange of news, and never more so than on Saturdays. That was the day the miners got their pay, the farmers came to town, and the Sobeys and their employees worked from shortly after dawn till eleven or twelve at night.

The stores sold Sussex Ginger Ale and Orange Crush; Surprise and Fels Naptha laundry soap, Palmolive, Lifebuoy, and Lux hand soap; Master Mason and Old Chum pipe tobacco; Buckingham, Winchester, and Turret cigarettes; Montreal Twist and Pictou Twist tobacco. Miners chewed tons of tobacco, though some shaved it with a knife, put it in their pipes, and smoked it. (It arrived in cans and Bill, as a boy, couldn't resist "this soft, sticky stuff, wrapped in wax paper. It had a beautiful aroma. I tried it. Never again. It was awful.") In a barn behind Number One, the Sobeys kept feed for pigs, cattle, horses, hens. They sold it to farmers, but they also bartered it for farm produce, just as local food merchants had done for generations. If Frank had more goods than he could store at Number One, he jammed them into his own and his father's basements.

Cecil McLaren was a legendary "meat man" in the Sobey organization. He'd learned his trade from an even more legendary meat man, Harry Harris of the old Number Two store in New Glasgow. "Harris was an excellent meat man," Frank said. "He knew his business. At night he'd figure out what he was going to buy, what he was going to cut out of a carcass, and so forth. We ended up with one of the best meat businesses in New Glasgow." McLaren said, "Harry Harris taught me up," and in time McLaren, too, would teach up meat man after meat man after meat man.

Before them all, however, J.W. was a pretty fair meat man. Frank said his father and two Westville meat operations – J. T. McQuarrie's and Hayman Brothers – bought beef together in neighbouring Antigonish County and on Prince Edward Island. "One fellow would go on one trip and have cattle either slaughtered there or driven in on the hoof," Frank said, "and then they'd each take what they needed. Late in the season they'd freeze this and put it in a barn in Stellarton and cover it with straw to hold the frost." The easygoing way that these old-time merchants kept track of how much meat each one took seems as antiquated now as the oak McCaskey Account Register in which Number One filed figures on who owed what to the business. "Each fellow'd just mark on a board the weight of the quarter he took," Frank said. "I never heard of them ever having an argument on settling up."

McLaren respected Frank for his business genius but he also respected him for an ability that, to an old-style meat man, mattered just as much. Frank knew meat. He was "pretty sharp" at buying live animals. McLaren explained that only about fifty-five per cent of an animal is marketable, and that, "If you break it down further from 'primal cuts' to 'shop cuts', you're then throwing away twenty-five pounds of bone for every hundred pounds." Making money out of meat began with assessing the breathing creature, with considering its conformation – how well it was filled out, whether it had hollows in its back – and its breed, age, and sex. And Frank, "He was able to go out and, what we say, take the clothes off them to see what was underneath them. Before they were killed."

Frank himself, however, said that when it came to sizing up live animals he was skilful only with lambs. "I could tell within a pound or so how a lamb would dress out," he said. "I could tell by the looks and feel of him, and by the breed. But we bought most of our beef from Canada Packers and Swifts. I don't think I bought two cattle in my life on the hoof, but all I had to do was walk through a refrigerator and I could tell what kind of beef was coming from the packers. If a hind quarter wasn't rounded and filled out on the back, you knew you weren't going to get as many pounds of the higher-priced cuts, like T-bone and sirloin." But as a carcass judge, McLaren was the master. "He was the most knowledgeable man we ever had on meat," Frank continued. "He could tell you right off the bat what you had to sell a piece of meat for, to get a certain percentage out of the carcass. He knew how to cut a percentage out of it, and as far as beef goes I don't think I ever did. I depended on McLaren for that, and before him on Harris."

McLaren regretted the passing of the art of butchery: "You used to buy the whole carcass of pork, not like today. It'd weigh 150, 200 pounds, and out of that you'd get your hams, your loins, your shoulders, your bellies. You'd cut it up into your fresh hams, your loin chops, your bacon. . . . The butchers today, they wouldn't know how to do that. The packing houses do all that for them now. They buy it all from the packers in primal cuts. [Supermarket butchers] aren't *meat-cutters*. If you took their power equipment away from them, they wouldn't know what to do. In them days, it was a different ball game. You cut by hand. You learned a hell of a lot faster on account of you learned where the big bones was. These fellows today, you'd be lucky to find one in ten who'd be able to tell the sex of an animal that was hanging up in carcass form."

After cutting up a pork carcass, "you'd take the fat, add some beef and make sausages. You'd also trim as much meat off the head as you could, then boil the skull and pick more meat off. That's how you made headcheese or potted meat." Bill Sobey, who was a teenager in the forties, said, "When I started in the food business at Father's store in Stellarton, we made our own prepared meats almost without machinery. We made pudding and sausages, loaves and pickled meats, cutting without power saws, using no power equipment except a grinder."

The Sobeys in summer stored their meat in big ice-boxes. They got the ice from Connolly Brothers, who had a pond on the site of what is now the Sobey-owned Aberdeen Mall in New Glasgow. From 1900 to about 1945, James M. Cameron wrote in *About Pictonians*, the iceman was as routine as "the coal man with his dump cart, and the grocery delivery man with his express wagon. . . . Plodding horses pulling green, painted, canvas-topped wagons, which dripped water from their load of ice blocks, were a familiar sight." Connolly Brothers' pond, which they once drained and then dynamited to eliminate dangerous gas bubbles caused by coal deposits, yielded two thousand tons of ice a year. The Sobeys bought their share in 200-pound blocks. "Our refrigerator," Frank said, "took about two tons each week, but in hot weather we'd have to replace it twice a week. We shoved the blocks up a slide and into a bunker at the top. We displayed the meat on open counters, marble slabs, and put it in the refrigerator at night. Those refrigerators worked very well."

Frank, thrifty meat man that he was, carefully rounded up trimmings from the other stores, and made sausages at the meat counter in Number One. He was genial, energetic, persuasive. Alex MacIntosh, now a corporation lawyer in Toronto but then a Stellarton schoolboy, said, "If you went in there, he'd always have a word for you, and an interest in what you were doing. I know he's a tough negotiator, but he's always been a gracious individual." Richard Giles, investment dealer, also remembered boyhood visits to Number One: "Frank's a salesman all the way. My mother would send me down to buy one pound of steak. Frank would cut off a slice and weigh it. He'd say, 'That's a pound and a quarter. That okay?' He trained all his meat men to do the same thing."

"Everything was delivered," Bill Sobey said. "Feed for the hens, and oats for the horses, kerosene, molasses and potatoes and groceries – everything – and invariably on the same truck at the same time." Recalling the days before trucks, Frank said, "I'd be out delivering groceries with a horse in the rain and slush up to midnight," and Billy Jamieson added, "I've seen me leave at ten at night with the wagon so full of groceries I'd have the molasses and oil cans tied to the axles." The horse did not disappear overnight. Half a dozen blacksmiths were still at work in New Glasgow as late as the mid-thirties, and it wasn't till then that a Model A Ford replaced delivery horses at the Sobeys' Westville store. "I'd go for miles out in the country by horse and wagon to deliver feed," Charles Higgins said.

The telephone slowly eliminated the delivery man's duty of taking future orders and the task of soliciting business door-to-door. But neither the phone nor the truck made delivery easy. On Saturdays at Number One, Frank said, "You'd have to deliver three or four hundred orders. All of these, of course, were put up by hand. Sometimes it'd be midnight before you finished. . . . Every Friday night we worked getting ready for Saturday. Saturday was the big day." Drivers still had to worry about kerosene splashing the groceries, and about such minor horrors as the one Cecil McLaren endured when he was sixteen: "They put some new gravel on the road at Pictou Landing in 1934. I hit it too hard and rolled the truck. The orders were all mixed up, and the tomatoes squashed, and the eggs all smashed. I had to do up every damn order again." McLaren also recalled that on some Saturday nights at Number Two in New Glasgow, "You'd be damned lucky to get through at two in the morning. . . . You had to work sixty hours, plus, every week."

Moreover, there must surely have been easier ways to make a living than to take a load of groceries into the miners' inky Stellarton ghettos on a Saturday night. The miners lived in small, unpainted, wooden, company-owned row-houses, built in the nineteenth century and the first decade of the twentieth. Few trees grew in the miners' districts, and Red Row had no streetlights till 1931 or sewer lines till the late forties. On spring nights, men with horses and dump carts hauled away the waste from the miners' outhouses. When the "honey cart" arrived, prudent wives closed the windows. It was a measure of the unpleasantness of the job that a good honey-cart worker could earn forty dollars a night, at least ten times more than a competent miner got for a day's work.

The miner's life made him fatalistic but free, stoical but playful, patient but occasionally violent. He lived within both a blanket of carefully unexpressed fear and a cocoon of secure arrangements. Payroll deductions paid not only for his blasting powder, rent, oil, coal, and union dues, but also for his doctor's fees, and his contributions to his church and the relief fund to help his family if an explosion should snuff him out.

With the hazards of their jobs making future moments doubtful, miners lived for the moments they had. With payroll deductions as insurance, they blew their take-home pay on pleasure. Frank carried not only chewing tobacco, groceries, and molasses into the mining districts, but also hops, malt, and yeast. No drinking miner's house was so small that he didn't have room to make his own beer. Many miners liked baseball, booze, and brawling - sometimes all at once.

Softball fever swept Stellarton in the thirties. The town had no fewer than five diamonds (one on the site of what would later be a

Sobeys Stores warehouse); and in 1938 J. W. Sobey, then sixty-seven, was manager of the Stellarton Monarchs, Maritime champs. Miners' neighbourhoods had their own teams. The Red Row 7-Ups played the Mulgrave Row Hawks and the Back Mines Moonshiners. Sometimes fists settled the outcome.

But Frank, in his eightieth year, would hear no evil about the miners. "We never had any trouble with the miners," he insisted. "They were fine people, and they were all our friends." He pooh-poohed thievery as a problem in the rougher mining districts. Kids, he said, still snitch stuff from all Sobeys supermarkets. (Just kids? "Well, sometimes pretty big kids.") He had been committed to Stellarton for eight decades, and if you were committed to Stellarton you were committed to miners. As Lawson Williams wrote in an historical pamphlet in 1964, "Stellarton grew on coal, lived on coal, and was owned by coal." David Hayman, a former mayor of Stellarton, said, "Way back when there was just the one Sobey store, Frank used to peddle meat all through Red Row and the Asphalt. That's how he got to know the miners. He was a jovial fellow. He was number one with the miners." Frank had known them in good times and bad times. He had seen some of their corpses. An explosion at the MacGregor Mine in 1952 killed nineteen, and Frank said, "It was just one puff. They died with their mouths open and their tongues cooked, sticking out of their mouths, and their hair burnt off. Just one blast."

Having once invested his savings in a toy factory that went belly-up, Antoine Turmel then turned to the business that would become the huge Provigo Inc. because, he said, "People will put off buying a suit or a pair of shoes when they are short of money, but they have to eat." Or, as Nathan Steinberg told author Peter C. Newman (*Flame of Power*, 1959), "If a man goes without food for one day, he will lie. If he goes without food for two days, he will steal. If he goes without food for four days, he will riot and kill. The food business is the most essential in the world, and the largest." It was for such reasons that Nova Scotian industrialist and financier Roy Jodrey told Frank, "You've got the best business in the Maritimes."

That, however, was in the fifties, after customers had begun to leave cash in most Sobeys Stores rather than debt. At Number One, customers ran charge accounts. Like other grocers, J.W. and Frank accepted both the paperwork and the debt risk of extending credit. The store did this before, during, and after the First World War; throughout the Roaring Twenties, which failed to roar in Stellarton; all through the Dirty Thirties, which were as dirty there as anywhere else; during the Second World War, the fifties, and even the sixties. Long after J.W. had died, long after the Sobey chain included cavernous cash-and-carry supermarkets in four provinces, and even after Number One had been replaced by a spiffy Sobeys supermarket, Frank stubbornly and, from a business point of view, illogically resisted pressure from his sons and executives to abolish credit in Stellarton. He felt he still owed that service to those who'd been buying food from Sobeys since he had first scoured the hills for live lambs.

The miners' indebtedness to the Sobeys rose in bad times, and the Sobey business languished or flourished with their fortunes. Explosions, depressions, strikes, even winter, which blocked the shipment of coal on the St. Lawrence River, were grim news for miners and therefore bad news for the Sobeys. "Miners had to eat, and they had to eat damn well," newspaperman Harry Sutherland explained. "Mining was hard work. If you were a grocer, they were your bosom pals, but you knew that when a mine closed, or they struck, times would be lean for you, too."

Fires and explosions closed the Allan Shaft in 1914, 1918, 1924, 1929, 1932, 1935, and 1941. Fire struck the Albion Mine in 1913, 1917, 1932, and 1945. An explosion hit the Drummond Mine in 1915. Three fires swept the Moss Mine in 1944 alone. And so it went. Some of these misfortunes killed men and some did not, but they all meant mine closures, the laying-off of miners, the choking of business for grocers. Moreover, in years that holocaust did not close mines, then strikes, lockouts, and union warfare did.

The miners' strike of 1925 lasted five months, and broke some small businesses. Soup kitchens, harbingers of the thirties, popped up in the miners' neighbourhoods. Miners' wives and children reported to them with lard pails and lunch buckets, and carried

The Allan Shaft, Acadia Coal Company's "Million-Dollar Mine", was the deepest shaft in North America, and its output was a major factor in the Stellarton boom during the early years of this century. A 1918 disaster killed nearly one hundred miners.

home soup and stew. A strike in 1934 dragged through the late winter and into May, and labour violence erupted in July. Again, in the spring of 1937 a strike closed the four mines of the Acadia Coal Company for six weeks. As though life weren't tough enough, union rivalry coloured the troubles with special nastiness. Even wives got in on it, attacking strikebreakers with their fingernails. Miners hung effigies of other miners on poles, stoned the houses of "scabs", hurled strikebreakers into a filthy pond, and, when the RCMP arrived, clobbered Mounties with rocks and overturned police cars. The Mounties apparently enjoyed no one's confidence. Miners sometimes met in the Jubilee movie theatre, which was next door to the Sobeys store. By then, Frank owned the Jubilee.

Behind the miners' despair lay the financial milking of the Acadia Coal Company. Acadia was by now a subsidiary of Nova Scotia Steel and Coal, which was in turn a subsidiary of Dominion Steel and Coal (DOSCO). In 1925 Acadia had boasted a cash surplus of

$1.7 million, but its corporate masters in Montreal then drained it to pay dividends on the stock and bonds of Nova Scotia Steel and Coal. Acadia never properly recovered from this blood-sucking, or from the fact that in January 1933 its immediate parent, Nova Scotia Steel and Coal, went bankrupt. Now the affairs of Acadia Coal – a proud, vigorous local company that outsiders had crippled – would be up to the untender mercies of the receivers-liquidators of Nova Scotia Steel and Coal. Acadia Coal was the backbone of Stellarton's economy, the inheritor of an industrial history that stretched back more than a century, but from 1933 to 1938, James M. Cameron wrote (*The Pictonian Colliers*), "The threat of insolvency and closure of Acadia was the prime factor, overshadowing all others, in the affairs of Pictou County."

On top of the specific crisis at Acadia Coal sat the general crisis of the Great Depression. In 1929, the average annual earnings of Pictou County coal miners stood at $1,034; by '32, they'd plunged to $558. Coal mining, never a pleasant occupation, had become a hell of a way to make a living. Selling groceries on credit had become a hell of a way to build a business. Frank said, "Bills got up to $200 and $300, and that was a lot when men were making only $2.50 a day on good jobs, so Father always had to carry heavy debts. A big percentage, of course, he never did get. It was a very hard time to make any money."

"In the thirties," ex-mayor David Hayman said, "the grocers kept the miners alive. They fed them. But most miners were honest, and as soon as they got back to work, they'd pick up the chips." For those who didn't, the Sobey rule was cash-on-delivery. "You *knew* the customers," Charles Higgins said. "You knew the good and bad credit risks. Sometimes when you were delivering, the manager'd say, 'If they don't pay up, take the order back.'"

For some, Pictou County was never as heavenly as its boosters claimed. The twenties, now remembered as a time of general prosperity, began there with a crushing depression. Massive unemployment afflicted the Maritimes. Unions collapsed, and Clifford Rose's experience was far from rare. "I tried a small grocery store [in New Glasgow], but we had to buy in the dear market of inflation and sell cheap when the slump came," he wrote in *Four Years With the Demon Rum* (1980). "So we were cleaned out."

He wangled a job as a temperance inspector in 1926. Backwoods stills and clandestine liquor traffic were rife throughout the Maritimes, but, according to Rose's colourful memoirs, his job was simply to raid "rum dives" in New Glasgow. They were "as thick as bees". He performed this service to feed his children, but the bootleggers - some of whom were women, known to their customers as "mothers" - argued that they offered their services to feed *their* children. Bootlegging, Rose thought, stemmed from "empty stomachs and the boredom of life". A more experienced cop gently told him how to keep his $75-a-month job: "Without bootleggers we wouldn't have jobs. Yours is to get convictions, but if you scare the Trade too much there will be no convictions to get. We can't afford to kill the goose that lays the golden egg." By 1929, Rose owned his own car, and "times are much better than they have been for some years." But in 1930 government killed the goose by ending prohibition, and the Great Depression descended. Unhappy times were here again, and for the East River towns the breathing-space had been short.

The ferocity with which the Depression struck the county may be seen in a desperate letter (published in *The Dirty Thirties*, 1972) that an elderly New Glasgow man sent to Prime Minister R. B. Bennett in 1934: "There is a great deal more destitution here than we have ever known. My house is besieged front door, back door and side door from early in the morning till long past the dewy eve. A couple of evenings ago I had a visit from three different widows who have boys between the ages of sixteen and twenty years without employment and who are absolutely destitute. My daughter . . . has given away all the spare clothes we have and I find myself reduced to one pair of trousers and two pairs of shoes. The odd pair of shoes would have been given away but no one can wear them, the sole of the right boot being an inch thicker than the left, to accommodate my game leg."

Hoboes drifted throughout the province. "Around '33, there

wasn't a day went by that somebody wasn't fed at our house," said Alex MacIntosh, now of Toronto. His mother, a close friend of Eliza Sobey's, was a widow. She ran a small farm outside Stellarton, and as the drifters "popped off the trains, she gave them odd jobs and fed them."

"The hoboes had a different feeling in those days," Frank said. "They didn't expect to get anything for nothing. My mother always said, and everybody said, they always asked if they could cut kindling – it was all coal stoves in those days – or gather up wood, or empty out ashes. They never just asked for something."

Stellarton had not only despairing drifters but also hundreds of despairing Stellartonians. "In the year 1933," MacIntosh said, "I don't think the mine whistle blew once in Stellarton."

Miners, like other destitute people, endured the humiliation of going to the town hall to prove they were so poor they deserved "direct relief". The poor got no cash. The town (and sometimes a miners' union) issued them orders, which they then traded with merchants for food and clothing. Since the town reimbursed the merchants for the orders, and since merchants were well represented on the municipal councils, the system guaranteed that unless a whole town went bust, the shopkeepers would eventually get their money. Federal, provincial, and municipal governments shared the cost of relief equally, but the towns had the unpleasant duty of deciding who'd get it. The County Council refused to pay it, on the grounds that the farmers, many of whom could feed themselves, were already overtaxed. Taxpayers who did not need relief squealed about giving it to those who did. Councillors got it in the neck from the hungry for being cruel, from the well-fed for being wastrels. Except for private households – among them the Sobeys' – Pictou County during the Depression was not always an example of charity.

Frank was mayor during the strike of 1937. "The men were pretty disturbed, and you couldn't blame them," he said. "It was a busy time for me and the councillors. The miners came into the town hall. One night they tore the paper off the wall and so forth, and practically crowded the council into a corner." Frank's next sentence, however, was a don't-get-me-wrong statement: "Having gone to school with miners' children and lived in a mining town, I would have to say that miners are the finest class of people you could find in Canada. I don't suppose there's any place where they suffered more than they did in Pictou County."

For employers, the thirties were not entirely bad news. Help was cheap. As a delivery boy in the Sobeys' Westville store, Charles Higgins earned three dollars a week for working every day after school, on Tuesdays till 9 p.m., and on Saturdays from 8 a.m. till nearly midnight. At eighteen he joined Number One as a full-time clerk. He says he put in a seventy-hour week and collected no overtime. "I'm paying you seven dollars a week," he remembers Frank telling him. "You're getting too much." The stores closed on Wednesday afternoons but that didn't mean time off work. "Frank bought carloads of plums, peaches, pears, maybe grapes," Cecil McLaren said, "and on Wednesday afternoons he'd just point at the fruit and say, 'Don't come back till you've sold it all.' "

Although some employees recalled long hours and overwork, the boss's memory was somewhat different. Frank said the staff worked till midnight only on rare stormy Saturday nights when orders piled up, and "Everybody seemed to work together very happily. In fact, the boys sometimes suggested we come back and work some nights, and if they came back I had to come back, and sometimes *I* was the one that got fed up with it."

"You *had* to work hard," Higgins said, "because there was always somebody on the doorstep, ready to take your job." But if you had a paying job, you could eat well. Twenty-five cents bought four pounds of smoked cod. Thirty-nine cents bought a one-pound T-bone steak. "I used to buy fresh salmon for twelve cents a pound," Frank said. But poultry, except at Christmas, was strictly for the rich. "Chicken," he continued, "was the most expensive food you could buy. It cost far more than sirloin. Today, it's the other way round." In his eightieth year, while driving his cobalt Mercedes-Benz, Frank picked up "an old fellow" who amiably complained that Sobeys Stores were now selling salt cod for $3.50 a pound and turkey for only eighty-nine cents a pound. Cod had once been "dirt cheap" and turkey "sky-high". For most of his life he'd been so poor he'd had to eat salt cod, and he'd fed it to all his kids. He disliked it. He loved turkey. Now, at last, he could afford turkey but his life was almost over. It hardly seemed fair.

Every December for a quarter-century, Frank drove to Antigonish to order Christmas turkeys directly from the farmers who'd reared, butchered, and dressed them. "I bought as many as 3,500 turkeys a season. We'd hang them all up in a barn with all the windows open at night to keep them fresh." Right into the fifties, when pre-packaged birds from the packing houses began to drive local farmers out of the business, Frank insisted on personally carrying out the annual turkey-buying mission in Antigonish. It was a Yuletide ritual he relished.

During the Depression, the food business in the East River towns was fiercely competitive. "There were so few dollars to go round," Frank explained, "and I can count, right now, ten food stores that were on the main street of Stellarton, not counting ours. A traveller [food salesman] would take all day in Stellarton alone. He'd go up one side and down the other." With ten competitors in Stellarton, and rivals in New Glasgow, Trenton, Westville, Antigonish, and Pictou, Frank found the price competition "pretty heavy. We had giveaways in those days, too, you know. Free dishes with so much of a purchase. Free silverware. We also had Dollar Days. You'd pay one dollar for a bagful of so many potatoes, so many sausages, so much sugar, and so forth."

If competition was tough at the retail level, it scarcely existed at the wholesale level. "The wholesalers had a kind of cartel going," Frank said. "They charged fifteen-per-cent mark-ups, and they had a powerful organization." One use of the organization was to strong-arm manufacturers into refusing to put Sobeys Stores on their "direct lists". Being on a direct list was a reward for buying in large volume. It meant you could cut out wholesalers, lower prices to customers. The Sobeys' biggest rival in the Depression was the Barkers Stores chain, which, since it had eight outlets and met other Lever Brothers requirements, was on the soap company's direct list for Solo shortening. The Sobey chain, with only six outlets, was not. Watching Barkers undercut his Solo prices while he paid the wholesaler's mark-up did not sit well with Frank.

The solution came from what a later generation might call the "Pictou County Mafia". Frank was now sufficiently important to have befriended Scott Cameron, a New Glasgow blacksmith who rose to become the dominant figure in Maritime Steel and Foundries Ltd. Moreover, Frank's young brother Harold had married Cameron's daughter, Helen. Now, Cameron's *wife* happened to be a sister of the sales manager at Lever Brothers headquarters in Toronto, and the local Lever Brothers salesman, H. R. Murphy, knew about all these connections. He dropped a word in his boss's ear, and Sobeys Stores magically appeared on the Lever Brothers direct list for Solo shortening.

The battle was not always so easy. "The wholesalers made it very tough for small operators to get on the direct lists of the food manufacturers," Frank said. "There were as many as twenty-five wholesalers in a province like Nova Scotia, and they all had salesmen on the road. New Glasgow alone had four or five wholesalers calling on all the independent stores. There was a wholesalers' guild here. My father-in-law belonged to it. That guild and all the wholesalers naturally did everything they could to keep the manufacturers from selling to the retail chains. But the wholesalers used a mark-up of fifteen per cent of the selling price. That was seventeen or eighteen per cent on cost. They were just taking too much. They all disappeared, and a new generation of wholesalers came along." (In the Maritimes, the Sobeys would one day own a sizeable portion of the new generation of wholesalers, and of what was left of the old generation as well.)

"I had awful fights to get on the direct lists of various companies," Frank continued.

By national standards, he ran a small chain; by any standards, however, he was stubborn, unapologetic, retaliatory. He acted as though gigantic food manufacturers needed him every bit as much as he needed them. "I went without Kellogg's Corn Flakes for a whole year," he remembered. "I tried hard to sell Quaker corn flakes and everything else, and then Kellogg finally put me on their list. Same thing with Carnation Milk. I refused to put it in. We were out of Carnation Milk for two years. I figured if I couldn't get along without Carnation, I shouldn't be running stores."

In one of the more flamboyant promotion campaigns of the thirties, Carnation used the Dionne quintuplets to peddle milk. When Twentieth Century Fox distributed *The Country Doctor*, a film featuring the five famous babes, Carnation arranged to stack cases of its milk in the lobbies of theatres where the movie played. By the terms of Frank's contract with Fox, he had no choice but to run *The Country Doctor* in the theatre he owned in Stellarton. Besides, he said, "It was a good picture. It did very well at the box office." But when it came to displaying "the milk from contented cows" in the Jubilee, he put his foot down: "I refused to let them put any milk in my theatre unless they sold me a shipment direct, which they did, and from then on I was on their direct list." It had been Carnation, not Stellarton's toughest merchant, who'd finally relented. "When they put us on the list," he continued, "they were under tremendous pressure from the wholesalers. The wholesalers even threatened to boycott Carnation products."

Sobeys Stores, from their birth as a chain, always handled their own warehousing and inter-store shipping. As early as the thirties, Frank was also wholesaling to other neighbourhood stores. He had his hands full in those days. He and his father put up a new store-front at Number One, and a new cash-register counter. The town buzzed about the improvements. Number One was both head-quarters for the little chain, and the busiest meat market in Stellarton. Number Two, New Glasgow, kept two delivery trucks on the move all week. Meanwhile, Frank found time to hustle round to all six stores at least once a week. He usually showed up late Thursday to paste newspaper ads for Saturday "specials" in the store windows, but staff never knew exactly when to expect him. The ads, incidentally, sometimes shared the window with circus posters. In return for the display space, Sobeys Stores got tickets to the circus.

Frank worked his staff hard, but he worked himself harder. "I devised a bookkeeping system, and charged everything out to the store, both at retail and wholesale," he said. "The idea was to find leaks. If your cost for so many goods was $100, and you sold them for $125 but only collected a $20 profit, you knew there was a $5 leak somewhere, through spoilage, theft, or whatever. . . . It made a lot of work. I used to take an adding machine home with me at night. I took stock every month. I had the store managers take stock and make up the sheets, and I always checked all these stock sheets myself."

His system was basically the same as the one A & P used throughout its vast empire. He stole ideas without a blush, applied them, sometimes improved them. He read voraciously, not only the *Christian Science Monitor* and the *Financial Post*, which he often devoured while lying in bed on the Sabbath, not only biographies of tycoons, magnates, and financiers, but also both American and Canadian magazines for the grocery trade. Moreover, the one-time drop-out taught himself to exploit the statistical services of Harvard University. He discovered that if he sent his own business figures to an office at Harvard, he'd get in return the figures on turnover, sales, and financing of U.S. grocery chains. A clever grocer could learn a lot from such numbers; and for Frank, all his life, education was ceaseless and pragmatic. It was just a matter of learning what you had to know in order to do what you wanted to do.

"All those years," James M. Cameron said, "the Sobeys were doing their best to keep those miners, and to expand at the same time. The fact that they succeeded suggests shrewdness." Cameron was not an unqualified admirer of the Sobeys; their acquisitive drive offended him. At the same time, he was the county's pre-eminent historian, and he said, "If anyone ever suggests there's a thick-headed Sobey, just let it go in one ear and out the other."

By the mid-thirties, all three of Eliza and J.W.'s children worked for the chain. Harold, while a student at St. Francis Xavier University, Antigonish, filled in for vacationing store managers in summer, and later took over the year-round management of Number Two in New Glasgow. Edith worked as cashier at Number One and helped with the bookkeeping. Moreover, by the time Frank's sons were just out of grade school, he had them bagging potatoes in the basement. The potatoes arrived in 75-pound bags, and it was the boys' job to dump them into bins so they wouldn't rot, then snap the sprouts off and put the spuds into sixteen-pound bags for sale as "pecks". When David was twelve, he kept two dozen laying hens. "I had big black Jersey Giants and some Plymouth Rocks," he said, "and I sold eggs round the neighbourhood." Frank encouraged David in this childhood enterprise, and indeed saw to it that all his boys started young in the food business, and at the very bottom. Bagging potatoes made cleaning mackerel look like skilled labour.

Frank's assumption of family leadership began when the Depression began. J.W., as he approached his seventies, found more and more time for the real pleasures in life: curling and baseball. He loved watching baseball with Sam MacIntosh, a butcher at Number One. A man who intimately knew the business remembered that "Old J.W., he'd wander in and say, 'Come on, Sam, let's go to the ball game.' Sam would say, 'I can't. Frank'll be mad at me. He'll fire me.' So J.W. says, 'Now don't you worry about that, Sam. I'll fix it up with Frank later. Let's go.' So off they go, and Frank, he's running around, ranting and raving and screaming, 'How can you run a meat counter without a meat man?' "

Asked how much influence J.W. had on the business in 1932, when Frank was still only thirty, Cecil McLaren said, "Let's just say the old man had a say in it, too." J.W. was happy to be an adviser, and an honoured handyman. He helped put up orders. He picked up the mail. He did important odd jobs. When rats crawled up through holes in the basement floor at Number One, it was J.W. who foiled them by filling the holes with a mixture of broken glass and cement. An old friend recalled J.W. as an affable codger, a popular but reticent gent who, while haunting Number One, seemed always to have a hammer in hand. Frank, meanwhile, looked like "a man who was all business". Older businessmen recognized him as a comer, just as a big-league baseball scout keeps track of boondocks talent.

J.W. may have taught his first son more than either of them realized then, including prickliness about violations of business confidence. W. R. Monteith of Saint John, N.B., was a clerk at the Stellarton branch of the Bank of Nova Scotia in 1929. His manager, he said, had "peculiar ways". The manager was so self-righteous he ostentatiously returned a bottle of wine that a customer had left as a Christmas gift. He was so stiff he'd never even said hello to J.W., but when the old butcher made a stock-market killing the banker gushingly congratulated him within earshot of other customers. The gentle J.W. went white with rage, not because the greeting was obsequious but because it put Sobey profit on the Stellarton grapevine. The banker's unctuous blathering was an intolerable invasion of clan privacy. "Frank's like his father that way," Monteith reflected fifty years later. "He believes in playing his cards close to his chest. To get what he wants, he never tells anyone more than he absolutely has to."

There was something else Frank learned from J.W.: the importance of feeding and grooming a business, the way one might feed and groom a colt till he becomes a marvellous horse. Some Pictou County men cared for their horses better than they cared for themselves, and fed them molasses to make their coats sleek and shiny. And Frank, at eighty, remembered his father had similar feelings about caring for a business. "I was never much interested in money," Frank said. That statement, all by itself, might inspire men with whom he had haggled to utter an astonished "What?". But he went on from there:

"I was more interested in building up a business. If you start thinking about what you're going to *make* out of it, what you're going to *get*, then the business will suffer. In my mind, the business always came first. Father and I operated that way all through the Depression years. We took very, very little out of the business, just living expenses, you might say."

By 1937, J.W.'s salary was $50 a week, and Frank's was $35. "I was pretty proud in 1937 because we made $3,700, after taxes,"

Frank said. "That was the most money we'd ever made in any year since father had started the business." But newspaperman Harry Sutherland remembered having said, "Dammit, Frank, even the New Glasgow *Evening News* made more than you did in '37."

What little the chain did make, however, father and son ploughed back into the business: "Father always used to say a business is like a farm, and of course he was brought up on a farm. He says if you don't keep putting money back into a farm, he says, the farm soon runs down. He says you have to keep improving your fields, removing rocks, putting in drains and fertilizer, and he says if you start taking money out of a farm you soon have a farm that's not worth very much. That's probably where I got the idea that a business was something that had to come first in your life. You had to cater to the business. You had to keep the business healthy, and I always felt that for every dollar we made in the business, we could go out and borrow two. That's how we expanded over the years."

It was this relentless strategy of ploughing back earnings that, in the sixties, caused some holders of Sobeys Stores shares to grumble about the paucity of dividends. It was this same strategy, however, that also kept Frank's salary low. "I never took more than $10,000 a year in salary," he said, "and our accountant came to me several times to say I wasn't charging enough up to expenses." He lived mostly on his investment income: "I was doing well on the market, and we were borrowing money for 5 or 5½ per cent, and a lot of stocks were paying yields of 7 or 7½. So instead of losing money on the spread between dividends and bank loans, which is what you're doing today, I was making money on that spread."

4

THE MOVIES, THE MAYORALTY, THE WAR

FOR WOMEN of the Dirty Thirties, movies were an escape from boredom and worry. In the movies, historian Margaret Farrand Thorpe explained (*America at the Movies*, 1939), "the adult American female" saw "the quickest release from a drab, monotonous, unsatisfying environment in dreaming of an existence which is rich, romantic, glamorous. . . . How can the American woman who buys her bread sliced and her peas shelled be expected to concoct her own reveries? At the movies she gets them ready-made, put up in neat two-hour cans." By the mid-thirties, Frank was selling the adult Stellartonian female not only her sliced bread and shelled peas but also her canned reveries. For he owned the Jubilee theatre.

But it wasn't just housewives who sat spellbound in darkness to escape the fears of the day. "During the most abysmal days of the early Thirties," Andrew Bergman wrote (*We're in the Money*, 1971), "as economic paralysis spread, snuffing out a shop here, a bank there, a factory somewhere else, movie attendance [in the United States] still averaged an astonishing sixty to seventy-five million persons each week. . . . It was evident that the total . . . included a great many people who could scarcely afford to be there. In those painful days, the marquees of America's Broadways and Main Streets attracted the dispossessed farmers, the failed bankers and all the sellers who had no buyers. Americans needed their movies."

And so did Canadians. Few American housewives needed reverie more than a Stellarton coal miner. If he could scrape up sixty cents, he could buy his girl a ten-cent bag of candy at the Sobey store, and then, for a quarter each, take her to a double bill at the Sobey theatre.

The Depression caught up to the industry in 1933. Theatres closed, admissions sagged, production dropped, but studio economy measures, government dollars, and a new moralistic outlook nursed the film business back to health. By the late thirties it was not merely robust, it was herculean. U.S. studios made more than five hundred feature films in 1937, which happened to be a good year for Frank, too. By '38 and '39, eighty-five million Americans each week crowded into seventeen thousand movie theatres. Many would remember the thirties as the greatest decade in the history of movie-making. They were the time in which Frank first made money by satisfying not only the bellies of Pictou County folk but their hunger for fantasy as well.

He had fallen for the Jubilee as a boy, even before he'd butchered his first lamb. H. L. P. McNeil, a New Glasgow shoe merchant who loved show business, built it before Frank was out of short pants, and it rose cheek-by-jowl with J.W.'s new butcher shop. The Jubilee was part of a fast flowering of theatres, most of which offered plays, vaudeville, and flicks, and often vaudeville and flicks on the same billing. N. W. Mason, a flamboyant New Glasgow character, had leased what was known as Mechanics' Hall in 1907, refurbished it, and grandly dubbed it the Empire Theatre. Mason billed the Empire as "the only theatre in town," but H. L. P. McNeil had already constructed the Itzit in New Glasgow, and shown flicks there in 1907. Mason, with partners, built the Academy of Music in 1912 chiefly for stage shows, and the Roseland in 1917 chiefly for movies. McNeil countered not only with the Jubilee in Stellarton in 1914 but, in 1917, with a supposedly bigger and better Itzit, which soon went bust. After that, the Itzit wasn't.

The talkies were a dozen years in the future, and the son of H. L. P. McNeil, also H. L. P. McNeil, recalled in 1981 that, to accompany the action on the screen, each local theatre had its own pianist, drummer, and violinist. "There was a man from Halifax who had a job painting railway cars here," McNeil said, "and each night he'd rush over to the theatre from work to play violin. His hands were still coated in varnish. This fellow was a terrific violinist." The Roseland boasted not merely a pit trio but a pit quartet, with a local schoolteacher blasting away on cornet.

But it wasn't till the birth of the talkies that theatre ownership intrigued Frank, and the talkies were slow to come. Even after the phenomenal success of *The Jazz Singer* with Al Jolson in 1927, industry leaders stubbornly dismissed sound as a fad, but audiences didn't. By 1929 the Roseland was being wired for sound and Frank, a 27-year-old hustler, hooked himself to an opportunity at the Jubilee.

Sound in the Roseland promised death to the Jubilee, which, in 1929, was floundering. H. L. P. McNeil was ill. His son, only nineteen, was doing the best he could, but he knew, as everyone knew, that the Jubilee could not survive without redecoration, new seats, new projection equipment, and, above all, sound. The theatre needed more money than the McNeils could muster, but Harry and Solomon Goodman sniffed possibilities. Romanian Jews who'd come to New Glasgow in 1904 (Harry) and 1909 (Solomon), the Goodman brothers were among the smartest East European immigrants ever to settle in Nova Scotia. When the Jubilee began to intrigue them, their department store in New Glasgow, the first in the county, was already a thriving fixture on the business landscape of the East River.

Frank kept his ear so close to the ground it was a wonder it didn't show grass stains, and he heard rumblings that the Goodmans might take over the Jubilee. So the young Presbyterian butcher-grocer from Lyons Brook dropped in on the middle-aged Jewish merchants from Zuckava, Romania. He found he had something in common with them: the crash of '29 had stung all three. "I had some pretty good stocks on margin with a brokerage house," Frank said fifty-two years later. "I had over $5,000 and Rene [his wife, Irene] wanted me to sell out and build a house. But no, I was

Sobeys' Number One and the Jubilee theatre, Main Street, Stellarton, circa 1940.

greedy. I said I'd hang on. Well, when the crash came, the dealer went broke. The account was eventually settled in 1935, and I ended up with $36 out of my $5,000." His father had taken a bank loan to pay the broker for his shares, and, "When the market broke, Father was left with this big loan. He went all through the thirties paying it off. I guess he'd have been better off if he'd been sold out, like I was."

In late 1929, however, "I went to see the Goodmans. They'd also been in the market, and they'd also got a bad crack. So they'd decided that instead of buying shares in outside companies, they'd now control their own investments." One such investment would be the Jubilee. Solomon Goodman planned to buy control from Jubilee Theatre, Ltd., then sell shares locally to raise money to revamp the place and put in sound. That's where Frank saw his chance. In effect, what he asked Goodman was, "If I sell a lot of shares, will you give me some?" Goodman bit, and in 1930 – with the Depression accelerating like an avalanche, the East River economy teetering for reasons of its own, and a greasy fog of apprehension settling on the streets of Stellarton – the incurably chipper young Frank Sobey went door-to-door at night to peddle $35,000 worth of shares in a sixteen-year-old theatre that was losing money. He persuaded merchants, doctors, railway workers, even miners that the Jubilee could once again be profitable. He was a "persistent porch-pounder", and he had a head start on all itinerant porch-pounders. He *knew* the potential buyers, and roughly how much each could afford to invest.

"I'd just go around town and sell $100 here, and perhaps $500 there," he said. "So, by selling shares, I got a few for myself, and the option on some more. I had a verbal option that, if the Goodmans sold out, I could get more." His selling theatre shares as a Fuller Brush man sold brushes was "my first experience in raising capital". But it was also early proof of something businessmen from Scotsburn to Bombay would notice about him in decades to come: he was a persuader. Though never a smooth talker, he got along equally well with the toughest "pit plug" (miner) and the slickest executive. Moreover, he was energetic, stubborn, and absolutely sure that, in the end, he'd make the other fellow see things his way, the right way.

He was a salesman.

He was a good citizen as well. "Stellarton *needed* a theatre, so Frank *was* being public-spirited," the younger McNeil said. "But he was also making a buck for himself." That would be the story of Frank's life: making a buck for his specific business and at the same time promoting general well-being. In his mind, the two causes were as intertwined as the seam and the cover on a baseball. What good was a theatre if the death of industry drove all its customers away? What good was a grocery store in a ghost town?

The all-new, super-improved, sound-equipped Jubilee reopened with an utterly forgettable talkie concoction entitled *Married in Hollywood*. But the theatre raked up money in 1930, a big year everywhere for movies, and proudly proclaimed itself "The Talkie House De Luxe, Stellarton". The gratified Goodmans soon bought from N. W. Mason the controlling interest in the Roseland and the Academy of Music in New Glasgow. Again Frank helped sell shares in the Roseland: "I went around after work peddling the shares here and there. It was hard, but if I made enough calls I was sure to sell to somebody. I guess it's just like insurance. The man that makes the most calls makes the most sales."

In 1933, Jubilee Theatre, Ltd., decided to pay its shareholders $35,000 in dividends, and to raise the money by selling bonds. Frank sold some of the bonds. But suddenly the Goodmans wanted out. Perhaps they sensed that the movie industry faced a rotten year. They sold back the bulk of their interest in the two New Glasgow theatres to N. W. Mason and others. Meanwhile, the younger H. L. P. McNeil hungered after the Goodmans' controlling interest in the Jubilee. So did Frank. Each claimed to hold an option on the Goodman shares, and legal swords briefly clashed. Frank won. In litigation he usually did.

To anyone other than himself and McNeil (who remained his friend and employee), his victory might have seemed Pyrrhic. After payment of the $35,000 in dividends, the company's balance sheet looked decidedly unpromising, and Frank got the Goodmans' interest for only $2,700. That, however, bought him not only control of the Jubilee but also its debts. They amounted to at least $50,000, and meanwhile he had to scramble just to raise the $2,700. Such figures are puny by the standards of the high-rolling, self-pampering financiers of a later time. Characters in Peter C. Newman's *The Acquisitors* (1981) doubtless spent $2,700 on a month's supply of cigars. But the place in which Frank Sobey needed $2,700 to control a theatre was Stellarton. The time was 1933, and maybe the mines would never open again.

"I had a hard time raising that money," he said. "I borrowed $500 on an insurance policy. Father went on a $500 note for me at the Bank of Nova Scotia in Stellarton, and my father-in-law went on another $500 note at the Royal Bank in New Glasgow. That's all they'd give him. Then I think I got a few dollars out of the business. In other words, I got the $2,700 together. . . ." He told neither bank he was borrowing from the other. Now he owned a theatre. "It was a nice theatre," he said. "It was set up for live shows, too, so it had dressing rooms, light panels, dropping curtains, and so forth. The shows mostly came from New York. Singing acts, comedy acts, chorus girls. The girls used to get about five dollars a day."

When Frank bought the Jubilee he inherited two apparently incurable problems. The first was that, at exactly the time a miners' strike had crippled the Stellarton economy, "We had some high-priced film contracts on hand." The second was the theatre's debt. He solved both problems with tactics so direct most men would not have had the gall to try them. The Jubilee got the first local run of all films from Fox Film Corporation (which in 1935 became part of Twentieth Century Fox Film Corporation) and, to solve his first problem, Frank went to the Fox office in Saint John, N.B. – Maritime headquarters, incidentally, for all major Hollywood studios – and warned the distributors there might soon be no more Fox outlet in Stellarton. "I told them that unless they did something for us," he said, "well, I just couldn't take any film from them. So they gave me half-price on their film for the duration of the strike. I think they let that deal run about a year. That helped us out a lot."

His tackling of the debt was even bolder. Northern Electric Company, Montreal, had installed the Jubilee's sound equipment and still owned it. Their policy was not to sell equipment but to rent it, and by 1933 Jubilee owed Northern Electric $27,000. It owed $25,000 more in federal income tax. Under Frank's management the theatre's revenues began to surpass its expenditures, but the debt load remained an albatross. "So I sent a certified cheque for $10,000 to the income tax department," Frank said, "and I told them that, if they wanted to, they could just take this in lieu of their taxes. I put on the cheque 'In lieu of all liabilities to date', and I told them that, if they didn't want it, to send it back, because Northern Electric were pressing me for their money. Well, they took the cheque, and cashed it, and that was that. Then I did exactly the same with Northern Electric. Certified cheque for $10,000 in lieu of all liabilities. Take it or leave it. They also took

Bill and David Sobey, 1929.

the cheque and cashed it. That way, I got the theatre to where we kind of had our heads above water."

Despite the squabble over the Jubilee's ownership, Frank continued to pay young Henry McNeil to run the Jubilee from day to day. "He was a good, careful operator," Frank said. McNeil was also a friendly fellow and, according to his wife, "People said being in Henry McNeil's theatre was like being in Henry McNeil's living room." Frank did the dickering with the studio salesmen from Saint John and at first paid himself a management fee of only $10 a week. "It took till 1937 before I got the theatre turned around and got any money out of it," he said. "By then, I was getting $37 a week for managing and buying films."

Just how able he was at running the Jubilee would not be publicly revealed till 1945 when Supreme Court Justice John Doull, in rendering a judgment in Frank's favour, said, "While Roseland has never paid a dividend, this [Jubilee] stock has been paying dividends for some years. Since 1935 there has been paid a total of $6 per share. . . . As a consequence there is seldom any of this stock offered for sale. . . . Under these circumstances, I cannot say that $5 a share for Roseland as against $15 a share for Jubilee is unreasonable. . . . [Sobey] had been successful in managing the Jubilee over a period of years and and knew the business."

He was an operator.

Halliwell's Film Guide to 8,000 English Language Films (1979) fails to list *Draegerman Courage*. It starred Barton MacLane - who usually played gangsters or crooked cops, and appeared in such Humphrey Bogart classics as *The Maltese Falcon* and *The Treasure of the Sierra Madre* - and Jean Muir. She was a leading lady of the thirties who starred in *A Midsummer Night's Dream, The Lone Wolf Meets a Lady*, and *The Constant Nymph*, among others. *Draegerman Courage* played at the Roxy in Westville in August 1937, and the theatre's newspaper ads called it "Warner Brothers Tribute to the Pictou County Miners!"

No one in the eighties remembered whether miners flocked to the Roxy to see *Draegerman Courage*, but Frank remembered scarcely anyone flocked to the Jubilee to see Miss Muir in *A Midsummer Night's Dream*. The film also featured James Cagney, Olivia de Havilland, Joe E. Brown, Dick Powell, Mickey Rooney, and as many other stars as Warner Brothers could sign up. Leslie Halliwell called it a "super-glamorous Hollywood adaptation", and in 1935 critic Robert Forsythe said, "The publicity push behind the film is tremendous. It is going to be a success or everyone at Warner Brothers is going to be fired." Indeed, the push was so strong the studio charged theatres extra for it. "I think it was about three hundred dollars for a week," Frank said, "plus a percentage of the gate." Stellarton, however, turned up its nose at Shakespeare-out-of-Hollywood. From a theatre-owner's perspective, "It was the worst picture we ever ran. We threw it out after three days." Yet *The Irish in Us* with Cagney, de Havilland, and Pat O'Brien, a film Halliwell dismissed as "a routine, good-natured, star action frolic", filled the Jubilee every night for a week, "and it only cost us twenty-five dollars." *How Green Was My Valley*, an effective tearjerker with Maureen O'Hara, Walter Pidgeon, Roddy McDowall, and Barry Fitzgerald, was another sellout. It, of course, was about a mining village - a Welsh mining village, it's true, but still a mining village.

The Jubilee's stiffest competition came from the Roseland and the Academy of Music. N. W. Mason, manager of the two New Glasgow theatres, was aggressive, showy, experimental. If movie attendance flagged at the Academy, he promoted boxing cards, featuring the likes of Fighter Jang, "The Moncton Cyclone"; Tye Cavanaugh, "The New Waterford Wonder"; and Joe Borden, "The New Glasgow Tar Baby". A tone of awe crept into the *Eastern Chronicle*'s (Jan. 9, 1933) description of Mason: "Some people are talking fight commissions, but the fighters must fight or they'll know that the Tex Rickard [Norman Mason] of Nova Scotia is a commission unto himself. The chief means to give the public their money's worth, and his word is law."

The chief used every gimmick he could concoct to suck the people of the East River towns into his movie houses. He gave away dollar bills, announced "Gift Nites", and "Monster 5-cent Matinees". In September 1933 - as though Randolph Scott in Zane Grey's *Sunset Pass*, "plus a big comedy EXTRA ATTRACTION", were not enough - he promised that on a Saturday afternoon he'd give two wire-haired fox-terrier puppies "to the lucky boy or girl". More important than Mason's flair, however, was the fact that the Roseland had exclusive rights to the first run in Pictou County of Metro-Goldwyn-Mayer films. That gave him his real edge on Frank.

MGM was the lion of the industry. Its motto was "More stars than there are in heaven", and its stable included not only Clark Gable, Greta Garbo, John Gilbert, Wallace Beery, Lionel Barrymore, Joan Crawford, Jean Harlow, and Spencer Tracy, but also musical-comedy luminaries Nelson Eddy and Jeanette MacDonald, comic teams Laurel and Hardy and the Marx Brothers, and, for horror films, Lon Chaney. MGM covered the waterfront. "MGM was at the top of the heap," said Eric Golding, a stocky, cheery man of seventy-four, "and Louis B. Mayer was king of the land." Golding looked more like fifty-four, but he had worked for MGM in Saint John, N.B. (Mayer's boyhood home, incidentally), for forty-eight years, and he said, "Anyone who wanted those big money names, the Gables and the Garbos, had to come to us. You didn't have to be a salesman for MGM, just an order-taker. . . . Now Frank, he had a deal with Fox."

Salesmen for Fox, when dealing with Frank at any rate, had to be considerably more than order-takers. Like other theatre-owners, he'd buy a year's films during one bargaining session. Some films would already be finished, some in production, some merely planned; but, in every case, the salesman could rattle off the names of the stars. Salesmen were usually far more knowledgeable about the industry than the exhibitors. ("Give me some of them Norman Shearer movies," a theatre-owner in Newcastle, N.B., once told Eric Golding, deftly turning Norma into a man.) But not only was Frank a haggler who wanted the best possible deal for himself, he was also a fan. He knew which stars he liked, which ones filled his house. "When the agents came over from Saint John," McNeil said, "Frank would get together with them, and they'd fight tooth-and-nail." But once they'd settled their business, they'd jump into a car, take a dirt road over the forested spine of Nova Scotia, and settle in at a place on the Atlantic coast where the fishing was good, the lobster dinners were gargantuan, and the rum was sweetly burning.

"We made a fortune on Shirley Temple," McNeil said. A Jubilee newspaper ad in early 1937 said *Stowaway*, with Shirley Temple, Alice Faye, and Robert Young, offered "more entertainment than there's tea in China." Alice Faye, once a singer with Rudy Vallee's band, was a Fox luminary throughout the thirties. She was earthy but feminine, a beautiful, sensible, wry blonde, and Frank preferred her above all the other actresses. Through Fox, Jubilee patrons also got to see Will Rogers, Don Ameche, and the romantic coupling of Janet Gaynor and Charles Farrell. "They were a team that just went on and on," McNeil said. "They were in *Sunny Side Up* [which reached the Jubilee in 1930], and that was the first movie that ever ran a whole week in Pictou County."

Fox, however, did not have a total monopoly in Stellarton. Frank struck a deal whereby the Jubilee got the first run in Pictou County of half of all Warner Brothers releases (Mason getting the other half), and on Saturday afternoons he ran cowboy epics from Republic Pictures Corporation. Thus, in 1937, to take one good year, the Jubilee showed Ida Lupino, Barbara Stanwyck, Miriam Hopkins, Merle Oberon, Madeleine Carroll, Constance Bennett, Claire Trevor, Ann Sheridan, Ann Sothern, Loretta Young, Ruby

Keeler, Errol Flynn, Joe E. Brown, Fred MacMurray, Cary Grant, Paul Muni, Douglas Fairbanks, Jr., Henry Fonda, Victor McLaglen, Peter Lorre, and Boris Karloff, not to mention the Ritz Brothers, Dick ("The Singing Cowboy") Foran, Warner Oland in *Charlie Chan at the Opera*, and Bing Crosby in *Rhythm on the Range*.

The Jubilee, like its rivals, ran roughly 150 movies each year during the Depression. Frank's all-time favourite was the Twentieth Century Fox production *Alexander's Ragtime Band* (1938), described by Halliwell as "an archetypal chronicle musical with twenty-six songs: well-paced, smartly made, bursting with talent". It starred Ethel Merman, Tyrone Power, Don Ameche, and the charming Miss Faye. Frank trained his projectionist to phone him at Number One just as his favourite scenes came up. Then he'd nip next door, abandoning groceries to catch Miss Faye and the others strut their magical stuff. He was thirty-six.

So much misery lay along the banks of the East River during the Depression that it might have puzzled some, half a century later, to hear Frank say, "We really had good times in the thirties. They were the happiest and best years of my life." But consider his situation in 1937. Though he was not rich - indeed, when he gave his son Bill a bicycle it was a used delivery bike he'd had straightened out after a truck had run over it - neither was he poor. From the theatre and the grocery chain he drew salaries totalling seventy-two dollars a week. That was good money in 1937.

After all, at any Sobeys store, a quarter bought a pound of bacon, or two pounds of pork sausages, four pounds of dates, a dozen eggs, or two tins of Catelli's pork and beans. Round steak, cut from western heifer beef, was all of twenty cents a pound. So were lamb chops and ham cuts. In response to hard times, Sobeys Stores sensibly urged at Christmas, "GIVE AN ORDER OF GROCERIES THIS YEAR - We will pack and deliver orders with appropriate gift card attached." Three dollars fetched enough Yuletide food to gladden the heart of any miner's widow with children to feed.

Good times were cheap, too. "We used to say, 'What will we

do?'" Frank recalled. "'Will we buy a quart of good Scotch for $3.50, or will we buy ten shares of Abitibi or Dominion Tar?' Very often the Scotch won out." He and Irene, along with Mr. and Mrs. W. R. Monteith - Monteith was a bank accountant in New Glasgow - often went to dances at Pictou Lodge. A Canadian National Railways log-cabin resort, it sat among fragrant, sighing pines overlooking Northumberland Strait. Revellers took their own liquor, hid it under their tables, and, while the moon sailed above the glittering Strait, danced to a syrupy band that played "Poinciana", "Boo-Hoo", "You Must Have Been a Beautiful Baby", "I Hadn't Anyone Till You", "Two Sleepy People", and the deathless "Bye, Bye, Blackbird". Often, as dawn broke, the dancers stripped and hurled themselves in the ocean. You could stay at Pictou Lodge for $5.50 a day, including all meals, but for overnight outings Frank preferred a celebrated seaside joint called "Belle Baker's".

If you wanted to be formal about it, Belle Baker's was the Harbour View Hotel, and Belle herself was Mrs. Oris B. Baker. She had a country home with half a dozen bedrooms, built by her father, and four cottages. They sat just above high tide at Marie Joseph on the Atlantic coast that Nova Scotians call the Eastern Shore. Frank discovered Belle's institution after a doctor told him he was working himself to death. "He said I'd have to take six months off," Frank said, "and I said no, I couldn't do that. 'Well,' he says, 'you sure better take *some* time off.' That's when I started to go fishing." He had another motive for his weekend retreats. He hated saying no to the bad credit risks who turned up at Number One on Saturday, so he'd duck out on Friday; but, "I'd leave word that certain people couldn't have any more credit. It was much easier to say no if I wasn't there."

Belle's place was famous not only as headquarters for fishing, duck-shooting, and hunting, but also for her cooking. Her lobster bisque and poached halibut were legendary, but she also whipped up memorable hors d'oeuvres, spiced crabapples, pickled beets, hot rolls, and a rhubarb pudding so ambrosial that a lieutenant-governor of Nova Scotia once begged her for the recipe. She charged $2.50 a day for room and full board. As just part of one meal,

Frank once ate three big lobsters. Belle's daughter, Mrs. Ian Morrison, Halifax, said, "When you think of what she gave people for $2.50, I don't know how she did it. Economics just didn't seem to enter into it."

"All the old fellows used to go to Belle's," Frank said. They included provincial cabinet ministers and bureaucrats, businessmen, travelling salesmen, professors, anyone acceptable to Belle. A. Garnet Brown - food broker, son of a food broker, and a minister in the Liberal government of Nova Scotia during the first half of the seventies - said he had known Belle Baker's, just as his father had known Belle Baker's. Small as the hostelry was, Brown said, it was nothing less than "a keystone of the Eastern Shore".

By 1937, Frank had many reasons to be pleased with himself. He had three healthy sons: Bill, ten; David, six; and Donald, three. (His daughter, Diane, would be born in 1939). After living with Irene in the old apartment above Number One and later in rented accommodation, he now owned a comfortable wooden home near the top of the respectable Allan Avenue. Just down the hill, at the corner of Stellarton's main street, sat the house where his parents lived, next to the curling rink, and a stone's throw south of that was good old Number One and the Jubilee. The older Sobeys' house was a solid, ample affair, with plenty of room to put up visiting relatives. In the thirty-three years since J.W. had moved to Stellarton, the town had been good to him. Now, Sobeys of three generations all lived within a few hundred feet of the family business, and of one another. Bill, as a tot, had decided to run away from home, and "to Mother's horror and Father's delight" he just ambled down the street and moved in with his grandparents for a couple of weeks.

The town knew the Sobey clan - which included Frank's sister, Edith, who worked at Number One as his secretary, and his brother, Harold, in New Glasgow - as a genial, hard-working, church-going bunch. Even Frank's dog was genial. He was the first of several black Labrador retrievers he owned, most of them named Monty. The family trained the first Monty to go to Number One, sit before the meat counter till the butcher gave him a slab of steak, wrapped in brown paper, and then carry it back to the Sobey kitchen in his mouth. He never put a tooth through the paper.

Frank did not escape Stellarton every weekend and, though often exhausted on Sunday mornings, he went to church so regularly he impressed even his Catholic neighbours. His family's church-going was conspicuous. He insisted they walk to Sharon St. John United Church. Church, family, and business all imposed their calm Sunday rituals. Returning from church, Frank led his children to Number One. While he checked the store, and tended the coal-burning furnace, his boys proved that church had not entirely washed them clean of fleshly desires. They snitched chocolate bars and jellybeans. (On weekdays, little Sobeys were privileged in another respect: they could get into the Jubilee free.) The family then continued north to J. W.'s house, where they picked up a pot of the vegetable soup that, decade after decade, Eliza Sobey prepared on Saturday nights. Frank's family downed the soup as part of their own Sunday dinner. It was as invariable a part of their Sabbath as sermons, as prohibitions against card-playing and tobogganing. If the routine varied, it was only to include even more family. On some Sunday afternoons, the Frank Sobeys walked along the railway tracks to the New Glasgow home of Irene's parents, where they had dinner and endured D. W. McDonald's prayers, or Frank drove them out to Durham and Lyons Brook to spend time with assorted McDonalds and Creightons.

During the six days of creation, the Sobey chain – which still promoted its delivery service by advertising "Our stores are as handy as your telephone" – was not flourishing, but its sales were actually growing. "We wish to thank all our customers for their patronage in 1936, which enabled us to handle the largest volume in our history," Frank proudly announced (*The Eastern Chronicle*, Jan. 7, 1937). "We are looking forward to serving you in 1937 with the best and freshest merchandise we can procure at prices that will invite comparison." He knew he was smart. The chain proved it. The theatre proved it. Times were tough, but they would change, and he confided to friends that he still dreamed of expansion.

Meanwhile, the community proved he wasn't the only one who

knew he was smart. Stellarton was in rough shape. Large sections had no sewers. Most streets were a mixture of dirt and ashes, with cinder sidewalks. Water lines were lead. Trees were rare. The town was smoky, bare, almost broke. On top of the disasters, strikes, lay-offs, and pay cuts that had crippled it, it suffered from the fact that the Acadia Coal Company, still languishing while receivership paralysed its parent company, owed the town $101,631 in back taxes. With these headaches in mind, a bunch of merchants called a meeting in a shop, and naturally they invited the able and youthful Frank Sobey. He feared they'd ask him to sit on the town council. Irene had gone to Montreal by rail – the fare was ten dollars, return – and she came home to discover she was now married to the youngest mayor in the town's history. "I think she was pretty disturbed," he said.

Reviewing what happened, the New Year's edition (1942) of the New Glasgow *Evening News*, said, "Back in 1937, after much persuasion from the general populace, a young Stellarton businessman was persuaded to take over the mayor's chair of the mining town. . . . Frank Sobey, slim, youthful, debonair, a hail fellow, well met, who was proving himself one of the smartest manipulators in the wholesale and retail grocery trade, took the seat on the rostrum and started things moving in Pictou County's largest mining centre." If proof were needed of Stellarton's respect for him, it lies in the fact that he held the mayoralty for twenty-two years. No one saw any point in running against him. He always won by acclamation, and resigned in 1959 to give someone else a crack at the job. The "debonair manipulator" had made false prophets of his schoolteachers.

Dealing with politicians, Frank was utterly pragmatic. A loyal man in most respects, he refused to be blindly loyal to either the Conservative or the Liberal party. An old New Glasgow man who disapproved of such fickleness sourly observed, "Frank Sobey ran with the Grits and hunted with the Tories." But Frank, who was nothing if not a hard-eyed realist, couldn't tell the difference. Neither Grits nor Tories had "clear principles". They just bounced along, trying to score points, changing policies day by day to win votes. He was born Conservative and usually voted Conservative, but he did not like the party's changing its name to Progressive Conservative in 1942. "I don't know what the 'Progressive' stands for," he said. "If it was 'Aggressive', I'd understand it better." Party labels didn't fool him. He saw John Diefenbaker as a Liberal at heart. C. D. Howe and Angus L. Macdonald might have called themselves Liberals, but they'd really been Conservatives. Rather than vote socialist, Frank would have chosen to burn in hell.

He considered running federally as a Tory, but decided he'd make a poor politician, because "I'd have had to be crossing the floor all the time." He voted for Liberals if they were suitably conservative, suitably businesslike, and suitably dedicated to getting government goodies for Pictou County. Thus, he supported a sometime business crony of his, H. B. McCulloch. McCulloch was a Liberal MP for almost twenty-two years and, as James M. Cameron put it (*Political Pictonians*, 1966), "He saw his job in a clear light - get 'things' for Pictou County and be re-elected." Frank liked him because "He'd developed a business [originally dry goods and ladies' wear] in New Glasgow, worked hard, had a good, sound mind. He had good connections with deputy ministers in various departments." Frank also voted for Lt.-Col. A. B. DeWolfe, a Liberal minister in the provincial government of Angus L. Macdonald and a man so cost-conscious he once made the shocking proposal that the government *reduce* his own departmental budget. He was Frank's kind of Liberal: "a good, sound, honest citizen, conservative in his thinking, like McCulloch and MacQuarrie."

J. H. MacQuarrie, the first Liberal ever to attract Frank's vote, was a son of the same Jim T. MacQuarrie who'd once bought beef-on-the-hoof with Frank's father. A lawyer who became Attorney-General, J. H. MacQuarrie had represented Frank in the squabble over control of the Jubilee. "Joe was a very fine fellow," Frank said. "I was in his office, and I said, 'Joe, I think I'll vote for you this time, but the family are pretty strong Conservatives and they'll likely vote against you.' " MacQuarrie said, "Frank, you go out and vote against me and we'll still be as good friends as ever." That generosity sewed up Frank's vote. Out on the street, Frank decided that if MacQuarrie had merely said, " 'Thanks, Frank,' I would have made a liar of myself." Frank remembered the conversation all his life. In Pictou County, a prominent Tory's voting Grit was not a trivial matter. Frank, however, never really saw himself as a Tory defector. It wasn't he who'd abandoned conservatism for Grits, it was the Angus L. Macdonald Grits, no matter what they chose to call themselves, who'd come over to his side, the conservative side. Besides, they were in power. They could be useful.

No sooner had Frank become mayor than he scuttled down to Halifax to see what he could get for Stellarton from the Grit government. It turned out to be a lot. He ended up at the desk of Robert Hugh MacKay, Deputy Minister of Labour, and he could not have found a more sympathetic, highly placed ear. MacKay, a Liberal politician who'd gone to his reward in the bureaucracy, was an East River boy. He was born at Riverton, next to Stellarton. He'd been a merchant in Westville and a manufacturer in New Glasgow. "I made a deal with him," Frank said. "The provincial government would pay eighty per cent of the cost of a work project." For a town full of jobless miners, the deal was a Godsend, or at the very least a Gritsend.

With the provincial money, the town replaced lead water lines with copper, then began to pave streets and install storm sewers. "I remember having 130 men out on the Westville Road one winter," Frank said. "We had thirty picks and thirty shovels. Some men went into the bushes and got a fire going to keep warm while the others worked. You'd be surprised how much was accomplished." But it wasn't only the chilly men with pick and shovel who worked on the provincially funded project. Frank charged part of the town clerk's salary to the scheme, part of the town engineer's salary, and, indeed, wages of just about all of Stellarton's municipal employees. "We even had the town truck charged up at twenty dollars a day," he said. "The only thing that ever bothered me was that I couldn't figure how I could get the policemen on. But the work project really did a lot for us. It took a lot of the cost of running the town off our hands. We actually *improved* Stellarton's financial position in this period [1937-38]."

Indeed, the project was so juicy a plum it embarrassed even Frank. Springhill and Cape Breton towns, also crippled by the times, were begging for government help, "and here we were actually making money on the project." He did the decent thing. He went back to MacKay, and said, "Now look, I don't want to get you people in trouble." MacKay said, "Frank, it's all right just as long as it never gets in the papers. If it does, every town in the province will be after me, and you're through." After that, Stellarton had two kinds of council meetings: the regular one, to which reporters were invited, and the real one. (This would not be the last time Frank would decide that the public's right to know about the spending of taxpayers' money might sabotage a cause he held dear. The press, he believed, had its functions, but these did not include messing up a good deal.)

Neither Frank nor his councillors got pay for their services to Stellarton. "They just figured they owed something to the community," he said. "They insisted that since I was in business here I had to so something for Stellarton. Towns were much better governed that way. It's a fallacy that you get better politicians by pay ing them a lot." He particularly remembered councillors Jim MacKenzie, a United Mine Workers officer, and "Long" Murdock MacKenzie, another miner who, at the height of the union violence, had survived the indignity of having some of his fellow townsmen hurl him into a filthy pond. "Without the help of those two I don't believe I could have carried on," Frank said. These two men had perhaps the least palatable of all municipal duties: "Jim and Murdock would spend hours in the town office, interviewing people for welfare, which was given out in grocery orders. They knew them all. They knew who needed help, who didn't, and who'd work for it, and who wouldn't. You'd get the welfare only if you worked for the town. A single man got one day's work a week, at $2.50. A married man got two days, and those with a family got three."

In addition to ability, Frank had luck. The work project was bonanza enough, but no sooner had he arranged that than the Acadia Coal Company suddenly came up with a lump-sum payment of more than $100,000 in local tax arrears. Frank and his council used the money to begin paving streets throughout the town, starting at the centre and fanning to the outskirts. "He had it all laid out, what he wanted to do each year," said David Hayman, a later mayor. "It got under his skin that he had to get permission from the province just to put down another chunk of pavement. I was with him in Halifax when this official says to him, 'No, we can't allow you to put more pavement down. It's too expensive.' Frank says, 'Yeah, well next year it'll be *more* expensive,' and he as much as told him, 'You don't know how to run a business.' One thing led to another, and the other fellow hit the desk with his fist. 'Mr. Mayor,' he shouts, 'you can't talk to me like that.' Frank jumps to his feet, and *he* hits the desk, 'Dammit,' he says, 'I can talk to *anyone* like that when I'm *right*.'"

By the forties, miners were buying the houses they'd always rented from Acadia Coal. Frank got the company to set up a wage check-off system for the payment of property taxes by the miners, and with the proceeds paved streets in their neighbourhoods. Hayman: "I remember he said to Murdock MacKenzie, 'Hey, how'd you like to get some pavement down in Red Row?' Murdock says, 'You gotta be kidding,' but Frank says, 'Nope. I mean it. That's a mess down there, and we're going to do something about it.'"

Frank was a bulldozer as mayor, but a pleasantly devious bulldozer. "He'd let the others talk it all out so he'd never be seen in a bad light by any of them," Richard Giles said. Giles was an investment broker whose father had served with Frank on town council. Just as Frank disliked having to refuse credit to hard-up grocery shoppers, he disliked openly saying no to someone who wanted something from the council. "Go ask so-and-so," he'd say. "Whatever he says is fine by me." Then he'd phone so-and-so to tell him what he really thought of the request.

He ran the town with a tight fist. Giles, in his youth, worked for a paving contractor, and he remembers, "Frank comes up one time in his suit and tie – this was on Acadia Avenue – and he says to the crew, 'You fellows are doing too much. Now you leave that section alone!' " He figured the gang was ripping up and replacing good pavement to make more money for the contractor. "For Frank," Giles said, "running the town was just like running a business." In every one of the twenty-two years Frank served as mayor, Stellarton showed a surplus.

During the Second World War, signs on local busses urged, "Back The Attack. Buy Victory Bonds. Don't Let Them [the armed forces] Down. Buy To The Limit. Victory Bonds." Mayor Sobey and future mayor Robert Munro led the war-savings campaign and, Frank said, "Stellarton was mostly at the top of the list of Nova Scotia towns our size. I used to borrow $50,000 at the bank and buy $50,000 worth of Victory Bonds. I'd sell them later. I was never a bond investor."

He and Munro, a hardware merchant who was locally renowned as a tenor, also collaborated to build the first artificial ice rink in Pictou County. "I told him I'd raise $50,000 if the town would guarantee $50,000," Munro said. "It was tough in those days for a town to raise even $1,000 for the Red Cross." Moreover, provincial law prohibited towns from guaranteeing bonds for rinks. Stellarton appealed once more to Frank's Grit buddy, Attorney-General Joe MacQuarrie, and Munro pushed on with his fund-raising. He recalled "the usual nattering that the promoters were lining their pockets, but the truth was we did it all for nothing. I wouldn't even sell the rink a water bucket." In 1948, Premier Angus L. Macdonald officially opened Stellarton's gleaming Memorial Rink. It was, Munro boasted thirty-three years later, "the only one in Canada with free skating on Saturday afternoons". What pleased Frank about it was that Stellarton had built it without any help from the province, and ran it so efficiently it paid off its loans. It pleased him when anyone made *any* legal venture work without government grants.

A believer in the Lord's helping those who help themselves, he encouraged a building co-op among miners in 1947. Ex-miner John Roach recalled that "Miners were not welcome on every Stellarton Street. There was a lot of snobbery in this town." The real problem, however, was that building lots in central Stellarton cost about five hundred dollars. "Well, Frank showed us this high ground on the outskirts. The town owned it, and the lots cost only sixty-four dollars. We built our houses after work." Older Stellarton people remembered Frank as the mayor who helped give them co-op housing, the rink, sewers, pavement, and thrifty administration, but he himself was proudest of having changed the town from grey to green. Governments had certain legitimate uses after all, and "I found I could get trees from the government nursery in the Annapolis Valley, and all through the war we put in an average of three hundred trees a year. Dan MacEachern, the town engineer, rigged up a watering truck. The driver could just press a pedal to make water flow out a pipe onto each tree. A lot of those trees are big now, six and eight inches at the stump.

"Dan was just a boy when he buried his parents," Frank said, "and he brought up the other kids. But some of them died and he buried them, too. I think it was TB in Dan's family. He suffered a lot of pain himself, and he told me the only thing that helped was black rum. One time, we needed him real bad but we couldn't find him. I had Sam Baker [the police chief] chasing round for three days. I bothered Sam four or five times a day. I said that if he couldn't even find the town engineer he wasn't much of a policeman. Later, Dan got real sick and it was Sam and me who took him to the hospital. He died. On the way home, Sam says, 'You remember when you raised hell with me to find Dan? Well, I had him hid. I had him hid for three days. I didn't want anybody to see him.' " Frank paused. Then he said, "That's the kind of fellow Sam was."

That's the kind of town Stellarton was. Frank would never leave it for long. Headquarters for Sobeys Stores would never move away.

Frank has boasted, "I never worked for anybody in my life, except my father and myself." He also allowed that, in his young-manhood, "you bloody well had to work." Still, he found time to play. He was not like his older friend, Nova Scotia industrialist and financier Roy Jodrey. Jodrey was a workaholic. Other men's urges to spend money on relaxation mystified him. His house was next door to his pulp factory in Hantsport, and he couldn't imagine a more relaxing activity than just listening to the hum of that plant. Frank, however, loved golf, fishing, shooting ducks and pheasants, rugged countryside, foreign travel, collecting Canadian paintings. He was sociable. He liked to take a drink, go to parties, dance a bit, occasionally play cards. "He had absolutely no card sense at all," New Glasgow lawyer R. B. MacDonald said. "The boys used to love to get him into a game. They'd win money off him." Frank paced himself, kept fit, took long walks. Even at eighty, MacDonald added, "Frank has such a damn *young* attitude about everything."

He was once capable of timely vanishing acts. In the war years, when he and Rene and the children spent their summers at a beach-front house at Chance Harbour on Northumberland Strait, Frank invariably disappeared on moving day. As summer began, Jim Johnson, a Sobeys Stores delivery man who could carry a hundred-pound bag of sugar under each arm, backed a company truck up to Frank's Stellarton house. "We'd load that thing with beds and refrigerators, everything," David Sobey said. "We had nothing at the cottage." They'd bring the furniture back home in September. "Father was never there during the move," David said. "He had a habit of disappearing at times, and no one could find him."

He was a restless man. "When you're in business," he believed, "you can't stay still." Nor could he stay still himself. He had to be on the move. He had to be busy. He had to be *doing*. In the late thirties he satisfied his urge to keep on going by buying a small car trailer. It had a chimney like the hat on the tin man in the movie *The Wizard of Oz*. The interior, David said, was built "like one of those old Peterborough canoes". The Sobeys threw a house party on the night Frank bought the rig and, as soon as everyone else had gone home, he said to Rene and their friends the Monteiths, "Come on, let's go down to the St. Mary's River." Halfway there, he unhitched the trailer, left the others, and drove back to Stellarton to get some essential gear that he'd forgotten in his excitement.

Frank Sobey, as mayor of Stellarton, and his wife were presented to King George VI and Queen Elizabeth during the royal couple's visit to Nova Scotia in June 1939.

They reached the river at dawn. The trailer enabled Frank and his family - the two older boys slept outside in tents - to beetle round eastern Nova Scotia on overnight fishing trips. It was on one such expedition, to the Margaree River in Cape Breton, that Frank caught a 28.5-pound salmon, his biggest ever.

The Sobeys met King George VI in Halifax on June 15, 1939, the last day of the first Royal Visit to Canada by a reigning monarch. The Nova Scotia government invited them to meet the royal couple because Frank was mayor of Stellarton, and the experience touched him to the depths of his royalist being. He had done his grandparents proud, and he and his wife drank in, for as long as they could, the vision of what the local press called "the Sailor King and his smiling Queen". The Sobeys were among the 150,000 Nova Scotians who, while the sun set behind Citadel Hill in Halifax, watched Their Majesties sail away on the *Empress of Britain*. Her hull was white, her towering funnels were golden. She flew the scarlet-and-gold Royal Ensign at her stern, and the Halifax *Herald* said she sailed "amid a wild cacophony of bells, ships' sirens, motor horns and cheers, and to the booming of guns". There was a ghostly touch to the majestic departure. For a while, shorebound spectators could see no one aboard the steamship - neither the captain, nor an officer or a crewman - except the King and Queen. He wore the gold-braided uniform of an Admiral of the Fleet, she was fragile in pale blue. They stood on the bridge, entirely alone, tiny and brave, waving farewell in a masterpiece of royal showmanship.

"For almost an hour the King and Queen stood on the heights above the deck," the Halifax *Herald* reported. "Their last glimpse of Canada and Canadians at home. They stood there until they could be seen no longer, as they sailed out past the [Royal Nova Scotia Yacht] Squadron, past the Martello Tower, past the little fishing villages, past sheer, granite Chebucto, to the open sea toward Britain, their other homeland." Soon the *Empress of Britain* was making twenty-four knots toward a continent that was plummeting into the most awful war in history. June 15, 1939, was a day the Sobeys would remember all their lives.

As the forties began, the Sobeys bought a new Plymouth and drove it all the way to the Pacific Ocean. Crossing the continent by car was a formidable adventure in 1940 but both Sobeys were competent drivers. His councillors could run the town for a while, and his family could run the business. Harold Sobey, who'd taken an army officers' course in Kingston, Ont., was home for a few weeks before going overseas. Now was the moment for Frank and Rene to escape. But as they rolled through New York, the Nazis were rolling through Holland, Belgium, and Luxembourg. Paris was about to fall. Crowds of New Yorkers stood outside newspaper offices to watch posters illustrating the dreadful advance of the blitzkrieg. "All this, and the stock markets were going to pieces," Frank said. "*Everything* seemed to be falling to pieces."

They pushed south to Atlanta. Holland surrendered. The British retreated. Dunkirk was a few days away, and the Sobeys thought they'd better go home. "So we sent a telegram," Frank said, "and they wired back, 'If you're enjoying yourself, keep right on going. There's nothing you can do.'" They drove through Dallas, Fort Worth, and El Paso, then popped down to Mexico and up to Los Angeles. "My wife was a terrific driver," Frank said proudly, after age had made her uncertain. "She used to drive as fast as any man. I remember she drove all the way from Fort Worth to El Paso in one day. That's about six hundred miles. She was going ninety-three and ninety-four miles an hour, which was as fast as the Plymouth would go. The road was straight, and there was very little traffic. Gasoline in Texas was ten cents a gallon, the lowest I ever paid for gasoline. We stayed at good motels for five dollars a night."

In California Frank proved he was not only a movie exhibitor but also, at thirty-eight, a movie groupie. He wangled Hollywood passes, and on the set of a forgettable farce he and Rene met Ginger Rogers and Ronald Colman. Colman was cool, but Rogers was "a nice girl". They also chatted with Frank's all-time favourite star, Alice Faye ("that Alice Faye was a smart one"), and British-born film actress Wendy Barrie. "Rene told me that if I could get Ginger Rogers actually to go out on a date with me, she'd let me go," Frank recalled. "Well, I didn't think that was too likely, so I said, 'How about Wendy Barrie?' Rene said, 'No.' " They settled for lunch together, with Dennis Morgan, co-star with Rogers that year in *Kitty Foyle*.

In Seattle they met Sobey cousins, and in British Columbia they stayed with Frank's Uncle Charles, who'd left Pictou County long before the previous war. Coming back east across Canada, twenty-two years before the official opening of the Trans-Canada Highway, Frank had to ship the Plymouth by rail over a chunk of the Rocky Mountains. He was glad to get home. They'd been away two months. It had been good to see the Sobeys in the far West. It had been exhilarating to chat with the women whose creamy faces glowed in his own Jubilee theatre. But his main business was the food business, and he had thinking to do. He'd used his vacation as a transcontinental exercise in enlightened snoopery. He'd been the phantom of the Piggly Wiggly, the lurker at the Big Bear, and the spy in the "cheapy" warehouse operations that billed themselves as "price-crushers" and "price-wreckers". He'd also haunted outlets of the great chains: A & P, American, First National, Kroger, Safeway, National Tea, and he came home with his head abuzz with purloined gimmicks, confiscated ideas, and dreams of

Frank meets a celebrity at Radio City Music Hall, 1940.

bigger and better stores. Most of all, he wanted a real Sobeys supermarket.

"This new revolution in distribution, the 'Super Market', burst on the scene early in the great depression," Rom J. Markin wrote in *The Supermarket: An Analysis of Growth, Development, and Change* (1968), "[and became] the merchandising phenomenon of the decade, despite hazards, rebuffs, and dire predictions of nonbelievers." Frank was a believer, but it would take him till 1947 to gamble on his belief by building his first supermarket.

Meanwhile, there was a war on.

The war caused a few furious spurts of industrial activity in Pictou County. Shipbuilding aroused the port of Pictou from generations of torpor. Foundation Maritime Company, Ltd., built twenty-four 4,700-ton steel cargo vessels there, and as Roland Sherwood wrote (*Pictou Parade*, 1945), "Giant cranes and shipbuilding frames pushed their gaunt shoulders against the sky, and long lines of cars stood parked on every street. . . . There sprang up row upon row of neat little houses, wide streets and well-kept lawns and gardens. For here, in this area, four hundred prefabricated homes were built to house those who came to work on the ships. . . .

There was no poverty, no idleness. . . . Everyone was busy, everyone had money. . . . The population doubled [to 8,000]; the streets were crowded; the post office jammed; the stores a bedlam; and long lines waited admission to the theatre and the liquor store. The banks stayed open at night to cash the workers' cheques, and sometimes in the crowding and the pushing and the jamming, you'd wish for the old-fashioned, slow-moving Pictou."

Coal surged back as a vital Canadian industry. In Stellarton, whistles blew, smoke flew, and shift followed shift into the pits. Logy with massive cargoes of coal, vessels and trains made their cumbersome way inland to satisfy the massive appetite of wartime manufacturers. Twice in the war years, Stellarton miners stumbled on reminders of the horror of their trade. In 1942, as they plunged further into the Foord Pit, they found the corpses of five men who'd died in an explosion more than six decades before; in 1943, they found fifteen more. No one knew it during coal's wartime revival, but soon all the historic pits of Stellarton would also be dead. Local coal was enjoying its last hurrah.

The war brought business to Trenton, too. The steelworks produced more than two million shells, and also made guns. That's where young Bill Sobey wanted to work, in the munitions factory where the money was good. His father wouldn't hear of it. Frank wanted his boys to learn the food business, and learn it they would. Bill continued in his boring part-time job at Number One until the manager, Roddie MacKenzie, fired him for shoddy sweeping. "I figured, 'Great,' " Bill said. "I was standing on the steps of the Jubilee, and along comes Father. He asks me, 'What are you doing out here?' Well, I says, 'I quit. I'm not working there any more,' and Father says, 'You get the hell back in that store.' " Forty years later Bill said, "I've been there ever since. Roddie still kids me. He says, 'Remember that time I fired you, Billy?'

"Boys, those stores were hard to run during the war," Bill added. Frank's brother, Harold, was overseas, earning distinction as a tank captain in the Canadian army. Moreover, Frank's other managers joined up. "The young people I had working with me, like Charlie Higgins, Roddie MacKenzie, and David Simpson, most of them joined the army," Frank said. "We were so short of people that I had Dot Bain running the store in Stellarton, and a girl by the name of Dee Gillis running the store in Trenton. The two New Glasgow stores were also run by ladies during the war. I lost my meat-cutter in Trenton, and I'd go over there every morning to cut the meat to get them going." He was a mayor, theatre-owner, and chain-store boss, but at forty he had still not escaped butchering. Moreover, at least once during the early forties his wife was a Sobeys Stores truck-driver.

The war stole even his secretary. Her name was Lois Creighton, and she'd succeeded Frank's sister as a kind of executive assistant at Number One. "You did everything," she said. "You did his correspondence. You did his banking. You did the bookkeeping. You did the payroll." But in 1942 the Royal Canadian Air Force posted her husband to Moncton. While visiting him, she decided certain women of Moncton were excessively friendly to air force men. "I wanted to keep my husband," she said. "I wasn't going to let any French girl steal him." She quit her job in Stellarton to protect her man in Moncton.

The moment Frank's good old boys drifted home, he pounced on them. Charles Higgins, who'd helped Sobeys Stores survive the worst the thirties could throw at them, went overseas with the Royal Canadian Army Service Corps in 1942. As soon as he showed his face at Pictou County at war's end, Frank hired him as a store manager. Frank pursued Cecil McLaren, the meat man's meat man, almost before McLaren was off the train. He, too, had gone to war with the RCASC. The troop train that returned him to New Glasgow in 1945 was also carrying hundreds of Cape Breton Island soldiers from Halifax to Sydney; and when it stopped in Stellarton, Irene Sobey came aboard to hand out sandwiches. That was at 11.30 a.m. "You know what?" McLaren said. "Frank was at my home at 1.30. He wanted me to go to work right then, that same afternoon. Well, I didn't want to do that, so I went in the next day." He went back to Halifax a month later for his formal discharge, a process that normally took several days. "But Frank called Halifax," he said, "and they started to pump me through

Frank and Irene Sobey at the christening of the corvette Stellarton *in Quebec City.*

the channels as soon as I got to the barracks. They discharged me that night." By morning, he was back at Number Two in New Glasgow, cutting meat.

The Sobeys spent their wartime summers in the boisterous cottage colony that faced Prince Edward Island at Chance Harbour. The beach was sumptuous there, and the water warm. It was a magical haven for children, and the Chance Harbour parents were an amiable gang of like-minded, party-going New Glasgow businessmen and their wives. The men included George Fleming (furniture), George Fanjoy (men's clothing), R. B. MacDonald (law), Bill and Harry Sutherland (publishing), Robert Thompson, and Tom Foster. Boston relatives of Irene Sobey often brought their children to Chance Harbour, and when the neighbours also had house guests it was not a place where you'd seek solitude in a tranquil wilderness. "We used to live it up pretty good down there," MacDonald said. "They were all great jokesters."

Frank swam naked after one raucous party. His friend and fellow member of the Gyro Club, George Fleming, beamed a searchlight on him so that, unless he wanted to suffer spectacular public exposure, he couldn't come ashore on the beach. "Frank ended up floundering in the eel grass and seaweed," MacDonald said. "He was all scratched and bitten." George Fleming's widow, Alice, recalled an itinerant booze-up on VJ Day in August 1945. The gang started at the Sutherland brothers' end of the beach. Then they worked their way along, stopping for more drinks at cottage after cottage after cottage. George got so tight he walked on the roof of Bertram Godden's car, and caved it in. Godden was both smaller and older than Fleming. But he was also a fussy ex-banker, and his formality made him imposing. When Fleming sobered up he couldn't sleep. He knew he'd have to confess, and he feared Godden's reaction. But in the morning, while stammering his apologies, big George put one hand inside the car and pushed up the ceiling. The roof snapped back into shape. "Poor George," his widow laughed thirty-five years later, "he'd been awake all night for nothing.

"Frank and Rene," she continued, "were just excellent neighbours. If there was a light on in our cottage, they'd never drive by without dropping in. They were full of friendliness and there was nothing they wouldn't do for you." Frank felt the same way about her and George, and the others. "I'd stay in the water half the day at Chance Harbour," he said. "The neighbours were a great bunch. If a storm came up and you were sleeping, someone always knocked on your bedroom window to get you out to help put the boats away."

5

THE WAR ENDS, AN EMPIRE BEGINS

AT WAR'S END, Frank was not hugely more successful than his Chance Harbour neighbours. They knew he was able, hard-working, a bit prosperous. They knew he was a smart mayor, a smart theatre-owner, the smart boss of six food stores. But he was still strictly a small-town businessman. Nowhere except along the river where he'd spent all his life was his name a household word. Would he ever satisfy his itch to build a great empire for his family? He was forty-three, and a man had only so much time. But now he abruptly took steps, made decisions, and laid foundations that would make 1945, '46, and '47 stand out later as the years in which, after maddening doubts, he finally launched his biggest dreams.

If Sobeys Stores had begun in 1907 when John William Sobey, at thirty-eight, first assigned delivery men to roam Stellarton with horse-drawn wagons loaded with red meat, then the parlaying of the stores into holdings worth tens of millions of dollars began almost four decades later when Frank Sobey, at forty-three and forty-four, made three crucial decisions. First, he dissolved the twenty-year father-son partnership in favour of incorporating Sobeys Stores, Ltd. The new company sold bonds to pay bank loans and finance expansion. Second, he used Sobeys Stores, Ltd., to acquire Barkers Stores, the chain that had been his head-to-head, town-by-town rival ever since silent movies. Third, he built the first slick, self-service, cash-and-carry supermarket - complete with miraculous new automatic doors – that Pictou County had ever seen. Ridiculed in advance by rival grocers, knocked by his own father, doubted even by himself, this store promptly gave him a flow of instant cash such as he'd never known before. Now he saw exactly where the future of his food business lay.

Moreover, while buying the store's site, he casually acquired the charter of the little local company that had owned the property. He rather liked its name: Empire Company Ltd. He kept it alive by tossing it a few stock-market investments. One day, Empire, with his youngest son Donald as president, would be the corporate umbrella for a vast family kingdom of investments and operating companies. But to get the Barkers chain in 1946, build the supermarket in '47, and also exploit chances to buy stock in Dominion Steel and Coal Company (DOSCO), Frank had needed more money than even he'd been accustomed to borrowing from banks. Some of this money came to him as the spoils of his bizarre and bitter victory in the county-rocking Battle of the Roseland.

Small-time takeovers are much like big-time takeovers. Whether the prize is a kingdom of publishing, a multinational mining concern, an industrial conglomerate, or merely the Roseland theatre in New Glasgow, the smell of the game is the same. Fighting to dominate an outfit is as old as blood-lust, the giddiness of victors, the bitterness of losers. Amicable takeovers, like arranged marriages, do occur from time to time. But when someone shouts "No", or mounts a counterattack, or otherwise tries to sabotage a takeover, you find on both sides the urge to Be On Top, and in the relentless cause of business expansion, the urge to beat the other guys. You also find loyalty, treachery, shifting alliances, rapid plot developments, secret meetings, and a windfall of work for lawyers. And greed, too, the polite word for which is acquisitiveness. The love of gain. Is there a businessman alive, big or small, who's not interested in making quick bucks?

The battle for the Roseland Theatre Company, Ltd., owner of both the Roseland and the seedier Academy of Music, began in the autumn of 1943 when majority shareholder N. W. Mason, Mr.

Show Biz of the East River towns, decided to make quick bucks by double-crossing men he'd known almost all his life. That, at least, is how they saw his plan, and they invited Frank to help them foil the traitor. But not only did Frank help them foil Mason, he also helped himself to control of the Roseland company. The ganging-up on Mason, his snarling responses, and the trail of lawsuits, appeals, and injunctions that stretched even into the months after his death - these made the case supremely gossip-worthy. Nearly forty years later, it still took little prodding in New Glasgow to get old tongues clucking about Frank's shrewd moves in the fight over control of Roseland Theatre.

The seven directors of Roseland Theatre owned 8,415 of the 9,600 outstanding common shares. They were solid, upright chaps, exactly the sort you'd expect to share ownership of the only movie business in town. Mason had served as mayor of New Glasgow for six years, Dr. Clarence Miller for four, and bookstore proprietor George White for two. Roy J. Bennett, shoe merchant, would be mayor for ten years. Four of the seven held only piddling amounts of Roseland stock, but director H. B. McCulloch, the Grit MP, had 2,392, and director Bertram Godden, the chap whose car roof was abused on VJ Day, had 704. Both men, as Mason would discover to his gall, were fellows upon whom Frank could count. Meanwhile, however, managing director Mason was clearly in the catbird seat. Ever since 1933, when the Goodman brothers had sold their theatre holdings, he'd had 5,100 voting shares. He was now eighty, and he was sick. He got an offer he could not refuse.

Mason was a famous old man. He'd been an actor, an impresario, a businessman, and a community leader. "He had played pro ball in the States, had acted on stage in Boston and New York, was a candy butcher, had the strength and virility of a horse, liked work, and loved life," James M. Cameron wrote in *More About New Glasgow* (1974). "He set up a candy and confectionery shop with ice cream parlour . . . [and attracted] trade by giving orchestral entertainment in the evenings. He staged impromptu shows himself in the window of the candy store by kneading huge blobs of molasses toffee." Mason had been a New Glasgow institution since before Frank's father had left the farm, since before Frank was even born. At forty-one, the mayor of Stellarton was a pup beside the ex-mayor of New Glasgow. Mason had pulled off myriad deals in his long life, but none looked so juicy as his last. He expected it to be a magnificent business swan song, and felt no alliance of his fellow townsmen on the board could possibly stop him.

Under his management, the company had had five grim years and five good ones. The common shares had never paid a dividend, and each year from 1933 to 1938 payment of dividends on the preferred stock had left Roseland in the red. Though business surged after that, federal taxes drained off the income. On November 7, 1943, however, Roseland Theatre showed a net profit for the previous year of $6,384.14, nearly $2,000 more than it needed to pay dividends on the preferred stock. "The company was in flourishing condition," Judge John Doull of the Supreme Court of Nova Scotia decided a year later. "True, it had not much more than made up its losses of the poor years," Doull continued, "but it had provided $52,737.55 for depreciation, and had about $10,000 cash on hand and some outside investments. The property had been put in good shape, a large sum having been spent in alterations in 1940." It's doubtful if even Mason's fellow directors appreciated the full value of the company. But Joshua Lieberman did, and so did Mitchell S. Bernstein. Theatre-owners from Saint John, N.B., they were the ones who made Mason the offer he couldn't refuse. He wanted to retire, and they could make his retirement wonderfully comfortable.

Mason had talked to his fellow directors about their buying his shares but decided he could do better with Lieberman and Bernstein. He was dead right. While negotiating with them, he heard from director Bertram Godden. Godden offered $30,000 for Mason's 5,100 shares and, considering Mason had paid only $17,100 for them in 1933, Godden doubtless thought this was a fair proposition. Whether the old promoter laughed in his rather stiff face is unknown. He probably did.

For, as Judge Doull said, "It soon appeared that Mason was being offered much more money. . . . In November, 1943 [Mason] took

Lieberman to a meeting of directors and told [them] this was the man to whom he was going to sell. The directors inquired the price and were told that it was $75,000," at which point, one imagines, six jaws dropped. "The directors who knew what the stock had cost [Mason] in 1933 thought it was a very high price," Doull continued. (Over at Frank's theatre, the Jubilee, the featured film that weekend was *It Ain't Hay*, with Bud Abbott and Lou Costello.)

The other Roseland directors, their jaws back in place, "asked Lieberman how he was going to get his money out of it." Not surprisingly and not soothingly, "Lieberman replied that he did not think that that was any of their business." Lieberman also flatly refused to buy out the minority shareholders at a fair price. The directors later tried to talk Mason out of the deal, and it was at this stage that they rang in Frank Sobey. Thanks to ancient bonuses for selling theatre stock for the Goodmans, he owned 360 common shares. Indeed, among non-directors he was the biggest shareholder. The other directors said that so far as control of the Roseland went, it wasn't Lieberman and Bernstein they disliked; they just wanted to sell their shares at the same time and at the same price as Mason.

Three directors now made Mason a counter-offer. They were Dr. Miller, H. B. McCulloch, and George White, but they were probably acting for other directors as well as themselves, and possibly for Frank, too. They may have suspected the $75,000 offer was a phony, a bluff Mason had cooked up with Lieberman. In any event, they offered Mason $50,000. W. F. Fraser, a New Glasgow broker in Mason's corner, promptly asked, "Why should he lose $25,000?" Good question. Game over.

Or was it?

On November 25, 1943, Mason agreed in writing to sell his interest in Roseland to Lieberman and Bernstein for $75,000. He and they both understood that what they were buying was not just his 5,100 common shares (and 55 preferred) but also the *control* that went along with them. The buyers slapped down $5,000 on the understanding they'd pay Mason the other $70,000 when he transferred control of Roseland to them. He was to do that on October 10, 1944, almost a year in the future. If Mason and the Saint John men had not been so cocky, they'd have moved both less slowly and less meanly. As things turned out, their meanness gave the minority shareholders more reason than they already had to torpedo the deal; and their slowness gave this same handful of crafty solid citizens time to find, aim, and fire the torpedo.

The fight turned vicious in February 1944. Lieberman and Bernstein, remember, were paying Mason $13.62 per share. It must therefore have been a masterpiece of judicial understatement when Judge Doull allowed that "The antagonism of [the other directors] to the change of management was not lessened when they received an offer of $3.50 . . . [from] Bernstein and Lieberman for any common stock held by shareholders." They must have been apoplectic. Their reward for riding out the bad years with Mason would be to get, for each of their few shares, roughly one-quarter of what he'd get for each of his many shares. On top of that, Frank had a reason of his own for wanting to wreck the Lieberman-Bernstein bid. As Doull put it, "Sobey did not want them as competitors [against his Jubilee] and no doubt he was anxious to obtain the management of [Roseland] at some future date."

Frank and his friends now moved cleverly, secretly, and, from Mason's point of view, infuriatingly. The board met on February 18 to reject the $3.50 offer. Only six days later, after at least some had huddled with Frank, they met again to spring something nasty on Mason: a Frank Sobey coup. It was as though Frank had just walked in off the street and plucked control from under the old promoter's nose. The secret lay in 5,400 shares of authorized but unissued stock. At the February 24 meeting, Dr. Miller, Roseland's president, read a one-sentence letter from Frank: "I offer, subject to acceptance on or before Saturday, February 26, 1944, seventeen hundred and fifty-one shares (1751), being controlling interest in the Jubilee Theatre Company Ltd., in exchange for five thousand (5000) Roseland Theatre Co. Ltd. ordinary shares in full payment." Mason was doubtless the only man in the room for whom the offer was a total and horrible surprise. (At the Jubilee, the Dead End Kids were starring in *Mug Town*, and Basil Rathbone foiled Moriarty in *Sherlock Homes and the Secret Weapon*.)

The other directors instantly voted to accept the proposition. Memory adds flourishes to old stories. Decades later, New Glasgow folk insisted that Mason had been in Florida when the board issued the treasury stock to Frank, and that the poor old fellow returned home to find control of Roseland had been "stolen" from him. But the truth was that, although he might as well have been in Florida for all the influence he had, he did attend the crucial board meeting in New Glasgow and cast his lonely vote against Frank's offer. He was, of course, outnumbered. Now, he suddenly no longer owned what he'd agreed to sell the Saint John men, the one thing they wanted from him: control of Roseland Theatre. Goodbye $75,000.

Who had concocted this ingenious and ultimately foolproof scheme to smash Mason's cosy arrangement with Lieberman and Bernstein? No one remembers for sure. Frank recalled that the disgruntled directors approached him, rather than the other way round, that it was they who first suggested he obtain 5,000 treasury shares in Roseland Theatre. But no matter what the source of the initiative, Frank and Bertram Godden, more than anyone else, were Mason's undoing. If Mason's deal succeeded, then Godden, with his 704 common shares, had much to lose. Doull said, "It probably makes no difference but I do not believe the proposal originated simply by Godden meeting Sobey on the street and making the suggestion." But then the judge added, "Although no doubt they did meet and action followed pretty quickly."

A Newfoundlander by birth, Godden had once been a bank manager in New Glasgow. Shortly before the crash of '29 he'd quit the bank for the investment business, which suggests career timing was not his forte. But Richard Giles, a younger man who later entered the same field, said Godden "just slugged away and his old clients stuck with him. He was extremely capable at acquisitions . . . at quietly rounding up certain stock for clients like Frank Sobey. In fact, he was just extremely shrewd, one of the most able men I ever knew in the investment business." Godden was "a non-member broker", which meant that although he was not a member of a stock exchange he had stock-exchange permission to do business through brokers who were members. He dealt a lot, for instance, with Dominion Securities, Ltd. "Godden," said an elderly, knowledgeable New Glasgow man, "was one of those fellows that sell stocks and bonds out of their vest pockets." He had no office. He worked out of his bedroom.

Having helped devise the scheme whereby Roseland Theatre grabbed the Jubilee and Frank grabbed 5,000 shares of Roseland, Godden quietly set about corralling shares to ensure his friend beat out Mason for control. At the moment, no one had it. The issuing of 5,000 common shares to Frank meant there were 14,600 outstanding. Mason still had 5,100, and Frank 5,360. An apocryphal story preserves the suggestion that Mason thought Godden the most contemptible of his enemies. During the court hearing over which Judge Doull presided, the lawyer representing Roseland directors cross-examined Mason. No transcript of the hearing survives, but in local fable part of the interrogation went like this:

LAWYER: "Now, Mr. Mason, you have suggested that some of these men treated you less than honestly. Surely you are not saying that Dr. Clarence Miller is a crook."

MASON: "No sir, I don't think Dr. Miller is a crook."

LAWYER: "Well, what about George White, Mr. Mason? Is he a crook?"

MASON: "No sir, George is not a crook."

LAWYER: "Roy Bennett?"

MASON: "Nope, not Roy Bennett."

LAWYER: "And Bertram Godden, Mr. Mason?"

MASON: (Silence)

LAWYER:"I ask you again, Mr. Mason. In your opinion, is Bertram Godden a crook?"

MASON: "I ain't sayin'."

But it was H. B. McCulloch who finally tipped control of Roseland Theatre into Frank's lap. A good golfer, curler, card-player, and political fence-mender, McCulloch was an MP for

One that didn't get away: a $28\frac{1}{2}$-pound salmon caught in the Margaree River, Cape Breton, 1940.

nearly twenty-two years. A rich businessman at forty, he'd drifted into politics at fifty-eight, perhaps out of boredom. Though he rarely spoke in Parliament, he won five consecutive elections. Moreover, he was an amiable, low-key master at generating goodwill towards his riding among the mighty in Ottawa.

"No mother with unwed daughters cultivated invitation sources more assiduously than did senior government officials seek bids to Henry McCulloch's yearly lobster dinners," James M. Cameron wrote in *Political Pictonians*. "The gatherings grew until at his final one the Commons Railway Room held some 150 Cabinet Ministers, Deputy and Assistant Deputy Ministers, departmental seniors, Senators, MPs, and Press Gallery newsmen. They regaled themselves on fresh lobster, sent by McCulloch's friend Broidy [Pictou County's pioneer shipper of live lobster] and rum sent by other well-wishers in Pictou County, served by the Parliamentary Restaurant staff. . . . The roster of the head table was a roll of the Privy Council of the times. . . . McCulloch reasoned that an official who had been treated to all the lobster he could eat, and looked forward to more of the same, would give the host a courteous hearing when asked. McCulloch's reasoning was crude. It was also correct."

McCulloch was in Ottawa when the Roseland board voted to issue Frank 5,000 shares in return for the Jubilee, but he doubtless knew about the deal. What is not so certain is whether or not the other directors knew about a neat understanding between Frank and McCulloch. Right after the board accepted Frank's offer, he got an option from McCulloch to buy 2,000 of the MP's 2,392 shares for $5 per share. "There is no evidence that the other directors knew of this option," Judge Doull said. Frank exercised the option. Now he had clear control. Days earlier, he'd controlled one theatre. Now he controlled three, the Roseland, the Academy of Music, and, once again, the Jubilee. If heads shook over this lightning development, none shook more violently than N. W. Mason's.

In March 1944 he turned eighty-one. His theatre staff gave him a set of canes, and he announced that he would play the lead role of Uncle Josh in yet another of his umpteen revivals of *The Old Homestead*. "So we will be on deck, or in our seats," the *Eastern Chronicle* promised, "to see N.W. again tread the boards, and a royal reception awaits him." Mason, however, also celebrated his birthday by suing. He sued Roseland Theatre, and all six of his enemy directors. For good measure, he also sued Frank Sobey. (*Let's Face It*), with Bob Hope and Betty Hutton, was playing the Roseland. So was *Is Everybody Happy?* with Ted Lewis and his orchestra. At the Jubilee, the feature of the week was something called *Wrecking Crew.*)

The case fascinated the East River towns not only because it attracted what the *Eastern Chronicle* called "a brilliant display of legal talent", including ace Halifax lawyers, but also because it bared the motives, tactics, and rivalries of county bigshots. The Battle of the Roseland was now a wide-open, courtroom dogfight among affluent gents who normally hid their differences. Other businessmen took sides. Some felt Mason had pulled a few dirty tricks himself, and was at last getting what he deserved. Others felt he was the victim of the boardroom equivalent of a gangland beating.

The *Eastern Chronicle*, which carefully observed that "the interest in the case lies in that it concerns so many prominent citizens," worried first about Mason: "For nearly half a century, Mr. Mason has been our showman and he has, during that time, guided the development of a large and engaging business. He is now eighty-one years of age, and his health is not very good, so it is but natural that he desired to retire and enjoy a well-earned rest from his long and arduous engagements." But at the same time the paper did not want to turn Mason's enemies into its own enemies. It therefore decided the safest course was simply to express bewilderment and sorrow over the whole nasty affair: "From the outside, he and his associates looked to be a particularly happy family, in keeping proportionately with the prosperity in which they shared. But a rift has come into the association, and the lack of confidence and regard for each other of the contenders was made plain at the trial. . . . We can express regret that a difference of a serious nature should have developed where so many of our business leaders are concerned."

Mason lost.

He wanted the court to cancel the entire deal that gave Frank the 5,000 treasury shares. He argued they'd been issued wrongfully, in bad faith, and for no other purpose but to sabotage his agreement with Lieberman and Bernstein. His lawyers claimed "the issuing of the shares to Sobey was not done *bona fide* in the proper exercise of the directors' powers for the general benefit of the company." Unfortunately for Mason, Judge Doull did not agree. He said, "I see no reason why it is part of the duty of shareholders to protect one shareholder who is endeavoring to sell his shares at more than $13 per share while others are supposed to be content with $3.50." Moreover, "If it is proper to issue shares, it is proper to change control. . . . I dismiss the action with costs."

Although growing feebler, Mason wouldn't quit. He appealed Doull's decision. Pending the outcome of the appeal, however, everyone agreed to mark time. Mason agreed not to call a meeting of Roseland shareholders or, if someone else called one, to vote for any change in the board membership. Roseland Theatre agreed it would "not approve, accept, register or act upon any transfer of the 5,000 shares issued to Mr. Sobey." And Frank, who'd apparently used the shares as security for a bank loan, agreed to "protect" the loan. Moreover, he would "not further mortgage, hypothecate, charge or create any liens upon the said 5,000 shares." Nor would he "vote upon, sell, transfer, make a gift of or otherwise dispose of or deal with, or use, or act upon" them. All these commitments, Chief Justice Joseph Chisholm said, "manifested a mutual willingness to maintain the status quo until the determination of the action so that the rights of none of the principal parties would be lost or prejudiced irretrievably." Until the courts reached a final decision, no one was to pull a fast one.

Mason tried anyway.

He introduced a player to the vicious game, and among Maritime theatre-owners the newcomer was a notoriously tough mug. His name was A. I. Garson. On March 8, 1945, Mason sold all but one of his 5,100 shares to Garson. Eric Golding of Saint John, who worked in the movie industry for half a century, said, "Frank Sobey met his match when he got up against A. I. Garson. He was a real shrewd operator." H. L. P. McNeil, the veteran New Glasgow theatre manager, said Garson looked "just like a movie gangster". He drove a Cadillac, and wore flashy silk ties and a belted camel-hair coat with huge lapels.

Garson, a Jewish businessman from Saint John, was associated with the Odeon chain. No one will ever know what Garson paid Mason for 5,099 shares in Roseland, but the moment he got them he acted as though he owned the joint. He fired off a bossy telegram to Frank:

> PLEASED TO INFORM YOU THAT I HAVE TODAY PURCHASED AND TRANSFERRED INTEREST OF N. W. MASON IN ROSELAND THEATRE COMPANY LIMITED STOP SUGGEST IMMEDIATE MEETING OF DIRECTORS AND YOURSELF WITH IMPORTANT OFFICIAL OF ODEON AND MYSELF TO DISCUSS IMPORTANT MATTERS STOP SUGGEST

YOU CONTACT ODEON WITH REGARD TO REBUILDING ACADEMY. REPLY NOVA SCOTIAN HOTEL REGARDS A I GARSON

Lawyers' swords clanged again (and in early April the Jubilee featured *Conspirators*, with Hedy Lamarr, Paul Henreid, and Peter Lorre). Since Mason had sold out to someone not bound by his commitments, Frank and his Roseland allies applied for a court order to free them from theirs. Without it, they feared, Garson might have them at his mercy. While they'd be restrained, he'd be free to vote his shares. Mason's counsel, however, tried a ruse to keep Frank and his friends on the hook. He argued that, since Mason was not voting the one share he had kept, he was still honouring his obligation, and therefore the others should honour theirs. Mason had never promised not to sell the bulk of his holding. "This is mere evasion," Chief Justice Chisholm ruled. The sale to Garson "violates the spirit of the mutual arrangement. . . . The applications of Roseland Theatre Company and F. H. Sobey should be granted with costs. The cost of these applications will be paid by Mr. Mason." Mason had lost again. The judge, however, recommended that everyone renew their earlier commitments, and that Garson now join Mason as the co-plaintiff in the appeal.

But even with Garson on his side, Mason was never able to get any court to invalidate Frank's control of the theatres. In December 1945 he finally won a court case, but by then he was dead. Lieberman and Bernstein had sued the executors of his will, and also Garson. They argued that Mason, with Garson's connivance, "fraudulently and maliciously" reneged on the original deal whereby they'd get control for $75,000. From Mason's estate they wanted either the control he'd promised them or $100,000. From Garson they wanted his 5,099 shares and $100,000 in damages. In reaching a verdict, Chief Justice Chisholm reviewed three centuries of precedent. He weighed whether or not "the foundation of the contract had been annihilated by the frustrating event." The event – and for the late N. W. Mason, "frustrating" had been a mild description – had been Frank's snatching control, and his rock-solid common front with the other six directors. Mason had had about as much freedom to do what he wanted as a chicken among foxes. Once the courts had ruled against him, he hadn't had the remotest chance of ever regaining the control he'd promised to sell to Lieberman and Bernstein. Chisholm therefore dismissed the action against Mason's estate and Garson, with costs.

Meanwhile Frank did something that not only stunned the local business community and guaranteed that his role in the Battle of the Roseland would be mooted for decades, but also plunged even himself into depression, regret, and second thoughts. Through none other than A. I. Garson, he sold his controlling interest in the Roseland, Jubilee, and Academy of Music to the Odeon chain. For $75,000.

Everyone who recalls Frank in 1946 also recalls that, the moment he sold the theatres, he was enshrouded in gloom. He was so upset he vanished from Pictou County. He visited his sister Edith and her husband, Angus Sinclair, in Campbellton, N.B., and there he fretted over what he'd done. What tortured him was not guilt – he was never a man with a pronounced sense of guilt over anything he did – but rather a hunch that he'd made a business mistake, and the distress of losing his foothold in an industry that had excited him since boyhood. As a matter of principle he disliked selling any going concern. He wanted to keep his cloud-built, profitable movie business, but he also wanted to expand his earthy, profitable food business. He hated the fact that he couldn't afford to do both. "Frank has two personalities," Edith said. "He wanted to buy the Barkers Stores [chief rival of Sobeys Stores], but he wanted the theatres, too." For the rest of his life, even after Sobey companies had invested in dozens of movie theatres, he'd occasionally wonder if he shouldn't have tried harder to hang on to the Roseland Theatre Company, Ltd.

An epilogue to the Battle of the Roseland occurred a full ten years later. It was yet another court victory for Frank, and involved his ancient role at the Jubilee. After Odeon had taken over the three theatres, his old company, Jubilee Theatre, Ltd., survived for a while. Frank still served as its secretary, and still drew the same $37 a week that he'd been taking ever since 1937. He collected this till July 6, 1946, but not during the following year; and when the new owners killed off the company in late July, 1947, he figured they owed him $2,035 in back wages. Frank's one-time employee H. L. P. McNeil was now working as a theatre manager for Garson-Odeon – "When Frank sold the theatres to Garson, I went along with the deal," McNeil recalled – and the reason Frank lost a year's salary was that the autocratic Garson had ordered McNeil to quit paying him. Garson figured that since Odeon had taken over, Frank's duties as secretary to the doomed and dormant Jubilee Theatre, Ltd., were trifling. Why pay him $37 a week for doing so little?

But Frank wanted his $2,035, and, as a matter of pride, he was damned well going to get it. It took him ten years but in 1956 the Nova Scotia Supreme Court ruled Garson had acted wrongly. He had not been the board of directors. He had merely been a shareholder (though a major one), and a secretary's job could not properly be "terminated by some particular individual telling the person who writes the cheques not to pay him any longer." The court told Jubilee Theatre's liquidators, the Eastern Trust Company, that Frank all along had been entitled to his money. By 1956, sales in his seventeen stores surpassed $8 million, and it's possible some people wondered why he'd fight on, year after year, just to get $2,035. He knew, however, that the money was his by *right*, and he had a principle to defend. It was the principle of not letting anyone push Frank Sobey around.

What Frank did with the $75,000 he got for selling the theatres is no longer perfectly clear. What is clear, however, is that he immediately made the two crucial decisions of his early middle age, and that they forced him to come up with much more money. He bought the Barkers chain of food stores, and he built his first modern groceteria. Both moves were locally controversial, and both confirmed his toughness and shrewdness. He drove so fierce a bargain on the Barkers deal that one of its previous owners, A. W.

(Bert) MacNabb, was bitter about it till he died. The second move was controversial simply because so many merchants thought the groceteria was too big, fancy, and newfangled to succeed. Some doubtless hoped that, for a change, the mayor of Stellarton would fall on his face.

Frank himself remembered, "I had just sold the theatres for $75,000. That enabled us to get heavier into the store business. I formed Sobeys Stores, Ltd., and it bought out Barkers Stores." David Sobey said, "I remember Father's terrible depression after he sold the theatres, but it was probably the best thing he ever did. With the money, he got Barkers Stores." But recalling 1946, Frank also coupled his gain on selling the theatres with his purchase of the site of his groceteria, and to confuse things further his lifelong friend Billy Jamieson distinctly recalled that what Frank did with more than half the money was to invest in the Dominion Steel and Coal Company Ltd. "As Billy says," Frank recalled, "I bought shares in Dominion Steel at that time. I'd followed it for years. They were making some money in the thirties, good money in '37, and the dividend was a dollar per share." Jamieson said, "He put $40,000 into DOSCO. He bought it at seven and a half, and inside two years it went to $21. He was getting the dividends, too."

A 4.5-per-cent mortgage from Canada Life Assurance Company Ltd. provided some of his money for the groceteria. Borrowing was the key to Frank's earliest strategy of expansion: "We had to keep the company profitable or we couldn't borrow. If we could make a dollar, we could spend three," by borrowing from the bank and issuing bonds. He could not issue bonds, however, without having an incorporated company; and therefore, on April 18, 1946, the father-son partnership became Sobeys Stores, Ltd. It would be the cash fountain for the irrigation of Sobey businesses for decades to come, but its first function was to buy the six Sobeys stores from their founders, and also the eight outlets, the Stellarton warehouse, and the New Glasgow bakery of Barkers Stores, Ltd.

Barkers was roughly as old as Frank's legal partnership with his father. Both were born in the mid-twenties, and for two decades they were hot competitors in the same towns. Each Thursday their ads faced off in the local press. Barkers' ads were the flashier of the two, and sometimes subtly knocked their rivals. They featured comic strips with deathless dialogue:

> FIRST WELL-DRESSED HOUSEWIFE: "There goes Bob with Betty. They've been married three years, and he seems crazier about her than ever!"
>
> SECOND WELL-DRESSED WIFE: "Well, why shouldn't he be. She's good-looking, sweet – and smart besides! And I know she feeds him well!"
>
> FIRST WIFE: "How do you know?"
>
> SECOND WIFE: "Because I know where she does her buying and that store has only the *best* food."
>
> CONCLUSION: "Of course, she is referring to BARKERS."

If this suggested that all the ugly, sour, stupid housewives, whose husbands were no longer crazy about them, bought inferior food at Sobeys Stores, it failed to save the Barkers chain. By war's end, Barkers' management had lost its zip. Its proprietorship was effete. Hope of rejuvenation was slender. Like everyone else, Barkers' owners had heard about Frank's Roseland killing. Maybe he was looking for ways to spend his bonanza. In any event, it was they who came to him, not he who went to them, and that might have been their first mistake. In the business jargon of a later age, he made up his mind "to play hardball". He played it so well that this takeover, only months after his theatre takeover, spawned equally sturdy legends about his sharpness and, in some eyes, his ruthlessness.

The two sides dickered over Barkers' real estate, equipment, accounts receivable, and inventory. Donald Archibald remembered Frank's toughness. Archibald, in 1982, was head of Archibald Farms, an Annapolis Valley outfit which, with an official quota of 189,000 birds, was one of Canada's biggest egg producers. Back in 1946, however, he was briefly a young member of a little team of Halifax accountants who assessed Barkers' inventory for Frank. "We went up to Pictou County and met Frank," he said, "and as

Supermarket shopping became instantly popular, as this early 1960s opening-day crush at Sobeys' North Sydney store shows.

soon as the Barkers shops closed for the day, we went through them all like a bat out of hell. We wound up at 2 a.m. . . . Frank was a very shrewd purchaser, a tough bargainer." He had not forgotten what the Highland farmers of Pictou County had taught him about haggling. Buying a dwarf lamb or a dented can of baked beans, you did what you could to drive the price down. "If any of the goods were damaged, or not quite top-notch," Archibald said, Frank and his accountants "just brutally discounted the value. Poor old MacNabb, he was quite bitter about the fact that the boys were being a bit harsh. I always figured maybe Frank was a bit *too* shrewd with him, but I guess that's all right." Business was business.

Frank, however, said he took little part in the negotiating. He left the real haggling to his accountants, notably Harold Egan and Leo Burke, and to Barkers' accountant, C. H. Glendinning: "I had to accept whatever the accountants agreed to, and so did Barkers." Moreover, he recalled, it was Barkers' accounts receivable that caused the fiercest disagreement, not inventory. "Where they took their big hosing was on their accounts." His tone suggested that that was exactly where Barkers had deserved to take their hosing. "We had some bad accounts [at Sobeys Stores]," he said, "but nothing like Barkers.

"So the accountants worked out a formula to grade the accounts by age. Thirty days or less, a one-dollar account was worth one dollar. A sixty-day account meant seventy-five cents, and so on. Anything a year old was considered worthless, and given to Barkers, but they collected very little money on these old accounts. As it all turned out, they didn't get fifty cents on the dollar [for the accounts as a whole]." What his accountants had done, while assessing Barkers' assets, was to impose the conservative bookkeeping policies of his own chain. "We still don't carry any account that's over thirty days as an asset," he said in 1981. "That's why, on paper, we don't make as much money as some. We operate on a very conservative basis."

Not only Barkers' accounts receivable but also its equipment was, in Frank's unhumble opinion, "carried way above what you might call normal value. They had a habit of charging everything up to capital. If they moved a refrigerator case from one part of the store to another, they charged the cost of moving it and setting it up as capital. So we had the equipment revalued. . . . When it came down to the final figure, after they paid off the creditors, they didn't get much money. There was just enough to pay off their preferred shareholders. There was nothing left for the common. They were in a very poor financial position. . . . I had quite a time getting these stores straightened around." In time, he straightened them around by selling some and replacing others with supermarkets.

The opinion of those among Frank's friends who remembered 1946 was that Barkers' management had been so inept that, without him, the chain would have withered away anyway. David Hayman, an ex-mayor of Stellarton, said, "Barkers were going down the hatch. Frank didn't hurt them." R. B. Cameron, a notoriously blunt, cigar-chewing New Glasgow industrialist, put it another way: "MacNabb got a hell of a high price, according to the way he'd been running those stores, but it was a low price according to the way Frank ran them." Cameron believed Barkers' previous owners became furious only after they saw what Frank could do with the business.

The price Sobeys Stores, Ltd., paid was $158,752.97, which included $78,000.00 for inventory, $38,615.50 for land and buildings, $20,687.40 for furniture and fixtures, and $20,065.57 for all those doubtful accounts receivable. The new Sobey company also bought the Sobeys stores from Frank and his father. The price was $112,021.82, including $39,678.59 for land and buildings, $25,789.00 for furniture and fixtures, $21,441.75 for accounts receivable, and only $23,441.75 for inventory. Since the price for Barkers' inventory was $78,000, it's probable that the Sobey business had never kept as much stock on hand as Barkers, and that its turnover was more brisk. The figures also suggest that the accountants were as severe in their assessment of the Sobey assets as they were with Barkers.

The new company now had fourteen stores (though it soon closed two Barkers duds and sold others), a bakery, and a good warehouse. The warehouse, Frank said, "was perhaps the most valuable asset we got in the deal." Enlarged and renovated, it would eventually become permanent headquarters for all Sobey businesses. It would one day inspire business journalists from Toronto to marvel over the old-fashioned thrift and unflashy style of Sobey men who directed a multi-million-dollar empire while working in their shirt-sleeves in "a converted warehouse" beside the tracks in a forgotten coal town.

Sales in the fourteen stores during 1945, just before the takeover, had totalled $1,642,775, and when Sobeys Stores, Ltd., sold its first modest ($150,000) bond issue in November 1946, the prospectus said, "It is anticipated that sales for the first year's operations . . . will show an increase over this figure." Actually, they didn't. They dropped back to $1,408,040. By 1951, however, they would more than double to nearly $3 million, and after that, year after year, Sobeys Stores, Ltd., would relentlessly sell more and more food. By 1971, sales figures would reach $92.8 million. By 1983, they'd pass half a billion.

The purpose of that first small bond issue – 4.5-per-cent, general-mortgage, sinking-fund bonds in amounts of $500 and $1,000 – was to pay the $142,500 in bank loans that had enabled Sobeys Stores, Ltd., to buy the two chains. The prospectus, however, pointed not only to recent borrowings but also to future triumphs. It said, "The Company has arranged to rent two modern groceterias which are now under construction, one in Truro and the other in New Glasgow." The one in New Glasgow would change Frank's entire thinking about how to make a lot of money by selling a lot of food. Now that supermarkets are part of the landscape of every North American's mind, now that they're as familiar as gas stations, telephone booths, jet airliners, and hamburger joints, it is difficult to imagine a time in which a man who announced he was damned well going to build a groceteria risked being called a fool. It took nerve to put one up on "The Back Street" (Archimedes Street) in New Glasgow in 1947, and then to wait for something good to happen, but that's what Frank did. It made all the difference, and drove the town's more hidebound grocers to the wall.

Reminiscing with his son Donald in 1982, Frank took a drag on his pipe and said that half a century earlier he had considered moving into Halifax with a no-frills warehouse store. A lifelong second-guesser of himself, he said, "I think I should have done that." But then, with pleasant resignation, he added, "When you get an idea, you either run with it or forget about it, eh Donald?" His having known anything at all about warehouse food stores in the early thirties showed how keenly he'd scanned the grocery-trade press. When he'd sniffed around Boston stores in 1925, warehouse outlets had not even been born. It was sudden hard times that spawned those primitive ancestors of supermarkets. By the standards of the day, their inventories were enormous, their prices low, their facilities crude. They were the "cheapies", and they were a revolution.

"In August, 1930, Michael Cullen opened his King Kullen Store in Jamaica, New York," Rom J. Markin wrote in *The Supermarket: An Analysis of Growth, Development and Change*. "By 1932 Cullen operated eight markets . . . and was doing an annual sales volume of $6 million in the grocery departments alone. The keynote was volume, attained through heavy advertising of brand-name goods. . . . The establishments were located in abandoned factories and empty warehouses. The floors lacked coverings; partitions were torn out and counters and display fixtures were made of rough boards. The units thrived in low-rent locations on the fringe of thickly populated areas."

Cullen called his stores "The Price Wreckers". The Big Bear Market, which described itself as "The Price Crusher", opened in 1932 on the first floor of an abandoned auto factory in Elizabeth, New Jersey. In its first year, this one gigantic cheapie sold $2,169,000 worth of groceries alone. The cheapies were messy, noisy, brazen in their ads. But the price was right, and hard-up women descended on them like locusts. Looking back, *Progressive Grocer* (October 1952) said, "Depression-weary housewives enjoyed visiting the markets, for the circusy, bizarre atmosphere that prevailed provided release for the suppressed emotions piled up within many women by the dreary monotony of Depression days."

Fifty years later, when Frank was chatting with Donald, the threat of another Depression had inspired chain stores to found stores similar to the original cheapies. Vincent R. Little, president of a Milwaukee wholesaling outfit that operated Pick 'n Save Warehouse Foods, told *Business Week* (March 23, 1981), "We are coming back full circle to the bare-bones approach of the original supermarket." Donald's brother David, chief executive of Sobeys Stores, Ltd., said that in the late seventies he'd considered linking the company with an American chain's opening of box stores in Toronto. Sounding like his father, he regretted having passed up the chance, but by 1982, Sobeys Stores, Ltd., had thirteen "Lofood" box stores of its own.

If the cheapie was father to the supermarket, the mother was the Los Angeles-style drive-in market, in which independent proprietors arranged their shops in a U- or L-shaped island in a sea of parking space. The word "supermarket" is older than Superman, and came from Hollywood. "Several prominent movie stars became interested in operating markets," Markin wrote, "so, naturally, this new 'market' concept deserved a new and glamorous Hollywood name." No one knows who coined it.

The mightier chains at first ridiculed the cheapies, then feared them, and finally copied them or, rather, built jazzier versions. In 1934-37, A & P replaced 933 shops in thirty-eight cities with 204 supermarkets. One study showed that while a typical A & P neighbourhood store grossed $943 a week, a typical super raked in $13,741. The closure of many small stores in favour of fewer supermarkets, Markin wrote, "was unquestionably the vogue of the times. This movement was to be the keystone of the chains' fight for survival. [In 1934-37] Kroger dropped 355 stores and added thirty-three supers. Safeway dropped 272 stores and added twenty-eight. The chains were convinced they must replace inefficient neighbourhood units in super-invaded areas with super-type markets of their own." Between 1929 and 1949, the number of A & P stores dropped from 15,418 to only 4,600, but annual sales jumped from $1 billion to $3 billion.

The movement immediately spread to central Canada. When J. William Horsey took charge of Dominion Stores, his job was somehow to rejuvenate the country's biggest but least profitable grocery chain. Dominion was a mess. It had 464 small, dingy, musty outlets in four provinces (including Nova Scotia). Some Dominions actually competed with others on the same city streets. Most still granted credit and made deliveries. Central control was feeble. Dominion had lost a million dollars in three years, and no longer paid its shareholders dividends. It appeared doomed. Horsey closed the losers, modernized the others, and built supermarkets.

"When Bill Horsey joined Dominion," Frank said, "they had a small store in New Glasgow with a counter, a cheese-cutter, a scale, and no self-service. Clerks served the customers, the same as in our own cash-and-carry stores. All the Dominion stores were like that, and Bill told me that one day he went into one of the stores in Toronto – on Yonge Street, I think – and the clerks were all running around, getting this and that for the customers. Across the street, Loblaws had a groceteria, based pretty well on the Piggly

Wiggly idea in the States, so Bill went in there to have a look. Well, it was full of customers, and *the customers were doing all the work.* They were fetching their own goods and taking them to the cashiers. Bill Horsey decided right then that that was the way Dominion had to go. So he went to the west coast and spent some time with the Safeway crowd. When he came back, he had four or five Safeway executives with him."

By late 1939, Horsey had chopped 133 stores. Fred Bodsworth reported in *Maclean's* (Aug. 6, 1955), "Every time Horsey arrived at board meetings, N. L. Nathanson of Famous Players greeted him with, 'Well, how many did you close last week, Bill?' " Horsey's brutal program worked. As early as 1940, Dominion was back in the black. "When the war ended," Bodsworth wrote, "Horsey's gross sales had jumped from $20 million in 1939 to $35 million, and net profit was around $200,000, even though he'd dropped [another] 118 stores."

Frank had seen the future of food merchandising during his transcontinental jaunt with his wife in 1940, but wartime restrictions forced him to postpone building a supermarket. Meanwhile, he fretted over whether or not the gamble would ever pay off. He nagged at his own dream. Credit, home delivery, the loyalty of wives to certain merchants were all part of the intimate economy of a tradition-conscious society. They were as familiar as the sight of steelworkers and miners trudging to work with lunch pails. Would the people of the East River towns patronize a big, gleaming, relatively impersonal, super-clean supermarket with automatic doors? Would they take to a place where you wandered around by yourself picking up packaged goods, paid for them strictly with cash, and then had to get them home on your own?

He just didn't know.

But as an inveterate horse-trader for thirty-odd years, he did know that just about everyone loved a bargain. He knew, too, that life was changing forever along the East River. He knew the automobile was here to stay, and you could pack a whack of groceries into any car's trunk. He knew the refrigerator was here to stay, and wives could therefore buy a whole week's groceries at once.

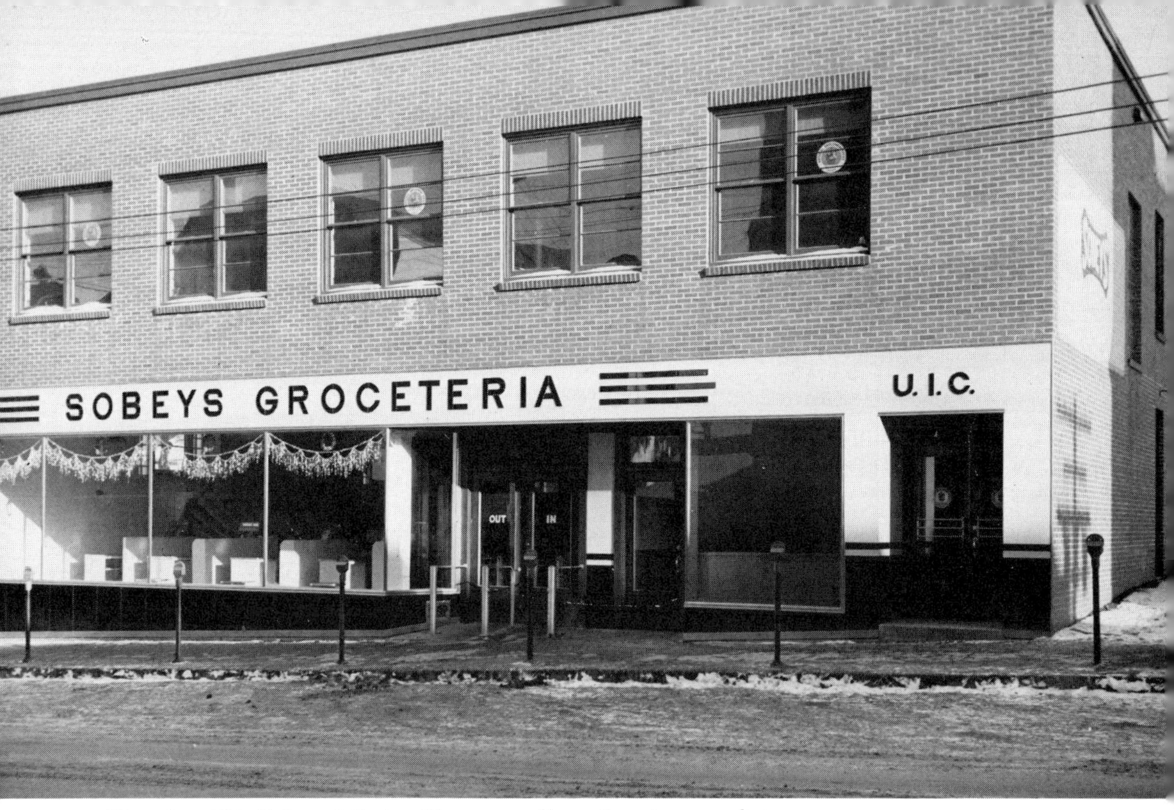

Number 25, Sobeys' first self-serve, all-cash supermarket on Archimedes Street in New Glasgow, opened its doors in August 1947. From its opening it was a runaway success.

He knew there were cities in which grocery-store credit was a doomed anachronism, like the Connolly ice business. Nor did he fail to notice the passage of the Unemployment Insurance Act in 1940 and the Family Allowance Act in 1944. The first "baby bonus" cheques reached local mothers in the summer of 1945. To a food merchant with a long view, such developments were worth pondering; and before any of his competitors, he figured that in Pictou County the supermarket's time had come round at last.

"Frank never lost sight of the work he had in hand," his brother Harold once said, "but there was never a time when he wasn't thinking in bigger terms, too." New Glasgow industrialist R. B. Cameron, who admired Frank as "a great Pictou County man", had a more vivid way of describing his friend's prescience: "Frank has that outhouse instinct that tells him whether to move or not to move." In the mid-forties, the signal that told Frank to move on construction of a supermarket was a fire in New Glasgow.

The wartime fire that wrecked the Empire Theatre building, corner of Archimedes and MacLean streets in central New Glasgow, also wrecked a chunk of wooden history that stretched back to the 1860s. The building was originally the Mechanics' Hall, where skilled tradesmen gathered for meetings and instruction, and amateurs and professionals mounted some of the town's earliest theatre. In 1907, that stagestruck hustler N. W. Mason, along with F. G. Spencer of Saint John, leased it, refurbished the interior, called it the Empire Theatre, and ran the place till 1912, when Mason built the Academy of Music. But even after the Empire died as a theatre, its name stuck to the structure. A bowling alley opened on the second floor in 1915, and in the twenties a plumber and a character named Paddy Nolan were street-level tenants. Nolan, once a local hockey star, ran an illegal rum shop there. He was a Tory, and the Tory government of the day left him alone. Grit bootleggers were not so fortunate.

The owner of the building, the rent-collector, was Empire Company Ltd. From 1920 on, its president was Frank's future ally H. B. McCulloch, its vice-president was H. G. Grant, and the secretary-treasurer was W. D. Chisholm, who also happened to be the plumber-tenant. Rents from five tenants in 1929 totalled about $1,000. Nolan, whose telephone listing was simply "Nolan, Paddy, Store, Archimedes, 210", paid $432.50, while the bowling-alley paid only $270. Either Nolan's dive was huge, or Empire shrewdly figured a bootlegger was more able to pay a steep rent than a bowling alley. In any event, the building never earned a fortune for its owners, and indeed, during the Depression, they pumped their own money into the company to cover deficits. Prohibition was over. Nolan was gone. In 1931, he was still in the phone book, but not on Archimedes Street, and not with a "store". Evidence of his undoing was beneath his name: listings for the new, legal outlets of the Nova Scotia Liquor Commission in Stellarton, Westville, and, alas, just along Archimedes Street in New Glasgow.

Fire gutted the Empire building late in the Second World War. One George McKay had long since bought out plumber Chisholm as the third partner, and he, Grant, and McCulloch promptly decided to pocket $1,000 of the insurance money each, to pay the company's debts, clear the ravaged lot, and sell the land. H. B. McCulloch, still the president, was the man to reckon with. So Frank reckoned with him, just as he did while nailing down control of the Roseland. The burning of the Empire presented the chance he both craved and feared: the chance to risk a bundle on building a supermarket.

All he wanted from Empire Company was land for a supermarket site. He got not only that, but also the company itself. He obtained its charter, if not by accident, at least casually. "Empire Company" did have an appealing ring to it, but the firm owned nothing other than the land. He had no intention of turning it into an outfit that, thirty-six years later, would boast assets of $268,150,000. By then, some would see the name as evidence of his gall and straightforwardness, as though he had tagged the company with a grandiose label to match his vaulting ambition to build an empire. But the truth was he'd simply bought a company that bore the name of a defunct theatre because neither he nor McCulloch had wanted the nuisance and legal expense of a real-estate transaction. "What was the use of spending money to make out a deed?" he asked.

By August 1945 Frank was president of Empire. His father and brother were the other directors, but it was he who called the shots. As early as a board meeting on September 15 he may already have decided that Empire's destiny was to become the investment arm of the family business. For it was then that Empire first decided to buy shares of Maritime Steel and Foundries Ltd. The Sobeys' New Glasgow friend H. Scott Cameron, once an ingenious blacksmith but now a dapper industrialist, bossed Maritime Steel. (The Sobeys also knew his sons, Clyde and R. B. Cameron, both of whom would succeed him as heads of Maritime Steel. Scott Cameron was Harold Sobey's father-in-law.) At that same Empire board meeting, the minutes stated, "The chairman [Frank H. Sobey] reported that an offer had been received from Mr. Frank H. Sobey for the purchase of the Company's land on Archimedes Street for $8,250." That money would be available for Empire investments.

Only months later, in March 1946 – after Frank had sold the theatres, plunged into the purchasing of Barkers, started the incorporation of Sobeys Stores, and planned his first supermarket – he and his father transferred to Empire the ownership of two buildings on New Glasgow's main drag, Provost Street. In May 1947, Empire sold them for $32,000. Its investment kitty was growing. "This was the money that started Empire Company off," Frank recalled. Early on, he'd also shoved "three or four thousand dollars' worth of Bathurst Pulp and Paper" into the company, and by February 1950 the investment sister of Sobeys Stores, Ltd., already boasted a portfolio worth more than $111,000. It included $77,550 worth of DOSCO, $11,000 of Eastern Paper Products, and smaller pieces of Consolidated Smelting, Maritime Steel, Massey-Harris, Fraser Companies, and Famous Players (the movies were still in Frank's blood).

Empire was in the insurance business during the fifties, but its prime function remained as an investment cache. Frank's pleasure lay in seeding it, fertilizing it, weeding it, watching it grow. He sold pieces of his personal portfolio to Empire, but since he believed that "to keep a company healthy you have to keep putting in more money than you take out," he took in return only demand notes and bonds that bore no interest. "I built Empire," he said, "by not taking any salary or money out of it. I loaned them money for years on which they never paid any interest. I never wanted money."

When, in 1971, he pocketed a million dollars by selling his half-interest in a Maritimes construction company he'd co-founded, he fed the money straight into Empire. When, in 1962, he parlayed a five-per-cent interest in the proposed Halifax Shopping Centre into $185,000, without having put up a nickel, he put that, too, into Empire. High succession duties were one motive for force-feeding the company, but the more important one was to build for the Sobey family a mountain of stock-market holdings. By 1973, when his youngest son, Donald, was president, these holdings, along with Empire's wholly owned operating companies, were worth $26 million. In 1982, after Empire had taken over other major Sobey companies and its assets had multiplied tenfold, he enjoyed giving his sons a gentle needle about what he'd done for them. Not that they hadn't contributed their own investment shrewdness. In his eightieth year, he reminded Donald that he'd put $6 million into Empire, and cheerily added, "If you'd been paying me interest, why I guess I'd be a wealthy man today."

But the company owed its birth and early nourishment to the business of selling food for cash, and that business shot miraculously ahead in 1947 when, on the burned-out site of the building that his courtroom enemy Mason had once called "The Empire", Frank built his first supermarket. He called it "Number 25".

Even Frank, in his bleak moments, feared Number 25 was too big to be profitable. The doubts would seem ludicrous by 1973 when Sobeys Stores, Ltd., opened a 43,200-square-foot supermarket in Dartmouth, N.S. After all, Number 25 was merely a 6,150-square-footer. In its time, however, it looked cavernous enough to be "Frank's folly". Number One, by comparison, had only 800 square feet of floor space. J.W., who had built Number One thirty-five years earlier, thought the new store was huge to the point of madness and predicted his oldest child would "come a cropper". Bill Sobey recalled his Uncle Harold's wondering, "How in the hell will we ever fill this thing with groceries?" Charles Higgins, the supermarket's first manager, said, "Frank told me that if we didn't do $5,000 a week, he could go broke. He was scared." Not merely scared, added Stellarton old-timer David Hayman, but "scared to death". So scared by the vastness of the place that he considered using part of it to sell furniture and, as David Sobey recalled, "He put up a partition at the last minute and rented off space." He had his fingers crossed. Hayman heard him tell Mrs. Sobey that if the supermarket took in only a certain amount of money, "Rene, I'm away." Whatever that figure was, he instantly grossed "an enormous amount more".

He was away.

Pictou County flocked to his doors, and they were the first automatic, electronic-beam doors in the county. Children loved to pass their hands across the beam and watch the doors magically swing open. Adults, too, were intrigued. Cecil McLaren, the supermarket's first meat manager, said that the doors were often defective in winter but that in August 1947, when Number 25 opened for the first time, "There must have been a hundred people just standing around watching them doors." Hundreds more *used* them. David Sobey, age sixteen when Number 25 opened, recalled the gentle stampede. Carnation Milk was a hot seller, and as customers snapped it up from a spot near the front of the store, he'd carry more cans up from the basement to replenish the display. "But on Saturday," he said, "the aisles were so jammed with shoppers, I'd have to take it up the back stairs, out the back door, through the parking lot, and in the front door."

No one was happier to eat his words than J.W. Sobey. After the first Saturday, he excitedly told hardware merchant Robert Munro, "Guess what? The groceteria grossed $10,000 in one night." Frank had prayed that sales at McLaren's meat counter would total $600 in the first week. "We done $1,000," McLaren said, "and she never went back. She went ahead all the time." The store had a fish tank, and "We sold a ton of salmon a week." By the early fifties, the meat counter was grossing $7,000 a week, and the whole store, which Frank had once feared might not take in $5,000 a week, was pulling in more than six times that amount. Older meat merchants, McLaren said, had predicted Number 25 "would never go. . . . It was in the wrong part of town. Well, McKay Brothers [meat and vegetables] were only the first to fold. At least six New Glasgow meat markets went under. . . . Number 25, that was the store that made Frank Sobey."

The supermarket did not celebrate its opening with splashy advertising supplements in the local press. The ads were modest, and played up only one attraction: low prices. At first, Frank advertised the spot as "Sobey's Wholesale Groceteria", to suggest a cut-rate operation. Other ads simply invited the public to "Visit Our Groceteria For Extra Low Prices. Everybody Wins Big Savings At Our Giant Food Fair." Announcing "Labor Day Specials", the store claimed, "Our Low Prices Are The Working Man's Friend. Shopping here for all your food needs is like getting a raise in pay because our low, low prices increase the buying power of your food dollars."

For customers, the beauty of Number 25 lay in low, low prices, but for Frank it lay in cash flow such as he'd never known before. "All of a sudden," Bill Sobey said, "there was money in the bank. It was just pouring in." He remembered his father marvelling to Harry Miller, the chain's accountant, "Harry, we sold all that inventory, and we haven't even *paid* for it yet!" Summing up decades later, Frank said, "This store proved so successful that it changed our thinking entirely on the grocery business. We were getting cash instead of delivering groceries all over town and putting them out on credit. That gave us a tremendous cash flow. A lot of our groceries were sold before we'd paid for them. We decided that was the way to go, and we've been in the cash business ever since."

Number 25 was such a bonanza that within only six months Frank opened another groceteria. In a rather solemn ad, Sobeys Stores, Ltd., claimed that the New Glasgow adventure had proved that "by eliminating both credit and delivery we are able to supply groceries at prices that provide a substantial saving to our customers each week. . . . We decided that our friends in Stellarton should have the same opportunity to shop on this plan, and for that reason we are changing Barkers' store at Stellarton over to a groceteria, effective Thursday, Feb. 5 [1948]. This store will be known as Sobeys' Groceteria from that date forward."

It sold 75-pound bags of Prince Edward Island potatoes for $2.59, prime-rib roast beef for 54 cents a pound, Delicious apples for 27 cents a dozen, and Campbell's tomato soup for 11 cents a tin. Headlines of the time said, "King [Prime Minister Mackenzie King] Blasts Communism, Promises Price Probe, Remains Ambiguous [about his successor as leader of the Liberal Party]," and "Housewives Continue to Use Buyer Resistance - Predict Beef Prices May Be Next to Rise." Sobeys Stores, Ltd., however, was not finding buyer resistance any problem at all.

Frank had a typically shrewd sideline at Number 25. He'd hedged his bet by putting a second storey on the building and renting it to no less reliable an occupant than the federal government. Even before erecting the building, he'd apparently bagged the unemployment insurance agency as a tenant, but exactly how he'd pulled this off would remain forever fuzzy. He himself thought his friend H. Scott Cameron, one of the first directors of Sobeys Stores, Ltd., had used his Grit connections to smooth the deal. In a county that thrived on rumours of political impropriety, others whispered that H. B. McCulloch – both the local Liberal MP and the chief figure among those selling the site to Frank – had surely done something nefarious in Ottawa to benefit both himself and Frank. But Frank's lifelong friend Billy Jamieson said such theories were nonsense.

Jamieson was working for the unemployment insurance service when the Empire building burned, and his superiors had already ordered him to find 6,000 square feet of New Glasgow office space. "I happened to be over at Frank's on a Sunday night, as usual," he said, "and I told him, 'Look, for years you've been talking about groceterias and how you'd like to get into them. Here's your chance. Buy that property, build your store, and put in space to rent to the government.'" In Jamieson's memory, that's all there was to it, just a reliable tip from a friend at the right moment.

But however the rental agreement came about, the fact that people were collecting unemployment-insurance money just upstairs from a groceteria was good news for the groceteria, and the rent the government paid was good news for the landlord. The landlord was not the newly incorporated Sobeys Stores, Ltd., it was Frank H. Sobey. The property was his personal possession because, he said, Sobeys Stores, Ltd., "couldn't afford it." The land was his. The building, which had cost him $60,000 to construct, was his. The rent from both Sobeys Stores, Ltd., and the government was also his. In 1982, when he was eighty, after thirty-five years had passed since the opening of Number 25, the property was still his. Why had he never, in all that time, sold it to the Sobey chain? "I can't get clear of it," he said shortly. "If I sold it I'd have to pay tax on the recaptured depreciation and capital gains on any profit. The tax department wouldn't let me sell it to Sobeys Stores at cost. I was locked in." He was not a man who easily admitted to sentimental feelings.

6

"YOU HAVE TO GET ALONG WITH PEOPLE"

"FRANK'S got a great knack with people," investment counsellor Richard Giles said. "He could turn it on with both frustrated miners and the country's top business leaders. It was almost uncanny, the way he could meet people, gain their confidence, and make a deal." Or milk them for information. New Glasgow paint manufacturer Bob Tibbetts said one of the Steinberg brothers, founders of the immense Steinberg supermarket chain (1980 sales: $2,247,272,000), had once complained, "That damn Sobey. He comes up to Montreal by train, and he asks me to show him round our newest store. We come to an innovation we're trying, and Sobey says, 'Hey, that looks pretty good. Exactly how do you do that anyway?' You know what? I was so damn flabbergasted I *told* him."

Frank was among the first of the ten investors who each put up $2,500 to help Tibbetts found his paint business in 1947, and in 1982 he was still on the board. "He used to pick the brains of Harold Egan [Halifax accountant and financial wizard] all the time," Tibbetts said. "They'd come to a board meeting, and Frank would say, 'Harold, I'm going to do this. What do you think?' Well, they'd go on and on about these deals that had nothing at all to do with Tibbetts Paints, and since Frank wasn't in Harold's office he didn't have to pay for his advice. I'd try to get them back on the track, but the meetings were getting longer and longer. I finally called them for 11 a.m. instead of 10.30. That way, they'd get hungry after a while and we'd adjourn for lunch."

"You just can't do anything," Frank believed, "unless you know people. And unless you can get along with people." He got along with the right people during the Battle of the Roseland, and with more of the right people during the incorporation of Sobeys Stores, Ltd. Tough on enemies, he was intensely loyal to friends, and in his old age he carefully acknowledged his debt to men who had long since died, including early directors of the chain. By the fall of 1946, the new company had on its board four bluenose bigshots: lawyer James McGregor Stewart, underwear manufacturer and Tory MP Frank Stanfield, steel-maker H. Scott Cameron, and Halifax businessman R. M. Colwell.

Cameron was president of Maritime Steel and Foundries Ltd., New Glasgow, which appointed Frank a director in 1944. That was his first board membership. Around 1907 Cameron, a young blacksmith, had gone to work for Maritime Steel's predecessor, J. W. Cumming Manufacturing, and by 1914, at thirty, he was pretty well running the place. Along with James T. Cumming, son of the founder, he nursed, dragged, and kicked the business through the Depression. Political connections helped, as they always do in Nova Scotia. "Cumming consorted with the Tories," James M. Cameron wrote (*Industrial History of the New Glasgow District*, 1960), "and Cameron with the Grits." In Cameron, the carefully chosen board of the young Sobeys Stores, Ltd., had a Grit. In Stanfield, it had a Tory whose younger brother, Robert, would be premier of Nova Scotia within ten years. And in Frank himself, of course, it had a born Tory with Grit friends.

A mechanical genius with marketing instincts, Cameron dreamed up the products that Maritime Steel made and sold. He was as clever at this as Frank was at selling food, and Frank admired him for proving that a Nova Scotian with imagination and unconquerable doggedness could defy geographical, historical, and economic odds to keep a local industry on its feet. Both men were self-taught small-town hustlers. Neither had been a college boy. J. McG. Stewart, on the other hand, had been a scholar of such brilliance that he'd taught Latin and Greek at Dalhousie University to put himself through law school. He was fifty-five when he joined the board of Sobeys Stores, Ltd., a Pictou County boy who'd made good, very good. He was the most influential lawyer in the Maritimes, a giant in his profession, a giant in the business community. Frank believed that three men - Stewart, industrialist Roy Jodrey, and Horace Enman, president of the Bank of Nova Scotia - did more to develop east-coast industry than "all the government incentives combined".

Stewart, who never discussed his childhood, had been crippled by polio, but he was a man of such spirit that when he coached rugger at Dalhousie he'd get out on the field on crutches to kick the ball around. He got his B.A. at nineteen and his law degree at twenty-four, and promptly joined a small Halifax firm that William A. Henry, a Father of Confederation, had founded in 1867. The partnership eventually became Stewart, MacKeen & Covert, with thirty-eight lawyers on its letterhead, the most powerful law firm east of Montreal. No one did more than Stewart to build its success, and Frank Covert, who succeeded him as "Mr. Lawyer" in Nova Scotia, idolized "the boss".

Stewart read Greek and Latin for pleasure. He was expert on Rudyard Kipling, stamp-collecting, and investments. Along with future Prime Minister Louis St. Laurent, he was counsel to the historic Rowell-Sirois Commission on Dominion-Provincial Relations (1937-40). When a business friend of Covert amiably sneered, "You think Stewart's infallible," Covert snapped, "As far as I'm concerned he's always right."

Stewart had an impeccable reputation, superb connections, an undying interest in his home county. "I once went into Halifax to see him about something," Tibbetts said, "and he knew more about me than I knew myself." Frank, who wanted to sell bonds for Sobeys Stores, Ltd., couldn't possibly have had a better name on his board. Stewart was a director not only of such stalwarts among Nova Scotian companies as Mersey Paper, Nova Scotia Light and Power, National Fish, and Moirs, but also of mighty national concerns - Sun Life Assurance, Canada Cement, and the Royal Bank, which named him their first non-banker vice-president. Nova Scotian entrepreneurs who wanted financing could not go wrong by consulting Stewart. He had the contacts. Indeed, he had such clout that, knowing he could always get a power of attorney from Frank Stanfield, he felt free to sign Stanfield's name on the first prospectus for Sobeys Stores, Ltd.

Frank: "Mr. Stewart said that to get financing I'd better get another director on. I said, 'Well, who?' He says, 'Get Frank Stanfield.' You had to get a form filled out, and the prospectus signed by all your directors, so I went out after Stanfield. I went to Truro, but he was in an election campaign. He'd gone to Windsor. I went down there, but I missed him. So I called up Mr. Stewart and told him I was having an awful time finding Frank Stanfield. Well, Mr. Stewart says, 'If I say Frank Stanfield will go he'll go, so I'll sign his name on the prospectus.' So that solved that, and we went ahead and formed Sobeys Stores, Ltd."

Stewart, he continued, "*was* the Royal Bank around here, and there wasn't a single important legal thing it did anywhere in Canada that he wasn't in on. If he said to the Royal Bank, 'Do this,' the Royal Bank did it. . . . Every time Horace Enman [president, Bank of Nova Scotia] came to Halifax he went to see Stewart." But Stewart's services to Frank did not stop at lending his eminent name to the board of Sobeys Stores, Ltd. For the incorporation, he nominated the entire professional team: the lawyer, Gordon Cowan, later Chief Justice, Supreme Court of Nova Scotia; the accountant, Harold Egan; and the bond salesman, F. Carleton Fisher, vice-president of Eastern Securities Company Ltd.

As a money-raiser for business, Eastern Securities was a Maritimes response to central Canadian disdain. The big Toronto and Montreal investment dealers - Wood, Gundy, A. E. Ames, Dominion Securities, etc. - weren't interested in underwriting bonds or selling shares to finance puny enterprises in the remote Maritimes. But Eastern Securities and Carl Fisher were. That was their business. Eastern Securities was your friendly corner investment dealer. They had a network of "storefront" offices where local agents sold small issues to local investors to finance small companies. "Carl could go out and sell two or three hundred thousand dollars' worth of bonds or stocks here and there, and that was a great service to the region," Frank said. "Unfortunately there aren't any small underwriters like that any more."

Frank was naturally glad other people bought bonds, but he wanted no part of them himself: "We had inflation of about two per cent in those days, and I figured that when you added that up over twenty years you were paying off your bonds with pretty cheap money. That's why I was never a bond-holder." Bonds were boring. They tied you down. "I never bought bonds. I never liked them. I always thought that if you had money it was far better to keep it in short-term securities. If you wanted it in a hurry, you could get it out."

Fisher was a tall, thin, balding gent. "He was very personable, very engaging, and very knowledgeable," Halifax lawyer Henry B. Rhude said. "Most people of his ability gravitated to Toronto or Montreal." Fisher was also a tough negotiator, but if he looked harried it was because he often had to do his negotiating with Frank. For each $100 that Eastern Securities retailed, they'd pay Sobeys Stores, Ltd., maybe $97, $98, or $98.50, pocketing the difference as their commission. To Frank, that discount was worth a haggle. So was the interest rate. So was the money the chain would have to pay into a sinking fund each year during the life of the debt. So indeed were such matters as who'd pay for Eastern Securities' lawyer, for the preparation of the prospectus, for the printing of the issue by a bank-note publisher.

"A fellow like Frank Sobey, he wants to keep as much of his money in the business as he can," Gordon Cowan, the chain's first lawyer, said. "Dealing with Eastern Securities, he'd try to squeeze them." But Fisher was not always squeezable. He knew that Frank knew the importance of making the issue attractive enough to sell, Frank recognized both his shrewdness and his marketing expertise, and the result of these hard-eyed sessions was series after series after series – in amounts of $200,000, $300,000, $500,000 – of bonds and preference shares. While Sobeys Stores, Ltd., grew, so did a friendship. Fisher was still on the chain's board when he died in 1967.

Then there was Harold Egan. A trim-looking man with horn-rimmed glasses and neat, sleek hair, Egan was almost as legendary as an accountant as Stewart was as a lawyer. He helped in the dickering over Barkers, the setting up of Sobeys Stores, Ltd., and the earliest bargaining with Fisher. In the early thirties, at Dalhousie University, he'd earned both his Bachelor of Commerce and his Bachelor of Arts degree in only three years; and the university promptly established rules to make sure no one, no matter how bright, would ever again pull off such a stunt. A Catholic, he was briefly the victim of outrageous bigotry. He wanted to be a chartered accountant, and took the course offered by the Maritime Business College. "But in those days," Mrs. Howard Elliot, his widow, recalled, "the Institute of Chartered Accountants never granted C.A. status to either Jews or Catholics. They failed Harold on the exams." Egan, however, had cannily kept his own copy of his answers, and it turned out he had the highest marks in the class. He took his case to none other than J. McG. Stewart, who won it for him. Egan got his certification.

Egan did much postwar business in Pictou County. In addition to his services to Frank, he helped to found Tibbetts Paints and reorganize Ferguson Industries, shipbuilders. Robert Tibbetts said, "Frank always thought I hooked him and Egan into putting up dough for Tibbetts Paints by telling him that Egan was in on it, and then telling Egan that Frank was in on it. They kidded me about that for years." Was the accusation true? Tibbetts grinned with great geniality. "Why, I'd never do a thing like that."

He said that Egan, at his peak, was "one of the finest financial brains in Canada. He could really show you how to run your business. He was famous for that, but he couldn't run his own." Jim Ferguson, Ferguson Industries, a contemporary of Egan's at Dalhousie, said Egan himself admitted he was better at organizing other men's businesses than at running his own. (Ferguson also recalled that Frank, who'd joined the shipbuilding firm's board in 1950, once complained that after he'd left a paper bag on his kitchen table, his wife, a meticulous housekeeper, had assumed it was garbage and "damned if she didn't throw it in the fire." The bag had been full of money, a day's take from one of the New Glasgow stores.)

The most important of Frank's postwar allies, however, was Horace Enman, the dictatorial president of the Bank of Nova Scotia. In the eyes of many Maritimes businessmen, Horace Luttrell Enman was as close to being God as a banker could be. "If he trusted you," said a New Brunswick-born stockbroker, "he'd give you the goddamn bank." Hantsport industrialist, financier, and investor John Jodrey, who succeeded his father Roy on the bank's board, said Enman was "a terrific banker. Dad would do anything in the world for him. He was a tall man with a marvellous personality. He really made the Bank of Nova Scotia." Born in Moncton, Enman joined the bank at fourteen, and from 1926 till 1943 he was Supervisor of Eastern Branches, with his office at Saint John. It was in that job, where he enjoyed unique regional authority, that he first earned reverence as the man who rescued, nurtured, and promoted Depression-starved Maritimes businesses. "This was the only bank with a divisional office for the Maritimes," said Arthur Crockett, a former deputy chairman of the board and, incidentally, a native of Westville. "Enman *ran* it." Another former deputy chairman, George C. Hitchman, said, "Enman was the only man outside Toronto who had real authority, and when they moved him to Toronto [as president and general manager], that was a tribute to the way he'd used it."

It was a tribute, too, to his uncanny judgment of men. Hitchman, who'd been with the bank more than half a century by 1981, continued, "He had a great ability to pick winners, finance them, and even encourage them to go into things. He'd *shove* them. You see, he *knew* them. He'd lived with them. He'd walk into a place, look around, and make up his mind just like that. He could do that because he knew people." The late Ralph Brenan, a New Brunswick industrialist, believed that "What Enman said *went*, and there wasn't too much consultation with Toronto, either. In many respects, he was the man who made Roy Jodrey, Fred Manning, Frank Sobey, a number of other fellows, and, yes, Ken Irving, too."

But Enman did not limit his services to the giants of Maritimes business (and indeed when he first helped them they weren't giants anyway). W. R. Monteith, who joined the bank as a clerk in

Stellarton in 1928, said, "One day a junior employee says, 'There's a fellow out there wants to borrow $500 to start a business, Mr. Enman.' Mr. Enman asks, 'Do you think he's honest?' and the junior answers, 'Yes, sir, I think so.' So Mr. Enman just says, 'Well, give it to him.' The customer's business thrived, and all his life he kept a big photo of Mr. Enman in his office with a message under it: 'The man who made me.' There were dozens of stories like that."

Frank had first gone to Enman almost twenty years before the bank gave him the short-term financing to buy Barkers. He was still in his twenties, and when he asked for a loan of a few hundred dollars to buy some Prince Edward Island potatoes, the manager of the bank's Stellarton branch said no. Frank promptly went to the Saint John office, where Enman sized him up and said yes. "I got the money," Frank recalled. "In fact I got more than I was entitled to." He told Enman that the Sobeys' new Trenton store was losing money hand over fist, and that the bank's Stellarton manager had insisted he close it. "He's a fool," Enman replied. "If we did that, we wouldn't have any banks. We hardly ever open a branch that doesn't lose an awful lot of money in the first few years. Once you close, you've lost your chance ever to regain that money." Enman was Frank's kind of banker, "and from that day on, he was one of the best business friends I ever had."

A forceful man with a fondness for the grape in his earlier years, Enman had his darker side. "I have rarely met a man who could inspire such loyalty," Crockett said, "but he could be nasty. He was a real Jekyll-and-Hyde." In the bank, some loved him, a few hated him. Everyone obeyed him. He was so competitive that shortly after the war he resorted to a ruse to keep the Royal Bank out of Trenton. By then he was sufficiently chummy with Frank to enlist him as his ally in the trick.

The Bank of Nova Scotia had closed its Trenton branch during the war, and Enman now got wind that the Royal Bank planned to open there. He knew even the exact morning the regional manager for the Royal would go to Trenton to assess sites, and on the afternoon before that visit he phoned Frank. He asked him to hustle over to Trenton, find any decent, midtown building, and put a

Horace L. Enman, Chairman of the Bank of Nova Scotia, 1955–59. From 1926 to 1943 he nurtured Maritime businesses as the Bank's Supervisor of Eastern Branches, and became a friend and ally of Frank Sobey.

highly conspicuous sign in its front window. The sign was to read "Bank of Nova Scotia Opening Here Soon". Frank knew just the building. His friend Andy Murray owned it, but when Murray and Frank arrived at its door that night the tenant was out and the building locked. They broke a back window, crept inside like cat burglars, and put up the sign. "The next morning," Crockett chortled, "the Royal Bank's top man in Halifax drove to Trenton, saw the sign, got mad as hell, turned around and drove back to Halifax. The Bank of Nova Scotia's been in Trenton ever since."

After the Enman-Sobey friendship deepened, the banker rarely visited Halifax without phoning the grocer to arrange a meeting there. Moreover, he issued a kind of standing order that Frank was *never* to visit Toronto without visiting his office daily. Frank would sit there while Enman jawed away on the phone and barked instructions to underlings, but during the calmer moments they'd cheerfully pick each other's brains.

"Mr. Enman also used to phone me from Toronto," said Frank, who was a whole lot better off than almost everybody else in the Maritimes, "and if I'd listened to him and taken all the money he wanted me to, for different business propositions, I'd be a whole lot better off than I am now." Crockett believed Enman not only tipped Frank on good investments but also steered him clear of bad ones: "He'd say, 'Frank, don't touch it,' and he saved Frank from stepping in a lot of holes."

From time to time, however, Frank did consider shifting some of his business to the Royal Bank, and he once consulted J. McG. Stewart about the idea. Stewart asked if he was happy with the Bank of Nova Scotia. Frank said yes, and the older man, despite his loyalty to the Royal, then said, "Frank, your bank is a bit like your church. If it lets you down, leave it. If it serves you well, stick with it." The Sobeys eventually did business with the Royal, and with other banks as well, but the anchor bank of the budding empire was the Bank of Nova Scotia; and long after Enman died in 1962, the relationship between it and Frank, and new generations of Sobeys, would remain both strong and personal.

The war had been a leash on Frank, and its end was his release. He tore off in several directions, sniffing opportunities to make a buck in field after field that had nothing at all to do with selling food. For most men it would have been more than enough, in only five years, to be mayor of Stellarton, fight the Battle of the Roseland, found Sobeys Stores, Ltd., buy Barkers, open pioneering groceterias, expand the chain, and set up Empire Company as an investment cache. But not for him. The years 1945-50 were a time in which he wasn't content merely to lay the foundation for an immense business structure. They were also a time in which the ex-butcher was at last free to become a hunter, a sharp-eyed, far-ranging tracker of that eternal quarry, the Good Deal. He itched to snare pieces of businesses that promised to grow. (In 1982 the fact that he was eighty had not even faintly dulled this hunger. It seemed to keep him young.)

He invested in the stock market in the late forties, just as he'd done since boyhood, but at the same time his speedy eye assessed main chances in the territory he knew best, the northern part of mainland Nova Scotia. He was a director of Maritime Steel, Tibbetts Paints, Ferguson Industries, and Nova Scotia Trust Company, and an investor in electric utility companies in nearby Colchester County, in Canada's only salt mine at nearby Malagash, and in housing-development and construction companies in his home county.

Cobequid Power and Northumberland Light and Power, which operated under one management, sold electricity to 2,900 customers scattered across central and northern Nova Scotia, and in 1950 Bertram Godden's business antennae detected that the little system might be up for sale. Naturally, he told Frank. "So I went over to Truro to see the owner," Frank said, "and after some talk he offered it for a certain price. Well, I was concerned. I didn't know anything about the power business." When he left Truro, the matter was still up in the air. He was fretting. Had he blown something good? Irene Sobey knew his mood. A slender, sensible, dark-haired woman in her early forties, she was beside him in the family car as they headed back to Stellarton.

"On the way back from Truro," he recalled, "I said, 'My gosh, maybe I should have bought that outfit.' Well, Rene says, 'Frank, if you feel you should have taken it, and that's really the feeling you got, why don't you take it?' So we turned the car around and we went back, and I took that company." In 1951, however, the Halifax-based Nova Scotia Light and Power Company, Ltd., whose illustrious board included J. McG. Stewart, offered to buy the system. "I made a fair profit," Frank said, "but I sold out because Mr. Stewart was anxious to get it for Nova Scotia Light. If I'd kept it and operated it, I'd have made a lot more." Again he seemed to regret that, decades before, he'd let a good thing go.

Cambey Construction ("Cam" for Cameron and "bey" for Sobey) was a partnership between Frank and Scott Cameron's sons, Clyde and Robert. When hundreds of shipyard workers left Pictou town at war's end, Cambey bought their hastily built houses, floated them up the East River on barges, used a crane to sling them onto trailers, then set them down on pre-built foundations in Stellarton. In the book *Stellarton*, Aubrey Dorrington claimed, "This was the first time in Canada that a large number of houses were transported in this manner." The partnership, however, did not survive. R. B. Cameron bought out his partners because board meetings bored him. He wanted to run the outfit on his own. He seemed born to dominate.

He would become notorious. As tough, pugnacious, hard-drinking, and blasphemous as any steelworker he ever employed, he would commit shocking verbal indiscretions, even at such solemn black-tie affairs as the Bank of Nova Scotia's annual banquet in Halifax. He'd prove capable of iron ruthlessness to some and touching generosity to others. "Frank's just a rock," he said in 1981. "He turned from being a natural amateur to being a damn good professional. . . . He's got it. He's got good judgment, and if his judgment lets him down, if he fails, then by Jesus he can take another look. He's an able enough operator that he can turn it around." Cameron had once considered moving Maritime Steel out of Pictou County, "but Frank thought up more goddamn arguments against it, and he must have been successful because I'm still here. He's a county man."

Frank's opinion of Cameron was less loquacious than Cameron's of him. Asked why he'd respected Cameron for so many decades, he gave a typically succinct reply: "Bob talks wild, but he decides right." Why was it then that these two mutually respectful lions of Pictou County industry, who were related by marriage – Frank's brother Harold had married R.B.'s sister Helen – never again tried to operate a business together? The reply of R.B., whose ego was not deficient, was a compliment to both: "No business in Nova Scotia would ever be big enough for me and Frank."

As early as May 1, 1947, three months before Number 25's electronic doors first swung open, two Sobeys stores had already offered hints that the future lay in groceterias. The chain had recently opened a small one in Truro, N.S., and now Frank reported to the shareholders that "sales have been holding around $4,500 a week, with a tendency to increase." Moreover, he'd just converted an old-style service store in Antigonish, N.S., into a little groceteria, and had thereby turned a loser into a modest winner. He now outlined a strategy: "If these groceterias on a strictly cash and non-delivery basis prove profitable, it is the intention of management to gradually turn most of our stores over to this type of operation."

But conversions weren't enough. He worried that, particularly in Stellarton and Westville, "the market may be saturated." To his mind, there was only one real answer to local market saturation:

move into another market. He believed any business that was not expanding was dying, and he would never lose that belief. In December 1982, at a board meeting of Empire Company, he grumpily noted that, although Sobeys Stores, Ltd., now had nearly ninety outlets, a whole year had passed since a new one had opened. He delivered an avuncular but pointed lecture to the dozen younger men who flanked the table. "When a firm stops expanding," he said, "it should sell out. . . . We need three or four more good Sobeys stores every year. . . . Look at K. C. Irving. He never stopped expanding, and he never closed a service station, no matter how bad it was. Now he's Number One in the Maritimes." Moreover, the money you spent on expansion was money on which you could legally defer paying income tax, "and I hate to see you paying millions to the government." Then, only half humorously, he recalled something his late friend Roy Jodrey had said: "You can't build a business and pay income tax."

Frank's boldest expansionary move in the late forties was to build a supermarket in hostile territory. Sydney, at the industrial heart of Cape Breton Island – and it was still a true island, with no causeway to the mainland – was 165 miles from Stellarton. The Sobeys were strangers there, and in the hotly competitive local grocery business, outsiders were not welcome. But when Frank couldn't find a good site, he did what he always did to solve a problem. He phoned a crony. He'd known Rubin W. Bolstad, the Toronto-based boss of Famous Players theatres, since his years as the Jubilee's owner.

Frank knew Famous Players owned a choice site in Sydney, but the local word was that it simply wasn't for sale. Sydney interests had tried to buy it and been turned down. "So I called up Rube," Frank said, "and he says, 'Do you need it bad?' I got it for $20,000." In the early fifties, after Sobeys Stores had begun to muscle their way into the juicy Halifax market, Bolstad would come through for Frank again, selling him a supermarket site on Quinpool Road even though Famous Players had already laid the foundation for a theatre there. Nor were these the only times that Frank called on Toronto to get exactly what he wanted in Nova Scotia.

Enman, a director of Canada Life Assurance, suggested he

approach the company for a mortgage on the Sydney supermarket. Back in '46, Frank said, "when the insurance companies were chasing me for mortgages," Canada Life had given him a 4.5-per-cent mortgage on Number 25 in New Glasgow. But now in 1949, when he went to Toronto to see A. H. Lennon, treasurer and future president of Canada Life, he discovered that "They wanted half of one per cent *more* in Sydney than in New Glasgow. Lennon wanted five per cent, and I wouldn't pay it. I guess you could say I had a row with him." Frank returned to Enman, described the row, gathered the banker could do nothing more for him, then went gloomily to his hotel room, picked up the phone to make reservations for the trip home, changed his mind and phoned J. McG. Stewart in Halifax.

Stewart suggested he see H. D. Burns, father of Charles Burns, the whiz Toronto stockbroker whose investment savvy was already helping Annapolis Valley industrialist Roy Jodrey become a multimillionaire. "I just had lunch with Charlie and his father," Frank told Stewart. But he beetled right back to the Bank of Nova Scotia building and up to the executive suite, and for the second time that day found himself in the presence of Herbert Deschamps Burns. Burns was still chairman of the Bank of Nova Scotia, and in 1949 a banker with even more clout than Enman. Not only that, he happened to be the president of Crown Life Insurance Company. He was from Digby, Nova Scotia.

"He called up a fellow by the name of Jamieson in Crown Life," Frank said. "I heard him say, 'I didn't say you *had* to give it to him [Sobey]. I told you to *try* to give it to him. Give it to him if you can.' So I went over to see this Jamieson, and he was shaking his head. He said, 'I just can't understand it. We have never before in our lives made a commercial mortgage in Nova Scotia, but now Mr. Burns wants me to do this.' " Frank concluded: "I got the loan I wanted from Crown Life." Burns, Enman, and Stewart, all older Maritimers, had all tried to help the up-and-coming, down-home operator get a 4.5-per cent mortgage on his second supermarket. They were a formidable trio, and you just can't do anything unless you can get along with people, and unless you're as stubborn as Scotch thistle.

In Sydney, the site, the building, and the mortgage were one thing. Selling groceries was another. The store was even bigger than Number 25, and its size aroused familiar nervousness. "Harold Sobey and I went to Sydney to open that one," Charles Higgins said, "and it seemed so huge we wondered how we'd ever fill it. By today's standards, of course, it was a hole in the wall." His job was to make it profitable, and by comparison with Number 25 the early sailing was rough. Local families ran most Sydney grocery stores, and another old Sobeys hand recalled, "There were a lot of good merchants there, and they weren't too anxious to see us move in. They wanted to drive us out, and they gave us a pretty hard time." The hard time was a price war that lasted months, resulting in a bonanza of ads for the local press, "But we had some plusses. . . . The stores in Sydney were a little dirty and smelly in those days, and our merchandising was better. Slowly, she started to come."

By the summer of 1949, Sobeys Stores, Ltd., three years old as a company, owned what Frank called "three large self-service stores", one in each of New Glasgow, Truro, and Sydney. It also had smaller self-service outlets in Stellarton and Antigonish; seven stores that still offered personal service in the old way; a bakery (once Barkers'); and "a peddling truck, wholesaling tobacco and candy to small stores and canteens". Sales were up $270,000 over the previous year, but the mightily significant fact was that "This increase was *all* made in the self-service stores. Our service stores showed a small decrease in volume."

Business was good, the future clear, the clan clannish. Frank, his brother, and his father, sole directors of Empire Company, held their board meetings in J.W. and Eliza's home, near the curling rink. Eliza still made soup on Saturday for Sunday suppers, and refused to pay for her groceries, on grounds they were part of J.W.'s salary. "You can charge these," she'd tell the cashier at Number One. Frank felt the incorporation required the abolition of such unbusinesslike practices, but Eliza was adamant. "She said she never paid for her groceries before," Frank said, "and she wasn't going to start now."

Frank's sister Edith, her husband Angus Sinclair, and their boy

Billy (a future director of Empire Company) often came down from Campbellton, N.B., to stay with Eliza and J.W., and the old couple returned the favour by journeying to the Sinclair home. The eccentric and beloved Aunt Mary – she who'd rounded the Horn, slept among snakes in Arizona, and intrigued the boy Frank Sobey with the stock market – continued to show up at her sister Eliza's house almost till her last breath. On September 11, 1948, she died in Fort William, Ont. Eliza was now the last of the Creighton sisters.

November 1949 was a terrible month in the life of the Sobeys. Angus Sinclair, husband of Edith, died on the ninth, and his grieving widow and four-year-old son came home to see her parents. J.W. was dying. Eighty years had passed since Janet MacIntosh Sobey had brought him into the world at Camp Aldershot, England. His young brothers Charles and Henry and sisters Margaret and Sara were still alive, but they were all on the Pacific coast. Now, in November 1949, there must have been a warm spell in Stellarton because Bill Sinclair would remember "Papa" sitting on the veranda of the house. J.W. died on the twenty-fourth. "Just before he went," his grandson Donald said, "he lapsed into a coma. Then he awoke. He said he was going to heaven on a staircase. He could hear a choir of angels." His church had served him well.

"He was an active curler and was one of the County's oldest curlers on the ice," the New Glasgow *Evening News* (Nov. 25, 1949) reported. The same edition carried a grocery ad under the heading "Signpost of Satisfaction. Your DOMINION Store." Dominion was huge, aggressive, and national, and would soon prove to be rougher competition than Barkers had ever been. Sobeys Stores, Ltd., countered the Dominion ad with "All the makings for Glorious Bakings" for Christmas – currants, raisins, walnuts, almonds, cut mixed peel, and 28-ounce tins of Libby's mincemeat for forty cents.

The Stellarton curling rink folded, and even Number One was doomed. Sobeys Stores, Ltd., would shortly tear it down, and replace it with "a very modern groceteria". Meanwhile, in December 1949, Frank and Harold held an Empire directors' meeting, and with the formal sort of flourish that boards feel necessary, "The president reported with deep regret the death on Nov. 24, 1949, of the vice-president of the Company, Mr. J. W. Sobey." They appointed their sister Edith to replace him. She and her son Bill moved in permanently with Eliza, and the three children of J.W. continued to gather in his widow's house to direct the affairs of Empire. Frank, when he found time, would treat Billy as a son. But his time was limited. As the half-century turned he was at last moving into the big leagues of Canadian business.

As the fifties began, the Bank of Nova Scotia was constructing Canada's most lavishly appointed banking temple. It was a fat twenty-five-storey structure, right at that choicest of all big-business locations in Canada, King and Bay streets, Toronto. Publicity material bragged about the exterior of "polished, Bedford limestone, dignified, beautiful, resistant to the stains of weather", the gleaming interior of Tennessee marble, Travertine marble, Breccia Rosata marble, and the mural sculpture, Canada's biggest, "carved of solid Hauteville marble" over a fourteen-month period, and all the other "appointments that are supremely right". This bank was "twice as high as Niagara Falls, with one and a half times the space of the Roman Coliseum!" Fifty-two-ton doors, the "largest ever", guarded the two-storey vaults, which were "designed to be atomic-blast proof". A time would soon come when this building, observed from the windy heights of neighbouring bank towers, would look like a quaint stone edifice, nestling beside the ant-like street traffic; but when it opened in 1951 it was the last word in efficiency, security, beauty, and justifiable ostentation. It was an old bank's new cathedral.

Frank had the privilege of exploring it even before it opened: "Mr. Enman used to get me to go through it with him, and he'd show me how they were putting in special telephone equipment so they could plug in here and there. That was all new in those days." The fact that Enman himself escorted the Stellarton boy around proved that Frank, as he approached his fifties, had graduated.

He was now something more than a smart operator in the bluenose sticks. He was moving among the mighty, and he was learning. He was about to become a director of the Dominion Steel and Coal Corporation. Nothing that happened to him in 1951 pleased him as much as his appointment to the board of this colossus of heavy industry.

Like the Canadian Pacific Railway, the T. Eaton Company, and INCO, DOSCO was an outfit whose very name had come to sound as Canadian as hockey, the wheat pool, bush pilots, and "Château" hotels. Marvelling over a coal mine beneath the ocean floor at Glace Bay, Cape Breton, in 1928, *Maclean's* writer George B. Pearson might just as easily have been marvelling over the whole amazing mess of industries that, from then on, would be known as DOSCO: "There isn't another one like it in the whole of North America – and it's Canadian!" In 1928, as DOSCO shakily arose from the carcasses of mercilessly milked companies, a Nova Scotian cabinet minister dismissed its stock as "pure, unadulterated water".

But by the fifties, the DOSCO pack – thirty-three firms in five provinces, and England – owned a shipyard, two shipping lines, three small railroads, nine mines, and nine steel mills and manufacturing plants. DOSCO outfits sold iron ore in Europe, steel rails in Central America, and for markets across North America everything from nuts and bolts to freight cars and transmission towers, from screws, rivets, and nails to ships, bridges, and chain-link fences. DOSCO employed 18,000 people, mostly in Nova Scotia, and the bluenose press habitually called it "the largest single industrial employer in the nation" and "the backbone of the Maritimes' whole economy". Every fifth Maritimer, down-home papers claimed, was more or less economically dependent on DOSCO.

The affairs of DOSCO and its subsidiaries, forebears, and corporate prizes among the East River towns had been inseparable from the health of Frank's stores and theatres, from his duties as mayor, his love of Pictou County, even his boyhood memories of horror at the pithead. DOSCO owned the steelworks and car plant in Trenton, and the coal mines in Stellarton and Thorburn. "I was brought up in a town and county," he explained, "which were almost totally dependent on DOSCO." The board of no great industrial concern, even of CPR, looked more tantalizing to Frank than DOSCO's. Its members included the likes of Toronto financier J. H. Gundy, Montreal industrialist Colin W. Webster, and others who regularly broke bread, cracked oysters, slurped Scotch, went yachting, played poker, and made deals with Canada's shrewdest financial machinators, richest industrialists, and most illustrious masters of the merger. The DOSCO board was part of central Canada's supreme capitalist clique. Did a grocer from Stellarton belong? Frank thought so. He never doubted his own smarts, and in the mid-forties began to buy DOSCO shares. He was rarely ashamed simply to state what he wanted, and what he wanted at mid-century was a seat on DOSCO's board. He told Enman flat out that he wanted a DOSCO directorship.

Enman had just become president of the Bank of Nova Scotia and, unknown to Frank, the rambunctious Lionel "Laddie" Forsyth was about to become president of DOSCO. Frank knew Forsyth. They were both directors of Nova Scotia Trust, and they'd had a drink or two together. Forsyth, the seagoing son of a square-rigger captain, was a legal wizard, sometime investment wizard, minor poet, major after-dinner speaker, ex-baseball player, ex-streetcar driver, ex-languages professor, breeder of Jersey cows, indifferent golfer, and a sawed-off 200-pound trencherman to boot. In *Flame of Power*, Peter C. Newman called him "a champion deflater of official stuffiness". The first Nova Scotian ever to head DOSCO, Forsyth would also prove to be the most successful president in its history. Under him, it would thrive. Under his successors, it would fall apart.

Stewart's fine hand undoubtedly played a part in Forsyth's appointment. Stewart was vice-president of DOSCO's bank, the Royal, and Forsyth was also a director of the Royal. So was DOSCO director Colin W. Webster. Moreover, Stewart and Forsyth (and soon Webster as well) were directors of Montreal Trust, trustees for Sobeys Stores, Ltd.'s first bond issue. Stewart, Webster, and the venerable J. H. Gundy, a DOSCO director, met regularly at board meetings of Massey-Harris Company; and Stewart and

Gundy were fellow directors of Canada Cement Company. Gundy, of course, was supreme at Wood, Gundy and Company, Ltd., which, among Canadian investment bankers, was the gentlemanly, if not always gentle, giant. Stewart had an Upper Canadian business grapevine like no other Maritimer.

Forsyth duly ascended to the presidency of DOSCO in December 1949, but a year later Frank's dream of a directorship had still not come true. The market price of DOSCO was temptingly high. He sold his 18,000 shares, and made a killing. Meanwhile, the Bank of Nova Scotia held its annual meetings in Halifax and Enman came to town. One morning, the bank directors gathered at the railroad station before travelling 150 miles in a private rail car to reach a lobster dinner at the luxurious Digby Pines. Enman, who wasn't keen on the expedition, had summoned Frank to Halifax to talk business, and now, as they paced the station platform near the chuffing, coal-fired, steam-driven locomotive, he was abrupt. When Frank said he'd sold all his DOSCO shares, Enman snapped, "Buy them back."

"Why should I do that?" Frank asked. "It'll cost me money."

"Never mind that. Buy them back."

"But the price is up. I'll have to pay more than I got for them."

"Doesn't matter. Buy them back anyway."

Frank bought them back, and in early 1951 he got the word: welcome to the DOSCO board. Now he understood why Enman had so imperiously ordered him to re-purchase his DOSCO holdings. DOSCO was a mighty customer of the Royal Bank, Stewart was a mighty figure at Royal, and Enman, who never visited Halifax without arranging to see him, had urged him to pry an opening for Frank on the DOSCO board. For the grocer from Stellarton, the second half of the century was off to a fine start. "It was Stewart, following Enman's suggestion, who got me that directorship," Frank said. "That was perhaps the happiest board I was ever on."

By the time the founding Sobey was dead and the expansionist Sobey had his DOSCO directorship, Bill Sobey, twenty-three, and David Sobey, nineteen, knew it was unlikely they'd ever escape the family business (Donald, fifteen, was still in high school). Frank seemed to feel their schooling was just something they had to get out of the way fast so they could get on with the job of learning the important stuff: how to make a meat counter profitable, a produce display mouth-watering, a store opening a palpable hit, and a chain ever bigger, ever better, ever tougher to beat. How to make a buck. Bill and David had attended Horton Academy, the Baptist-run prep school in Wolfville, and had discovered that going home for the "summer holidays" meant not just fun in the sun at Chance Harbour but also working their young butts off for Sobeys Stores.

Their first job, as small boys, had been sprouting and bagging potatoes in the basement of Number One. When Donald was old enough to perform this same drudgery, he said, "I'd go to the store at 7.30 a.m., and between then and 10.30 at night, I'd get out of there only for lunch and supper. I hated it. I thought, *I can't make my living this way*." Bill remembered putting in a solid day with the potatoes, then going home to collect his pay. Frank was in the bathtub, and he told the boy to search his trousers for change. "There's only twenty-four cents here," Bill said. His father cheerfully replied, "Fine, that's your pay. That's what you're worth." David, as a boy, was proud to ride along with a delivery man and carry boxes of groceries up to customers' houses, "but I don't think I ever got paid for it." Not long after that, "I was allowed to take orders on the phone, and box them." The war was on, men were scarce, and any eager lad could make himself useful.

School had its demands, to be sure, but young Bill and young David were never entirely free of what Bill called "clerking around, sweeping floors, cleaning up". Bill was twelve when the war started, but long before it ended he could drive "one of the old, silver-panelled, Ford delivery trucks. Drive in, back out. I'm not the best driver in Nova Scotia but I've never met anyone who could beat me backing up." Later, "I was a meat-cutter for four years. I did all those old jobs, making sausages and puddings, cleaning turkeys. One whole summer in New Glasgow I didn't do much more than clean mackerel and salmon."

Nor did David escape gutting fish. At Number 25, where he

worked in a meat department for the first time, "Cecil McLaren had me on fish non-stop. I bet I cleaned more mackerel than anyone else in the history of that store. I cleaned so much mackerel I was sure Cecil disliked me for some reason." Cleaning mackerel seems to have been an initiation ordeal for new boys in the meat department at Number 25. "But it was great training," he added. "You couldn't get better training than in the meat departments." One reason why it was good training was that – thanks to a system McLaren instituted at Number 25 and Frank promptly imposed on the whole chain – each meat manager had to sit down every Saturday night to calculate the profit or loss on his counter's operation during the previous week.

David's earliest job of considerable responsibility was as manager of the small store in Westville. "I was also the only meat man there," he said, "so I had to do all the work." Like his father and grandfather before him, he used his spare moments to make sausages.

Other young Maritimers helped in their fathers' businesses. Boys joined their fathers in dories, hay fields, apple orchards, woodcutting, barn-building, manure-shovelling, and a dozen other tasks in the old routine to assure family survival. Some stayed home and succeeded their fathers on the farm or the fishing grounds. Some went away, and learned other skills in other places. There was nothing unusual in any of this. Why shouldn't Frank's sons have worked in the stores for a while? Hadn't he and his brother and sister all helped old J.W. run the business? Indeed, it would have been gossip-worthy in Stellarton if the Sobey boys had *not* worked for their father.

What made Frank's relationship with his sons rare, however, was that he would not countenance their simply making themselves useful to the stores for a while and then shoving off to separate careers. He wanted them with him for good. Their sweeping up, slitting mackerel, and delivering groceries weren't quite like the meaningless summer jobs of other youths. These joe-jobs were the beginning of his preparing them to help run a business dynasty for the rest of their lives. To him, the grocery trade was a family calling – as medicine, law, science, and warfare have been for others – and making the chain grow was a duty to Sobeys yet unborn. He sent his older sons away to study at the feet of the masters so they could return to him stronger and wiser than they'd been before, and better versed in the secrets of the mighty supermarket movement. Besides, it was their turn to pick a few brains.

It was typical of Frank that he sent Bill and David to separate masters, one in Ontario, the other in New England. Different masters had different techniques. Loblaw might know things that First National did not; but First National, in other respects, might be sharper than Loblaw. So Bill went to Loblaw in Toronto in 1946-47, and David went to First National in Boston in 1953.

Frank knew that the miracle chain of Canada was the Loblaw Groceterias Company. In just thirty years it had grown from a two-store partnership into a 119-store empire. It sold more food per outlet – and earned more profit per dollar of sales – than any other large chain in the world, and U.S. food-merchandising executives were constantly dropping in on Loblaw's headquarters in Toronto to learn the latest wrinkles and tricks of the trade.

To get his oldest boy into the Loblaw organization, Frank once again used a perfectly placed connection. George Huffman was the Loblaw general manager. "I'll put him [Bill] in a store out on Bloor Street West," Huffman told Frank. "That's handy to my home, and I can keep an eye on him." Thus, even before Frank built Number 25, his son Bill, at nineteen, went to work in Toronto for the industry leader. He was there not only to get the best possible on-the-job training, but also to suck up information for use back home. He stayed a year, returned to the East River towns, and joined the team that was opening Number 25.

By 1953 it was David's turn for a period of educational exile, and Frank knew exactly where to place him. Frank had befriended the senior management at First National Stores, a Boston-based merger of supermarket chains which, in David's memory, "was then *the* food chain." Indeed, Frank and First National were so chummy that the U.S. chain had already offered to get him store plans and equipment, and now it came through with a job in Boston for David. David was married by then, and for a while the young couple lived in a third-floor Boston tenement with exposed lead pipes, a space heater they feared would ignite the whole building, and a bathroom so infested with cockroaches that "When I went in there, I'd flick on the light and just stand there for a moment to give everybody time to clear out." First National, however, was decidedly less primitive: "It was a chance to work for somebody else, and to see how they did things. I moved around from store to store. I did everything, from the basement up, filling shelves, cutting meat, you name it."

He was twenty-three when he returned home, and his wife was expecting their first child. Frank figured he was now ready for a tough job, and sent him to manage the first store that the chain built in Halifax. It was on Gottingen Street in the North End, a section of town that was known neither for affluence nor for gentility. "So far as making a go of that store went," David said, "you either did it, or you didn't." Apparently, he did. "I had a great three years there. You really learned the business. . . . It wasn't big but it was one of the top-volume stores in Halifax, and we sold more Carnation Milk than anyone else in the city."

Meanwhile, Bill Sobey was getting to know the Maritimes. By July 1959, Sobeys Stores, Ltd., boasted twenty-three stores in Nova Scotia and New Brunswick. Two were under construction, and three more were planned for '59. Moreover, almost all the outlets were modern supermarkets. The faithful Charles Higgins, working under general manager Leslie Sharp – a one-time Loblaw man whom Frank had lured away from Toronto – had "opened" most of the new stores, but Bill had helped him. "I used to travel a lot with Bill on store openings," Higgins said. "You had to go in when there was nothing there but the bare walls. You ordered the stock, lined it up on the shelves, hired staff, placed the newspaper ads, the whole thing." Bill also worked closely with his uncle Harold, vice-president of Sobeys Stores. "I thought I was a hot-shot buyer," Bill said, "and he was a great tempering force on me."

Though Harold was nine years younger than Frank, they had a fair bit in common. Harold, too, had married a Pictou County

Scot, slaughtered lambs, delivered groceries to the Bullpen behind the Albion Mine. His children, too, got their free fill of candy from a Sobeys Stores building on Sunday afternoons, and on some Sundays dropped in with their parents on Eliza "Nanna" Sobey. Both brothers were personally frugal or, in the words of Harold's son John Robert Sobey, "very tight". Harold was loath to blow money on clothes for himself and, while his children bought their gloves at relatively expensive shops, he bought his at the local emporia.

But in other respects the Sobey brothers were quite unalike. Harold hated debt, while Frank thrived on it. Harold paid his bills the day he got them, and never borrowed from a bank to buy stocks on the market. Frank was a careful but relentless borrower. His idea of an exciting life was to use the other fellow's money to invest and expand some more, then do all these things all over again, and never stop. (Not, at least, till interest rates got so steep that some other strategy of expansion made better sense.)

There were differences of personality, as well. Harold was the easier fellow to be around. He was tall, good-looking, instantly likeable. His smile put strangers at ease, and at New Glasgow's hangout for businessmen, the City Club, there was no more popular figure than Harold Sobey. H. R. Murphy, a soft-drink bottler in New Glasgow in the early fifties, said that Harold, who'd inherited his father's passion for curling, was a miraculously sunny skip. Murphy played on Harold's rink, "and it wouldn't matter if you made ten bad shots in a row. He'd never blame you, and he stayed so cheerful." Frank had admired Harold's easy ways with people and had once told him, "I wish I was more like you."

Harold's duties to the chain in the late forties and fifties lay chiefly in buying and merchandising. "He's often been underrated," investment counsellor Richard Giles said. "He was actually very skilled at these jobs." For a time, Harold also supervised the stores, and as the chain expanded he did much of the hiring. "Maybe it was his army training, or maybe he just had a knack for it," Frank said, "but he could always find good people, and then continue to have good relations with them." In his late forties, however, Har-

Harold Sobey and his parents, 1940.

old decided he'd had enough of peddling groceries for one lifetime. By then, Frank's third son, Donald, was doing the bookkeeping for Empire Company. Donald never would learn the grocery business as his father, his brothers, and his uncle had. Instead, he would prove that when it came to investing Sobey money, he had Frank's shrewdness.

If Frank used friends to place his sons with efficient chains, he also used friends to tell him who was worth stealing from efficient chains. He knew in 1952 that the time had finally come to ask a non-Sobey to join his top management. He wanted an expert work addict from away, a man who'd already proved he knew all there was to know about opening and operating modern groceterias. "Father's always had a talent not only for getting the right guys," David Sobey said, "but also for recognizing the right time to get the right guys." The right guy to get in 1952 was a Toronto-born Loblaw vet named Leslie Sharp, but Frank didn't know that till he'd done some detective work by phone.

Sharp, in 1952, was Loblaw's top district supervisor. His territory was Number One district, affluent North Toronto. Earlier, he'd been up to his ears in Loblaw's ulcer-making postwar expansion program. "I worked six years," he said, "and hardly ever even got to bed." He'd had enough. He fell out with the Loblaw organization, served notice, and went into business for himself as a food broker. He'd been doing that for all of two days when, in the middle of the night, he got a phone call from Stellarton, N.S. A fellow named Frank Sobey wondered if he'd like to move down there to help build a supermarket chain. The upshot was that Sharp became general manager of Sobeys Stores, Ltd., in November, and stayed for nineteen years.

When Frank hired him, his resignation was so recent that Loblaw still hoped to get him back. Who'd been Frank's tipster? Who had phoned long-distance to tell him Sharp had quit? Raiding the gardens where managers grow is such a provocative activity that Frank, even thirty years later, was reluctant to name the caller. "I knew we had to get an experienced chain-store man in," he said, "and there were one or two companies that I depended on. I knew their heads. So I got a call one night from one of these people. I'd rather not say who. I don't want to get anyone in trouble." Later, having calculated that much water had passed under many bridges since 1952, he allowed that his informant had been one of the top men at the Montreal headquarters of Kraft Foods, Ltd., a man who made it his business to know every skilled food merchandiser in Canada.

"He told me about a man with Loblaw's. He says, 'He's one of their best but something's happened at Loblaw's. I don't think he'll go back, but they want to see him Monday morning.' " Frank now called George Huffman, Loblaw's general manager. "How did you ever hear about that [Sharp's unhappiness]?" Huffman asked. "We can't afford to lose men like Les Sharp." But Huffman confirmed not only that on Monday morning Loblaw president George Metcalf would try to persuade Sharp to return to the fold, but also that Metcalf might not succeed. That's when Frank phoned Sharp, and Loblaw's never had a chance. "I got Les to come down and see me that weekend," he said, "and we made a deal."

"I had good experience and that's what he wanted me for," Sharp said. "They had maybe sixteen stores [in 1952], some self-service, but some still the old-style service stores. The biggest was only about six thousand square feet, and none was as big as the groceterias I'd supervised in Toronto. Well, the idea was for me to take this little chain and turn it into a completely modern chain of supermarkets, and to develop a team not only to do this but to run the stores as well. I found the job hard to get a handle on at first, but things moved pretty swiftly. . . . I pretty well built the stores, but I got a great deal of support from the family. Frank's son Bill was a great help."

Sharp worked as hard as he'd ever worked for Loblaw's, "but it was different. More freedom. Frank, he'd give you your head. . . . He'd never lose heart, you know. Sometimes we'd lose a tough battle. You'd tell him about it, and it wouldn't fizz on him." If he was a good boss, however, he was also "tough to work for". He demanded exceptional effort, and "If he gave you a job to do, you did it, make no mistake." Moreover, Frank was "a tremendous debater". Even if he shared your opinion, he'd often pretend he didn't. "He'd take the other side just to test you," Sharp said, "just to hear you express what you thought."

Sharp quit in June 1971. Dominion Stores, in a fit of ferocious price-cutting, was giving severe jitters to the entire supermarket industry, and nowhere more so than in the Maritimes. "They'd slashed prices on something like two thousand items," Frank said, "and the pressure got very bad. We were finding it tough to hold our volume, and it was almost impossible to make money. In one or two quarters we actually suffered losses." For the general manager of any chain smaller than the belligerent Dominion giant, 1970-71 was a harsh time, and indeed the warfare was rough on Dominion executives as well. Sharp decided he'd be happier on his own, and moved to Halifax to set himself up as a food broker. That's what he'd intended to do in Toronto nineteen years earlier, when he'd received from Frank the telephone call that changed his life. Meanwhile, he had done for Sobeys Stores all that Frank had hoped he'd do. When he left, the chain boasted sixty-four supermarkets, and annual sales nudged $100,000,000.

Who would replace Sharp? With Bill Sobey as president of the chain, David Sobey as executive vice-president, Frank himself as chairman of the board, and a team of capable men in senior management, was another outsider even necessary? Frank thought so, and at sixty-nine he was still the boss. "My father said a business is like a farm, because if you don't put more back into it than you take out, then you're in trouble," he explained, "but he also said a business is like a farm, because every once in a while you've got to take in a new bull. It's been my policy to move people up within the organization, but once in a while you need to inject some new blood, just as you do with a herd of cattle." Sharp had been a Loblaw man. This time, Frank thought, he'd better get his new blood from Dominion Stores.

He did not put an ad in the Careers section of the *Globe and Mail*. He did not hire a head-hunting agency. He did not pay a professional at assessing executive potential to get strangers to endure probing interviews and multi-page tests of aptitude, attitude, and character. Instead, this seasoned grocer once again used the most primitive of all techniques of personnel research. He consulted a smart friend. William Flavelle McLean, fifty-five in 1971, was the Toronto-born president of Canada Packers, Ltd. Frank liked the man, and he liked the company.

"I have great respect for their operation," Frank said. "If you ever hired anyone from Canada Packers, you got a good man." The working day at Canada Packers' head office in Toronto began at 7 a.m., and in Moncton Frank had once heard a sales supervisor tell the firm's regional sales crew, "When you work for Canada Packers you work twenty-four hours a day, seven days a week. If the business is there, you go get it." Frank knew that the man at the top of Canada Packers would know about the men near the top of Dominion Stores, Ltd., "So I went to see McLean. He said he'd get his people working on it, and he got back to me about ten days later."

McLean told him the two hottest bets as future presidents of Dominion were A. C. Jackson and J. Skiffington Murchie. Frank just happened to phone Murchie first, and the Dominion Stores man now did what the Loblaw man had done almost twenty years before. On a weekend, he went from Toronto to Stellarton for clandestine talks with some guys named Sobey. A Dominion Stores decision was now working in the Sobeys' favour. The chain had long rewarded its top management with hefty, regular bonuses, which the executives had come to regard as part of their salaries. But Dominion's price war was such an all-out blitz that, to help pay for it, the owners had slashed the bonuses to hot-shots like Murchie. Frank knew all this. Just as he had once known Sharp was sore at Loblaw's, he now knew Murchie was sore at Dominion, or at least disgruntled.

"Murchie is still with us," Frank said ten years later. Indeed he was. By then, he was the first non-Sobey ever to serve as president of Sobeys Stores, Ltd. Moreover, it said something for the astuteness of Frank's informant, McLean, that Jackson, the man Frank never did get around to calling, had risen to the presidency of Dominion Stores.

Luring the right man from a rival concern could be as tricky as the games spies play. You had to know whom you could trust, because, for instance, "There are an awful lot of men some companies would love to get rid of." Nor was Sobeys Stores, Ltd., invariably the aggressor. "We lost our top meat man two or three years ago," Frank said in 1981. "Loblaw's offered him twice what we were paying. The Western Co-op – they're in Alberta – they got our warehouse man." So he lost a few, but he won more, because "I always kept my feelers out so I'd know where to go if I had to get a top man. I know the people who know how to assess who's available. I could find a good man right now easier than the boys [his sons] could."

In the year Frank nabbed Les Sharp, 1952, he also revelled in one of the sweetest adventures of his middle years. He and Irene drove to Sarasota, Florida, winter headquarters for the Ringling Brothers circus, and arrived while Cecil B. de Mille was directing *The Greatest Show on Earth* for Paramount Films. Here was a chance for Frank to taste again, at one sunny location, both entertainment passions of his youth – the circus and the movies – and he made the most of it. "Sarasota seemed to be nothing but circus people in those days," he said. "Rene and I would go into a supermarket, and there'd be a midget, a trapeze artist, and maybe a clown or two, all buying their groceries." They stayed at the Ringling Hotel, which boasted a three-storey hall for aerial acts; saw John Ringling North enter the lobby on a horse; and joined circus professionals and Hollywood stars at nightly parties. "At one of them," Frank said, "a beachball hit Dorothy Lamour in the face."

On the movie set, however, security was tight. Rubberneckers from Stellarton, Nova Scotia, weren't welcome, but Frank solved that little problem in his usual way. He phoned a crony, Rube Bolstad, president of Famous Players, in Toronto. Bolstad phoned a publicity man in Hollywood, and in a matter of hours the Sobeys had an undated day-pass to the set. On the advice of "an actress or somebody", they avoided the front gate. Day after day, Frank and Irene traipsed through the back entrance for circus workers, stagehands, cameramen, and the likes of Betty Hutton, Cornel Wilde, James Stewart, Charlton Heston, Dorothy Lamour, Gloria Grahame, and North America's top circus clown, the sad-faced Emmett Kelly.

The movie, as it turned out, was a typically lavish de Mille epic, but also mediocre. (Though critics knocked it, Frank stoutly defended it. It "did big business in Stellarton.") The Sobeys returned to the Sarasota neighbourhood winter after winter, staying at Lido Beach. His son Donald visited Lido Beach in 1957, and recalled, "There was nothing on Longboat Key at all, just a little old bridge to get there." Within twenty years, however, so many pricey condo developments and golf clubs lined the shore that only a few undeveloped beach-front acres remained on the entire island. Toronto real-estate wheelers – including Isadore Sharp, boss of Four Seasons Hotels – had their eye on that land in the late seventies. "A stockbroker told the Four Seasons people the Sobeys were always interested in a partnership," Donald said, "and we joined with them on this. They had connections in Sarasota, which we'd always liked both for its growth potential, and as a place to stay."

The group paid $6 million for the Longboat Key acreage, and

sold it for $13 million a year later. After carrying costs and taxes, the Sobeys pocketed nearly $700,000. Only months later, the group paid another $6 million for subdivision land in south Sarasota. "We sold that out for $20 million only eighteen months after we bought it," Donald said. "After taxes, we [the Sobeys] made about $1.8 million on that one." Except for putting up money, "None of it was any of our doing. We were just sitting around the table." But they had picked shrewd operators to sit with. The magical era of the circus had long since passed, but for Frank and his family Sarasota was still rewarding.

By 1953, Frank wanted J. McG. Stewart to give him another lawyer. Not that Gordon Cowan wasn't capable. A Rhodes Scholar who'd taught law, he worked for Stewart, MacKeen & Covert (under its various names) for a quarter-century before becoming Chief Justice of the Trial Division in the Supreme Court of Nova Scotia. Cowan was uncannily well organized. Frank Covert said that he had "a brilliant mind" and that, before his judgeship, he was "a great, all-around lawyer, specializing in corporation law". But Frank thought Cowan behaved like a judge long before he became one. He recalled that, while discussing haggling tactics before sessions with Carl Fisher over the terms of the bonds Eastern Securities would underwrite for Sobeys Stores, Ltd., "Cowan would say, 'Frank, you can't ask for *that*.' " Cowan wanted to figure out what was fair to both sides before they clashed. What Frank wanted in his corner was not a dispenser of mere fairness but a tough guy who'd fight strictly for *his* interests, a lawyer who agreed with him that the way to start negotiations was to demand the unreasonable. Cowan, he said in 1982, "was a nice, mild, honourable little fellow" who belonged on the bench rather than in the rough-and-tumble of business warfare. "So I spoke to J. McG. Stewart, the fellow who really got me started," Frank said, "and he gave me Harry Rhude."

Henry B. Rhude, Halifax-born war hero, joined Stewart's law firm during what Frank Covert called its "golden years of recruitment". Rhude had survived four years as a navigator aboard RCAF bombers, and at war's end had the Distinguished Flying Cross. He was still only twenty-one. Thanks to a bout of tuberculosis, it was in Camp Hill Hospital that he wrote his bar exams. Stewart snapped him up, and Rhude was admitted to the bar in 1951. He worked as though he knew it was a privilege to be alive. "When he was articled with us," Covert wrote in his unpublished history of the firm, "I went into the library one day, and there were five articled clerks there. I left them with five problems to divide among them. The next morning there were five answers on my desk, all from H. B. Rhude, all helpful and correct, and at that time the doctors would only let him work for half a day!"

Covert singled out Rhude and J. William E. Mingo as the partners who, more than all others, "made life easy for me." They were the cream of the talented crop at the leading law firm east of Montreal; and Frank Sobey had both of them working with him at once. Mingo was counsel for the provincial Crown corporation Industrial Estates Limited during the years (1957-69) that Frank was IEL's president. Rhude, after meeting Frank in 1953, became *the* corporation lawyer for the Sobeys' multifarious business interests, and remained so right down till the mid-seventies. He was at the heart of every important decision, deal, sale, or acquisition that the Sobey empire made. "Harry," Frank said in 1983, "knows more about our financing than any of us do."

But in Rhude's memory their meeting thirty years earlier had not come about simply because Stewart had responded to Frank's request for a tough lawyer. "The truth is, I met Frank in a bar at the Mount Royal Hotel in Montreal," he said. "I was with Harold Egan, and Frank breezed in and bombarded me with questions. I must have answered a couple to his satisfaction because a day or two later he showed up at my hotel room with Roy Jodrey." Rhude remembered the visit because it had profoundly embarrassed him. He was twenty-nine in 1953. Sobey, fifty-one, and Jodrey, sixty-four, were among his firm's most valued clients. The young lawyer, in the middle of a Montreal afternoon, faced them in his pyjamas beside an unmade bed. His work habits seemed to leave much to be desired. He told them that although he'd been out of hospital for two years, he was still under doctor's orders to take a nap each afternoon.

"Frank liked younger people," Rhude said. "He liked their energy, but I never understood why he took to me. Why it started is still a mystery." What some Halifax lawyers saw as a bigger mystery was why this fruitful lawyer-client relationship lasted a quarter-century, given that the Sobeys were known to be notoriously difficult clients. Rhude simply said, "Frank has quite a capacity for engendering loyalty."

"I was using Harry all the time," Frank said. "I'd be in Montreal maybe, and I'd get into trouble or something. I'd phone Harry at four or five in the afternoon, and he'd be with me in the morning Same thing in St. John's, Newfoundland, when we built the Avalon Mall [in the mid-sixties]. And breaking into those financial markets in Upper Canada, we put a lot of things together and we learned a lot together. Harry was a hard worker, and he was a mover. He was my right-hand man. He was at my elbow. He was with me." No clan chief could have asked for more.

Covert, however, recalled Rhude's having once confided to him that his dealings with Frank were not as happy as he'd like them to be. The older man, who'd become something of a guru at Stewart, MacKeen & Covert, said, "One of your problems with Sobey is that you haven't put a goddamn cent into his company." When Rhude said he had no money to invest, Covert said, "Well, borrow it." Rhude eventually became president of Sobey Leased Properties, and a director of Sobeys Stores, Ltd., the Empire Company, and half a dozen other firms that the Sobeys owned either wholly or partially.

7

UP AND DOWN WITH DOSCO

IN THE EARLY FIFTIES, Frank found his obligations as a DOSCO director immensely pleasurable. For one thing, they required him to visit Montreal each month, at DOSCO's expense, for board meetings; and even the most hidebound Pictou County loyalist was bound to concede that Montreal offered titillation the East River towns could not provide. For another thing, a man of Frank's acquisitive drive could not help finding it stimulating to be closeted with such elite custodians of inside business information as C. L. Gundy, Colin Webster, Lionel Forsyth, and the other financiers, industrialists, and corporation lawyers who comprised the DOSCO board. For yet another, he now befriended the manager of DOSCO subsidiaries in Nova Scotia, the day-to-day bosses who weren't afraid to turn back their sleeves, work up some sweat, get their hands dirty, or, in the case of Harold Gordon, check out a burning coal mine.

Gordon was a hefty, handsome, Scottish-born Cape Breton Islander. He was a blunt, growling man with huge hands, and according to C. Arnold Patterson he "looked like a Nordic God." Patterson, later the proprietor of radio station CFDR in Dartmouth, N.S., was DOSCO's public relations chief (1958-63), and he remembered Gordon as "a real he-man. He wasn't a domineering man, he was a *dominant* man. He was a crackerjack engineer, too." His home was Sydney, but Stellarton had known him as the fearless boss of the Acadia Coal Company. "Gordon was perhaps the most courageous man I ever knew," Frank said. "He was brought up in the mines. If there was trouble, if there was an explosion, he was the first man in and the last out. At the Springhill explosion [1956], I went over and Louis Frost – he was the chief engineer – was lying on a cot. He'd got a whiff of gas coming up the slope, and he said you had to keep your head close to the pavement and crawl up. There was only a foot of air below the gas. Well, Harold Gordon was the last man to come out of that mine. . . ."

Now Gordon was chief of all DOSCO coal mines in Nova Scotia (which meant ninety per cent of them). He was not easy on union leaders, but the miners held him in such respect that, so far as labour strife went, his term as the czar of Nova Scotian coal mines was a fairly calm period in their turbulent history. "If you said anything against Mr. Gordon in Stellarton," newspaperman Harry Sutherland said, "a miner might punch you in the face."

Frank's friends in DOSCO's top management also included W. F. Knoll, Sr., of New Glasgow, who ran the empire's Trenton Industries, Ltd., manufacturers of coal-mining machines; Charles Appleton, chief of coal sales, a Stellarton man whom Frank had known since boyhood; T. H. McEvoy, chief of steel sales; Clement Anson, who ruled the steelworks in Sydney; and Robert Nelson, the Quebec-born dictator of Halifax Shipyards, Ltd. "Nelson was tough and totally bilingual," Patterson said. "He was fluent in both English and profanity. He was a tall, impressive guy, a major figure around Halifax, and he ran the shipyard like a personal fiefdom. . . . Whenever you arrived in Halifax, you'd find a twenty-year-old bottle of Bell's Scotch in your room from Bob." Frank said Nelson was "a real character, but a great operator. He made money for the company all through the years."

Like Frank, most DOSCO bosses were roughly as old as the century. They'd fought their way up through DOSCO's thick ranks. Nelson, for instance, had started at the shipyards as an accountant in 1928, the year of DOSCO's corporate emergence. McEvoy's entry in *Canadian Who's Who* (1962) said he'd been "associated with DOSCO and predecessors since college days." Most of the

The Board of Directors of Dominion Steel and Coal Corporation in the early 1950s. Left to right: Charles Burchill, Charles Hunt, William Knowle, Dr. Waterhouse, Laddie Forsyth, C. B. Lang, Kim Cope, Arthur Cross, Gammie Jones, Frank Sobey, Colin Webster. Frank Sobey was named to the Board in 1951.

managers had also spent the bulk of their lives in Nova Scotia. Anson was born in England and educated in Australia and at McGill University, but he'd married a Sydney girl in 1928 and, during his climb to the top of the steelworks there, had become thoroughly Nova Scotian. Even McEvoy, born in Ontario and now, as chief of steel sales, a Montrealer, had Maritime connections. His wife was a New Brunswicker, and his alma mater was St. Francis Xavier University in Antigonish, N.S.

"McEvoy was short, square, powerful," Patterson said. "He was also one hell of a salesman. Anson had a terrific ego, but I guess you could say most of them had strong egos and strong characters." They were solid company men but not company patsies. They did conspicuous local do-gooding and President Forsyth liked that. He wanted them to be noticeable. "Forsyth bought them all Cadillacs," Patterson said. "He ran a very decentralized kind of operation. These guys were intensely loyal to him. They were his buddies. They were oligarchs really." Frank revelled in their company.

He liked opinionated men with practical skills. As a boy, he'd dreamed of being in the construction business, and spent happy hours with his Meccano set and exploring the electrical innards of the Jubilee theatre. Now his DOSCO pals included engineers, metallurgists, mine managers, and a shipyard boss; and to make them even more stimulating, most ran domains that earned profits for DOSCO. No one knew then that DOSCO was doomed.

In Montreal, "We used to go out to dinner, and naturally drink a little too much." Lionel Forsyth was a member of what Peter C. Newman described in *The Canadian Establishment* (1975) as "the most snobbish club in the country", the Mount Royal Club, where the ashtrays came with silver toothpicks. "The legend persists," Newman wrote, "that the main reason Max Aitken, the future Lord Beaverbrook, left Montreal for England in 1910 was that he couldn't get into the Mount Royal. Izaak Walton Killam, Aitken's old business associate, didn't even try; he just sat in his mansion across Sherbrooke Street and glared out – though he did make it into the St. James's and the Toronto clubs." As late as 1974, the Mount Royal still had only 530 members, but Frank had succeeded where Aitken had failed. Forsyth managed to get him a membership in the early fifties.

"Laddie was a great personal friend," Frank said. "Any time I was in Montreal, he wanted me to have lunch with him at the Mount Royal Club. He had one bad habit. He liked to drink too much. He'd say, 'Well, let's not have too much to drink. Let's just have a double and let it go at that.' So we'd have a double. Then just before we went in to lunch, he'd say, 'Let's have one for the road. You can't fly on one wing.' So we'd have another double. He could hold his liquor, and I never saw him any the worse for liquor, but I think it was hard on his system."

Another member of the Mount Royal was James Muir, president of the Royal Bank. Frank was sufficiently close to Muir that he could see him on short notice, which he once did with his friend Roy Jodrey. They were walking in Montreal, and Jodrey was fretting about a million dollars that he owed the Royal. Jodrey had borrowed the money to buy shares in British Columbia Power, and when the company had been bought out by the government, he had deposited the cash from the sale of his shares into the Bank of Nova Scotia rather than into the Royal. "The banks wanted their loans paid down," Frank explained, "and this was just in one of those tight-money times when they wouldn't give you any money to buy stocks or inventory." Jodrey feared that if he paid off the million, the bank might refuse to reloan it to him when he needed it. "So I suggested he just go right in and see Mr. Muir," Frank said. "Roy wanted me to come in with him, so I did. Well, he told Mr. Muir his problem - that if he paid the million off, he was scared he wouldn't get it back, and he might want it for something. Mr. Muir pounded his fist on his desk, and he said, 'Mr. Jodrey, you can pay it off today and have it back tomorrow, or any day you want.' Roy went out very happy. He said to me, 'That Muir, he's quite a fellow, isn't he?' Those fellows, Muir and Enman, they really *ran* their banks."

Forsyth, as a boss, was avuncular and flamboyant. Each summer he stayed at the elegant Keltic Lodge in Cape Breton and summoned all his bluenose chiefs, the DOSCO general managers in four counties, to join him there for good talk, good food, and good booze. "I always like to have my family with me," he said. Wives, too, were welcome, and Frank and Irene rarely missed these jolly sessions.

What made these gatherings doubly pleasant for Frank was that Horace Enman had his own palatial summer retreat at Ingonish, and often joined the DOSCO gang. One morning after breakfast, the president of the Bank of Nova Scotia, the president of DOSCO, the president of Sobeys Stores, Ltd., and Clem Anson, boss of the Sydney steelworks, were sitting together on the steps at Keltic, and Enman asked, "Why don't you fellows buy some DOSCO shares?"

"Where will we get the money?" Forsyth wondered.

"I'll put up the money," the bank president promised.

Remembering the conversation and subsequent investment, Frank said, "So we went out and we bought 100,000 shares. Clem Anson took ten per cent, and Laddie and I split the rest. But Mr. Enman spoke to me on the side. He said I'd have to go on the note because although Laddie was a great operator he wasn't careful about his own private business affairs. So I said I'd go on the note. I guess Mr. Enman told the bank to make the loan all right, but somebody neglected to see that the note was endorsed. So after Laddie died [on January 1, 1957], the Montreal Trust Company told me there were these 100,000 shares of DOSCO – I think they were at the Bank of Nova Scotia on St. James Street – but nobody seemed to be on the note. So I told them to speak to Laddie's secretary because she knew about the transaction. They took her word for it. I got my share. Clem Anson got his, and Laddie's estate got its share. The stock had gone way up in value. . . . Well, that's how we sometimes did business."

But if Frank found his DOSCO connection meant lunch at the Mount Royal Club, exquisite dining in "the Paris of North America", and hobnobbing at Keltic with useful men he admired, he also found that it had its dark side. For DOSCO was not just an industrial giant, it was the most tragedy-ridden industrial giant in Canadian history. Once he was an insider there, he was an insider on economic realities that threatened to kill his home town and on mine disasters that did kill his fellow townsmen. On April 28, 1950, one year before he joined the DOSCO board, an explosion and fire ripped through the very shaft that his father, dead only four months, had helped to build forty-five years before. Half a dozen men suffered severe burns, and Stellarton regarded their survival as miraculous. Seven more fires plagued the Allan Shaft in the following year.

But despite the danger, Frank insisted, Stellarton miners preferred the Allan Shaft above all other mines: "They seemed to feel it was a fine mine to work in, and the men who were paid so much per ton could make more money there than anywhere else. The miners looked on explosions and falls just as the hazards of their occupation, and when the Allan Shaft was closed on account of fire, they were the ones who were fussing to see it open as soon as possible so they could go back to work."

Frank had been on the DOSCO board little more than a month when the fire that broke the Allan's back occurred. "During the war," he said, "they'd broken from the Allan Shaft into the old Foord Pit. This was a great seam of coal. It was supposed to be forty feet thick, the thickest in the world, but it had been closed down since the explosion of 1880. When they got in there [during the Second World War], they found bodies - or remains of bodies - and took them out. Maybe it was a bad thing to go back into the Foord. This coal was very gassy.

"Anyway, I was in Montreal at a DOSCO meeting [in June 1951], and Harold Gordon phoned us from Stellarton. He said the Allan Shaft was on fire again. He said he'd just come out. They called the floor of the mine 'the pavement', and he said, 'I can fight fire in the roof or I can fight it on the pavement but I can't fight it when it's *fallen* from the roof. The pavement's so hot you can't stand on it.' He ordered all the men out, and closed the Allan Shaft for good. That finished it, and the jobs of hundreds of men."

Scarcely seven months later, on January 14, 1952, the smell of fire in the MacGregor Mine at Stellarton caused a crew of nineteen miners to go below to seal off the burning section. An explosion killed them all. Once again, the mayor happened to be out of town on DOSCO business. This time, he was at the Isle Royale Hotel in Sydney with Forsyth, Gordon, William Knoll, and, among others, Alec Sample, the resident superintendent of the MacGregor. Frank and Sample had known each other all their lives. "We were having lunch," Frank said, "and a call came in from Stellarton. Harold Gordon took the call. He rushed back and said there'd been an explosion at the MacGregor. He and Alec jumped into a car and tore off for Stellarton. Alec said his son was down there. I remember he said that if he'd only been home, it would never have happened, or, if it had, he'd have been down there with them." Overman Winston Sample was among the dead. They were the cream of the pit.

"These men just died in a flash," Frank said. "Their tongues were out and swollen, and the hair was all burnt off their eyebrows and heads. Alec McKinnon [Alexander McKinnon, Minister of Labour and Mines in the Nova Scotia government] came down to Stellarton, and I remember I went around with him to see the families of all these men that same day." The MacGregor, as a working mine, lasted just five more years, and closed forever in 1957. "So here we were," Frank said. "We'd had twelve hundred men working in those mines. Now they were closed. There wasn't a man working in a mine in Stellarton."

In "The Old Mining Town", Stellarton historian Aubrey Dorrington lamented the death of coal mining:

> The squeaky crunch of hobnailed boots
> On a frosty winter's morn
> And the lonely whistle of a miner boy
> Are sounds that we now mourn. . . .
>
> The whistle for work is heard no more,
> Its throaty voice is mute.
> We listen in vain on the steps of our home
> To hear another toot. . . .
>
> In bygone days when we were young
> The mines, they worked full blast,
> But times have changed, they're all gone now,
> Too bad they didn't last.

Frank would do more than anyone else to see that his proud coal town would not become a wistful ghost town. But in 1957 he, Roy Jodrey, and Forsyth's bluenose chiefs faced a stock-market takeover that they all feared would turn DOSCO into a ghost corporation. Their fears were justified.

When Laddie Forsyth, sixty-six, died on New Year's Day, 1957, Nova Scotia lost its most spectacular and forceful champion at DOSCO, and in a matter of weeks Upper Canadian plotters were concocting a scheme to sell the company. The sell-out was a Canadian classic. It involved two of the permanent themes of our history: first, control of our industry by foreigners (in this case, British); and second, political and financial intrigue in Toronto and Montreal to exploit Maritimers. It also involved superstars of Canada's corporate elite in secret plans, subterfuge, misleading statements, rumour-mongering, backroom arm-twisting, barrage attacks of business propaganda, private vilification, public acrimony, and threats of lawsuits. The knowledge that Forsyth had been a prophet was little comfort to his friends. Again and again he had warned Frank that once Nova Scotians lost their toehold on DOSCO, it would be finished; and what followed the sell-out was the slow, painful dismemberment of the flagship of heavy industry in eastern Canada.

The outfit that raided the shares and debentures of DOSCO was the glamorous A. V. Roe Canada Ltd. Roe was a postwar wonder baby, the miracle of Canadian aircraft production. But that, Frank recalled, was a limitation rather than a recommendation. "They were good aircraft people," he said, "but they'd had no experience in running steel plants or coal mines." Sir Roy Dobson, who'd helped build warplanes for the Royal Air Force, had founded A. V. Roe in 1945. He'd had to borrow $1,000 from a Canadian friend to pay the legal costs of its incorporation. Its birth lay in the merging of three government-owned plants, and throughout its galloping expansion in the fifties its chief nourishment was government contracts. By 1957, A. V. Roe companies employed more than 21,000 workers, and annual sales shot past $200 million. *Time* magazine ranked it among "Canada's industrial mammoths", and the *Financial Post* (Aug. 17, 1957) predicted its gobbling of DOSCO – "the largest such transaction in Canadian history" – would make it the nation's biggest industrial employer.

The real owners of this massive industrial kingdom would be in England, and, if the price was right, key Canadians on DOSCO's

Fellow Nova Scotian industrialist Roy Jodrey, who led the fight against A. V. Roe's takeover of DOSCO in 1957, shown here with his wife Belle.

board wanted them to have it. The Hawker Siddeley Group, through a Canadian holding company, owned 83.9 per cent of Roe's outstanding shares, and in the summer of 1957 their most bitter enemies in Nova Scotia were Frank Sobey and Roy Jodrey. Jodrey was another grade-school drop-out, a man with such natural business genius that now, at sixty-eight, he was the amiable patriarch of the richest family in the province. "Roy became a great friend of mine," Frank said, "and he was perhaps the most astute investor I ever met. He could read a balance sheet quicker and pick out the flaws quicker than anybody I ever knew." Jodrey had joined the DOSCO board only in 1955, but he'd been buying stock of DOSCO (and its predecessors) for roughly forty years, and his companies and children now owned a whopping 105,000 shares.

It later seemed to Frank that Forsyth's body had scarcely cooled when certain DOSCO directors began to engineer the sale of their own company. "We had a meeting after his funeral in Montreal," he said. "Lang [C. B. Lang, an ex-president and the chairman] called it. The general managers had all got together and they thought Clem Anson should be president." But with the exception of Arthur Cross, who knew DOSCO's problems better than anyone else alive, the directors from central Canada did not think Anson was right for the job.

"Mr. Lang was in the chair," Frank continued, "and I said well maybe Clem Anson would make a pretty good president, and the man next to me said we'd have to keep a lot of controls on him. So Lang spoke right up. 'Well,' he says, 'I guess we can't agree on that. I'll take the job till we find a new president.' So that was sort of bulldozed through. It took Roy [Jodrey] and me by surprise. It was put through so fast we didn't get mad till after the meeting." Lang was born in Thornton, Illinois, worked for steel companies in the Calumet district, and arrived in Montreal in 1914 at the age of twenty-six as manager of a rolling-mill. By 1957 he'd been a steel man for half a century and a DOSCO man for twenty-seven years. He was as tough as horseshoes, and not highly likeable. Indeed, in Frank's opinion, "Lang was very adamant and a very spiteful man."

DOSCO was supposed to be looking for a new president, but "There never was a sincere search. Lang just said, 'I'll have to go back in,' and that's when he started to negotiate with A. V. Roe. The board put him in on a temporary basis, but instead of running the company, he tried to sell it. Which he did." The president of A. V. Roe was Crawford Gordon, Jr. - Sir Roy Dobson was now chairman of the board - and "Gordon made a deal with Lang to take over DOSCO."

Meanwhile, Frank and Jodrey, unaware of what Lang, other DOSCO directors, and Crawford Gordon were cooking up, conducted their own small search for a man with the talent and stamina to fill Forsyth's shoes. For a while they thought they'd found him. Just as Sobey relied on tips from shrewd insiders to find top grocery executives, Jodrey now got word from a banker, George Hitchman of the Bank of Nova Scotia, that the right man for the DOSCO job might well be D. G. (Bud) Willmot of Toronto, the dynamic forty-year-old president of an outfit called Anthes Imperial, Ltd. Jodrey companies were major shareholders of the bank, and Jodrey was on its board. Hitchman, later deputy general manager but then an assistant general manager, not only told him how able Willmot was but also told Willmot he should get together with the two Nova Scotians for dinner. Through Enman,

Frank also knew Hitchman. "So we got Bud to come down to Montreal," Frank said. "Roy just had a small room in the Mount Royal Hotel with one bed and two chairs, so I said we'd better get a suite. But Roy [notorious for his ability to pinch pennies till they screamed] says, 'To hell with that. If this isn't good enough for Mr. Willmot, then Mr. Willmot isn't good enough for DOSCO.'

"So we talked to Bud in this little room. We talked along the lines that DOSCO would buy out Anthes Imperial, and Bud would come in as president and run the whole outfit. I think we had Bud a little favourable on the deal." But Lang and C. L. Gundy – who was not only president of the awesome financial house Wood, Gundy and Company, Ltd., but also, as it later turned out, one of the DOSCO directors who favoured the A. V. Roe takeover – shot down the suggestion before it got off the ground. "Bud had done his financing through Dominion Securities [rival to Wood, Gundy]," Frank said simply. "Maybe that had something to do with it."

Frank and Jodrey had proposed that DOSCO buy Anthes Imperial in order to get Willmot, and more than a decade later Molson Industries confirmed their judgment of Willmot's management mastery by using the identical recruitment technique. In *The Canadian Establishment*, Peter C. Newman said that between 1949 and 1967 Willmot had turned Anthes, originally a St. Catharines, Ont., heating-supply and plumbing operation, into a consistent money-maker, "and when Molson's began to diversify, its directors paid $74 million to buy out Anthes so they could get him [as chief executive officer]. In addition to a hefty salary boost, Willmot received some $10 million worth of Molson stock yielding $350,000 in annual dividends." Newman called Molson's wooing of Willmot "the most expensive recruitment in Canadian corporate history".

By the spring of 1957, the investment community was buzzing with rumours that someone was out to get DOSCO. The year 1956 had been the most profitable in DOSCO history; 1957 was shaping up even better and in June, Frank recalled the following August, "a large broker" approached him and Jodrey with a deal "to go in and tie up the shares of DOSCO. He would arrange a group to gain control, but we'd put him in charge of finances. We didn't think it was good for DOSCO. . . . The company had been left a sitting duck for financial snipers." It took till July for the first takeover rumours to drift into print, but weeks before that the number of DOSCO shares traded on Canadian exchanges was moving around like a barometer's needle in unsettled weather: only 17,907 for the week ending May 24, but 84,269 for the week ending June 7; down to 25,826 the following week, but 95,510 for the week ending July 5. The trend was up.

The business press speculated that both unnamed German interests and A. V. Roe were angling for control of DOSCO. Lang and Roe officials now performed an intricate dance of denials. "I have no comment," a Roe executive said in July. "I don't know where these rumours start. It's weird and wonderful." Lang's statements managed to pooh-pooh the idea that Roe was out to get control of DOSCO but did not degenerate into outright lies. The evasion was readily apparent only after the takeover machinery was rolling. His handling of grapevine news about the DOSCO board meeting he called for Thursday, August 8, was a classic example of the verbal sleight-of-hand big businessmen sometimes feel they must practise.

When DOSCO secretary G. C. Broadbent phoned Jodrey on August 4 to tell him about the meeting, Jodrey asked what was on the agenda. Broadbent's unbelievable reply was that he didn't know. When Jodrey phoned Lang on August 6 to ask what A. V. Roe would offer for DOSCO shares, Lang's unbelievable reply was that he didn't know. (Jodrey's sources were so good he knew anyway.) Both Jodrey and Frank were sure the purpose of the August 8 meeting was to consider the offer, and so many others shared this belief that on the morning of August 7, while the Nova Scotians were Montreal-bound on the Ocean Limited, Lang issued a press statement to squelch speculation. The statement was cute.

The meeting, he said, was merely a "regular" gathering of DOSCO directors, not a "special" meeting to consider an offer for control of the company. DOSCO had received no such offer. He'd been "very much disturbed" by published reports about a special meeting, and denied stories that linked DOSCO to any transaction with

A. V. Roe. The business reporters had popped their questions too early, perhaps only minutes too early. Lang had tricked them. With the superb timing one might have expected from manufacturers of jet engines, A. V. Roe got its letter of intent into Lang's hands that very afternoon, and the next morning, scarcely twenty-four hours after Lang had denied stories of a special meeting to consider an A. V. Roe offer, the directors of DOSCO got together for a special meeting to consider an A. V. Roe offer.

The "weird and wonderful" had come to pass, and the offer was seductive: for each DOSCO share, A. V. Roe would pay 1¼ A. V. Roe common shares plus a cash bonus of $10.25. The aircraft firm offered a similar deal for DOSCO's convertible debentures, and for anyone who wanted a mouth-watering market price for his DOSCO shares there would never again be a better day. The *Financial Times* of Canada calculated that the cash value of the offer on August 8 was $38 per DOSCO share. Since DOSCO was trading at $29, the stampede began. In the week that ended on Friday, August 9, no fewer than 226,433 DOSCO shares were traded on Canadian stock exchanges. A. V. Roe claimed it had not yet acquired any DOSCO stock, but Frank said "friends of theirs had."

The offer appalled Frank and Jodrey. In this, they stood alone on a board that central Canadians dominated, and they spoke out bitterly during what Frank remembered as "stormy meetings". As directors, they resented the fact that Lang had popped the offer on them so fast he had not even bothered to provide the August 8 meeting with A. V. Roe financial statements. As investors, they felt that no matter how good the deal looked to greedy grabbers of fast bucks, DOSCO had such immense assets by comparison with A. V. Roe that the takeover was, in Jodrey's words, "nothing but a scientific steal". As Nova Scotians, they distrusted absentee management of DOSCO by aircraft manufacturers. As Nova Scotians, they feared what ownership of DOSCO by cold-blooded Englishmen might ultimately mean to the towns and workingmen down home; and Frank knew that every one of the late Laddie Forsyth's bluenose chieftains hated the very thought of working for new masters at A. V. Roe. Again, as Nova Scotians, Frank and Jodrey also fumed over the way Montrealers and Torontonians had gotten together behind their backs to engineer the sell-out to the English.

They now knew they'd been shut out of negotiations that some of their fellow directors had been secretly conducting with A. V. Roe for weeks, if not months; and the line-up of directors on August 8 seemed to prove how thoroughly the others had snookered them. Neither was on DOSCO's inner cabinet, the executive committee. It included R. J. Wysor, a steel expert from Charlotte, North Carolina; C. L. Gundy of Toronto; Colin Webster of Montreal; the American-born Montrealer, President Lang; and C. J. Burchell of Halifax. Wysor was at first neutral, but the other four clearly favoured the A. V. Roe offer. So did directors F. C. Cope of Montreal, DOSCO's solicitor, and Jean Raymond, scion of an old French-Canadian family of distinction. In short, the DOSCO directors who were quickest to declare their approval of the terms of A. V. Roe's takeover included four Montrealers, one Torontonian, and one 81-year-old Nova Scotian (Burchell), and four of the six were on DOSCO's executive committee. One of them, the *Financial Times* said, was "reputed to own or represent twenty-six percent of DOSCO ordinary." He was Colin Webster.

Webster and Gundy, moreover, had connections at exalted levels in Toronto. They sat on boards with the likes of E. P. Taylor, who, as the supreme figure of Upper Canadian business life, was becoming as legendary as hockey's "Rocket" Richard, and with Taylor's lawyer crony, J. S. D. Tory, the merger-master who'd helped marry Simpsons Ltd. to Sears Roebuck, and the Ferguson interests of Britain to Massey-Harris. It was convenient that Tory was a legal counsel for Wood, Gundy and at the same time a legal counsel and director for A. V. Roe. Tory, Webster, and Gundy dined at the same clubs in Toronto and Monreal, but had so little interest in Nova Scotian business that none had joined the Halifax Club, venerable hangout for bluenose businessmen. There was an old, upper-crust, Upper Canadian camaraderie among these men, and it preceded the arrival of either Frank or Jodrey in any of the important boardrooms of the country.

James W. Gogan, director, executive vice-president, and secretary of Empire Company Limited.

Gundy's role was particularly galling. To raise $24 million to pay the $10.25 per DOSCO share, A. V. Roe would sell preferred shares of its own. Racair Ltd., the Canadian vehicle by which Hawker Siddeley of England controlled Roe, would buy $20 million worth, but the remaining $4 million would be offered to the public. The underwriter was Wood, Gundy, and its cut would be $160,000. Moreover, Wood, Gundy was A. V. Roe's fiscal agent, and it had the lucrative assignment of getting the shares Roe needed to grab control of DOSCO. A senior partner in a smaller investment firm said, "In a deal like this, you get so many cents for every share you round up. . . . They [Wood, Gundy] got an over-ride on everything, an over-ride on the turning of shares, and maybe a fee for advice. . . . They'd pay certain agents and, well, they just masterminded the whole operation."

Jodrey was famous for his habit of assessing financial statements, listening to others discuss a proposition, and then asking a blunt, earthy question: "Okay, but where does the deal sugar off?" Neither he nor Frank believed the A. V. Roe offer would ever sugar off adequately for some ten thousand DOSCO shareholders, but they could see it sugaring off for Wood, Gundy. C. L. Gundy's firm was negotiating for Roe, selling Roe securities to the public, and recommending to DOSCO shareholders they accept the Roe offer. It was obvious enough to those shareholders that Gundy was a DOSCO director, but, in the opinion of the dissident DOSCO directors from Nova Scotia, he hadn't properly clarified his interest in either Roe or Wood, Gundy. Even if everything Gundy did to promote Roe's acquisition of control in DOSCO was strictly legal, it struck them as more than a bit thick.

Nova Scotia erupted with outrage and fear in the weeks that followed the August 8 DOSCO meeting. In Pictou County, where disaster and age were already closing coal mines, whole towns shuddered under the suspicion that Roe's acquisition of DOSCO would hurt Trenton Industries, Ltd., Eastern Car Company, Ltd., and Trenton Steel Works, Ltd. Some wondered what Roe would do to the Halifax Shipyards, while others argued the takeover might end up crippling Cape Breton industry. Miners and steelworkers worried. The Nova Scotia Federation of Labour worried. The mayors of Sydney, North Sydney, Pictou, Westville, Trenton, New Glasgow, and Stellarton (Frank was now in his twentieth year as mayor there) not only worried but worried noisily. In Nova Scotia, the late summer and early fall of 1957 were a time of protest meetings, platform rhetoric, angry editorials, and futile appeals to government to stop A. V. Roe in its tracks.

While social concern and provincial loyalty inspired Frank and Jodrey in their fight against the takeover, so did their anger as private investors. Together they controlled 150,000 DOSCO shares, and no matter what the stock market indicated, they felt those shares were worth far more than $10.25 each plus stock in an outfit that had yet to prove it could survive without juicy government contracts. DOSCO was thundering along at the most profitable rate in its history. Under Forsyth's regime, it had poured tens of millions of dollars into capital improvements. No one knew yet how grave the problems were in its Cape Breton coal operations and the Sydney steelworks, but what Frank certainly did know was that DOSCO's profit for the first six months of 1957 was a record-busting $7,563,355.13. He also knew that the company's net working capital was among the massive plums that A. V. Roe was trying to grab. It stood at more than $50,000,000. Jodrey said Roe was trying to buy control of a $300-million industrial empire for $60 million, that for the first time in Canadian history a goldfish was swallowing a whale.

Jodrey was blind with rage. A man whose parsimony was legendary, he now blew $50,000 in out-of-pocket expenses on a hopeless battle to sabotage the takeover. A man whose fame rested on shrewd stock-market investment, he now stuck like rockweed to a decision that, in lost market values, would cost his family more than $2 million. A man who refused to get a suite in the Mount Royal to interview Bud Willmot, he now rented a suite in the Ritz-Carlton as headquarters for a propaganda war against A. V. Roe. At sixty-eight, he fought the takeover for twelve angry, sweaty weeks. He hired lawyers, secretaries, writers. His weapons were telegrams, newspaper ads, letters to shareholders, a direct appeal to Prime Minister John Diefenbaker, threats of lawsuits, every trick of persuasion his guile and memory could devise. And he lost. "That was the *only* time I ever knew him to let his pride overrule his judgment," Halifax developer Charles MacCulloch said later. "It took a lot out of him. He wasn't the sort of man who enjoyed public posturing. . . . It was something that always amazed me."

It amazed Frank as well. His head was cooler than Jodrey's and perhaps his nature was more cynical. Jodrey was trying to round up enough DOSCO shares or proxies – the company bylaws required him to get twenty-five per cent, or almost 800,000 – to force a special shareholders' meeting. This, he hoped, would not only tie up some of the shares Roe wanted but also result in the airing of questions he hoped would fatally embarrass the takeover campaign. But Frank knew Jodrey would lose. Forever a realist, he saw by late August that they'd never beat the big boys who'd engineered the deal. Forever a man to make the best of a rotten situation, he advised his older friend to throw in the towel, accept the offer, take what profit he could. Frank: "I told Roy, I says, 'Look, we might as well back out 'cause we're beat.' I says, 'You'll lose a million on this.' Well, it was the first time Roy ever got mad at me. He says, 'If I can't afford to lose a million dollars, it's a funny thing.' You know, if I'd told him he might lose ten dollars he'd probably have thought about it. He was really mad." Frank was nowhere near as rich as Jodrey. It would have been a funny thing if he *could* have afforded to throw away a million.

Jodrey's team met at the Ritz-Carlton on Friday, August 30, to draft a letter to all DOSCO shareholders. Frank's accountant friend Harold Egan was there, and so was Nova Scotian industrialist Mowbray Jones. The letter was to go out over the names of Frank and Jodrey, but the heated atmosphere in the suite bothered Frank. He wondered if people weren't losing their heads. Jodrey had never ordered a hotel suite in his life. He was upset, strangely excited. A doctor was giving him tranquillizers. So far as the letter went, Frank said, "Mowbray Jones was putting in statements that I thought were too strong, stuff that would just cause agitation and resentment, without really helping." The language struck Frank as excessively personal and trouble-making.

He did not say, perhaps for fear of hurting Jodrey's feelings, that he now opposed the whole purpose of the letter: the appeal for enough proxies to force a special meeting of shareholders. He said he was concerned about what Premier Robert Stanfield might think of the letter; and then, as he'd done to avoid the embarrassment of confronting bad credit risks at Number One a quarter-century before, he vanished on a Friday night. He made himself unavailable.

With their mailing deadline closing in, the others couldn't find him. Egan read the letter by phone to Stanfield, who not only said it was okay by him but also promised to try to reach Frank to tell him so. Stanfield couldn't find him. Jones kept phoning Frank's hotel, the Windsor, but he couldn't find him either. Meanwhile, the letter was being printed over the names of both Frank and Jodrey, and an hour before midnight Jodrey phoned the Montreal manager of National Trust and, in effect, said, "Let 'er rip." National Trust began to mail the letter to 10,000 DOSCO shareholders at 7.30 Saturday morning.

It was not till Sunday that a senior officer of National Trust got two telegrams from Frank. The first, sent at 7.30 a.m., said:

> HAVE NOT YET SIGNED LETTER. DO NOT MAIL UNLESS FURTHER ADVISED.

The second, sent at 5.32 p.m., said in part:

> NOW ADVISED THAT LETTER MAILED SATURDAY BY YOU WITHOUT CLEARANCE FROM ME. MY REASON FOR NOT RELEASING LETTER WAS THAT I WISHED ALL REFERENCE TO REQUEST FOR SHAREHOLDERS MEETING DELETED. AFTER GIVING CAREFUL CONSIDERATION TO MATTER I WILL NOT HOLD TRUST COMPANY RESPONSIBLE FOR THIS MISADVENTURE PROVIDED YOU FORWARD LETTER IMMEDIATELY ENCLOSING COPY OF MY EARLIER WIRE TODAY AND COPY THIS WIRE TO THE PRESIDENT AND EACH OF THE DIRECTORS OF DOSCO.

National Trust did as he asked.

Jodrey was not happy with his Stellarton cohort. Their mutual friend Ralph Brenan, a courtly New Brunswick industrialist, was talking about Frank when he said, "Roy depended very, very much on the support of some of the largest shareholders. They didn't say in my presence they would sign the letter but they didn't say they wouldn't. When the time came, they wouldn't sign. . . . His big disappointment wasn't the money. It was that the people on whom he depended – and had assumed were supporting his view – in the final analysis did not come through." But Frank's reasons for not coming through were understandable. Jodrey had already built his family's massive corporate empire, and it was bound to grow more massive. Frank, age fifty-five, felt he had only begun, and one did not build an empire by flailing away at a lost cause that could only burn up money.

He *knew* the cause was lost. Before October 1, expiry date of the Roe offer, there simply wouldn't be time to round up enough support, from shareholders scattered all across North America, to force the meeting. Moreover, it was brutally clear that most DOSCO directors, men with whom he'd shared the boardroom in the Canada Cement building for six years, intended to sell their own shares to Roe. In early September the Montreal *Gazette* said,

Arthur H. Crockett, Deputy Chairman, the Bank of Nova Scotia, 1972–83, and a current director of Empire Company Ltd.

"The directors concerned are reported to own or control at least fifty percent . . . of DOSCO shares. . . . The majority are said to have been agreeable to the offer ever since it was broached, and several are conjectured to have explored the possibilities of such an offer prior to its actual transmission."

But the clincher that convinced Frank no one could stop the Roe juggernaut was that Wood, Gundy, now working for Roe, had previously sold $12 million worth of convertible bonds for DOSCO. "If it weren't for those bonds," Frank said, "we could have blocked it. But Wood, Gundy knew exactly where they were, and it's easy enough to buy bonds from institutions if you pay a dollar or two extra. . . . They were buying from every place they could even before the offer came out. . . . Wood, Gundy was buying the bonds, which Roe converted into common stock. That made our position untenable." It was when he explained this to Jodrey that the older man lost his temper. Frank felt that if you couldn't fight City Hall, the smartest thing to do was to resign yourself to trying to get along with it.

Jodrey fought on, and eventually 2,385 shareholders, representing 565,525 shares, lined up on his side. They weren't enough. He needed 800,000 to force DOSCO to call a special meeting. By late October A. V. Roe owned seventy-six per cent of DOSCO's common shares. Jodrey announced that he'd hang onto his, and, as a minority shareholder, "do my best to see that nothing is done by the new controlling owners which will adversely affect DOSCO or its shareholders." He'd lost the battle and he'd lost a bundle. Now he lost even his directorship of DOSCO.

"Between Roy and [C. B.] Lang," Frank said, "there had developed a very strong resentment, and Lang reached an understanding with A. V. Roe that one of the conditions of the takeover was that they'd put Roy off the board." Jodrey's tactics had infuriated Lang, and Lang was dying. After anger had dissolved in the flow of events, Roe officials confided to Jodrey that his dismissal had been something like granting a vengeful man his last wish. On November 1, the new controllers of DOSCO called a shareholders' meeting for the exclusive purpose of bouncing Jodrey. Many minority shareholders felt this was an outrage, and the meeting was among the most bitter and tempestuous gatherings of Canadian businessmen of the time. On a standing vote among those at the meeting, Jodrey won twenty-four to twenty; and, as Frank recalled that ugly morning, "I was the only director who stood up to vote against Roy's being expelled from the board."

What counted, however, was the poll of shares. A. V. Roe weighed in with 2,370,476 in favour of kicking Jodrey out, while his side could muster only 134,224. "I now state," Lang said, "that it is in order for a motion to be made to elect another person as a director to replace Mr. Jodrey." The other person was Sir Roy Dobson. Lang died the following February, and in 1959 Sir Roy, chairman of A. V. Roe, invited Jodrey back to the DOSCO board. Frank had done a little peace-making.

He had not lost his seat on the DOSCO board, and "I got to know Sir Roy Dobson. He was a very fine fellow, a very able, strong character. I was walking up the steps of the Halifax Club with him, and I said he should put Roy back on the board. He says, 'Why? He was pretty nasty to us.' Well, I says, 'He's a fighter, just like you are. When he gets into anything he'll fight right down the line if he thinks he's right.' He looked at me, and he says, 'Perhaps you're right.' So it wasn't long after that till Roy was put back on the board."

Meanwhile, on February 20, 1959, Prime Minister John Diefenbaker killed production of the Avro Arrow, the most advanced fighter plane in the history of Canadian aircraft production, the crowning glory of everything A. V. Roe had ever built. Roe immediately laid off 13,800 employees. Now, only sixteen months after gobbling DOSCO, it began its long, sickening slide. Even its name disappeared in 1962, when it became Hawker Siddeley Canada, Ltd. Roe stock, which reached 25½ in 1957, was down to $3.50 in 1968. DOSCO stock, which surpassed $30 in August of '57, sold at $7 in March of '68. By 1969, Hawker Siddeley Canada, Ltd., hadn't paid dividends on its common shares for eleven years, and its annual shareholders' meetings were like investors' bearpits.

The DOSCO that Nova Scotians had known was doomed. In 1966, Hawker Siddeley Canada bailed out of the iron-mining business. In 1967 it bailed out of the coal business, and the Cape Breton Development Corporation, with federal funding of nearly $100 million, took over the Cape Breton collieries. And on October 13, 1967 – known thereafter as Black Friday in Cape Breton – one T. J. Emmert, the latest DOSCO president, announced the company would soon close down the steel-making business in Sydney. Federal MP David Orlikow (NDP, Winnipeg North) said the shutdown was "cold-blooded economic murder", and Nova Scotia premier G. I. (Ike) Smith denounced Hawker Siddeley as "completely lacking in any sense of corporate responsibility to the community in which it has operated." The makings of Black Friday were in London, England, among the real owners of Hawker Siddeley Canada. They were losing money in Canada.

"On the [DOSCO] board," Frank said, "it eventually came about that anything we put through was subject to the approval of the Hawker Siddeley people, and this became a very unhappy situation for me. . . . We seemed to be in trouble with the steel plant and so forth, and I think the company was losing interest in the steel operation in Sydney. It came to the point where they said they were going to close the steel plant down. I was very upset about this, and said so to the board. We had some stormy sessions. But they closed the plant, and I couldn't see any prospect of doing anything with it. I got off the board."

Frank conceded that Hawker Siddeley, with its manufacturing experience, had run the Trenton industries efficiently and, in the time of oil-rig construction, also Halifax Shipyards. But, "DOSCO would still be operating today [1982] if it had been left with the same management [Forsyth's team]. When the A. V. Roe people bought it out, they were not in the steel business. They were in the airplane business. They worked mostly with government, and costs didn't mean so much to them. They upset the operations of DOSCO and got costs up to a point where it became unprofitable." They "loaded it with executives who didn't understand the steel business" and, in short, cursed DOSCO with inferior management.

By the time Frank resigned, any anger Jodrey had felt over his position in the takeover battle a decade earlier had long since dissolved in the healing brew of their mutual interest in answers to Jodrey's favourite question: "How can a feller make a dollar?" The Jodreys and the Sobeys were among the most powerful business families in the region and, when they combined on a deal, as they did from time to time, a formidable team. Jodrey died at eighty-four in August 1973. His friends buried him in a graveyard overlooking his beloved Gaspereau River. Frank was there at the graveside.

8

IT'S MANAGEMENT THAT MATTERS

TALKING about Frank's investment habits, retired broker N. Douglas MacDonald of Halifax said, "Jesus, he was into so many things, but, you know, he normally didn't buy something today just to turn it over tomorrow. And when he bought into a company, he'd already know pretty well what was going on there, and he'd do it in a big way. In anything he did, he had his eye on the future, and quite a distant future, too." George C. Hitchman, who rose to become deputy chairman of the Bank of Nova Scotia, said, "When Frank Sobey bought stocks, he made sure he knew the people in the companies in which he was investing. He learned about them and he learned about their business." In investing, as in hiring executives, Frank often ignored professional advisers in favour of his own trusty network of knowledgeable friends, his own discreet espionage, and, finally, his own judgment. Without rancour, veteran Toronto broker Charles Burns said that Frank, unlike many heavy investors, "feels no loyalty to any particular stockbroker. He's loyal only to Frank." Frank had his own ideas about where to put his money. "If you always listen to a broker," he said, "you can go broke."

All his life he "played" the market in small ways, but in bigger ways his investing was a matter of discovering on his own that a company was promising and then, decade after decade, pumping money into it. This led to directorships that enabled him to watch how efficiently his money was used. "You've got to put your eggs in a few baskets," he said, "and watch them." One of his earlier eggs was Malagash Salt Company, Ltd. He knew about Malagash Salt before he tried to buy it. At a spot roughly seventy-five miles east of the East River towns, it owned Canada's only rock-salt mine. The head office was in New Glasgow, and the directors were New Glasgow men. Frank knew them, and in the late forties he also knew that Malagash Salt, after twenty-two troubled years, was at last showing a profit. Highways departments had discovered that salt was better than sand for fighting ice on roads, and by 1949 Malagash was selling its product to governments in the Maritimes, Ontario, and Quebec.

"They were making a little money," Frank said, "and operating conservatively. They were in pretty fair shape. So one day Bertram Godden [his ally in the Battle of the Roseland] comes to me, and he says, 'Why not buy control of Malagash Salt?' " It wasn't just the company's recent improvement that made the idea intriguing. Frank suspected Malagash Salt was ripe for a takeover by a national company, and, sure enough, while Godden scuttled around Nova Scotia to buy shares on his behalf, the Canadian Salt Company, Montreal, also began to gulp shares of Malagash. Canadian Salt was a new outfit that already embraced the salt division of Canadian Industries, Ltd., in Windsor, Ontario, Alberta Salt Company, and Manitoba Salt Company. They wanted Malagash Salt, and they wanted it badly.

One luminary at Canadian Salt was Ray Milner, a New Brunswick-born, Halifax-educated lawyer who'd settled in Edmonton and done exceptionally well for himself. He was now chairman of Western Natural Gas Company, Ltd., and Northwestern Utilities, Ltd., a director of assorted oil and coal companies in Alberta, and also of the Royal Bank, where he undoubtedly knew J. McG. Stewart. "Ray Milner, along with Nesbitt, Thomson [the Montreal investment house], started buying against me," Frank said. "I knew all along they'd be interested. Well, anyway, they got forty-nine per cent of Malagash Salt, but I had forty-eight per cent." To dissolve the stalemate, a Canadian Salt delegation journeyed to Halifax.

The party included Ray Milner, a major shareholder; Norman C. Hobson, managing director of Canadian Salt; and E. Gerald Smith, vice-president of Nesbitt, Thomson. "We met in a room at the Nova Scotian Hotel," Frank recalled, "and Mr. Milner said, 'Well, I guess initiative [Frank's] deserves to be rewarded.' " Frank then sold his Malagash shares to Canadian Salt, bought 5,000 shares of the bigger company, and joined its board. Since he'd recently become a DOSCO director, this was his second national directorship in as many months. Moreover, the Malagash Salt adventure had been profitable. "By June 1951," John R. MacQuarrie wrote in *Malagash Salt* (1975), "the worthless Malagash stock was suddenly being wooed at $130 a share, and on June 9 control of the company went to the Canadian Salt Company, Montreal."

Canadian Salt soon proposed to sink a salt mine on the Canadian side of the Detroit River, but lacked the resources to finance so massive a project. It therefore sold control to the Morton chemical interests in the United States. Founded in 1885 as Joy Morton and Company, they had become the only nationwide U.S. marketer of salt, with vast salt operations in Louisiana and the West Indies, and a famous marketing slogan: "When it rains, it pours." When Morton took control, most of Canadian Salt's Canadian shareholders sold out at $8 per share, but not Frank. Instead, he bought even more Canadian Salt. President Daniel Peterkin, Jr., of Morton "told me he was disappointed all those Canadians sold. He sold me 5,000 shares at $8. These shares were also trading on the market, and I'd buy a few every once in a while." He remained on the board.

Canadian Salt wanted to dig its mine on a huge tract of land that DOSCO owned near Windsor, Ont.; and Frank, as a director of both companies, now served as the liaison man for a gigantic real-estate transaction. DOSCO had bought the land from U.S. Steel, who, before pulling out, had constructed a wharf and started to build a blast furnace. The property included a railway, hundreds of acres, and the tiny village of Ojibway. Just across the river, Detroit loomed into the sky, but the negotiations began 1,600 miles east beside another river. Frank owned a cabin in Guysborough

County on the banks of the St. Mary's, a fine salmon stream in those days, and he was fishing there with Norman Hobson of Canadian Salt and DOSCO president Laddie Forsyth. "We were sitting on the bank at the Ford Pool, and Norm started to talk about the Windsor property," Frank said. "Laddie had previously asked $12 million, which I thought was a hell of a big price. But he got it. After some talk, Norm decided to recommend to the board of Canadian Salt that they buy the land, and everything on it, for $12 million."

Canadian Salt planned to sink their mine on part of the property and develop the rest, but it had nowhere near $12 million. At a board meeting in Montreal, Frank recalled, "Someone asked, 'Where will we get the money?' and that's when Daniel Peterkin [president of the Morton interests] said, 'Well, we'll find the money,' and they did. A foundation the Morton crowd had set up bought the land. They tried to develop it, and years later they did perhaps come out of it all right. They sold a piece to the group that was developing a racetrack. It's all almost part of Windsor now, and the racetrack's still there. Anyway, I used to tell Dan, 'You made a mistake paying that much. You were standing on the wrong side of the river. Your trouble was, you were looking across the river at Detroit.' That was only scrub land in those days, just a good place for shooting pheasant."

Sinking the mine was a fiendish problem. Water can be fatal to a salt mine. The shaft sits on the salt. By dissolving the salt, water causes the shaft to warp. At Ojibway, "the thing was so difficult they had to get an outfit in from Texas to freeze the ground right down to the salt. They put pipes into the ground, two or three feet apart, and forced ammonia down. At one point, they struck a four-inch stream, and they froze that. It took a year to do all the freezing. The compressors were going for a whole year." The mine didn't open till 1955, but in time it proved a money-maker.

The sinking of a shaft at Pugwash, N.S., was even tougher. After test drilling, Canadian Salt decided that Shea's Island at Pugwash, just along the coast from Malagash, was an ideal mine location. "The drill holes showed rock all the way," Frank said. "Dan Peterkin told me this would be the only mine he knew of in North America where you could get salt without getting into trouble. This was going to be the cheapest salt mine ever built, just straight through clean, solid rock. They figured it would cost $500,000. I says, 'The Bank of Nova Scotia will give you that. I'll call Horace Enman. He says, 'Fine.' " The test drilling, however, had struck not solid rock but gypsum and granite boulders that "floated" in a geological gruel of sand, mud, and water. Canadian Salt began to sink the shaft one rainy day in June 1955, and soon realized they were dealing with what a visiting geologist called "the Muck of Ages".

The company could eventually find no other solution than to build a cement pillar in the earth. The pillar was like a skinny skyscraper in reverse, and though no one knew it at first, it would take no less than four years to construct. "On September 10, 1955," John R. MacQuarrie wrote in *Malagash Salt*, "Archie Patterson, a grout expert, originally with the Cementation Company, but now an employee of the new mine at Ojibway, came to Pugwash on loan for a few weeks. He would be here four and one half years. The first concrete pad was poured in the shaft the next day." By June 1957, the renowned Cementation Company, owned by South Africans but with headquarters in Doncaster, England, was in charge of the agonizingly slow shaft job.

The method of construction was to drill holes, then pump in the grout – a porridge of cement and water – at pressures of more than one thousand pounds per square inch. Thus, it was hoped, cracked rock would become solid, sand would become sandstone, and the whole shifty geological structure would become sufficiently stable to tolerate a man-made hole to the salt. "When a batch of grout hardened," Frank said, "they'd dig through the cement and do the same thing all over again, and they did this till they got this big blob of cement right down to the salt." The blob housed the shaft, and at least three hundred railway boxcars of cement went into its construction.

"It is always a tough assignment, the chipping, or moiling, of the pad concrete," MacQuarrie wrote. "Explosives must not be used lest a fracture be caused far back of the shaft wall in the

Henry B. Rhude, a director of Empire Company Limited.

already unconsolidated ground, and thus start a leak." He felt that to sink a ten-by-twenty-foot cavity to a depth of 385 feet, without once using explosives, was surely "something of a record". At that level, in March 1959 - four years after Canadian Salt started work on this supposedly cheap, easy mine - the shaft hit solid salt for the first time. "I remember Norm Hobson," Frank said. "He kept saying, 'Frank, when they hit the salt, you and I are going to go down there with a bottle of Scotch.'" Asked whether the job had cost much more than the original estimate of $500,000, Frank snorted, "More like $5 million."

Such spectacular setbacks did not shake Frank's faith in either the management or the future of Canadian Salt. "I kept buying," he said. "They split the stock three for one, and that made 750,000 shares outstanding. Ray Milner was getting old, and he promised if he ever sold he'd give me first refusal. One day I was in our Truro store and I got a message to phone him in Edmonton. I bought 15,000 from him. Then they split three for one again. Now there were 2,250,000 shares outstanding. I was still nibbling. I ended up with about ten per cent, and I put it all into Empire." By 1977, twenty-six years after Frank had parlayed the race for control of Malagash Salt into a share of the national company, Empire Company of Stellarton owned 212,043 shares of Canadian Salt, worth more than $3 million. But later that year Empire sold them to help pay for investments that Frank's son Donald felt were more promising. "I was against selling," Frank growled. "It was Donald's idea."

Most brokers in the mid-fifties thought Dominion Textile Inc. was a dull investment, and maybe a loser. Frank didn't, and by 1981 Empire Company would own more than a million shares of Canada's biggest textile manufacturer. They'd be worth nearly $20 million.

Dominion Textile first began to fascinate Frank in 1956. The price was $6.50 a share, the dividend 60 cents. Yet he could borrow from the bank at interest rates as low as five per cent. Moreover, "I figured Canada just had to have a textile industry, and Dominion was the biggest and the best." Ronald H. Perowne, chairman of the company in 1981, speculated that Frank, a quarter-century earlier, had said, "Let's take a look at these guys. If they're fighters, if they can hold off the Japanese, they'll beat the pants off any other textile business in Canada."

Frank had indeed decided to take a look at these guys. The chief builder of the company in the first half of the twentieth century had been Sir Charles Blair Gordon. Now his son was president. George Blair Gordon was a private-school boy from Westmount; and Peter C. Newman (*The Canadian Establishment*) mentioned "his preference for playing polo". But Blair Gordon had not been allowed to gallop straight to the top of Domtex. He worked first as an electrician at a paper mill in Port Arthur, and when he joined Domtex in 1923 it was as a lowly fitter's helper. "He still has a scar on his brow," Newman said, "from an inkwell hurled at him by a striker in Montmorency Falls in 1938." Gordon knew the company from the bottom up, and inside out.

But before Frank would sink money into Domtex he had to satisfy himself about Gordon, about other Domtex bosses, and even about its potential bosses. To him, management was the crucial factor in any business. Capital and labour mattered too, of course, but good management came first. If you had it, everything else fell into place. If you didn't, nothing fell into place. A shrewd investment was primarily a bet on shrewd management. Moreover,

"When I buy into a company, I always like to see the management have some of their own dough in it. There's nothing like a man having his own money in the business he's running." You had to be careful, though. The stronger managers were, the less likely they'd be to relinquish power in their old age, to make room for fresh blood. "Sometimes they hang on to the end," Frank said. "When you see that happening, you look around for another company to invest in, maybe a smaller one with younger management."

It was with such convictions in mind that in the summer of 1956 Frank went to Montreal to investigate Domtex personally. "I went in to see Mr. Blair Gordon," he said. "I didn't even know who he was. I just asked to see the president. I told him I was looking at the stock and thinking of buying some, and he says, 'Well, I think a lot of the company, too.' I said this was the biggest textile company in Canada, and Canada would always need a textile company. We couldn't afford to depend on offshore for all our textiles. He agreed. He said he had 20,000 shares himself. So I said, 'Who have you got behind you, to run it if anything happens to you?' That's what you should always ask. What's coming along behind the fellows in charge?" Gordon told him about vice-president and managing director Ryland Daniels, who'd joined the company in 1930; and vice-president Edward F. King, then a boardroom crusader for improvements in Domtex marketing. (Daniels later succeeded Gordon as president, King succeeded Daniels, and Ronald H. Perowne, who succeeded King, said, "Frank Sobey's a great one on lines of succession.")

"Mr. Gordon gave me quite a lot of confidence in the organization he'd built up behind him," Frank said, "so I went out and bought 20,000 shares, but, in buying, I run up the price a bit, and had to pay seven dollars." Asked if he'd had $140,000 to pump into Dominion Textile in 1956, he said, "The banks had."

"Frank Sobey had a great characteristic in common with his friend Roy Jodrey," Toronto investment dealer Charles Burns said. "They both mastered the art of credit. To do that, of course, you first have to be smart enough to buy into things of real value. You convince the banker. You gain his confidence. Those two could do that. They could establish credit and borrow almost unlimited amounts, and, more important, it never *worried* them that they owed lots of money. Listen, I once had a partner who owed a bank $30,000, and it fussed him so much he sold his stock in our company to pay off that loan. Sobey wouldn't have given a damn about the bank loan. You know that Dominion Textile he bought at six or seven dollars? It soon went to thirty."

Frank became a director of Domtex in June 1962, when the board expanded from seven to eleven. The expansion, Edward F. King recalled, was "part of an effort to dilute the influence of the old guard." King was named executive vice-president that same year, and saw his mission as that of revitalizing an old company. "Things had been too easy during the war, and later had been allowed to slide." He'd first joined the board in 1953, and had since seen elderly directors fall asleep at the meetings, "like at the Bank of Montreal now [in 1981]." Frank, King said, "came on at a crucial time." Domtex faced make-or-break decisions in the sixties about whether or not to pour tens of millions of dollars into the construction of gleaming new plants, the revamping of old factories, facelifting, updating, improving systems, and replacing outdated equipment with the most advanced the company could buy.

"Management felt that if we were going to stay in business, we simply had to have modern plants," King said, "and Frank was with us on this. He was a great guy for wanting dividends for the shareholders, but he was never so greedy he didn't support ploughing money back to finance things to build the company's future. We spent a lot of money in the sixties, and that's why Dominion Textile is so strong now." More avaricious and less visionary Canadian textile companies withered away.

Frank believed that any management team good enough to attract his money was also good enough to deserve his support. As a director, he invariably backed management, and this became an investment principle in his family. The Sobeys have often taken a large position in a company because they knew, first, that its management was able; and, second, that the very size of their investment would help protect that same management from pernicious takeovers. "We've never voted against management in our lives," Frank said. He remembered King having repeatedly warned him that " 'If anybody ever takes over Dominion Textile and changes the management, you should sell your shares and get out.' It's a *people* business, in a tough, competitive industry, the same as the grocery business."

"Frank was my kind of guy," King said. "The first time we met, it was a Frank-and-Ed sort of thing. We used to kid each other a lot." King became president in 1966, and chairman in 1969. Ronald H. Perowne, who succeeded him in both positions, said that King, like Frank, "sees the world the way it is, not the way you might want it to be. They're both realists. Ed King is pretty bing-bang-bing, a tough guy to work for. He was a boy when he started here. He was fifty-four years with the company. He sure made me keep my nose to the grindstone, and I'm still doing it forty-four years later. . . . Do you know that seventy-five per cent of the guys here who make $100,000 a year or more are at their desks before eight o'clock every morning?"

A brawny man with white hair, and a pink, lumpy, amiable face, Perowne, at sixty-four, was fond of Frank and proud of Domtex. Frank, in 1982, had not been a Domtex director for ten years (his son David had replaced him on the board), but Perowne clearly remembered him as "the type of director who says, 'Let's have the meat and potatoes before we talk about the asparagus.' He's too bloody smart to be thrown off by the fancy trimmings. He backs you if you're hard-working, stick to your last, and communicate well. He was always urging us to expand in the U.S. He'd say, 'Why don't you guys go on down there? You're the biggest in Canada. You should be there, too.' It pleased him to see us getting involved in other parts of the world, and he kept asking, 'What's the competition up to? Do you know? What are you going to do about it?' He was a damn good director."

By 1981, Dominion Textile ran twenty-five plants in Canada, six in the United States, six in Europe, one in Hong Kong, another in South America. It employed 13,700 workers, chalked up annual sales of $865 million. Empire Company, Stellarton, N.S., owned more than a tenth of its outstanding shares. "Over the years," Frank said, "I just kept on buying shares at various prices, and I think we now have well over a million shares, just picked up that way, all done on the basis of our confidence in the management, as we knew nothing about the textile industry. Nor do we today."

When D. G. (Bud) Willmot went to Montreal in early 1957 to discuss the DOSCO presidency with Roy Jodrey and Frank, they naturally wanted to know all about him. He was a confident, prepossessing fellow, well-built, well-groomed, well-spoken. He was only forty, but for nine years he'd been president of Anthes Imperial, Ltd., St. Catharines, Ont. It made soil pipes, water pipes, oil tanks, brass valves, furnaces, boilers, and radiators; and during young Willmot's time at the top, it had never stopped expanding. Now it owned plants not only in St. Catharines but also in Winnipeg, Edmonton, and Calgary, not to mention warehouses in Montreal and Toronto. Its employees totalled 886, and its operating profit during 1956 was $1,277,699. As Willmot talked on about his firm, something occurred to both Nova Scotians at the same time. It was simply that Willmot was a natural-born money-maker.

"While I chose not to make any moves toward DOSCO," Willmot recalled, "both Frank and Roy Jodrey found the Anthes Imperial story interested them, and both purchased shares." Frank said, "After Bud left the hotel room, Roy turns to me and he says, 'That's one smart feller. I think we should buy some of his shares.' We went right out and bought a thousand shares each." Frank continued to purchase the stock year after year: "I kept on buying Anthes, and gradually it went up to $45 [from about $10], and I was still buying a few shares from time to time, and then they split it, and I still bought a few shares, and they kept on splitting, maybe two or three times. So my investment in Anthes turned out exceptionally well. All along, I was buying it because I felt Bud Willmot was a real top operator. A money-maker." When Molson Industries bought the company out, Frank was both a director of Anthes Imperial and its second-largest shareholder. "I made a lot of money on that Molson transaction," he said. Willmot now became president of Molson Industries, and Frank a director; and, by early 1973, Empire Company of Stellarton owned more than $4 million worth of Molson Industries stock.

As a director, Willmot said, Frank demonstrated "a nose for the things that appeared to have potential, and he was not afraid of the speculative step. He had a very definite entrepreneurial instinct." One director invariably opposed any proposition that involved the smallest risk of losing money but later, after the risk had paid off, pretended he'd favoured it all along. "Frank wasn't like that," Willmot said. "He wasn't a nay-sayer. Moreover, if a venture was properly presented to the board, he would always support management."

By the mid-seventies, Frank had retired as a director of Molson Industries. Empire Company, under the presidency of his youngest son, Donald, was selling its Molson stock in favour of other investments. This, however, did not mean an end to the Willmot-Sobey connection. In the spring of 1975, Willmot led a group that took over Jannock Ltd., a Toronto-based outfit with investments in everything from fish-packing to brick-making, from steel-fabricating to sugar. "I remember I told Donald," Frank said, "I told him, 'Perhaps you should buy Jannock because Bud's in there now. I know he's a money-maker, and he'll find people to turn that company around.'"

"Yes," Willmot said in 1981, "I invested in Jannock a few years ago, and that did attract the interest of the Sobeys. Also, Donald Sobey knew our president, the new president of Jannock, Gordon MacNeill." MacNeill was from Sydney, N.S., and sat with Donald on the board of the Toronto-Dominion Bank. In 1977, Empire Company bought 210,150 shares of Jannock, which by early 1978 had a market value of $2,679,413; three years later, Empire owned 803,200 shares of Jannock, which, along with warrants, were worth well over $12 million. Donald Sobey and, of course, Bud Willmot were both on the Jannock board. Moreover, Willmot had recently brought Empire Company into a partnership agreement with A.P.L. Oil and Gas of Calgary, which had just begun to drill producing wells in western Canada. Willmot, at sixty-five, regarded Donald Sobey, forty-six, as "a fine, intelligent chap". And something of a money-maker, too.

If betting on Willmot was an example of Frank's faith in an able Torontonian, his betting on highway-builder Ashley Colter of Fredericton was an example of his betting on an able Maritimer. In Colter's case, a fresh political breeze in Nova Scotia improved the odds. The Liberals had been in power twenty-three years when the Tories, under Robert Stanfield, beat them in 1956, and a ring of construction companies had had all that time to perfect a tendering racket. "If you were a contractor and you wanted to build a highway, you had to belong to the Construction Association," Frank said. "If you didn't, the Highways Department wouldn't look at your tender. But you couldn't join the Construction Association unless you'd built ten miles of road in Nova Scotia. So that completely shut out any new companies."

Once Stanfield was in power, he asked the trusty Fred Blois to investigate quaint customs in the Highways Department. Blois was a manager in the Stanfield underwear factory, a man who'd worked for Tories in every election since 1911, and a former member of the legislature. What he found in Highways, Frank said, was a bidding pattern: "One fellow would be low one time. To protect him, the other bids would be well above his. Then maybe the high fellow would be the low bidder on the next job. They seemed to be making sure that everybody was getting his share. Well, Fred Blois wanted to break this game. He was very anxious to get a new company into the road-building business in Nova Scotia." Which was where Frank and Ashley Colter came in.

One of Frank's closest friends was New Brunswick industrialist Ralph Brenan, a fellow director of Fraser Companies, and it was Brenan who introduced him to Colter. Colter was just the man Frank was looking for. He owned Diamond Construction, and had done the groundwork and paving for the Halifax International Airport. "I phoned Fred Blois to tell him I was going to form a construction company with Ashley Colter, but Colter was in Mexico," Frank said. "Well, I formed the company anyway, and when he came back I told him about it, and he says, 'That's fine, just fine.'"

With Tories in power, the new company - Waverley Construction, which would later buy out Tidewater Construction - soon won road-building contracts. But the Sobey-Colter partnership also did big jobs for Gulf Oil at its refinery on the Canso Strait, and for Frank's friends at Scott Maritimes, Ltd., when, in 1964, they decided to build their huge pulp mill near his house on the Abercrombie Road. "Ashley and I founded this company by each of us putting in $6,000," Frank said, "and we borrowed the rest of the money with the two of us going in on the note. Ashley never took any salary out of it, and I never took any salary out of it. We never took five cents out of it. We didn't charge it for telephone calls or travelling expenses. We paid those ourselves. The bank called me up once in a while when the company had a big job and needed more money, and wanted my signature on the notes. But I paid no attention to running the company. I left that to Ashley. He was a very fine gentleman, and very honest. I've had excellent experiences when I've gone in with people on a fifty-fifty basis. I guess I only went in with people I felt I could trust."

When Ashley Colter fell ill, his son Burton, who'd helped run the company, proposed that the Colters buy Frank's half-interest. "I got something like a million dollars," Frank said. "That was a good profit, and it all went into Empire. I always tried to build up Empire. I always felt that the best way for a family to hold onto capital was to have it all in one place so you could make substantial investments in companies that had good management."

He sometimes assessed a man's management ability on the basis of a single meeting. While trying to flog bonds to expand his supermarket chain in the late fifties, he met L. L. Lang, president of Mutual Life Assurance of Canada, Waterloo, Ont. Lang bragged about his son, Howard J. Lang, chief of National Steel Car, Hamilton, and Frank decided to visit the younger Lang. "National Steel Car's property was right up against Dofasco [Dominion Foundries and Steel Company Ltd.]," Frank said. "They had a lot of good property, and Howard Lang told me that some day Dofasco would have to come to him and make a deal for some of it. If Dofasco wanted to expand, there was no other way they could move." Frank thought Lang was a smart cookie, and immediately bought shares in National Steel Car. "He was an exceptionally good operator," Frank said, "and I went on buying quite a few shares. I did very well with that investment. I told Roy Jodrey about it, too, and he bought a lot. He did well out of it, maybe even better than I did. Well anyway, that's how you sometimes pick things up, and smell things."

Pondering National Steel Car, Waverley Construction, Anthes Imperial, Dominion Textile, Canadian Salt, and certainly Sobeys Stores, Frank found his thread again: "You know, business is people, more than anything else. If you can get the right people to run a business, then they'll make it successful. The type of business doesn't really matter. If they're the right people, if they have it, they can make any business work."

The incorporated Sobeys Stores, Ltd., was a decade old in 1956, and earned a net profit for the year of $134,145, which was ten times the profit it had reported for its first year. Sales for '56 totalled $8,296,075, up forty per cent over 1955. Frank declared, in late '55 at Saint John, N.B., that "We opened the largest and finest store we ever attempted, on a property acquired from Simpsons-Sears, Ltd., and operated along with them as a joint shopping centre. We are very pleased with the efficient layout, design, and operation of this store, and it has already proven its ability to earn a profit."

The fact that Sobeys Stores, rather than Dominion, had joined Simpsons-Sears in Saint John was entirely due to Frank's hustle. Till he went up to Toronto and changed their minds, the department store's brass had favoured Dominion. He talked first with Morgan Reid, a senior executive, who told him that in the United States it was Sears policy "to go with the local operator" rather than a national supermarket chain. Armed with this information, Frank next visited Edgar Burton, chairman of the Simpsons-Sears board. "We know what Dominion can do for us," Burton said bluntly. "We don't know what you can do." Frank wouldn't quit, and perhaps Burton saw in him a bit of his own father. C. L. Burton, paramount figure in the history of the Robert Simpson Company Ltd., had written (*A Sense of Urgency*, 1952) that, "As soon as one thing is done, another immediately takes its place. It is the awareness of this ceaseless continuity of things requiring to be done that marks, in my view, the man with the whole sense of urgency." That's what Frank had, a whole sense of urgency. With regard to Simpsons-Sears' gambling on a Sobeys supermarket in Saint John, he said later, "It took some pushing, but I persuaded them."

Now the chain was not only interprovincial but also increasingly urban. If Saint John was paying off, so were Sydney and Halifax. Frank was proving that even in tight-money periods he could keep his chain not merely healthy but steadily expanding. Year after year after year, sales and profits had surged ahead. As fiscal 1956 closed, Sobeys Stores didn't owe a nickel to the bank. It had just sold a $500,000 bond issue, its biggest yet, to Eastern Securities. For Frank, however, none of this was good enough. He wanted the business to grow even faster. To finance his expansionary dreams, he'd need more money than Eastern Securities could ever raise on behalf of a small, family-owned company. In 1958 he therefore founded Sobey Leased Properties Ltd., to tap sources of bond financing in central Canada; and in 1959, Sobeys Stores, Ltd., "went public" in a way that enabied it to raise share capital without endangering family control. In the development of the Sobey chain, these were the most significant steps since incorporation in 1946.

Sobeys Stores, Ltd., by the late fifties, had gone about as far as it could go in pursuit of long-term debt financing. "We had quite a few bonds out already in trust deeds," Frank said, "and we couldn't put out new bonds ahead of these." Moreover, Eastern Securities was edgy. By comparison with equity and assets, the chain's debt was now so big that its debentures were getting hard to sell. Yet it needed fast money to sustain its fast growth. "So

J. W. Ritchie, a director of Empire Company Limited.

Sobey Leased Properties," lawyer Henry Rhude said, "was a matter of finding a new way to raise money."

Here's how it worked: Sobeys Stores would build a supermarket, turn it over to Sobey Leased Properties, and then rent it back according to a twenty-five-year agreement. The chain would pay sufficient rent to enable the leasing company to meet payments of interest and principal on a twenty-five-year first-mortgage bond. The rent might be higher than normal at first, but with continuing inflation it would soon be competitive and within twenty years it would be dirt cheap. Moreover, payments on the mortgage would drop throughout its life. "We issued bonds for eighty per cent of the value [of the supermarket or, later, mall]," Frank explained. "They were twenty-five-year bonds with a payback of four per cent of the principal for each year. I wanted them that way because I always knew what I could do in the coming few years but I did not know about the more distant future. By paying four per cent off each year, the bonds would be down by twenty per cent in five years, and we only had to pay interest on the outstanding balance."

Under earlier financing methods, security for a bond might lie in inventory, accounts receivable, or such intangibles as an idea or a reputation. Sometimes it was tough to raise sixty-five-per-cent financing. But the buyer of a Sobey Leased Properties bond got not only a first mortgage on real property but also an assignment on the supermarket lease. In the case of shopping centres, there'd be a department store and dozens of smaller shops, and all these leases would also be part of the assignment. With such security to offer, the chain got eighty-per-cent financing to fuel its expansion.

"The Sobeys find the land, build the store, and lease it from one of their companies, and they do all this with their own resources or interim bank financing," J. William Ritchie, Scotia Bond Company, Ltd., explained. "And *then* they go for the long-term financing. When somebody asks about the security, you can say, 'There it is, it's standing right there, and here's the appraised value.' It makes for a tighter, more understandable financing, and it's a pattern they've developed very successfully, going right back to the late fifties."

Frank founded Sobey Leased Properties simply to open more supermarkets and sell more food, but as shopping malls swept the continent, the new company offered a path into real-estate development. Dominion Stores shunned the same path. It chose to lease property. When it purchased land, it then sold it to a developer on the condition Dominion would rent the key location for a supermarket. It avoided the special headaches of financing, building, and operating shopping centres, and chose to stick to what it knew best, selling groceries.

Frank, however, wanted his empire to sell groceries *and* own real estate. "Being Frank Sobey," said Gordon Cowan, his lawyer before Henry Rhude, "he asked himself, 'Why let somebody else make money out of a development in which the anchor is a Sobeys Store?' He wanted it both ways. He needed capital but he wouldn't sell off land. He sold bonds and debentures to finance all this, but he kept the voting stock in the family. They've been doing a good job of merchandising but they also have all this immense amount of real estate that they paid for out of borrowed money. That's one of the main strengths of the Sobey organization, while Dominion has been in trouble down here [in the late seventies and early eighties]."

Whose idea was Sobey Leased Properties? Frank remembered that DOSCO president Lionel Forsyth had tipped him off that Montreal Trust, of which Forsyth was a director, had helped Petrofina, of which he was also a director, to establish a separate leasing company to own Petrofina service stations. Forsyth suggested he consult Herman Stockwell of Montreal Trust, and it was Stockwell who not only made Frank see the light with regard to leasing companies but also committed Montreal Trust to take the lead by subscribing to $100,000 in first-mortgage bonds of Sobey Leased Properties' first bond issue in 1959, provided that Frank could place the balance of $400,000.

To sell the real-estate bonds, Frank himself went straight to the handful of big institutional markets in central Canada. The money he now sought was more than Eastern Securities could raise in the Maritimes. But selling the bonds required every ounce of his salesmanship and stubbornness. "Selling the first issue in central Canada for a small Nova Scotian company twenty-odd years ago was not easy," said George C. Hitchman of the Bank of Nova Scotia. Had Frank sold them himself? "You're damned right he did," Hitchman replied. "I know. I knew pretty near every move he was making. He could *do* it. It wasn't millions he was dealing in, but it wasn't chickenfeed, either."

"It was always very hard for Nova Scotian companies to raise big sums," Frank said. "It was hard to get anything over, say, $300,000, because the investment houses up there just didn't want to put money down here. The big underwriting companies might take Nova Scotia Light and Power or, say, Maritime Tel, but, from their point of view, what else *was* there down here?" Harold Renouf, the diminutive accountant who became chairman of Via Rail Canada in 1982, recalled a bond-selling pitch Frank delivered to the top officers of Sun Life in Montreal. The response was so discouraging that Frank walked to a window, pointed down at the excavation for the foundation of yet another Montreal skyscraper, and blurted, "The trouble with you fellows is that you'd rather put money into that hole than help the Maritimes." No one knew what to say. Then the president of the firm cleared his throat and allowed that he and his cohorts did indeed prefer to back projects right under their noses rather than a thousand miles east. "I understand that," Frank replied, "but how do we build stores in the Maritimes when you want to sink your money in a hole in the ground in Montreal?" The appeal, in this case, did not work. He struck out.

It had been Roy Jodrey who'd inspired him to try to beat the odds in central Canada: "I ran into Roy in Toronto one trip. He says, 'Look, every time you come up here, put a few thousand dollars' worth of bonds in your pocket. You go find a friend in a bank or a trust company, or you're talking to a banker or somebody, and you say you're going to put out a bond issue. You suggest he might want to buy some for his institution, and maybe just to be polite he says perhaps he will. So then you pull them out of your pocket, slap them down on the table, and say, "There they are. How about it?" You get him to take the lead.'

"The fellow agrees to put up *some*," Frank continued, "but only on the condition you raise it all so you can go ahead with the project." He was fifty-seven when he set out to sell Sobey Leased Properties' first bond issue. Once he came to an agreement with Montreal Trust, Sun Life followed suit. "We had a mortgage from Canada Life on our New Glasgow store," he said, "so I tried them next. They weren't interested. I tried Crown Life. They weren't interested. So I went over to London, Ont., to see London Life. They weren't interested. Well then I drove to Waterloo to try Mutual Life, but the fellow in charge of their investments could hardly credit the idea that Montreal Trust and Sun Life were taking pieces of this issue for a company way down in Nova Scotia. So I said, 'Why don't you call them up?' He called Sun Life and Mr. Stockwell at Montreal Trust, and then he said, 'Well, we'll take $100,000, providing you can sell the balance.' That's the way you had to go about it. You go to insurance companies, pension funds, anything you can think of. I sold $100,000 one day to the Canada Council, on the telephone. The man I was talking to was Douglas Fullerton. That was to complete an issue. I had to get the whole thing out."

As early as 1953, Frank locked voting shares of Sobeys Stores, Ltd., inside a holding company to preserve his family's control. In August 1952 the major shareholders were Frank, with 4,463 shares, and his younger brother, Harold, with 3,001. By January 1953, however, Frank's personal holdings had shrunk to 210 shares, while Harold still had his 3,001. Frank had shoved the bulk of his shares and a few hundred of his sons' into a new outfit, Sobeys Stores Holdings. It owned 5,003 shares, more than the total held by all individuals, including Harold. In his late forties, Harold found selling groceries no longer gave him the satisfaction Frank still derived from it. He wanted to go his own way, and to take with him the proceeds of his substantial share (roughly a third) of the supermarket business. Frank wanted to see him content, to raise capital through the first public issue of Sobeys Stores stock, and, at the same time, to continue to protect the family's control over the chain. With the help of Carl Fisher, Henry Rhude, and particularly John N. Cole in the Montreal office of Wood, Gundy, he accomplished all three objectives in the spring of '59.

Frank and C. L. Gundy, president of Wood, Gundy, were both directors of DOSCO, and Cole recalled Gundy's saying to him, "You'd better go down to Halifax and have a talk with Frank Sobey. He's thinking of going public." When Cole went to Halifax there were 10,600 issued and fully paid common shares of Sobeys Stores, Ltd., and 14,750 preference shares. To give Frank what he wanted, they split the common and redeemed the preference shares. The common became 234,000 A shares, and 106,000 B shares. These were identical in every respect but two: only the B was voting stock, and it wasn't for sale (though within a year, Frank would sell a block to Weston-Loblaw), nor was it necessary to pay dividends on the B stock. Wood, Gundy immediately bought 125,000 A shares at $15.75 each, and sold them to the public at $17. "It was a successful operation," Cole said. "The timing was good. It caught a market that was interested in this sort of thing, and it was tidied up in no time. Everybody was quite happy about it." Out of the proceeds, $318,760 went to redeem the old Sobeys Stores preference shares; $787,500 was collected by the family; and $862,490 went straight into Sobeys Stores, Ltd.

Frank and Harold, in return for their old common shares, each received portions of the new A and B stock. They struck a private deal. Harold got Frank's non-voting stock, which was being publicly traded; Frank got Harold's voting stock, which was not being traded, and put it into Sobeys Stores Holdings. Thus, each brother got what he wanted. Harold continued to offer counsel as a director of Sobeys Stores, Ltd., and Empire Company, but now he had liquidity and the freedom to handle all his investments as he chose. Frank consolidated family control.

Less than two years later, on the night of Friday, December 30, 1960, his mother died at home in Stellarton. She was eighty-nine, and had survived her husband by eleven years. "The two were married on the first day of this century," the New Glasgow *Evening News* reported on New Year's Eve. "Had she lived until tomorrow, she would have marked the 60th anniversary of her wedding." She was a "well-known and highly respected resident". At the funeral in her beloved Sharon St. John United Church, "the Stellarton Local Council of Women sat in a body as a tribute to Mrs. Sobey," the congregation sang "Safe in the Arms of Jesus", and the pastor took his text from Isaiah 40:31: "But they that wait upon the Lord shall renew their strength; they shall mount up with wings as eagles; they shall run, and not be weary; and they shall walk and not faint."

In addition to her two sons and her daughter, Eliza Creighton Sobey left eight grandchildren and six great-grandchildren. There were therefore plenty of Sobeys to carry on the business her husband had founded more than half a century before, which was just as well. For Frank had plunged himself into a mission that, for a dozen years, would drag him further and further away from the management of the chain he had so painstakingly nurtured. As president of the provincial Crown corporation Industrial Estates Ltd., he took it upon himself to help rescue the shipwrecked hulk of the Nova Scotia economy.

9

FOR NOVA SCOTIA: INDUSTRIAL ESTATES LIMITED

PESSIMISM enshrouded Nova Scotia in the mid-fifties. The war seemed to have been but an interlude in a decline that had begun in a time beyond memory. Had the Depression ever really ended? Nova Scotia heard only faint echoes of the postwar boom in distant parts of Canada. The province languished in the exhaust fumes, and its people saw little else to do. Canada's population rose by 6,630,000 between 1926 and 1956, Nova Scotia's by only 180,000. As fast as children were born, older children left, and newcomers were rare. Canada welcomed 164,857 immigrants in 1956; Nova Scotia got 1,679 of them.

It would have been bad enough if Nova Scotia had merely been holding its own with the rest of Canada, but since the war it had failed to do even that. In relative terms, its economy was still going downhill. Its measly share of Canada's manufacturing industry had actually declined since 1946. Between 1949 and 1956, Nova Scotia's per-capita spending on what economists call "new, durable, physical assets", such as factories and housing, was only 58.8 per cent of Canada's. Such figures seemed abstract, and bloodless, but they were background to realities that were harsh enough to a miner in a town where there were no more mines. "It's hard to remember the realities now," Yarmouth businessman Seymour Kenney said in 1980, "but we just weren't an industrial province. If you drove for fifty miles along the whole French Shore [the western tip of

Nova Scotia], you'd see hardly a gallon of paint on the buildings."

More lifeless figures: in 1946 personal income, per capita, in Nova Scotia was $678, or eighty per cent of the figure for all Canada; but only ten years later it was $971, or a mere seventy-one per cent of the national figure. Canadian wages averaged $66.44 a week in 1956. Nova Scotian wages, at $52.90, lagged even behind those in New Brunswick and Newfoundland. To make the picture even less promising, it had mostly been federal government money that had kept Nova Scotia from plummeting even further.

But it was central Canada's domination of that same federal government that Nova Scotians blamed for their plight. They felt Ontario and Quebec had been double-crossing them ever since 1867, had been imposing tariff, trade, transportation, political, and financial policies to milk Maritimers and crush local industry. Older Pictou County men could rhyme off the names of a dozen factories that, just since the twenties, central Canadian muscle had squeezed to death, and the Halifax *Chronicle-Herald* greeted A. V. Roe's raid on DOSCO by recalling that "Industry after industry here has been acquired by Central Canadian interests of a competitive nature . . . and closed down to [strengthen] the purchasing companies' operations in Toronto, Montreal, and elsewhere. There have been cotton mills, boot and shoe factories, the once-bustling Rhodes-Currie car plant at Amherst, the sugar refinery at Dartmouth and many others." Central Canada's gift to Nova Scotia was "a trail of empty buildings".

The unkind suggested Nova Scotia's stagnation actually stemmed from bluenose defeatism and entrepreneurial lethargy, but whatever the reasons, Premier Robert Stanfield faced a staggering challenge when he first came to power late in 1956. "We felt we had to run very hard just to stand still," he told author Geoffrey Stevens (*Stanfield*, 1973). "In agriculture we had a system of small farms, which people were constantly leaving. Fishing was in a state of revolution. The so-called inshore fisherman was pretty well disappearing in most parts of the province. That involved a large expansion of the trawler fishing industry and the centralization at certain points. The forest industry had to be re-organized substantially. The coal-mining industry was failing rapidly."

Pictou County had known since the Depression that coal's long-range menace was oil. Sixty-nine per cent of Canada's energy came from coal in 1926 and only ten per cent from oil, but by 1960 the figures were sixty-eight per cent for oil and seventeen per cent for coal. The railroads, once a huge market for coal, converted to diesel oil, and in every major coal field in Nova Scotia, the number of colliers dwindled and the number of unemployed miners rose. Only massive federal subsidies kept the industry breathing. The problem lay not just in declining markets, but also in the mines themselves.

They'd been worked so long in Cape Breton that men now had to trundle for miles under the Atlantic seabed just to reach the coal. The dollar costs were high, the coal itself was excessively sulphurous, the main markets were far up the regularly icebound St. Lawrence River. In Cumberland County, the awful disasters of 1956 and 1958, which together killed 114 men, not only finished Springhill as a mining town but also focussed world attention on the horrors that lurked in Nova Scotia coal shafts. In Pictou County, no one who was not a miner, an ex-miner, or a miner's boss better understood the horrendous threats to the coal industry than the mayor of Stellarton.

"Travelling time from the pithead to the face got longer every year," Frank said. "The cost of hauling coal to the surface was increasing. The cost of pumping was increasing, the cost of keeping air in the mines. As the mines got older, there were more areas to be ventilated, and more areas where they had to keep up track. In Stellarton they had real problems with gas. They called the floor of the mine 'the pavement', and after a fire or explosion had closed a mine for a while, they'd have to go in, lift the tracks, and do what they called 'brushing'. The pressure was so great, you see, that the pavement kept rising, so the job of the 'brushers' was to keep on cutting off these bumps and heaves that kept rising in the pavement." Brushers cost money.

Stellarton's prospects were bleak even by Nova Scotian standards.

If the hoot of the mine whistle sounded less and less frequently, so did the moan of the train whistle. The town's second industry was Canadian National Railways, but as an employer CNR was shrinking, and as a market for local coal it was vanishing. As recently as 1948 the local yard maintained sixty-one coal-fired steam locomotives. By 1955 not one was in service. Soon, local runs would all be gone, like the "turnip" watches the conductors had sported for generations.

Pictou County coal production dropped from 650,000 tons in 1948 to 271,000 tons in 1957. As 1957 began, the MacGregor Mine was still producing 600 tons a day when, on January 23, miners detected the old smell of fire. Was an explosion imminent? No one wanted to wait to find out. The mine was pretty well worked out anyway, and on February 3 a crew began to seal forever the mouth of the MacGregor. That ended a century and a half of coal mining in Stellarton. Without mining, the town was like a movie house without a projector. DOSCO had estimated that 2,700 Stellarton people, half the population, were "wholly dependent" on the coal industry.

Frank hustled off to Halifax. Twenty years before, he had persuaded a Liberal cabinet minister to fund the works program that had helped Stellarton lick the Depression. Now, he called on the first Tory premier in almost a quarter-century. Somebody, he felt, had to do something for his home town; and at first that was his only motive for visiting Stanfield. He had no idea that he was now on his way to an unpaid job that would gain him a slew of national honours; embroil him in sensational controversy; take him to London, Paris, Stockholm, Tokyo, and Bombay; force him to mingle with British lords, French diplomats, and American super-tycoons; and for a dozen years leave him as the spotlighted boss of a campaign that would bring to Nova Scotia hundreds of millions of dollars' worth of industry. He would make sure that Pictou County got its share, or, as some would complain, a bit more than its share.

"Frank and Harold Egan came in to see me," Stanfield said.

"Clearly Frank had been using Harold as a consultant on town affairs, and Harold was a very bright fellow." Frank had land in mind as a publicly owned site for future industry. It lay on the outskirts of town near Westville, and in his boyhood the streetcar company had run an amusement park there to drum up traffic. In days when women's skirts still swept the ground, and his father's work on the Allan Shaft was done, and Stellarton was beginning to enjoy its fleeting heyday, Bear Brook Park had boasted a merry-go-round, dance pavilion, bandstand, duck pond, rustic bridge, and shooting gallery. Now the land was bare, but it was on the railway and fronted on a paved road. The Acadia Coal Company, DOSCO's Stellarton subsidiary, owned it.

"So Mr. Stanfield told me to go ahead and get it," Frank said. "I went after Harold Gordon and I got it for nothing – one thousand dollars, but I don't believe we ever paid it. I also told Mr. Stanfield I'd like to get Harold Egan working with me to get some type of industry for Stellarton. So he gave me a few thousand dollars to spend in that way, or, rather, he agreed to pick up the bills. I don't think we spent more than a thousand." Bear Brook Park would become Stellarton's industrial park.

But Stanfield was already committed to something bigger than Band-Aids for one town. Unlike most premiers, he came from a manufacturing family. "Stanfield's Unshrinkables" were Canada's most famous long-johns, and the Stanfields had been proving since before the turn of the century that manufacturing for export was possible in Nova Scotia. But it needed imaginative goading. "People had been talking for thirty years about getting government involved in industrial revitalization," E. A. Manson said. A druggist from Sydney, Manson was Stanfield's first minister of trade and industry. "But no one had ever done anything," he continued. "When I went in, there were just two fellows in the industry department. No one was travelling. They were just sending out a circular letter. The first thing I did was to cancel the bloody thing."

Stanfield had promised that a Tory government would found a "Nova Scotia Industrial Development Corporation". He had no precise idea of what it would be or do, but during his first session he pushed through the legislation to create it. Half its financing would come from the provincial treasury, and to encourage Nova Scotians to invest in their own future the other half would come through the sale of shares to the public. "I objected to that at caucus," Manson recalled. "We were going to sell shares for five dollars each to individuals, labour unions, and so on. I said, 'Christ, it's just like a Red Cross campaign.' I just couldn't see the damn thing. I didn't know what the answer was , but then a fellow named General Appleyard came to town."

Major-General Kenelm Appleyard, a former British Army officer, was an acquaintance of Roy Jodrey and Edward Haliburton, a fruit-grower and ex-journalist who was now minister of agriculture. Appleyard toured the Annapolis Valley, found himself comfortable in this "new England", and chose to make the industrial recovery of Nova Scotia a retirement hobby. An engineering and industrial consultant, he so impressed Harry Halliwell, financial editor of the Toronto *Telegram*, that Halliwell called him "a professional engineer with the soul of an artist and the social conscience of a missionary."

But it was more important to the Tories that Appleyard was chairman of an outfit called North Eastern Trading Estates. Government financed it, but businessmen ran it, and it had apparently done for northeastern England what Stanfield's greenhorn cabinet wanted to do for Nova Scotia. Manson went to England to see Appleyard, and the general came to Halifax to see Stanfield. "We met at Bob Stanfield's house," Manson said. "There was General Appleyard, Bob, Ed Haliburton, Ike Smith [Stanfield's chief lieutenant and minister of highways], and myself, and we killed a bottle of Scotch." Over the Scotch, Appleyard persuaded the Nova Scotians to commission another military man from England to do a discreet survey. Colonel M. D. Methven was the general manager of North Eastern Trading Estates, and his assignment in Nova Scotia was to address town councils, find out if they'd give industries tax holidays, and report to Manson on whether or not the industrial-estate system might rejuvenate the sluggish bluenose economy. His conclusion, Stanfield said, was that "We might have some failures but experience in the United Kingdom suggested other industrial tenants would come in to replace them."

Meanwhile, Stanfield invited business luminaries to a series of secret meetings at the Lord Nelson Hotel. The guests included Manson, Smith, financier J. C. MacKeen, corporation lawyer Frank Covert, Frank Sobey, and several others. Both Methven and Appleyard opposed selling shares to the public. Frank and Harold Egan were also sure the idea would flop. To attract industry, the new agency would make deals that would not always guarantee profits. Without the promise of profit, who'd be crazy enough to invest? "We became more and more nervous about this," Stanfield recalled. "If we invited Nova Scotians to invest, they might suffer losses, or at best wait a long time for returns. The annual shareholders' meetings might be, well, embarrassing."

But the Tories not only had promised a company in which the public would be involved but had also incorporated it. Shutting the public out now would give Opposition Leader Henry Hicks a chance to make the new cabinet look like fools. But in *Stanfield*, Geoffrey Stevens wrote, the premier "saw the logic in Sobey's argument. 'We will just tell the opposition we were wrong,' he said, with characteristic candour." Frank, however, believed it was G. I. Smith who said, "All we can do is say we were wrong." (Whoever suggested the confession, Frank liked the attitude: "If Richard Nixon had only said the same thing they'd never have got him.") Stanfield himself, twenty-four years later, said that, when it came time to face the Liberals in the legislature, the Tories simply said that although they'd proposed one plan, "We now have a better idea." The better idea was Industrial Estates Limited, a provincial Crown corporation with total government financing. The initials IEL would become the most familiar acronym in Nova Scotia, the tag for an outfit that the business press would hail as Canada's most imaginative effort to revitalize a provincial economy.

The hotel meetings laid down IEL ground rules. Government would provide the money ($12 million to start) but it would keep its nose out of IEL. Businessmen would run the agency, and they'd do it as unpaid volunteers. "We would have no political discussions with any members of the government with the exception of Mr. Manson," Frank said. Manson was the sole cabinet minister on the IEL board, and "He was a great help, and certainly shielded us from political pressure." Not government but IEL would announce its agreements with industry clients, and only after they'd been signed and sealed. But to whom would go the honour and crushing workload of serving as president?

Frank got the job by a fluke. The position that would win him fame, if not fortune – he said later that the effort he put into IEL rather than his own business "cost me at least a million" – landed in his lap because another man had turned it down. Stanfield had Frank in mind only as vice-president, but the president he sought was Frank Covert. Covert was a senior partner in what was then Stewart, Smith, MacKeen, Covert, Rogers, Sperry and Cowan, and he was already succeeding his idol, J. McG. Stewart (who'd died in 1955), as the most important lawyer in Nova Scotia. "No matter where they originate or where they eventually end up," Peter C. Newman wrote in *The Canadian Establishment* (1975), "the lines of established business power in Nova Scotia lead to Frank Manning Covert."

But in addition to the obvious reasons for choosing Covert as president of IEL, there was a not-so-obvious one. Covert was a big Grit. Having a Liberal at the top of the controversial new agency would remove any suspicion that the Tories had favoured one of their own. Stanfield wanted Covert, Manson said, "to clean up the political act". Moreover, if so prominent a Liberal were the top dog, the irascible Liberal leader, former premier Henry Hicks, might go easy on the controversial new agency. "Hicks would have been hellish embarrassed to attack IEL if Covert was head of it," Manson said.

"I had long talks with Covert," Stanfield said, "but he said he was too busy." Manson insisted, "We had actually *made* Covert president. His name was in the documents as president. He was going to have to sign the papers, but we couldn't go ahead that night because he resigned two hours before the incorporation." Why? Manson, who was as Tory as Covert was Grit, believed for-

Frank Sobey and lawyer Frank Covert, mid-1960s.

ever after that Covert had succumbed to pressure from Hicks. But Covert said in 1983 that what had actually influenced him to turn the job down was a friendly remark from an arch-Tory, his eminent law partner Henry P. MacKeen. MacKeen was so thoroughly Tory that Stanfield would later approve his appointment as lieutenant-governor. "I set up the whole thing [the legal work for the incorporation of IEL] for them," Covert recalled, "and Stanfield asked me to take on the job. But I came back to the office one night, and I talked it all over with Harry [MacKeen]. I was anxious to do something for the province, and I thought IEL sounded like a good thing. Then Harry said, 'You know why they asked you, don't you? It's just because you're a prominent Liberal. If you take it, the Liberals won't criticize it.'

"Then, on a Sunday morning," Covert continued, "I talked with Stanfield, and I said, 'You've just chosen me because I'm a well-known Liberal.' Stanfield turned his back to me for a moment, and walked around a bit, and then he said, 'It wasn't just that. There were other reasons, too.' After that, I talked to Egan and Sobey. I told Sobey he should take it. I helped select the board for it, too. They were mostly Tories." Another Halifax lawyer said, "You know, one of Covert's finest services to IEL was that he gave them Bill Mingo as their counsel." In the stable of able lawyers at Covert's firm, none was more able than J. William E. Mingo. "I handed IEL over to him," Covert said. "It became his biggest client, and he developed a tremendous expertise in handling it."

When Covert refused the job, Manson said, "It was a hell of a shock. I almost dropped dead. You couldn't have a company without a president. So that's when we asked Frank Sobey." Frank agreed on two conditions: that he could have one friend, the ace accountant Harold Egan, as IEL's secretary-treasurer; and another friend, the ace banker Horace Enman, as chairman of the board. (Enman was chairman of the Bank of Nova Scotia but no longer president.) Once Frank had Egan, he wasted no time putting the arm on Enman, who happened to be at his summer home at Ingonish. "The next day," Frank said, "Harold and I went down to Cape Breton, and we persuaded Mr. Enman to come on as chairman. So I headed up Industrial Estates." All this happened within a day or two of Covert's withdrawal.

"Frank Sobey was a big man to take it over under those circumstances," Manson said, "and it was a big sacrifice for him. It was the biggest job in Nova Scotia. Nothing like it had ever existed before. He deserves all the credit in the world."

"Frank had been honoured," New Glasgow newspaperman Harry Sutherland said. "Here was this guy who'd been a butcher kid in Stellarton, and Mr. Stanfield was asking him to take on this stupendous job. . . . You know, if you look over the hills from here, you see Truro [home of the Stanfields]. We played hockey against Truro. The Stanfields were rich and Frank's father was not, but I imagine old J.W. curled against them from time to time." As a boy, Stanfield had gone to the same summer camp as Harold Sobey, and remembered him all his life "as a pleasant kid. I liked him." Frank Stanfield, brother of Robert, had been on the board of Sobeys Stores, Ltd., for a decade, and in 1953 Robert had asked Frank Sobey to run for the Tories in a federal election. "He was friendly about it but he wasn't prepared to run," Stanfield said, "and that probably showed good judgment on his part." It had not been a good year for Tory politicians in Nova Scotia.

By the time IEL started, Sutherland continued, "Frank had some money." Both Stanfield and Frank knew that, when it came to the mission of an outfit like IEL, "money talks to money"; and that a smart businessman would always prefer to talk not to a politician or bureaucrat but to another smart businessman. "Mr. Stanfield would have known all about Frank's ability," Sutherland said. "With Frank, you had to do it right or go out of business."

But at first Frank and his IEL cohorts didn't do it right at all. IEL's first task was to find a general manager, but for perhaps the only time in Frank's life, he let himself be talked out of using his system of brain-picking by phone to find the perfect executive. IEL felt that if it was going to be a big-time operation it should use big-time recruitment methods, and at Enman's urging it hired a reputable head-hunting agency. The agency winnowed the applicants down to half a dozen, and gave the short list to Enman.

"Mr. Enman says, 'I have talked to one fellow, and I think he's our man,'" Frank said. The man was from Ontario and his name was J. B. Essery. With Enman, he joined Frank and Egan for breakfast in Halifax. He impressed the grocer as he'd impressed the banker, and he won from IEL an annual salary of $30,000 and a year's contract. "I let Enman overshadow me on that," Frank said, remembering the fiasco that followed. But he also blamed himself: "I guess one of the worst mistakes I made was hiring [Essery]. He turned out not to be the man for the job." Frank fired him roughly six months after hiring him. Liberals had already objected to Essery's salary, huge by the standards of 1957, and now they attacked the government with such vicious glee that, as Manson recalled, "I finally just had to stand up and admit we made a mistake. That was the end of it. It was never mentioned in the House again."

Stanfield remained unrattled. For years to come, whenever Frank would warn him that certain IEL decisions might give him political headaches, Stanfield would reply, "Let me worry about that. You fellows have a job to do. So do it." Long after the Essery mess, Frank reported to Stanfield that he'd heard Conservative lawyers in the Halifax Club were grumbling over the fact that Bill Mingo, a Liberal lawyer, was getting IEL business. "Is he doing a good job?" Stanfield asked. When Frank said yes, the premier's response was this: "If gossip in the Halifax Club starts to influence how I run my government, it'll be time for me to get out and somebody else to get in." That attitude was why Frank came to respect Stanfield more than any other politician he ever knew.

Next he had to tell the premier about something even more unpalatable than the speedy dismissal of IEL's high-paid manager. It was the little matter of Essery's contract. IEL owed him another six months' salary, and it would also have to pay to move his family and furniture back to Upper Canada. With regard to the political embarrassment, Stanfield simply said, "We can take it." With regard to replacing Essery, he said, "That's your problem. Do what you have to do."

Frank knew exactly what he had to do, and it involved neither a head-hunting agency nor a stranger from Ontario. He directly wooed "a boy from Stellarton whom I knew very well". F. L. Blair was sales manager at the Toronto headquarters of Canada Packers, and boss of the company's Chicago sales office, as well. He ran the biggest sales team in Canada, roughly seven hundred men. "And they were all hard workers," Frank said. "They were early risers and hard drivers. When I was looking for a man [for Sobeys Stores, Ltd.], I very often tried to get one that Canada Packers had trained." But prying Blair loose from Canada Packers required all of Frank's determination, and all his talents of cajolery.

He knew Blair wanted to spend his last years in the service of his home province. He knew Blair owned a food-wholesaling business in Newfoundland, and he offered to give him a week off each month to look after it. This was not rashly generous, for Frank also knew that a lifetime at Canada Packers had turned Blair into a work addict. Three weeks of his work would be worth at least a month's of another man's. The trouble was, Blair stood to gain from an excellent company pension plan, and unless Canada Packers' president, William McLean, agreed to his leaving, he couldn't join IEL without jeopardizing the pension. So Frank worked not just on Blair but also on McLean.

"Pretty near every day I spent half an hour or so on the phone talking to Bill McLean and trying to get him to let Fred go," Frank said. "I told him Fred was tired, and he says, 'I know he's tired, he's been working hard, but we've got other things in mind for him.' " Meanwhile, months were slipping by, and as IEL's first birthday passed, the agency still had no permanent general manager. It drew new sneers and fresh ridicule, but Frank hung tough. He knew whom he wanted, and at last "I persuaded Bill to give Fred a leave of absence." Fred Blair came home to Nova Scotia. IEL was off, and somewhat running.

IEL was a Nova Scotian adaptation of a British idea. In a time when its future seemed rosy, the *Financial Times* of London (July 2, 1965) observed that thanks to "a British rather than an American-trained pilot" an "economic backwater" called Nova Scotia was "fast moving back into the mainstream." The pilot was General Appleyard, whom Stanfield preferred to call "the midwife of IEL", and the model was North Eastern Trading Estates. The *Financial Times* of Canada (Oct. 28, 1963) called IEL "a landlord-type organization that helps industry by offering a wide variety of incentives," which was accurate but incomplete. For it was also a promoter of spectacular confidence (and, in time, a victim of that same confidence).

Stanfield told the first board meeting on September 25, 1957, that IEL's purpose was "to encourage the promotion, expansion, diversification, and development of industrial activity in Nova Scotia". It would leave resource development and heavy industry to the government, and concentrate on light or secondary industry.

IEL would buy land for future industries; provide power, water, sewers, and roads; build factories for lease or sale; lend money for purchase of machinery and equipment; and "assist, by all means at its disposal, any suitable industry in any or all phases of its operations. . . ." Stanfield also said, "By deliberate intent, we have created a company which will speak for itself, which will operate independently of government direction and interference. . . . Finally, and I would like to emphasize this, the government will permit the company to operate as an autonomous corporation. . . ."

IEL advertisements shouted, "Industrialists! Have Industrial Estates Ltd. finance and build your plant in Nova Scotia! The company will develop the site of your choice, finance and build your plant, lease it to you at low rental and, if and when you wish, sell it to you at book cost." Not only that, IEL offered to finance up to sixty per cent of a client's cost of equipment, and to arrange tax concessions from municipalities. All of this, in Canadian terms, was innovative to the point of being revolutionary. Other provinces and the national business press began to monitor the Great Bluenose Experiment.

Frank had two prohibitions for IEL: first, it should never accept a client with insufficient capital to run a business and repay its debt; and second, it should never, ever, take an equity share in any client industry. "The establishment of a business that is not properly financed is not doing a service," he said in 1965, "but, rather, a disservice, because the community is worse off if the business gets into financial difficulties - which mostly results in unpaid bills and disappointed employees being left in the area." On the second point, he simply believed that it was not only wrong but stupid for any government to put up taxpayers' money as risk capital in a private venture. IEL would eventually break these two rules, and then its bubble of glory would burst.

Frank was also adamant that, no matter what the general manager's salary, neither he nor any other director should receive a nickel more than a flat fee, which eventually rose to all of thirty-five dollars, for attending IEL meetings, plus expenses incurred on IEL business. He had ideas about public service that many might now regard as quaint. In his time, in his father's time, a man entered public life only after he'd proved himself by making money. You became a politician for the honour of serving the community where you'd made the money, even if the service meant you might lose some of it. As mayor, he had never expected a salary, and neither had the men on town council. As president of IEL, serving Nova Scotia as he'd served Stellarton, he did not expect a salary, and neither should the businessmen on the board.

Not getting paid also had practical advantages. Mingo reflected that it was all very well for Frank to talk about the virtue of working for nothing but it also "increased his clout tremendously. The more people pay you, the more they can demand of you. If you're not getting paid, then you can really throw your weight around. Frank demonstrated that technique in spades, specially when he ran into resistance, from Stanfield maybe, or Manson. It enabled him to come late, leave early, deliver his message, and not have to argue his points. It made him efficient." Moreover, Frank figured, if he got a salary while other directors remained unpaid, they might expect him to do all the work. Serving for nothing, "I could ask any of the directors to go on a trip to see somebody for IEL."

Stanfield named IEL's first board, but after that the company elected its own directors at annual meetings. "Though officially any person could be appointed . . . so long as he was not bankrupt or had not been found lunatic," economist Roy E. George wrote (*The Life and Times of Industrial Estates Limited*, 1974), "in fact appointments have been limited to Nova Scotians, and there seems to have been an understanding that directors would be drawn from various districts of the province." The directors were a chummy lot. They invariably reappointed everyone who wanted to stay on. Most did. Not counting the cabinet ministers who succeeded one another as the link to government, and three general managers, IEL had a total of barely thirty directors during its first fourteen years. A decade after its birth, five of the original nine volunteers were still on the board: Frank, Harold Egan, Yarmouth building contractor S. W. Kenney, Annapolis

Valley egg-producer D. F. Archibald, and Truro dairy-products distributor C. G. MacLennan. Moreover, Halifax financier J. C. MacKeen and R. G. Urquhart, mayor of Sydney, had been listed as directors ever since the second annual report.

The trouble was, IEL critic Roy E. George complained, "Almost all . . . were drawn from the Nova Scotian business community, mostly owners or executives of distributing, building, contracting or real-estate developing businesses. Since the province's industrial sector is under-developed . . . experience of the directors in the operation of manufacturing industry, with which IEL was solely concerned, has been slight." George felt the IEL board needed out-of-province experts on manufacturing. Frank, however, believed that "If Nova Scotia was going to go ahead, it had to be developed by Nova Scotians," and IEL directors were "good Nova Scotians with no political axes to grind. They were independent."

Moreover, most worked hard for IEL. Even George conceded, "There seems little doubt that some directors have voluntarily given a great deal of time and effort to the affairs of IEL." Frank gave more of himself to IEL than many men give to full-time jobs. "He was an odd guy," Mingo said. "He had tremendous physical energy. He'd get up at 6 a.m., work for an hour, phone you at 7 and ask you what you'd done for him that day. He was very shrewd, and *very* demanding, and he was spending much more time on IEL business than he was on Sobey business." To do this – and also to free himself for trips to board meetings in Toronto and Montreal – Frank had to loosen his grip on the reins of the family business. His sons took over more and more responsibility for the burgeoning chainstore-mall-investment empire. "He threw the business at them," Mingo said, "and I think that was good for them."

Donald Sobey agreed: "It was a great thing for us that Father went into IEL, because it gave Bill, Dave, and myself a chance to work without him looking over our shoulders every day. We could make *decisions*. . . . He was home often enough to correct the course if we'd gone wrong, but we nevertheless sometimes had to make moves and guide things without him right up till the last point." Some successful fathers, Donald suggested, dominate family companies so fiercely their sons lose for life the ability to make decisions.

David Sobey, still in his mid-thirties when Frank had hurled himself into IEL, had a slightly different slant on things: "We were pretty young, and I wished I had more counsel from him. His leaving then was not the best thing for Sobeys Stores, Ltd., but you certainly knew you had to get up and do your own thing. I was just coming into the head office, and I needed him. He was out of here almost completely, but, you know, he had a tremendous capacity for knowing what was going on. He certainly knew how to put you under pressure. He could come back at you fast." Frank had a trick of arguing against David's plans, not because he disagreed with them but because the argument itself put the heat on in advance. "You knew then," David said, "that once you made the decision you'd have to work like hell to make sure it turned out right." On the other hand, Frank sometimes argued simply because he thought "the boys" were wrong. "He once said," David recalled, "that one of the hardest things he ever did was letting us make mistakes."

Frank's dedication to the IEL cause may be seen in the fact that, all told, he attended 140, or better than eighty-two per cent, of the directors' meetings during his term as president, a further 139 IEL committee meetings, and board meetings of the IEL subsidiary, Springhill Development Corporation. Directors frequently deliberated all morning, sent out for sandwiches at noon, deliberated all afternoon. But particularly for Frank and Harold Egan, attending meetings was only the smallest part of the job. Getting a battery factory to move from Salem, Massachusetts, to the most famous hard-luck town in Canada was an early example of how they operated outside the boardroom.

Springhill, N.S., was a synonym for horror, a catchbasin for misery. On November 1, 1956, an explosion in No. 4 Colliery killed thirty-nine men. On December 26, 1957, a black gift for Boxing Day, a fire gutted the town's commercial district. Meanwhile, DOSCO had announced it would never again open No. 4, and 450 miners were out of work. The huge old No. 2 still employed nearly 900 men, but a clergyman warned Springhill would be "a ghost town" if No. 2 ever closed. It closed. On October 23, 1958, the last great Springhill "bump" doomed the last great DOSCO colliery in town, and killed seventy-five miners. If Nova Scotia's industrial future looked bleak, Springhill's looked black. If Nova Scotia needed treatment, Springhill needed intensive care. It was an economic paralytic.

Stanfield therefore decided to waive IEL rules in Springhill's case. "The special assistance offered to industries to locate in Springhill was much more than offered by Industrial Estates Limited," Frank wrote in IEL's second annual report. "A subsidiary company, Springhill Development Corporation Limited, was formed to handle the Springhill situation." Under its authority, he set out to buy a factory.

Stanfield, he remembered, told him, "Look, if you can get some kind of industry for Springhill, make a deal you wouldn't normally make. We've got to get something in there." Shortly after that, W. N. White, marketing man in Nova Scotia for Surrette Battery, tipped off IEL that the company was up for sale. Frank and Harold Egan hustled down to Salem and reached John J. Surrette's office on a Friday afternoon. They were too late, but maybe they weren't. Surrette had given his partner an option to buy the business. If he couldn't get money to buy the other fellow out on Monday morning, then the other fellow would buy him out; and since Surrette didn't have the money, it appeared Springhill would never get a battery factory.

"So here we were on the Friday afternoon," Frank said. "Surrette called in his auditor, and Harold and I talked to him. We called up Surrette's banker in Boston. We called White in Nova Scotia. We got good reports, and everything seemed fairly good. So we said, 'Well, where will we get the money?' " That night they phoned Horace Enman in Toronto, "and Mr. Enman said, 'I know the president of that bank [Surrette's, in Boston], and I'll call him up, but you buggers [Frank and Harold Egan] will have to sign the note.' I said, 'Personally?' He says, 'Yes.' So Harold and I signed the note personally. When we came back and told Mr. Stanfield, he said, 'Get it out of your names fast,' which we did.

"Here's how it worked: we bought out the partner, and took Surrette's shares as collateral. We made an arrangement with him that when the loans were paid off, he'd get all the shares. So we founded Surrette Battery of Springhill, which bought out the American company." All of which explains why the balance sheet for the first annual report (for fiscal 1958-59) of Springhill Development Corporation shows a "Contingent Liability" of $127,500 "Re: Surrette Battery Company Limited and John J. Surrette".

Now, however, Frank had yet another sticky problem. The battery-making machinery was in Salem, and he had to get it to Springhill. But the duties that Canadian border officials imposed on such equipment were so steep the whole deal suddenly looked rotten. Frank went to Ottawa to see fellow Nova Scotian George Nowlan. "A shaggy St. Bernard of a man and a topnotch Minister of National Revenue," Peter C. Newman wrote (*Renegade in Power*, 1963), "[Nowlan] was surely one of the most charming politicians ever sworn into a Canadian cabinet." What charmed Frank about Nowlan, however, was not his shaggy-dog looks but his speedy solution to the border problem:

"At first, Mr. Nowlan says, 'There's nothing I can do for you. I can't do anything about the tariff structure. That's set by the government.' 'Well,' I said, 'that's too bad.' I talked to him for a minute, and I was just going out the door when he whistled and called me back. He says, 'I can lower the value of the shipment.' So I said, 'That's all I want to know. We'll put a value of a few dollars on it,' which we did, and we got it in pretty cheap. So Surrette Battery was a pretty safe deal." And Nowlan was a friend indeed. By 1961 Surrette Battery, Springhill, was employing fifty workers, and twenty years later it was still in business.

IEL soon lost its second general manager. Fred Blair had agreed to take on the job for only two years and, though fighting illness, stuck it out for an extra six months. "Fred's health wasn't so good," Frank said, "and he also had his wholesale business to look after,

The IEL Board, June 1965. First row (seated) left to right: General K. C. Appleyard, W. S. K. Jones, S. W. Kenney, G. I. Smith, R. L. Stanfield, F. H. Sobey, J. C. MacKeen, C. G. MacLennan, J. W. Gillis, S. G. Allen. Standing, left to right: D. F. Archibald, B. J. Waters, R. S. Brookfield, H. J. Egan, Ross Macleod, R. W. M. Manuge, R. G. Urquhart, Claude Carter.

so after about the fifth time he resigned, I said to Fred, 'Well you really mean it, don't you?' and I accepted his resignation."

Blair had achieved a fair bit. During his term IEL helped to establish sixteen light industries: five in the Halifax-Dartmouth area, two in Springhill, and one in each of Stellarton, Weymouth, Lunenburg, Truro, Stewiacke, Yarmouth, North Sydney, Oxford, and Kentville. Moreover, IEL was now collecting significant rent – $103,658.52 for the year ending March 31, 1961. Not bad for an outfit with a full-time staff of five, and only a part-time agent in each of Toronto and London.

The Springhill *Record* used Blair's retirement as an excuse to lodge a complaint against IEL and Stanfield's government. The battery factory and other sputtering efforts to settle new industries in Springhill just weren't good enough: "It seems to have been forgotten that nearly six hundred men are still walking the streets in Springhill, assisted by advances from the Disaster Relief Fund, which is rapidly diminishing. The situation in Cape Breton seems to have stolen the limelight – and the fact that more men are walking the streets here than in Cape Breton seems to have been forgotten." This was an early expression of criticism IEL could not escape. No matter what outside praise it gained, no matter how carefully Stanfield selected directors to represent different corners of the province, no matter how conscientiously IEL tried to sprinkle its clients, it was forever being pilloried for favouring one district over another. Every corner of the province resented what every other corner was getting, and IEL could never dissolve local paranoia. Remembering the ceaseless flak much later, Frank said, "We had to let our clients choose their locations. People who can be pushed around for the wrong reasons aren't good operators."

Still, it had escaped no one's notice in the early sixties that both the president and the first effective general manager of IEL were Stellarton men, and that the first industry the agency attracted went to Stellarton. This was Donato Faini & Figli (Canada) Ltd., an Italian-owned knitting mill. Truro grumbled. Wasn't it the leading textile town in the province?

By 1968, IEL had also brought to Stellarton a typewriter factory, an envelope factory, and, in a splashy (and eventually disastrous) foray into equity ownership, Clairtone Sound Corporation, Ltd., makers of stereo sets for the carriage trade. Moreover, within a year Frank would announce what he regarded as IEL's crowning achievement: its successful persuasion of the Michelin tire empire of France to build factories in Bridgewater, N.S., and, more important to him, at Granton, Pictou County. Not only that, he'd taken a personal hand in 1963-64 in getting Scott Paper Company Ltd. of Pennsylvania to choose Point Abercrombie, Pictou County, as the site for a massive new pulp mill. "We weren't involved with

IEL in a formal way, not as a client," Walter Miller, president of Scott Maritimes, Ltd., said. "But it extended all the courtesies and helpfulness it could. They stood by with advice, consultation, and assistance, primarily through Frank Sobey himself." It was IEL that arranged for Scott Maritimes to get a break on its property taxes.

Miller was a regular guest in the Sobeys' new home. In 1963 Frank decided to live outside Stellarton for the first time in six decades. He bought land on the shore of Pictou Harbour, roughly halfway between Stellarton and his birthplace at Lyons Brook; and, there, he and Irene built an airy brick house with pillars that give it a vaguely Dixie Land look. It boasted gold-plated bathroom taps, an outdoor swimming pool, and enough wall-space to hang his growing collection of fine Canadian paintings.

One of Frank's first guests at the mansion he called "Crombie" was Lord David Garnock, of the ancient firm of John Crossley and Sons, Ltd., suppliers of more than half the British rugs and carpets sold in Canada, exporters to more than a hundred countries. Prompted by IEL, the British-owned Crossley would shortly enter a Canadian marriage with the American-owned Fieldcrest Mills to spawn Crossley Karastan Carpet Mills, Ltd., of Truro, N.S. That was an IEL triumph, and if the IEL president was to hobnob with such corporate giants from abroad, then the unpretentious white frame house on Allan Avenue, home to his children and dogs for thirty-odd years, would no longer do.

Frank and Irene invited bankers, industrialists, and senior bureaucrats to gatherings at Crombie, and, since the new Scott pulp mill was just along the road, Walter Miller came, too. A. Garnet Brown, food wholesaler and provincial cabinet minister (1970-78), said, "Nobody had more influence in locating that mill in Pictou County than Frank did. It was originally going to Sheet Harbour [in Halifax County]." What was good for Pictou County, as a rule, was good for Frank. He was a half-owner in the construction company that got the job of clearing and levelling the huge site for the mill. He and Miller became fishing and golfing buddies. Frank was a director of another pulp industry, Fraser Companies, and it was typical of him that he'd grill Miller on Scott's woodland management and then ask Fraser executives why they weren't doing the same things. Fraser's president finally asked Miller "to please quit telling Frank all those stories."

The location of Scott Maritimes, Michelin, Clairtone, and the smaller industries in what was once Bear Brook Park aroused criticism that Frank wielded excessive influence on behalf of his own bailiwick. But according to Stellarton-born Lance Hale, later of Halifax, the reaction to such criticism along the East River was, "Goddamn right. We knew Frank wouldn't let us down." As so many said, Frank was a Pictou County man.

Fred Blair's retirement meant that for the third time in four years Frank had to find a general manager. He knew whom he wanted: Robert W. M. Manuge. "I went in to see the premier," Frank said, "and asked him if he had anyone in mind. He said, 'No. Have you?' I said, 'Yes,' and Mr. Stanfield just said, 'Why don't you go get him?' He didn't even ask who it was, so I told him Bob Manuge." But Manuge was canny. He wanted the confidence of the entire board and wouldn't take the job till every director agreed to his appointment. Some had nominees of their own. Frank knew that if he called a board meeting, "They'd all start talking, and we'd never get it settled." He therefore leaned on each director in private. "I only had a couple of days," he said, "and I had a hell of a time." Still, he prevailed. In June 1961 Robert Manuge, thirty-nine, went to work for IEL. Its most spectacular years now began. They would bring fame not only to Manuge but also to Frank, to Stanfield, and indeed even to Nova Scotia. "If Frank had done nothing else than bring in Bob Manuge," Manson recalled, "he'd have justified his existence at IEL. Manuge was the best salesman I ever heard."

He was also a driven man. He was the fourteenth of fifteen children of a struggling lumber dealer in South Brook, six miles from Springhill, Cumberland County. He hated his childhood in that rough-edged, poverty-stricken, culturally isolated community. Observers have suggested that his near-fanatical drive stemmed from an obsession with acquiring so much money and prestige that the horrors of his South Brook years would no longer haunt him.

At sixteen, Manuge had kicked the manure off his feet, moved to Amherst, N.S., taken night courses in business, landed a job with Canadian National Railways, and picked up social graces from "a very fine lady who treated me like a son". She was a cousin of multimillionaire financier Izaak Walton Killam. By 1952 Manuge was in Montreal as divisional manager for Hussman Refrigeration Company, Ltd., which sold coolers to supermarkets. He was still only thirty-one, and it was in that job that Frank, ever watchful for good men he might one day steal, first noticed him.

By the time Blair quit, Frank had not only heard Manuge's persuasive sales pitches, sometimes by phone at 7 a.m., but also crossed swords with him. Sobeys Stores, Ltd., had tried to claim damages after its Hussman refrigeration equipment had failed during a weekend, but Manuge discovered that the real cause of the breakdown had been an outside power failure. The chain cancelled the claim. Frank liked men who got up early, and stayed up late to do their homework.

When Frank first pursued him, Manuge had just quit Hussman to join Bolands, Ltd., a Dartmouth-based supplier to IGA grocery stores, and for a while there was a pretence he was only taking a leave of absence from Bolands. "We look forward to the day with anxiety and with pleasure when his services with IEL have been brought to a satisfactory conclusion," Roy W. Boland said, "and he will be back with us in our expansion program." But Bolands, Ltd., like Hussman and indeed South Brook, was already far behind Robert William Merlin Manuge. He promptly joined the right clubs, the Royal Nova Scotia Yacht Squadron and the venerable Halifax Club (only $150 for entrance, and $58.30 for subscription in those days), and plunged into the career of his life as Nova Scotia's fast-talking, glad-handing, quick-stepping, high-flying industrial missionary. It would take him roughly two million miles by air to reach hundreds of industrialists, bankers, and factories in thirty-three countries.

Frank Sobey, Charles MacCulloch, Morley Taylor, Robert Manuge, and J. C. MacKeen, 1965.

He had the bland, even features and slicked-back hair of a Grade B movie star, but there was nothing bland about his manner. No politician was better at pressing the flesh. His elaborate courtesy camouflaged his zeal. He seemed to be curiously beseeching but at the same time reasonable, deeply appreciative of your problems, and willing to let you in on an awfully good thing. His conversational style was a rare mix of confidential disclosure, formal correctness, and public oratory, and it all worked on many powerful men. He was effective in public, effective behind closed doors. "He knew how to handle himself with heads of companies," Frank said.

Manuge had been on the job scarcely six months when *Marketing* (Nov. 16, 1961) said IEL's aim was "to replace the tradititional picture of Nova Scotia as a fog-shrouded land of patient dory fishermen with one of great industrial potential," and that "The drive took on new impetus this year when Robert Manuge was hired as general manager." *Time* (Jan. 19, 1962) said, "When [Manuge] learned that more than 100 companies had built plants in Ontario without even considering Nova Scotia, he hired a man in Ontario to make Nova Scotia's case." Media admiration was just beginning. By 1963, the press was calling Manuge "dynamic", "suave", IEL's "chief sleuth" and "star salesman", a "down-east supersalesman".

Manuge made as many calls as he could without collapsing, as the pushiest salesmen have always done, and he wrote thousands of letters. He claimed IEL sent hundreds for every client it landed. But it was the glamour of his jet-setting that gave IEL its aggressive, worldly image. Some Nova Scotians sceptically wondered why he had to travel so often, and in such lavish style, but others liked to see a bluenose supersalesman hustling the world on their behalf. He earned a reputation, later pooh-poohed by his critics, as a man who got industries to settle in Nova Scotia simply by cornering tycoons aboard international jets.

On a Montreal-New York flight, he befriended the wife of a top executive of Citroën, French auto-makers; and later, through her husband, he gained an acquaintanceship with François Michelin. That was the beginning of negotiations that in 1969 inspired Michelin Tire to establish its North American beachhead in Nova Scotia. Moreover, on a Far Eastern flight, Stephen Kimber said (*Financial Post Magazine*), "Manuge charmed Indian industrialist Govind Jolly into establishing Anil Canada Limited, a $30-million hardboard manufacturing plant, in tiny East River along Nova Scotia's south shore." Jolly had confirmed the story. "We were having a drink in the lounge of a Japan Airlines jet going from Tokyo to Hong Kong," he told the Halifax *Chronicle-Herald* (March 27, 1965). "We started talking business, and I soon began to find things out about Nova Scotia. It was a most fortunate meeting."

IEL put up $7 million to finance the site, building, and some machinery for Anil, which turned out to be its most bizarre adventure. No Indian firm had ever before involved itself in so substantial a manufacturing enterprise in North America, and this alone earned IEL publicity in the New York press. Moreover, it's doubtful if any factory in Canada ever had such a spate of exotic inauguration ceremonies. On February 2, 1967, the Halifax *Chronicle-Herald* reported, "While onlookers shivered in bitter cold officials of Bombay-based Anil Canada Limited and the province's IEL broke coconuts and burned incense in a special Hindu christening of machinery at the Indian company's new hardboard plant. . . . Coconut milk and red dust were sprinkled over a control panel." Then, only two months later, the austere-looking Robert Stanfield, the dapper Robert Manuge, and assorted bureaucrats received garlands of roses at the plant, and "had their foreheads dabbed with vermilion paint in the traditional Hindu 'talik'."

As if two ceremonies weren't enough, the Moslem president of India, Dr. Zakir Husain, showed up on June 30, 1967. He was bound for Expo 67 in Montreal, but he went to East River so he could "officially" open the plant by clouting a coconut with a hammer and spilling the milk on some machinery. Anil Canada was well and truly opened, but its elephant was not long for this world.

"Balkrishnan" weighed three and a half tons, and his job was to carry wood in Anil's lumberyard. He arrived in a splash of publicity three weeks after Dr. Husain, and he was fine in summer. A victim of the Canadian winter and perhaps of some neglect, he caught a condition like pneumonia. As he weakened, lady animal-lovers who belonged to the Kindness Club of Halifax began to knit huge bootees for him. Before he could try them on, he expired. Some years later, so did Anil Canada, which was bought by Masonite of Canada.

Frank and Manuge, on the face of things, were an unlikely team. Frank disliked speechifying. Manuge revelled in it. Frank distrusted the press. His idea of a good newspaper was one that printed your releases exactly as you sent them out, and kept its nose out of your affairs. Manuge basked in media attention. When Frank got media compliments it was for being shrewd, astute. His were the talents of a man at work with other men behind closed doors. He was something of a fixer. Manuge was the flashiest of front men. Frank behaved like the plain-spoken Stellarton man he had always been, but Manuge seemed to have invented his supersalesman personality.

Despite personality differences, Frank and Manuge had important things in common. They had both quit school early in favour of business courses and making money. As Manuge liked to point out even a dozen years after they'd left IEL, "We're both self-made men, and we're both self-starters." Moreover, they both had abnormal energy and, like the Canada Packers men Frank admired, they started to work early every morning, often at 6 a.m. "If I get up early, it's to answer a phone call from Mr. Sobey, who has already started his day's work," Manuge told a New Glasgow audience in 1967. He called Frank "the master salesman of Canada". Such comments were not a matter of sucking up to the boss. In 1982, Manuge's regard for Frank still verged on hero-worship.

"From the moment I started at IEL," Manuge said, "I could phone him at any time of the day or night, and he'd *always* be courteous. He never complained about me waking him up, and he never said he was too busy, and to call him back later. This was vitally important, because if he'd been brusque I'd have quit calling him." Manuge admired Frank's boardroom ability "to cut his way right through the underbrush to the tall timber."

"Bob turned out to be a real top man at IEL," Frank said. "He was like a high-spirited horse. He had a good mind and he was a worker. You didn't have to be pushing him all the time. I was in touch with him practically every day, but when you get a man like that you give him freedom to operate. Bob wasn't scared to travel. He spent more than half his time travelling. He liked breakfast meetings with potential clients, and that was smart. There's no booze on the table at breakfast, and since they've got to get to their offices, they don't waste time."

Frank knew, however, that even Manuge could not get his foot into corporate doors without help. He knew that only the president or chairman of a company had authority to locate or enlarge a plant; that politicians weren't much good at arranging interviews with corporate biggies; and, finally, that corporations always appointed an amiable fellow to hear out visitors from government and send them away with nothing but a warm feeling. Big businessmen reserved their time for discussions with other big businessmen, and big bankers. So sometimes it was Frank who got IEL's man in to see the boss and sometimes, in the early days, it was Horace Enman. "Whether in England, or any part of the United States," Frank said, "Mr. Enman would use the Bank of Nova Scotia to make an appointment." Later, Enman's successor as IEL chairman, J. C. MacKeen, often served as the door-opener. He was the senior director of the Royal Bank, and "we used the Royal, especially in Paris." When it came to setting up the right interviews, arranging the right contacts, and even providing transportation in foreign cities, Canadian banks could be immensely helpful.

"Bob Manuge was a great one for talking to the industrial-development departments of the banks," Frank said. "He got to know the Royal Bank people in Paris, the Bank of Nova Scotia people in London, and some of the banks in Hong Kong. That way, we found leads and followed them up. We also had directors like Jack MacKeen who were ready to work, and ready to travel on a moment's notice." Moreover, in November 1961 IEL named what the *Globe and Mail* called a "spanking new advisory board", an international network of highly placed bluenose old boys to give the agency prestige, advice, information, and sometimes an entrée.

They included J. S. D. Tory, Toronto, the same merger-master who'd helped engineer the DOSCO takeover; Henry Borden, Toronto, president of Brazilian Traction, Light and Power; Charles Gasvie, a prominent Montreal lawyer who'd been president of the St. Lawrence Seaway Authority; K. M. Sedgewick, Montreal, investment counsellor, executive vice-president of W. C. Pitfield & Company, Ltd.; Ross MacLeod, New York, vice-president and general counsel, New York Life Insurance; and in 1962, Alfred C. Fuller, the founder and, at seventy-eight, still the chairman of the Fuller Brush Company, Hartford, Conn. These men were examples of the very brain drain that IEL hoped to stanch. All except

Tory were Nova Scotians by birth, and he was the son of a Nova Scotian. "They gave us some knowledge of big industries across the continent," E. A. Manson recalled. "They were an unpaid Fifth Column. For instance, MacLeod was from Sydney but he lived in New York, and when Manuge was going down there he'd phone him up. So MacLeod acted as the advance agent for Manuge."

By 1962, IEL had hired Ernest K. Birmann, formerly the industrial commissioner of Barrie, Ont., as its full-time man in central Canada, and Sir Robert Hadow, an ex-diplomat, was its part-time man in London. In '63, it named Colonel Robert Solborg as a Special European Representative. Solborg's life had been so hair-raising that he gave IEL a touch of panache. The son of a Czarist army officer, he was himself a cavalry officer and in 1914 was knocked off his horse by an Austrian's lance. He soon popped up in Trenton and New Glasgow to oversee the construction of railway cars for the Russian government, but then in 1917 the revolution broke out. Since he could not go home without risking a Bolshevik firing squad, he took a job at the local steelworks. He had another good reason for lingering near the East River. His marriage to Virginia Underwood of New Glasgow made him a Pictou County boy. During the Second World War, he worked as a spy for the British, was captured and tortured by the Gestapo in Paris, escaped, and finished the war in the U.S. army. He earned honours and decorations from eight countries, and spoke eight languages. Now, in 1963, his home was Paris. He was the ex-president of the European subsidiaries of Armco Steel Corporation, Middleton, Ohio, and a man who knew his way around.

Back in Halifax, Manuge worked up colour brochures in assorted languages to spread the word about Nova Scotia's universities, government labs, superior social environment, transportation advantages, and indeed every conceivable asset from a "temperate climate" to a "stable, intelligent work force". One IEL publication trumpeted that "The great port of Halifax, at which ships of all nations call, is the nearest year-round, ice-free port on the North American mainland to Britain, Europe, Africa and points beyond – and nearer to Rio de Janeiro and Buenos Aires than is New York."

IEL advertised all over the world, and it sent out this flood of stuff about "The New Nova Scotia" from a Halifax office with only a handful of staff.

"I told the premier once, and I've always believed this," Frank said, "that if IEL grew to the point where it had more than a dozen people, it would become ineffective. It would just become another arm of the government, which would be duplicating work of the department of trade and industry." With regard to administrative costs, Mingo said, "He believed in running things on a shoestring. That was his philosophy. It was one reason why IEL never had an in-house lawyer. He'd have to be paid for whatever time he wasn't actually working on IEL cases. It was why Frank insisted on running IEL with a paid staff of Bob Manuge, a guy to fill in when Bob was away, and a couple of girls." Not everyone approved of the tightness of Frank's ship. In 1974 Professor Roy George complained, "In 1968, with assets approaching $100 million and over fifty clients, there were only twelve staff, of which half were secretaries! An aversion to empire-building is commendable, but should not be carried to absurdity."

But Frank had wanted a catalyst. After he quit, he said, IEL became what he'd always feared it could become: "a milk cow". In the sixties he'd had all the staff he'd needed. He'd also had Harold Egan.

It was a tribute to Stanfield's determination not to let partisan considerations infect IEL that Harold Egan, its first secretary-treasurer, was a dyed-in-the-wool Liberal. He had stumped for the Grits. Egan's widow, Mrs. Howard Elliot, said he was "a lovable, stubborn Irishman" and a work addict: "Everything Harold did was work and home, home and business. We used to go to Barbados every winter, but after a week there, he'd just be going out of his mind. He'd be on the phone down there, talking to Frank up here." Mingo worked closely with Frank and Egan on deal after deal, year after year, and he said, "They were a great team. They were the ones who sent IEL on its creative streak. They were both highly imaginative businessmen."

Harold was a detail man. Frank preferred to grasp the concepts, strike the basic deal, let others tidy up, and push on to something else. In typical negotiations, Frank and Egan would bargain together with a potential client, Frank would leave, then Mingo would join Egan. "Frank appeared to have a short attention span," Mingo recalled, "but maybe this was just because he had so much on his plate." In any event, "He couldn't have operated without Egan. He depended on him as a crutch. Frank never read anything. Harold read everything. Frank would call him up, and Harold would brief him."

Frank had certainly been a detail man when he'd worked nights on the books of Sobey Stores in the thirties, but now he was the boss. To look after the numbers and legal clauses, he relied on the best professionals he could find. In March 1968 he underwent a grilling by the Industry Committee of the Nova Scotia legislature, and when he couldn't answer questions about the details of IEL operations, he simply said, "I'm not a figure man. I'd like to have a good figure man with me, or a lawyer that can figure. . . ."

Thirteen years later, when Frank was seventy-nine, American lawyers interrogated him for hours in a Halifax hotel room, and Frank's cavalier attitude towards the pesky details of his own business affairs seemed to strike his inquisitors as scarcely believable. One of the lawyers, Robert A. Moore, represented Hannaford Brothers, Ltd. - a New England supermarket chain which so feared a takeover by Sobeys Stores, Ltd., that it had launched a civil action to put a ceiling on share purchases by the Sobeys. In reply to one question, Frank couldn't even tell Moore whether or not he was actually an officer of Empire Company Ltd. "I may be," he said blithely. "It runs in my mind there were some changes made in the officers' listing of Empire. . . . Perhaps they shoved me upstairs. I don't know. It'll say right there [in the 1981 annual report of Empire]." He was chairman of the board. "So that as chairman of the board," Moore persisted, "you're an officer in Empire Company. Is that right?" "Yeah, yeah, if I am," Frank replied. "If it says [so] there, I am."

Frank also told his inquisitors in the Hannaford case, "If I get a lawyer to make up something for me and he says that's okay, I

Premier Robert Stanfield and IEL's first Secretary-Treasurer, Harold Egan, May 1964.

sign it. If I find a letter is not okay, perhaps I get a new laywer. . . . I don't go and read those fine prints. I wouldn't hire the lawyer if I did." Recalling Hannaford's having presented him with a twenty-one-page legal agreement, he said, "I don't like to sign long documents 'cause I haven't got the time to read them, and if I do read them, after I get over two or three pages I forget what was on the other page, and I have to go back and see. . . ." Now he put a needle into the profession of those who were wasting his day: "No money in it for legal counsel when they have a short agreement. . . . Yeah, twenty-one pages. That's ridiculous, you know, stupid."

At IEL, Mingo said, "Frank was very good at absorbing instructions verbally, but if you passed him more than a page and a half, he wouldn't read it. . . . Suppose we strike a deal here in the office at two o'clock on a Saturday afternoon. Well, Frank would say, 'Okay, can we sign this in one hour's time?' It might be a very complicated deal, but he acted as though it were the sort of thing you could draw up on the back of an envelope." When Mingo explained why the paperwork might take a while, Frank would abuse the legal profession about complicating things to drive up their bill. He'd start, "You lawyers . . ."

But the penalty for not having a complicated document might be more severe than Frank's bad-mouthing lawyers. What he really wanted, Mingo said, were dozens of out-clauses "so that if the deal soured, or he wanted to change it, he could turn the screw on somebody. . . . He was not good at shouldering blame, so you knew that if he didn't have the right out-clause when the time came to use it, then it would be 'the lawyer's fault'." Frank didn't know he wanted so many loopholes, but any lawyer who hoped to continue working for him swallowed some abuse and provided them. "He knew what he wanted," Mingo said, "but there were a lot of other things he didn't know he wanted. He expected the people who worked for him to understand him better than he understood himself."

He was, in short, a prickly client, but despite his harangues he was trusting. His habit of simply signing on the dotted line gave a lawyer the leeway to be innovative and creative. That, in Mingo's opinion, made Frank "a good client. I learned an awful lot from him." (Advised in 1981 that Mingo had enjoyed his IEL years because Frank had allowed him to be creative, Frank said, "If a man doesn't enjoy what he's doing, he should find another line of work, and if a lawyer isn't creative, what good is he?") On leeway, Mingo said, "It was Frank who gave Bob Manuge his head, and Bob hasn't been able to work for anyone since."

By 1981, Mingo was a man whose judgment had been confirmed by appointments to the boards of the Bank of Canada and at least nineteen companies. His judgment of Frank was that "He really is larger than life. He's no common variety type of person. I'm a great admirer of his." On a rainy Saturday afternoon in May, at Mingo's roomy office at Stewart, MacKeen & Covert, Halifax, he remembered the IEL of the sixties and, Grit though he was, he applauded Stanfield's invention: "I think the team of Stanfield, Sobey, Egan, and Manuge was brilliant. They were a really gifted crowd, and I don't think anyone in the province appreciated quite how gifted at the time."

Few government-funded agencies anywhere have ever received the press flattery that IEL inspired in the mid-sixties. The announcement of each new industry it lured to Nova Scotia aroused breathless compliments. Accolades rolled in from across the continent. As early as November 23, 1962, *Marketing* headed a story "How IEL ousts the dole from Nova Scotia". On February 23, 1963, the

Halifax *Chronicle-Herald* said IEL "remains the most effective self-help organization that we in Nova Scotia have yet established." On September 6, 1963, *Time* lauded Stanfield for "the thirty-odd manufacturing plants which have sprouted across the province under the government-sired [IEL]". When the Tories almost obliterated the Opposition in the election of October 1963 - the new Assembly consisted of thirty-nine Conservatives and four Liberals - the Halifax *Chronicle-Herald* suggested IEL was already so sacred a cow that what did in the Grits was daring to knock it.

Before the year was out, the *Financial Post* (Nov. 18, 1963) said, "Something called IEL is handling the formidable task of restoring Nova Scotia to a more prominent position in Canada's economic picture [with] startling success." On November 28, 1964, the *Globe and Mail* noted a debate in the Ontario Legislature about Ontario's weak industrial promotion, and then commented, "When the industrial progress of Nova Scotia begins to worry mighty Ontario, the mouse has indeed begun to roar." Only weeks later, the *Atlantic Advocate* headed a story "Industrial Estates and the Remarkable Frank Sobey", and went on from there: "Nova Scotia is riding the happiest economic wave in its history as [IEL], like a ship laden with good tidings, brings home cargo after cargo of new industries."

The *Financial Times* of London (July 2, 1965) lauded IEL for having brought "forty new industrial plants to the Canadian province and [creating] jobs for about 4,000 people." The *New York Times* (Aug. 29, 1965) blared, "Rise of New Vigor Stirs Nova Scotia"; the *American Banker* (Oct. 6, 1965) declared, "Nova Scotia Leaps into Mainstream"; and when two bluenose cabinet ministers explained how IEL worked to an audience in Los Angeles, *Hollywood Citizen News* ("The Voice of the Golden Westside") burbled, "We wish California could be operated with Nova Scotia's businesslike efficiency." And so it continued, year after year.

Stanfield went to the polls again in May 1967. This time, he whupped the Opposition by merely forty to six. You could attribute his victory to the fact that almost everyone agreed with G. I. Smith, his chief cabinet lieutenant, that IEL had "done more to make the name of Nova Scotia well and favorably known throughout the world than anything since the days of wooden ships and iron men, and our ships and men were known wherever ships and men could go."

By the time IEL celebrated its tenth anniversary, in September 1967, it had spent more than $75 million to help industries from eight countries settle or expand in Nova Scotia; and Smith boasted that, directly and indirectly, it had created nine thousand jobs. Some industries had faltered but only four failed, and IEL found new owners for each of the four. Scattered about the province were IEL-assisted plants that churned out everything from fish to fibreglass, from paper boxes to aluminum cans, from boats to glue, from cement to rugs, sweaters, industrial belting, electronic equipment, flour, envelopes, and even automobiles.

An early IEL success was Formex Company of Canada, which arrived in Kentville in 1961. It made a fabric blanket for use in paper-making machines, and Frank's friend Roy Jodrey, who was not an IEL director but was a knowledgeable pulp-and-paper man, had a hand in getting the American owners of Formex to consider his beloved Annapolis Valley as a location for the $3-million plant. In the same year, IEL helped National Sea Products (through its subsidiary Lunenburg Sea Products, Ltd.) to finance a major expansion that gave Lunenburg what the Halifax *Chronicle-Herald* (Sept. 27, 1961) called "the most modern and efficient fish-processing plant in North America, and probably one of the most modern in the world." This, said Lunenburg mayor R. G. A. Wood, "ensures our future." After that, Canada Envelope came to Stellarton, Crossley Karastan Carpet Mills and Canada Cement Company Ltd. came to Truro, and by 1964, IEL had thirty-six clients. But the publicity coup of them all was the arrival at a former sugar refinery in Dartmouth of an assembly plant for Sweden's Volvo automobiles.

"Volvo" is Latin for "I roll", and in early 1963 the press bandwagon for Volvo and IEL rolled and rolled. Volvo was not only the first auto-manufacturer to establish a factory anywhere in Canada outside Ontario but also the first European car-maker ever to run an assembly plant in North America, and the Halifax *Mail-Star* (Feb. 21, 1963) was beside itself with ecstasy. Under an eight-column front-page headline, "Swedish Auto Manufacturer Will Open Dartmouth Plant", it ran a five-column colour photograph of a brown four-door Volvo with red, white, and blue wheels. "Automobiles like this," the caption helpfully explained, "will be assembled at [the Dartmouth plant]." A front-page editorial described Volvo's coming as "the most heartening news Nova Scotians have heard for a long time. . . . Would that there were more days like this in the Halifax-Dartmouth region."

The paper sent a man all the way to Gothenburg, Sweden, so he could report, among other things, that Volvo chairman Gunnar Engellau had "quiet, Viking-blue eyes, a trim athletic build and a mind that works as smoothly as the engines of the 100,000 quality motor vehicles his company produces annually." Once again Stanfield made *Time* (March 1, 1963): "Glowed Premier Robert Stanfield, 'This is something we haven't had before, and we hope other industries will follow.'" Rumours spread that Japanese, French, Italian, and Austrian auto-makers were now eyeing Nova Scotia favourably and that it was out to become "another Detroit".

Prince Bertil of Sweden drove the first car off the Dartmouth assembly line on June 11, and by then the arrival of Volvo had silenced all but the most partisan or axe-grinding of IEL's critics. Moreover, it had served as a signal to other international corporate giants, and they came to Nova Scotia thick and fast. Not only that, Nova Scotians learned in December 1963 that their government and IEL had snatched from western provinces the biggest plum of all: a $30-million heavy-water plant, Deuterium of Canada, Ltd., for Glace Bay, Cape Breton Island. IEL was putting $12 million into it. In view of the fiasco the plant was doomed to become, it's ironic to recall how overjoyed Nova Scotians were that the province would now share the glamour of the atomic age.

It was a measure of Nova Scotia's triumph that Premier W. A. C. Bennett, national NDP leader Tommy Douglas, and other western politicans expressed bitterness about Deuterium's decision to settle at Glace Bay. Russ Brown, a Saskatchewan cabi-

J. S. Murchie, a director of Empire Company Limited and president of Sobeys Stores Limited.

net minister, complained of "rank discrimination", and a Vancouver newspaper wondered nastily how long all Canada must shell out taxpayers' dollars to enable Cape Breton Islanders to live in Cape Breton. Dismissing such talk, the Cape Breton *Post* (Dec. 7, 1963) said IEL had "initiated and developed the project months before western Canada had heard about it."

That wasn't true. As Linden MacIntyre, the Halifax *Chronicle-Herald*'s Cape Breton correspondent, explained in an exhaustive series in 1971, Jerome S. Spevack, father of Deuterium of Canada, Ltd. (DCL), had originally proposed a plant in Alberta. Moreover, Dr. J. L. Gray, president of Atomic Energy of Canada, favoured a British Columbia competitor of DCL. MacIntyre said, "A Toronto lawyer, Alex MacIntosh, steered Mr. Spevack to Nova Scotia in the first place – and he was later one of Mr. Spevack's nominees on the board." MacIntosh was a Stellarton boy.

If Cape Breton was happy about DCL, Pictou County was giddy about Clairtone Sound Corporation, Ltd. The fabulous news broke on November 19, 1964, and the New Glasgow *Evening News* devoted most of its back page and its entire front page to the story. In screaming-red two-inch letters, suitable for the arrival of a divine being, it announced "CLAIRTONE COMING TO COUNTY", and offered up platitudes from every dignitary it could find. Those of the New Glasgow mayor were typical: "This could be the beginning of an economic expansion of undreamed-of possibilities for our area. Industry begets industry. The fact that Clairtone has chosen our area cannot help but cause other industries and businessmen to look in this direction."

The Halifax *Chronicle-Herald* also celebrated the announcement with a red headline and breathless prose: "Nova Scotia has been chosen – against all comers – as the base of a new $8-million expansion by Canada's fastest-growing manufacturer of domestic sound equipment. Clairtone Sound Corporation, Ltd. of Rexdale, Ont., is . . . moving, lock, stock and barrel, to a futuristic production plant to be built in Pictou County. . . . By April next year [1965] the first phase of the 250,000 square-foot operation will be in production, making television sets as well as a wide range of high-quality stereophonic, high-fidelity, radio-phonograph combinations. Initially, between 600 and 700 people will be employed [but] the eventual staff may be in the region of 2,000."

The first talk about Stanfield's chances of becoming prime minister occurred in 1963, the year IEL announced the coming of Volvo, Crossley Karastan, the Reynolds can factory, Canada Cement, and Deuterium of Canada. In *Maclean's* (Nov. 16, 1963), a writer speculated, "If John Diefenbaker quits the Tory leadership fairly soon, and if the Ontario Tories don't want Manitoba Premier Duff Roblin to replace him, and if the Prairie Tories reject Ontario Premier John Robarts, and if some darker Tory horse doesn't make a marvelous spurt for the wire, then the next leader of the federal Conservatives will likely be the bony premier of Nova Scotia, Robert L. Stanfield."

As IEL triumph followed IEL triumph, the speculation grew until Stanfield won the leadership of the federal Tories on September 9, 1967, formally quit as premier four days later, and entered the Commons as Leader of the Opposition on November 15. For another decade he'd be centre-stage in national politics. IEL, to a large degree, had changed the course of his life.

IEL also brought drastic change to the lives of Frank and Irene Sobey. "He was a bit shy at first," Mingo said. "It was a large step for the former butcher boy. It put him on stage." In the sixth decade of their lives, the Sobeys found themselves travelling to world capitals with Stanfield, and entertaining important foreigners at home. "She never got much public credit," New Glasgow newspaperman Harry Sutherland said, "but Irene Sobey had to feed every industrial bigshot who came to their house." Sometimes the entire IEL board met at Crombie.

If IEL made Stanfield a national figure in the political world, it made Frank a national figure in the business world. When the Dartmouth *Free Press* (April 28, 1966) called him "A man of action, a genius at pushing through red tape", it was echoing praise the business press had been heaping on him for years. Newspapers repeated Stanfield's blush-making appraisals of Frank. He had been trying to quit IEL for years, the premier said in 1967, "but we have pressed him to stay. . . . We cannot buy or hire his kind of talent."

Honours followed the attention. The first honour, also a burden, came in January 1963, when Prime Minister John Diefenbaker phoned him in Stellarton to ask him to join the Atlantic Development Board. Only a few weeks later, however, the Diefenbaker Tories fell to the Pearson Liberals, who promptly replaced the Tory chairman of the ADB, Fredericton publisher Michael Wardell, with one of their own, Halifax lawyer Ian MacKeigan. Frank thought the Liberals would bounce him, too, and he went to Ottawa to tell Secretary of State J. W. Pickersgill he'd quit whenever it suited them. But, he recalled, "Mr. Pickersgill said, 'Who told you I wanted you to resign?' So I was reappointed to the new board that the Liberal government set up." It pleased him that when it came to these unpaid directorships, he had sufficient stature that both Grits and Tories wanted him. He stayed with the ADB for four years.

"The Atlantic Development Board," MacKeigan said, "was funded with $100 million [in August 1963], and it later rose to $300 million. We had a very free mandate to spend that in any way we pleased to advance the economy of the Maritimes. . . . Our basic philosophy was to build infrastructure – industrial parks, highways, power, sewers." The agency also produced "a whole flock of studies" on economic development, transportation, tidal power. MacKeigan, later Chief Justice of Nova Scotia, was proud of his ADB years: "We did a challenging, interesting and, I thought, effective job. . . . It was the most effective board I ever sat on. They weren't just rubber stamps for the staff. They were all very good, capable, shrewd, businessmen, and Frank Sobey was typical of them.

"He was a common-sense tester of things. The staff might come in with ideas for, say, laying waterlines to a fish plant. He'd dig into it and say, 'Look, you want to spend X dollars on waterlines. Hell, it'd be cheaper to hire tank trucks and haul the water in from the lake.' He had a businessman's functional analysis, and he was ideal for assessing the feasibility of a project, what kind of market it would serve, and was it worth it? Frank was just a damn good businessman. He was also a great guy to pal around with on those trips."

At the ADB, Frank learned to dislike the federal bureaucracy, and to like Pickersgill. "I phoned him one night at ten o'clock regarding a temporary building for Clairtone," he said. "I wanted to put it up fast with Atlantic Development Board money, and he agreed. The next day I had a contractor on the job, and drew up an agreement to build this building, which cost quite a lot of money. It took pretty near two years for Mr. Pickersgill to get this through cabinet - and through the various departments, and Treasury Board, and so forth - before we got paid. That's how Ottawa works. The Ottawa office [of the ADB] became so large and cumbersome we were powerless to do much. Everything we did was slowed up by them. All they wanted to do was call in outside consultants to make studies and more studies. There were so many studies on various areas and various things in Nova Scotia that the shelves in Ottawa and Halifax must have been crammed with reports no one ever looked at again. But they cost the taxpayers a lot of money." After leaving the ADB in 1967, he advocated its removal from Ottawa and re-establishment in the Maritimes; but it soon disappeared in the morass of the Department of Regional Economic Expansion.

Frank would never forget a hair-raising ADB adventure in

Labrador. The board met at Goose Bay–Happy Valley and then went on to Labrador City, but Frank stayed behind because Pickersgill had invited him to join a party flying further north the following morning. Since accommodation was limited in Happy Valley, the Secretary of State and the president of Sobeys Stores, Ltd., spent the night on cots in a community hall above the fire station. The next day they climbed aboard an Otter seaplane with the manager of the Goose Bay airport, Paul Martin (son of External Affairs Minister Paul Martin), one MP, and one pilot. "This plane had been used for hauling in barrels of gasoline and so forth to the north," Frank said. "The handle was broken off the door, and we had it tied shut with a chunk of rope." But off they all went to look over Labrador's northernmost cod fishery. They soon landed beside a schooner.

Crew were catching, splitting, and salting cod. The hold was jammed with fish, and the deck was filling up fast. Knee-deep in offal, the visitors sat down at a rough table and took lunch with the crew. They later flew out to Ironbound Islands, several miles off the coast, to see another fishery. "We spent some time there," Frank said, "and then, in order to take off, we had to taxi out towards the west, and then head east into the wind to lift off the water. There was quite a chop on the ocean, and I thought one of the wings was going to hit the waves. The wings came within six inches of the waves, I'm sure. Well, we went on from there to Chimo and another Eskimo village, and we were very late getting back to Goose Bay. We were lucky. There'd been a bad storm there, and if we'd been on time we couldn't have got in. At one point Mr. Pickersgill asked if I'd noticed the airport manager who was with us because this fellow was just hanging onto his seat. He said he was scared to death the whole trip. I guess I just didn't have enough sense to be scared."

The adventure wasn't quite over. The next night, the government sent in a Viscount to fetch Pickersgill back to Ottawa, and Frank went along for another ride. A Viscount seated up to fifty-four passengers, but they had the plane pretty much to themselves: "Paul Martin's son stretched out on the floor, Mr. Pickersgill stretched out on two front seats with the backs down, and I did the same. There was also a hitch-hiker with a pack. He wanted to get some place, so we took him along."

They reached Ottawa near midnight. Pickersgill's wife and daughter met him with a Volvo. "Industrial Estates had established a Volvo plant in Nova Scotia," Frank explained, "so Mr. Pickersgill had naturally bought a Volvo. He insisted on driving me in to the Château Laurier hotel, but I knew the Château was a long piece out of his way, so I insisted on getting a taxi. Well, he wouldn't hear of it. The car was crowded because we had a lot of luggage, but he took me all the way in to the hotel. That's the kind of fellow Pickersgill was. I thought an awful lot of him. A couple of members of the board asked me later, 'How is it that Pickersgill asked you, the only Conservative on the board, to fly north with him?' Well, I couldn't explain that."

But not all the honours that came to Frank in the sixties involved him in the dining customs of Newfoundland fishing schooners. Others found him sipping tea with Queen Elizabeth, and kneeling in academic robes while a university chancellor intoned Latin phrases over his bald, bowed, and briefly humble head. By 1964 he was a director of the Fathers of Confederation Memorial Citizens Foundation, which promoted and oversaw the Confederation Centre of the Arts, Charlottetown.

The Queen opened the building in 1964 - to mark the centenary of the Charlottetown conference that preceded the confederation of Canada - and the Sobeys were among those who met Her Majesty and the Duke of Edinburgh at an afternoon tea on October 6. They also attended the State Banquet ("Gentlemen, white tie and decorations; ladies, evening gown and gloves"), and then went home to Pictou County, where Frank got word that the University of King's College, Halifax, wanted to bestow upon him a Doctorate of Civil Law. Not only big-business friends showed up at the university on November 20 to see him get the degree, but also a contingent of Pictou County folk who'd known him since his days as the hustling son of a Stellarton butcher. Like supporters of a small-town hockey team that's playing against a city for a national title, they flocked to Halifax to be with him during an historic moment in his life. Pictou County remembers its own.

But no other trophy or piece of parchment made Frank prouder than the Canadian Industrial Development Award. He picked it up on September 21, 1965, only ten months after getting his honorary degree, at a banquet in Quebec City. Its sponsor was a trade-and-industry council of all provincial governments, and since the judges were tycoons from across the country it was recognition by his mightiest peers. It was for "significant contribution to the industrial development of Canada in the public interest", and no Nova Scotian had ever won it before. Its few previous winners included C. D. Howe, and Frank's friend Frank M. Ross, the former lieutenant-governor of British Columbia (and, incidentally, step-father of the rising young Liberal, John Turner). Frank and Ross were both directors of a mutual fund in Vancouver and together had explored the Peace River country in a small plane. The man who'd nominated Frank for the award, however, had been Roy Jodrey.

Next, *Maclean's* chose Frank as a man of the year. On January 1, 1966, it named fifteen "Outstanding Canadians of 1965". They included Toronto opera star Teresa Stratas; Quebec crime-buster Claude Wagner; Vancouver architect Arthur Erickson; Montreal distiller Samuel Bronfman, head of the first Canadian-owned company with sales of a billion-plus; and Stellarton industrial promoter Frank Sobey. For success in business, he told *Maclean's*, all you need is "good-quality management, good-quality labor, and money. If you have the first two, you can usually get the third."

Irene Sobey, however, knew Frank's success had taken qualities less easy to define. The day before he got his honorary degree, she was alone for a while at the Nova Scotian Hotel, Halifax. News of Clairtone's plans had just burst on her home county like a cloud of happy gas. Month after month, IEL – her husband's IEL – had been springing sweet news on Nova Scotia. For her and Frank, 1964 had been a year of trips with the Stanfields to London, Paris, Stockholm, and the Volvo plant at Göteborg, and going to meet the Queen. In five more days she'd celebrate the fortieth anniversary of her marriage to the restless youngster who, in the time of iceboxes, Model Ts, and earphone radios, had mapped out for her what he was going to do with his life. Now, on hotel stationery, she scrawled a note to herself:

"This has been such a year that I am very sorry I did not keep a diary for every day. Yesterday, the announcement of Clairtone came as an electric thrill to Pic. Co. And such headlines. And so much credit to Frank Sobey! I am so proud of him. . . . Tomorrow, Frank gets the honorary degree. Gee! What a man I married. The Lord has been good to me. Mary [Irene's sister] always used to say that if I went down cellar for an apple in the dark I would come up with the largest and juiciest one in the barrel. *And I sure did.* If I die tomorrow, I really *have had something.* . . . The Lord really laid his finger upon him. He gave him such a clear, far-seeing mind. Frank has done wonders with His help."

Even in its glorious youth, IEL was never free of sniping and suspicion. It endured attacks because it did too little for this or that county, and too much for corporate giants from away. In the fall of 1963, after the announcement that, thanks to a $12-million loan from IEL, Canada Cement would set up a plant in Brookfield, near Truro, Liberal leader Earl Urquhart said, "A company with assets of $112 million should not be financed out of public funds." He added his improbable hunch "that Canada Cement was asked to take a loan from our government so [IEL's] publicity boys could add this name to the list of industries assisted."

(The real story, Frank recalled, was that a clause in an outstanding Canada Cement bond issue effectively prohibited the company from putting out another one, "So I made an arrangement for a loan of $12 million to them. But it was at a quarter of one per cent *over* what the Nova Scotia government was paying for money, *plus* there was an annual service charge of $10,000 from Canada Cement till the loan was paid off." The deal was "profitable for the government", and Brookfield got its cement plant. During his IEL years, and long after, Frank resented charges that his IEL had ever been extravagantly generous to industry.)

Liberal finger-pointing at the Canada Cement deal, and at "unnecessary inducements" to get the gigantic Reynolds metal interests to establish a can factory in Dartmouth, looked like mere partisan carping in 1963 and '64, but, particularly in the case of Clairtone, such complaints would return to tarnish IEL.

In February 1967, Eileen Stubbs, a municipal politician in Dartmouth with Liberal ambitions, smote IEL hip and thigh. She complained it had wangled property-tax deals for its clients that deprived Dartmouth of revenue. She charged it with "mismanagement and misallocation of public funds, miscalculation of industrial development, inefficiency in industrial planning, and lack of controls on investments made with public monies." She referred to IEL's "industrial charlatanism" and demanded a Royal Commission, because "It is time someone knocked down this sacred cow. It's not a child, but the bastard of government."

The *Globe and Mail* (Jan. 5, 1966) had more rational reservations. Most provinces, following Nova Scotia's lead, had either set up IEL-like organizations or were talking about doing so, but nevertheless, the *Globe* said, "The heavy direct involvement of the Nova Scotia government is looked at somewhat askance by officials in other provinces, who consider that Nova Scotia is putting itself in a highly vulnerable position. Many of the IEL-sponsored companies have little of their own money invested in the facilities, and they are free to depart at short notice. . . . This would leave IEL holding a costly investment in empty plants." (Frank argued, of course, that this was the beauty of the whole IEL principle of leasing out factories rather than investing in companies. If the worst happened, it was better to have an empty, usable plant than debts for worthless investments.)

A suspicion about Frank and his friends on the IEL board rippled about the province. It was that they were huddling at secret meetings to concoct ways to use IEL funds to enrich themselves. Such rumours were inevitable. Some people, in Nova Scotia as elsewhere, forever believe that all successful businessmen are basically pirates; and that only someone as naive as Stanfield would give a gang of pirates control over tens of millions of dollars in public monies. For the most cynical, it was enough to know that IEL director Seymour Kenney had secured contracts to construct facilities for IEL clients; that Harold Egan owned a big chunk of an IEL client that was building pleasure boats in Mahone Bay; that Frank and Egan were directors of IEL client Tibbetts Paints. It didn't matter that the boat-building business went bust and Egan lost half his shirt. It didn't matter that he and Frank had been directors of Tibbetts Paints for a decade before anyone had heard of IEL, and had helped found it with their own money. Surely their "conflict of interest" was the tip of the iceberg of IEL corruption.

But the truth was, it was legal for an IEL director to own a piece of an IEL industry so long as he declared the interest and abstained from voting on matters that affected it. Even Professor Roy E. George, not a fan of Frank's IEL, conceded in *The Life and Times of Industrial Estates* that "No improprieties have ever been demonstrated." He added, however, "But this does not still the rumours, and it's impossible for a director upon whom suspicion has fallen to establish his innocence."

The mill of sordid whisperings was one reason why George thought IEL needed some non-Nova Scotian directors: "Because Nova Scotia is a small and, by North American standards, an old society, its business community is closely connected by intermarriage and long-standing friendships. It is therefore inevitable that IEL directors, drawn from within the province, will be involved in deciding on proposals for business deals which involve themselves, or their relatives or friends. At best, this makes their positions difficult, leaving them open to suspicions that they are using their offices to feather their own nests or the nests of others with whom they have connections."

IEL's obsession with secrecy fertilized the suspicion. "The difficulty is this," the Halifax *Chronicle-Herald* (Jan. 29, 1963) explained. "How to reconcile the public's need and right to know how the public's money is spent with the corporation's right to conduct its business in the most efficient and effective manner possible." There would never be an answer. The problem was built right into IEL's entire function as a publicly funded corporation dealing with privately operated industries. IEL could not breach the trust of private companies by spilling information their rivals might exploit; and it did not want to tip off its own rivals, the other provinces, about the companies it was wooing. Frank believed only fools blabbed about a deal till it was in the bag. He ran his own businesses secretly, and he'd run IEL secretly. Moreover, while the Liberals and the press knew it was their duty to root out IEL mistakes, Frank knew that trumpeting those mistakes would make it all the harder to attract industries to Nova Scotia. Such activity was unpatriotic.

While IEL's mistakes were small, he had the upper hand. After all, it was supposed to take uncommon risks for the common good. But Clairtone was a big mistake, the one the government's enemies had long awaited, and in October 1967, as reporters' questions about it got persistent, Frank got mad. "All you're looking for is a little bit of headlines, which we're not interested in," he blurted. "So I'm not interested in talking to any reporters who are trying to deter and hurt development in Nova Scotia. . . . We can let the Toronto people do that." This outburst wounded the Halifax *Chronicle-Herald*, which liked to boast, "If it's good for The Maritimes, the *Chronicle-Herald* is for it." It defensively explained that its IEL coverage had been "careful, indeed discreet, and its editorial attitude was one of whole-hearted support."

"Amen to that," replied the *Cape Breton Highlander* (Oct. 11, 1967), a feisty weekly. "Perhaps if our media had a little more red blood and a little less discreetness, public figures wouldn't become outraged when a reporter dared to ask what was happening to public money. . . . The people have a right to know how their business is being conducted. It must be possible to do this without making it impossible to conduct that business." But in the case of IEL, it really wasn't. Few cared, until Clairtone.

When riled, Frank could snarl at politicians, too. A committee of the legislature explored the Clairtone embarrassment in March 1968, and the "prosecuting attorney" was Liberal leader Gerald A. Regan. His exploitation of the government's most expensive bungles (Clairtone, Deuterium of Canada) would help him lead the Liberals to power in 1970, and he remembered the hearings as "halcyon days for me. It was exciting, challenging, and I was on the way up. . . . As a witness, Frank Sobey was open and cordial, so much so I was startled. After the first day, he came over and gave me a good cigar. I took it, which the press reported, and some of my friends in the party criticized me for this later." But when Regan's questions about Clairtone got rough, Frank did what E. A. Manson said he could do. He took off the gloves. "I am sorry to have to say, Mr. Regan," he retorted, "but you're trying to make political capital . . . at the expense of industrial development in Nova Scotia. I don't mind mentioning that to your face."

Clairtone Sound Corporation was a glamorous company with two glamorous founders. The business press treated Toronto entrepreneurs Peter Munk and David Gilmour as movie magazines treated Rock Hudson, with awe-struck approval. "Munk was simply a great salesman," Mingo said. "My, he was a promoter. My, he had energy. My, he had charm. My, he had imagination. I remember he had to get some goods through U.S. Customs fast so he could raise some cash. I heard him ring up U.S. politicians and officials, and in two hours he arranged a Customs hearing that it would have taken most businessmen two years to set up." Munk and Gilmour were young men in a hurry, a terrible hurry.

Like Frank, Mingo continued, "Munk believed that if you wait till you've got everything lined up exactly right, then maybe you'll never get off the ground." Even after Clairtone's ship had begun to sink, and to drag with it some of Frank's own reputation as a business genius, Frank stood by Munk in public. "It's a good job we have people like Peter Munk in Canada," he told the committee of the legislature. "He's a builder. . . . It's people like Peter Munk that created all our industries. . . . They created our railroads. Invariably they lost most of their capital in doing it, because they went too fast. . . . The people that sit back without courage, and do a lot of talking and a lot of criticism, make no contribution to the industrial development of our country. That's all I want to say."

Clairtone, in 1964, put superior sound equipment inside superior cabinets and, with superior advertising, sold stereo sets to people who thought they themselves were sufficiently superior to deserve better sets than the ones that ordinary people bought. Everything worked beautifully, including the sets. Munk and Gilmour had started in 1959 with $3,500. In '62, sales hit $6.7 million; in '63, $8.9 million. Now the Toronto stock-exchange magazine touted Clairtone as a dynamic child of Canadian entrepreneurial flair. The company introduced the world's first transistorized (tubeless) stereo consoles, and at the National Furniture Show in Chicago unveiled "Project G", a stereo with black, spherical speakers that projected sound in all directions. Ads urged, "Listen to Sinatra on Clairtone - Sinatra does."

But although Clairtone owned a cabinet factory in Ontario, it still had no electronics plant. It needed a new factory to build sets from start to finish, and D. W. "Pat" Samuel tipped off Munk and Gilmour about IEL. A New Zealand-born war hero, ex-pearl diver, and polo player, Samuel had arrived in Vancouver as a car salesman, then shot to the presidency of Volvo Canada. Since IEL had just persuaded Volvo to establish its Dartmouth plant, Samuel knew what the agency might do for Clairtone. The upshot was that in August 1964, IEL chairman J. C. MacKeen and David Gilmour met over tea at a New York hotel. In his book *Clairtone* (1978), Garth Hopkins described Gilmour's subsequent report to Munk:

" 'What he [MacKeen] is saying in essence, Peter, is that Industrial Estates . . . will build the plant . . . and provide the extra working capital. . . . That, plus tax holidays, faster depreciation allowances, worker-training grants, and I don't know what else from federal and local governments, makes a wild package!' " (The package wasn't quite that mouth-watering, but it was tantalizing. IEL would finance the plant and sixty per cent of the cost of production equipment, and also provide a grant to train workers; and the federal government would indeed offer income-tax holidays, plus accelerated depreciation allowances.)

Four days later, Hopkins wrote, "With a speed and efficiency that impressed even the tireless Clairtone pair, the IEL team, headed by President Frank Sobey, had put together a detailed presentation of the financial and other advantages to Clairtone of moving to Nova Scotia." By November 1964, Pictou County had the joyous news. Thanks to IEL's taking $7,945,000 worth of first-mortgage bonds, Clairtone and the county would live happily ever after. Clairtone, like Santa Claus, was coming to town.

"One must admire the courage of Frank Sobey," the *Pictou Advocate* enthused. "He is apparently willing to stake his own great reputation on this huge venture. . . . It is saying much for [his] courage that he was willing to have this great venture established . . . practically within hailing distance of his own home." The heart of Pictou County, of course, was where he'd always preferred to see mighty industries settle.

Amid the celebratory commotion, only one story suggested danger, and it was cast not as a warning but as a tribute to Munk's refreshing style. He told a Halifax *Chronicle-Herald* reporter that, not once but three times, Clairtone had been so short of cash it had barely escaped bankruptcy. Munk, the reporter gushed, "is known for his unorthodoxy, but rarely has a businessman spoken as frankly about a side of a successful company's operation which most executives like to leave discreetly veiled by the past." In fact, Clairtone had never, ever, had enough cash to be safe. Munk and Gilmour weren't much interested in safety. They wanted phenomenal expansion. Sales, and sales alone, spawned growth.

"Munk was too good a salesman for his own good," Mingo said. "He could sell anything to anyone – including himself. A small example: he'd go down to luxury department stores in the States and say, 'Tell me what you want. I'll give it to you.' So Clairtone had to keep changing its production line." A small example, yes, but part of the reason why Clairtone was not only a rags-to-riches story but also a Perils of Pauline story. One day Clairtone would be tied to the tracks, the train would be rampaging toward her, and her previous rescuers would decide to leave her where she lay.

The aid to Clairtone in 1964 was unusual. IEL normally built plants, then leased them out. But Clairtone could not qualify for federal tax breaks unless it owned its own plant and equipment, so in this case IEL provided nearly $8 million in mortgage financing. "This is a very involved deal," Frank explained at a press conference. "Normally, we arrange to build and lease. But for tax purposes, we worked out an arrangement with Clairtone. There are a lot of ways to skin a cat." There would also be a lot of ways to lose taxpayers' dollars, but for the moment everything was coming up roses.

It took IEL only ten weeks to erect a temporary plant for Clairtone in Stellarton, and in June 1966, Munk officially opened the permanent "space-age" factory. This seven-acre plant was the biggest ever built in the Maritimes. "We got Eastern Construction to build it for only $7.50 a square foot," Frank recalled. But if the construction was thrifty, the formal opening was flamboyant. Munk laid on a nine-car train to bring dignitaries up from Halifax.

"That's when I first got scared of Clairtone," Frank said. "It was when I saw that train. Good, sound business people don't have to do things like that. I thought right then that Clairtone might be heading for trouble." Close to a thousand people attended the ceremony, and heard Munk say all the right things. Nova Scotians had "spirit and dignity". They were "under-rated and misunderstood by the rest of Canada and this continent". A bluenose industrial revolution was dawning, and "the winds of change were blowing."

Munk had already mesmerized the Stanfield government with a vision of Nova Scotia as "the Ruhr Valley" of Canada. The vision included the revival of the coal and steel businesses, and the birth of electronics and automobile industries. So far, however, Clairtone's own plunge into auto-making had been about as exciting as a water-logged firecracker. The company had used a million dollars that IEL had put up in order to buy control of Canadian Motor Industries. The brainchild of Pat Samuel, CMI was supposed to build an assembly plant for Japanese cars at Point Edward, Cape Breton Island. In March 1965, news that the plant would rise in June had aroused the usual media euphoria, but by Christmas there was still no CMI factory. Moreover, only eight months after Nova Scotians had learned that Clairtone controlled CMI, Clair-

W. H. Richardson, vice-president of Empire Company Limited.

tone no longer controlled CMI. "A major reorganization," the *Globe and Mail* reported in December, had transferred control of "financially troubled CMI" to three Japanese companies.

"The CMI situation upset me, and upset Harold Egan," Stanfield remembered. "Looking back on it, we should have said, 'Okay, that's off. We're prepared to help you [Munk and Gilmour] in the stereo business, but cars are a different matter.' We didn't call it off. Things went from bad to worse. . . . This eroded Clairtone's capital position and eventually we had to get the Japanese to come in."

As the Japanese took control, Cape Breton got bad news. The *Monetary Times* summed it up: "Construction of the CMI plant has been postponed for 18 months or two years, and postponed with it is the prospect of 2,000 jobs for Cape Breton. Clairtone is now a minority shareholder. And the government of Nova Scotia, which once jockeyed with Ottawa for the credit of bringing CMI to the province, has emitted a long, deep sigh of relief."

When news of the Japanese takeover broke in December 1965, IEL and Clairtone were secretly working out a deal to pump another $3 million into the stereo plant. IEL made it clear that none of the money was to go to CMI. It was also clear that Clairtone was now in the business of manufacturing not only hi-fi sets but also colour-TV sets. In *Clairtone*, author Hopkins speculated that Harold Egan, acting on his own, told Munk that the only way Clairtone would ever get another $3 million from IEL was to move into colour TV. Hopkins felt, "The answer to the still-unresolved question of whether or not IEL forced Clairtone into colour television and out of cars (thereby probably sealing its ultimate fate) undoubtedly died with Harold Egan."

But others felt that "the still-unresolved question" had never really been unresolved at all; that the answer lay in the hypnotic Munk, who needed no prodding from Egan to pursue support for the colour-TV adventure; that, in fact, the IEL board initially disliked the idea; and that it was only after Munk had entranced the provincial cabinet that IEL came through with the $3 million. "Harold Egan never encouraged them [Munk and Gilmour] to go into colour TV," Frank recalled. "In fact, Harold was very nervous about getting into colour TV. It was something they didn't know anything about."

Moreover, Robert Manuge insisted that the Stanfield government, in an unprecedented intrusion into IEL affairs, had forced a reluctant IEL to back Munk's colour-television dreams. In a letter to Frank in 1983, Manuge stated unequivocally that "Industrial Estates Limited at no time suggested that Clairtone go into the production of colour TV sets, nor did we wish to finance this move, or the move into Canadian Motor Industries Holdings Limited re. the sales of Toyota cars. In fact, you wrote to Peter Munk and told him that we would not perform this financing. Peter went over your head and appealed directly to the government of the day which, for the first time ever, asked you and the Board of Directors of IEL to go along with Mr. Peter Munk, thus setting the stage for a chain of unfortunate events. Had Clairtone stayed with hi-fi sets only, I doubt if they would have gone bankrupt."

This story, however, contradicted testimony from Egan's own mouth. Fifteen years before Manuge's letter, in March 1968, Frank told the committee of the legislature, "The television market looked very good, and they [Clairtone] sold us the idea that the plant had the capacity, and I think it had, to handle TV, and we advanced some additional funds to enable them to get into the TV market. . . ." At this point Egan chimed in: "Well, the fact of the matter is, Frank, nobody was more enthusiastic about colour TV, and getting into it, than we were. . . ." Egan also testified that the provincial cabinet had never given directives to IEL. IEL decisions were exactly that, IEL decisions.

Egan was fudging. The atmosphere was intensely political. Liberal leader Regan hoped to ridicule Tory bungling so effectively he'd lead the Grits to power; and Egan, Grit though he was, preferred to see IEL shoulder the blame for Clairtone's fate rather than the Stanfield cabinet. Remembering the heat of the hearings, Frank said, "We protected the government all through that."

But however one divides the blame for Clairtone's move into colour TV, it's likely everyone involved soon thought it was a hot idea. It wasn't. A brutal slump in the industry would leave IEL exactly where it should not have been: too far ahead of its time. By late 1966, the new plant in Stellarton was working round the clock. It had 1,250 employees. They were churning out stereos and TV sets that, in the last quarter of the year alone, chalked up sales of almost $9 million. That, however, was Clairtone's last happy season. It rolled into 1967 with a huge inventory of expensive TV components and unsold sets. Rumours spread that shoddy workmanship had caused the return of "rejects" from across the continent, and in March a labour dispute threatened to halt production. Frank and Harold Egan could see the sky darkening over Clairtone. They were now on its board. (For the $3 million IEL had given Clairtone in early 1966, it had taken back 300,000 shares, thereby breaking its policy rule against taking equity in a client company but buying two directorships.)

IEL had sunk more than $10 million into Clairtone, and felt that was its limit. Hutton & Company, Wall Street, now agreed to head a syndicate to underwrite $2.5 million (U.S.) in Clairtone debentures, but even before it could get its prospectus into print Munk knew that Clairtone, to meet its 1967 targets, would need at least *another* $2 million. Back he went to IEL. His answer came in July 1967, from Frank and Egan. It was not what he wanted to hear: IEL would come through with the $2 million, but only if he and Gilmour surrendered control of Clairtone. Munk was appalled but powerless, and in late August IEL became the dominant owners of a manufacturer of stereos and unmarketable television sets. No one was happy about this, least of all Frank. Rather than see a government-funded agency buy control of Clairtone, he'd have let it go bankrupt.

IEL had bought a bummer. Negotiations to sell Clairtone to the gigantic Singer Corporation collapsed in August 1967 because Clairtone's mid-year figures were so grim. IEL was paying $2 million to take over an outfit that had lost $800,000 in six months. Frank, almost alone, now urged that Nova Scotia cut and run. Every ounce of his business experience told him it was right to let Clairtone sink or swim on its own.

One reason why Munk had asked IEL for more money was that he knew Clairtone could not make the first interest payment on the Hutton debentures. Frank believed Hutton was so big, so expert, and had so much face to save, that it would not let the Clairtone industry disintegrate. If Clairtone failed to pay interest, then Hutton would foreclose, take over, make the business work. After all, they controlled the huge Wurlitzer interests, with all their expertise. Moreover, General Instruments was a major Clairtone creditor. Frank argued that if IEL refused Clairtone further money, then Hutton and General Instruments would pick up the Clairtone pieces and find a way to protect their investments. But Hutton had persuaded the government that its foreclosing would weaken Nova Scotia's international credit rating. That danger, Frank insisted, was a phony.

Moreover, he believed governments should never bail out business failures. A bankruptcy, dreaded though it might be, could purge a failure of its fatness. Sure, it caused temporary hardship. But new owners with smart managers would come in, pick up the wreckage cheap, fit it together properly, restore jobs. Fifteen years later he had not changed his mind. He was eighty. He was sipping a cold beer on a steamy Florida afternoon at his apartment in a "leisure village" for older folk, and he'd been reading about Canadian government efforts to rescue industries that made Clairtone look like a pipsqueak.

"The government is making terrible mistakes when they bail out lame ducks like Massey Ferguson, Canadair, De Havilland, and the electronics industry," he said. "All they're doing is bailing out the bankers. They say they're saving jobs. They're not saving jobs. If you let a company go bankrupt, then someone else takes over the assets. It then becomes more competitive. It increases its market share and makes the jobs. Some companies went bankrupt two or three times. When James Dunn got control of Algoma Steel, he was buying their bonds for thirty cents on the dollar. Just about all the big Canadian paper companies went under in the thirties, but they came back. Maritime Steel went through financial reorganization twice. That's why it's strong today." After DOSCO announced closure of the Sydney steel mill in 1968, Nova Scotia formed a Crown corporation (Sysco) to own and run it, and that was "an awful mistake. It could have been unloaded twice to private interests. Now they're in too deep. Their financial charges are as great as their wages."

He paused to light his pipe, summed up: "You know, once you start making business decisions based on what politicians want, you're headed for trouble."

What the Stanfield cabinet had wanted in 1967 was to see IEL pump money into Clairtone to save hundreds of jobs in Stellarton. It was ironic that the man who objected was Frank. For he was Stellarton's favourite son, and ten years earlier his concern for Stellarton had been part of IEL's birth. But he thought the government's decision was plainly wrong, and though he respected Stanfield more than any politician he'd ever known, he told him so. The advice didn't take. Clairtone got its $2 million, and IEL got its Clairtone.

Under IEL control, Clairtone's slide became a breakneck plunge. Net losses for fiscal 1967 rocketed to $6.7 million. The agony of Clairtone continued till its foreclosure sale in October 1972. By then the province had bought IEL's interest in Clairtone for $19,105,190. "That meant simply that the government assumed all financial obligations of Clairtone," Garth Hopkins explained. "By the time the company ceased operations, those obligations

Robert Stanfield makes a presentation to Frank Sobey on his retirement as Chairman of IEL in 1969.

totalled more than $26 million. Perhaps $3 million was recovered from the sale of assets and of the Stellarton plant."

Hindsight on the Clairtone fiasco would never be unanimous. Ad-man Dalton Camp, who'd helped sell both Clairtone stereos and Robert Stanfield, told Hopkins that Munk and Gilmour were so congenitally enthusiastic "they would assert with all conviction that such-and-such was true, when it was demonstrably not true. . . . That factor caused them to over-rate their real position in the U.S. market and blinded them to certain inherent disadvantages in moving to Nova Scotia." Gerald A. Regan had exploited Clairtone's failures and then, as the new premier, presided over its dismemberment. In 1981, recalling the mess from his perch as a federal cabinet minister, he reached the unsurprising conclusion that the blame lay in bad decisions by the Tory government of the sixties.

"The worst piece of judgment, no matter who was responsible for it," he said, "was to allow two struggling, scrambling, young entrepreneurs who'd built up a pretty exciting business in the hi-fi field . . . to allow them, at the very moment they were moving here and almost before they'd settled in, to get into colour TV. And instantly to open the treasury of the province to enable them to do this. If Clairtone had stuck with what it first came to Nova Scotia to do - make stereo sets - it would be here today. The colour-TV venture undermined the whole business." Regan concluded his analysis by graciously offering that, as premier, he'd made the odd mistake himself.

"Clairtone just got caught in the first wave of the TV industry moving to Japan, and also in that sudden sag of interest in colour TV," Donald Archibald recalled. He'd served as an IEL director throughout the Sobey years. "They just ran into something that was beyond them," he said. "I always felt much of the Clairtone thing was a result of things that were just beyond Nova Scotia's control."

Frank, however, still believed some things had not been beyond Nova Scotia's control. "Clairtone cost the province more than $20 million," he said, "because the cabinet wouldn't let me pull the rug on them." To a Stellarton man, Clairtone had not been a total disaster. Simpsons-Sears took over the plant and turned it into a distribution centre that employed more than a hundred workers. That was far short of the two thousand that Munk had talked about one thrilling November day in 1964, but in Pictou County it was not to be sneezed at. "I always figured that having that plant in Stellarton would pay off," Frank said, "and it has."

Behind the Clairtone affair lay cockiness not just on Munk and Gilmour's part but also on IEL's and Stanfield's. "IEL had had very distinct successes," Stanfield said. "Everybody associated with it became somewhat overconfident. I can't recall anything they thought they couldn't correct. We *expected* some failures, but by the mid-sixties people in both government and IEL felt they could cope with anything." Overconfidence was also the prelude to the financial catastrophe of Deuterium of Canada.

But so were the looming clouds over Cape Breton Island. The *Globe and Mail* (Jan. 5, 1966) reported, "Dominion Coal Co. Ltd., in the past five years, has closed three mines. . . . Mine employment, now about 7,000, has fallen steadily from 11,200 in 1956. The company plans to close another mine in January, with a further loss of 450 jobs." The Cape Breton *Post* (Feb. 26, 1966) said, "We have seen industry after industry remove from this area in the past twenty years. The plate mill, the nail mill, the benzol plant, the tar and chemical plant, the cement plant have disappeared from the Cape Breton scene to be relocated in Central Canada. . . . No planning has been done in an effort to avert what everyone in government circles piously seems to think will happen: the early end of coal operations and the later end of steel operations." Stanfield and Frank both knew how pessimistic DOSCO was about the future of Cape Breton.

"We weren't as cautious as we should have been," Stanfield said, "but Cape Breton was in a hell of a state, and maybe that justified some foolhardiness. Also, we were very much interested in getting into the nuclear age." Mingo said, "He knew he was grabbing at straws, but the Cape Breton situation was so bad he *had* to grab at straws."

The Canadian government had committed itself to nuclear reactors fuelled by natural uranium and controlled by heavy water. Dr. J. L. Gray, president of Atomic Energy of Canada Ltd. (AECL), had staked his reputation on the system, and early in 1963 AECL called for bids for the supply of 1,000 tons of heavy water for use in Ontario Hydro reactors. Whoever got the contract would build Canada's first heavy-water plant. The race was on. Deuterium of Canada, Ltd. (DCL), child of American scientist Jerome Spevack, was only one of several bidders, and his first proposal involved building a plant in Alberta. Then he got wind of IEL.

Spevack, as far back as 1940, had worked with Harold Urey, the

Nobel prizewinner who'd discovered deuterium. He'd helped develop the first atomic bomb, and later invented an "improved" process for making heavy water. With batteries of lawyers, he fought to protect his process from theft. It wasn't till June 1963 that he and his wife, Ruth, also his business ally, met IEL. By August they had a deal: IEL would put up $12 million by buying second mortgage bonds from their company, Deuterium of Canada, Ltd., and at the same time would take forty per cent of DCL's shares. Before IEL put up the $12 million, however, DCL would have to raise the rest of the $18 million for the $30-million plant by issuing first-mortgage bonds on the private market.

The story leaked. In a headline five inches high, the Cape Breton *Post* (Aug. 31, 1963) announced that Cape Breton was "on the threshold of the nuclear age". Cape Breton, Linden MacIntyre recalled in the Halifax *Chronicle-Herald* in 1971, "seized on the news as shipwreck victims would welcome the vision of a rescue boat. Every chartered group, politician - anybody whose name had the slightest whiff of prestige - immediately began to bombard the new Liberal federal government with resolutions and pleas. The heavy-water contract had to go to the as-yet-unnamed messiahs who were going to lead Cape Breton out of the desert. Nova Scotians demanded the heavy-water plant and they got it."

But before they got it, they almost lost it to Western Deuterium, Ltd., of Victoria, which Gray favoured for various practical reasons. Dynamic Power Corporation, Ltd., of Calgary was another formidable contender. To beat such competitors, Nova Scotia succumbed to Ottawa pressure to guarantee Canadian control of Spevack's DCL. DCL and IEL struck a new deal in October 1963: IEL would now get 25,001 of the deuterium company's 50,000 shares, or effective control. IEL would still not have to put up a nickel to buy the $12 million in second-mortgage bonds till DCL had raised $18 million by selling first-mortgage bonds on the Canadian market. The plant, it was expected, would pay for itself in seven years. Early in December the news broke that DCL had entered the lowest bid - $20.50 per pound - for the heavy-water contract, and that negotiations with AECL had begun.Surely, for

Nova Scotia, this was the most fabulous industrial breakthrough of the century.

IEL had never before taken equity in any client company. In this case, however, it had no choice, and it was therefore far from being solely to blame for what eventually happened. The abuse IEL endured for the debacle was, in Frank's unapologetic opinion, misplaced. "That was one deal we knew was too big for us to handle," he insisted. "It was not an IEL project. It was a project of the Nova Scotia government. I remember G. I. Smith [Stanfield's lieutenant in cabinet and successor as premier] spoke to me at a 'do' in Truro. He said they were talking to Spevack about his heavy water, and he says, 'You fellows in Industrial Estates will have to negotiate this deal, because we have no negotiators in our government.' That's how we [IEL] got involved in heavy water."

The decision to build the plant at Glace Bay was highly political, and IEL became a conduit for money that Stanfield promised Ottawa the province would invest in DCL. IEL's position, he recalled, "was forced on us by the federal government. They said the plant had to be Canadian-controlled." In Frank's memory, Nova Scotia's federal cabinet ally was J. W. Pickersgill: "He told me once he was going to quit if we didn't get the plant. He said it was the only time he ever went into cabinet with his resignation in his pocket. Jack Pickersgill got that plant for Glace Bay." But so did Labour Minister Allan MacEachen, Cape Breton's man in cabinet, and indeed Prime Minister Lester B. Pearson. Mingo said, "Stanfield got to MacEachen and Pearson, and he agreed to this deal whereby IEL would take control of Deuterium. I think he promised this over a handshake at 24 Sussex Drive [the prime minister's official residence]. Anyway, it was a commitment he was bound to honour. So now the province was doubly committed, politically and financially. As early as February of '64, Harold Egan and Frank Sobey realized they'd unleashed a tiger."

By then, it was alarmingly clear that DCL had no hope of quickly raising $18 million. But Burns and Roe, the New York engineering firm supervising the plant's construction, now reported the job would cost only $28.5 million. That was so encouraging that in March IEL accepted Egan's recommendation that it allow its $12 million to go into the project *before* DCL came up with its $18 million. Now Nova Scotia was truly on the hook. No matter what financial and technical horrors lay ahead, there'd be no backing out.

The heavy-water plant bloomed into an endless nightmare for Spevack, Stanfield, Frank, and indeed all who'd helped bring it to Glace Bay. It was hardest of all on Egan. "He was the only one who really thought the whole thing through," Mingo said. "He was the only one with the mind and time to understand all the problems, but understanding them didn't mean his judgment was right. Everyone relied on Harold. Harold let everyone down." By June 9, 1968, Egan had been fighting the tentacles of the DCL octopus for five years, but the monster had just kept growing. The accountant came home tired that night. He had a chest pain. His wife wanted to call a doctor but he said no, he'd just go to bed for a while. Stanfield was set to debate with Pierre Trudeau on national television later in the evening, and Egan asked his wife to awaken him when the duel began. She let him sleep through it. Near midnight, she checked him. He was dead, at fifty-six. Had the financial horrors of the heavy-water plant hastened his death? His friends thought so.

If the DCL blunders, accidents, chaos, and squabbling hadn't broken so many hearts and cost so many tens of millions, they'd have been hilarious. Imported labour meant imported unions. They and feisty Cape Breton workers clashed so destructively with the Texas-based prime contractor, an outfit with obtuse attitudes toward labour, that fifty strikes hamstrung the project in 1965-68. Equipment arrived late. Equipment arrived faulty. Valves and pump bearings had to be replaced. Delays in engineering sucked progress out of the construction schedule for months on end. With depressing monotony, the actual bills made liars out of cost estimate after cost estimate. The weather ganged up on the job: the winter of 1966-67 was among the nastiest in memory. Finally even the ocean conspired against DCL's success.

DCL used salt water at the plant to save the cost of piping in fresh water, but the salt corroded millions of dollars' worth of equipment. Experts later argued that if only the plant had been pushing the seawater through the pipes faster the corrosion might never have occurred. To compound the damage the slow flow caused, there was the damage no flow caused. Bunglers allowed stagnant seawater to sit in the system for months, and it wrecked stainless steel that had cost more millions. "The start-up attempt in late 1968 and early 1969," Linden MacIntyre wrote, "revealed serious corrosion and leaks that allowed deadly hydrogen sulphide to move around within the system and to escape into the atmosphere." Or, as E. A. Manson, the former industry minister, put it, "We turned the thing on, and it just leaked all over. If those leaks hadn't been in the pipes, we'd have had it then." In hindsight the pools of salt water, silently eating new steel, symbolized something: that everything that could possibly have gone wrong at the plant had indeed gone wrong, and that men at every level had no idea what they were doing.

"I don't think any of us, nor anyone else in Canada, understood the technological complexity of what we were getting into," Stanfield said. "I know I certainly didn't. I thought it would be just like building a big power-generating plant." If anyone at DCL did grasp the technological problems it was Spevack, but he was difficult. Imperial Oil, Stanfield said, had once bid on the heavy-water project but Spevack's prickly, litigious reputation had scared them off. "I used to tell them we'd done them a favour," Stanfield said wryly.

Frank acknowledged that Spevack was "a terrific scientist" but said he was both unreasonable and ignorant of money matters. Nor did Mingo doubt Spevack's scientific credentials. "It was just that he thought he was Jesus Christ," Mingo said. "His ego was that big. He was on a mission to save the world, but he also wanted all the benefits from the mission." Spevack believed the U.S government had stolen his earliest patents for making heavy water. Now he jealously guarded his improved process. Mingo thought he wanted to license his method around the world, not only to get rich but also to survive in history as "another Newton or somebody";

and when IEL bought control of DCL, Spevack insisted on so many stipulations that the control wasn't really control. IEL could not fire his appointments to the board, much less dismiss him as president. Without his approval, IEL could do no financing. "He had special rights written into the deal in a thousand different ways," Mingo said, "and that led to all kinds of tension and friction between him and the Nova Scotians."

One Spevack appointment to the DCL board was Alex MacIntosh, the Toronto corporation lawyer from Pictou County who'd first steered the Spevacks to the Nova Scotia government. "I guess that was one of the worst things I've done for the province," he said with rueful cheerfulness over lunch in the Toronto Club in 1981. In the fall and winter of 1963-64, MacIntosh remembered, "I was acting for Spevack, but I was also regarded as someone with a little common sense. The Spevacks were an interesting pair. They were inexperienced in business but absolutely adamant about their own positions.

"Frank worked very hard to obtain that [AECL] contract for Nova Scotia. He made trips to Ottawa, and in the negotiations in Nova Scotia he demonstrated infinite patience. I've heard people say he has no patience but I saw him at meetings that went on till early in the morning. I saw him in a negotiation [with Spevack, among others] that would have tried the patience of almost anyone. It certainly tried mine. He was a very good negotiator, and very patient."

But Frank reached the limit of his patience in 1966, and so did both IEL and the Stanfield government. Recognizing the futility of DCL's efforts to sell bonds, IEL had loaned it $15 million on top of the original $12 million. The province had put up all the money, and was about to put up all the money for an expansion Ottawa had authorized. Moreover, it was now clear that Spevack's insistence on secrecy meant there was slender hope of ever selling the plant. Nova Scotia decided to sever the Spevack connection. It bought him out with $3 million, payable over six years.

But it had not heard the last of him. By 1970, everyone knew that only massive federal help would ever get the plant producing, but the feds feared Spevack would sue them for stealing his know-how. Nova Scotia had agreed to pay him $3 million, with the final payment due in 1972; but now, in 1970, he refused to grant the release the province needed in order to bring in the feds unless he got the full balance first. The province asked the redoubtable Halifax lawyer Frank Covert to deal with Spevack.

"He was quite violent and abusive over the phone," Covert said, "so I finally said, 'Well, Mr. Spevack, I thought we could at least get together to discuss it, but if we can't, I'm afraid I'll have to advise the government to introduce legislation cancelling your contract without payment.'" Weeks of negotiation followed. Spevack was stridently unbending, but every time he swore he'd not sign the release till he got the full contract amount, Covert threatened legislation to cancel the contract. Finally, Ruth and Jerome Spevack met over tea at Covert's house. "After I had the tea in my cup half gone," he recalled, "I said, 'Mr. Spevack, I have not more than five sips of tea left. When I have finished, the interview is over. There will be no second chance. You have very little time.' After one sip, I said 'four more', then 'three more', and 'two more'. Then Ruth Spevack said, 'Darling, you'd better sign.' He signed, and I delivered the notes payable and spread over the years." The coast was now clear for AECL.

"Atomic Energy of Canada rode reluctantly to the rescue in 1971," Geoffrey Stevens wrote (*Stanfield*). "AECL still needed the heavy water and it decided that, rather than build a new heavy water plant from scratch (at an estimated cost of $135 million), it would be further ahead to put $95 million into the Glace Bay plant and try to make it work. Besides it was the only way to protect the $135 million in taxpayers' money that the province had already expended. AECL borrowed the $95 million from the federal government, took over the plant, and by the summer of 1972 had finished pulling it apart." In 1976, thirteen years after Cape Breton heard it was entering the nuclear age, the Glace Bay plant produced its first marketable drum of heavy water. The total bill? Roughly $250 million in public monies.

Looking back, Stanfield did not gloss over the fact that the heavy-water adventure had been an epic financial tragedy. He mildly observed, however, that one might also consider "what's been poured down the sink in the case of [provincially owned] Sydney Steel" in the years since he'd quit the premiership. Putting the best possible light on the story in 1981, Mingo said, "If it hadn't been for Deuterium, there'd never have been the second one [Canadian General Electric's more successful heavy-water plant on the Cape Breton side of the Canso Strait]. . . . Secondly, the Glace Bay plant, after all, *is* there." By 1983, however, there was little consolation in that. Construction of other heavy-water plants, doubts about the efficiency of nuclear energy, a slackening in the surge of the industry had made false prophets of all the experts who'd predicted a decade earlier that Canada would soon face a crucial shortage of heavy water. Now it was a crucial glut that the Glace Bay operation confronted. Once, the plant hadn't been able to make heavy water; now it couldn't sell it. It was stockpiling for a better day.

Perverse glee characterized much Nova Scotian reaction to the Deuterium and Clairtone fiascos. News of these failures drowned acknowledgement of IEL's successes. How good it was to see how the mighty had fallen! Liberal leader Regan hammered at the "two crown jewels of IEL" as "colossal flops". In April 1969, Regan's sniping got so far under the skin of G. I. Smith, Stanfield's successor as Tory premier, that Smith snarled he'd tolerate "none of this drivelling nonsense from a weakling who wants to sink back into the morass and stagnation from which Nova Scotia was rescued by this government in 1956." In happier times, Smith had been a calmer man.

But IEL made an astounding comeback. Just as its reputation hit bottom, Frank announced the most triumphant coup of his whole career there. During the two years that IEL had been wiping egg off its face and mud off its escutcheon, it had been carrying out secret negotiations in France. Now, on July 29, 1969, Frank revealed that the Michelin tire empire of France had chosen Nova Scotia as its manufacturing beachhead in North America. In the biggest red headline the East River towns had seen in the five years since the first Clairtone announcement, the *New Glasgow Evening News* screamed "MICHELIN TIRE COMING TO PICTOU COUNTY". A front-page editorial the next day said, "To Mr. Sobey and all those who worked so diligently, we say thank you for another job well done."

Unlike Clairtone, Michelin was not a trendy hothouse flower. Unlike Deuterium of Canada, it was not a plunger into untried technology. Michelin men had been making tires since 1889, thirteen years before Frank's birth. Michelin now had massive holdings sprinkled round the world, factories on three continents, and a daily production of 30,000 tires in France alone. Michelin would be coming to stay. Its first two plants in Nova Scotia would cost up to $100 million, have a million square feet of floor space, and initially employ 1,300 workers. One would rise at Bridgewater, and a bigger one at Granton in, of all places, Pictou County.

Frank said it was Robert Manuge, more than anyone else, who hooked Michelin (and Manuge agreed). Not only was "Nova Scotia's globe-trotting salesman" the first in the IEL crowd to hear that Michelin planned a North American manufacturing base to expand its assault on the U.S. tire market, he was also the man who followed up his knowledge with fifteen trips to France. The French liked his elaborate, energetic, courtly style. "Bob initiated that deal," Mingo said, "and it was François Michelin's appreciation of Bob that got that deal." At the same time, "When you turned Frank loose on a potential client, he could be pretty forceful, and maybe not entirely open." Mingo doubted, for instance, that Frank had warned Michelin that "unions are practically a part of religion in Pictou County." The Michelin organization hated unions, and in time did indeed face a union crisis at Granton. "Frank charmed them into Pictou County," Mingo continued, "and that's been their principal problem in Nova Scotia."

Frank did some of the charming at home. A notoriously careful outfit with a near-paranoiac obsession with secrecy, Michelin insisted Manuge refer to their dealings as "Project Y", and also sent secret agents to scurry around Nova Scotia to explore potential plant locations. Some French visitors ended up at the Sobey house for dinners. "I had quite a problem persuading Michelin to come to Pictou County," he said. "They were worried about the labour force. I knew they'd never go to Halifax, but I had a hard time selling them on the idea there was enough skilled labour here."

He and Michelin's chief, François Michelin, had curious similarities. It was as though Michelin were a Gallic exaggeration of Frank. Each headed a business that one family had tightly controlled for generations, though Michelin's was vast and worldwide. Each was secretive, though Michelin was more so. (Michelin Tire was so secretive it refused to let Charles de Gaulle's bodyguards accompany him into its headquarters, and barred trusted suppliers from its factories.) Each was paternalistic and anti-union, though again Michelin was more so. Frank had insisted on setting up an employee pension fund for Sobeys Stores, Ltd., as far back as 1950, and felt personally responsible for seeing that long-time employees were comfortable in their old age. Moreover, though the chain had suffered strikes that had not endeared him to the labour movement, he'd learned to accept the fact of unions. François Michelin abhorred them.

"He operated as a one-man operation, on a very austere and economical basis," Frank said, almost enviously. "He was the main industry in that town [Clermont-Ferrand], and he had a record of *never* letting employees go. . . . He has continued that policy here. This year [1980-81], when tire sales were down, he put the men to work cleaning and painting the plant at Granton and putting some men on training courses. You know, when he moved Pictou County men to France for training, he moved their families with them, provided English schooling for the kids, and paid their way home at Christmas."

Each believed in simple offices for executives, but Michelin carried this belief to the edge of fetishism. "When Manuge arrived in France to meet Michelin officials, he was disconcerted," Stephen Kimber wrote in the *Financial Post Magazine* (April 26, 1980). "The head office was pedestrian, spartan, and bare. Top officials did their work at desks created by placing boards across filing cabinets and the place had all the corporate ambience of a company on its way into receivership." Another journalist said he saw a senior Michelin manager "shaping bits of used wire into paper clips".

Even Frank, a martinet about routine office expenditures, was surprised by the monastic appearance of François Michelin's office. "It had a bare hardwood table and bare hardwood chairs," he said, "and that was it. Everything was as clean as could be. We worked at a plain table with hard chairs. The toilet was the old-fashioned kind. The water-box was up high, and you pulled a chain."

During the final negotiations, Manuge and Mingo were in Clermont-Ferrand while Frank lingered in London. Manuge said, "He once told me that in any bargaining session you should always leave the back door open," but in this case Frank stayed behind not to retreat through the door but to enable himself to enter it at the right moment. "When you're into negotiations you can get yourself locked into a position where it's hard to back down," he said, "and then you need somebody else, somebody like myself, to come in, and maybe discuss different approaches."

IEL's main assistance to Michelin would be a seven-year, $50-million loan, $18 million of it for equipment, and the balance for plant construction. The interest rate was lower than rates in North America because Michelin insisted it could get cheaper money in Europe. The Nova Scotians knew that unless Michelin provided a guarantee for this massive investment, the deal would inspire Grits back home to pummel IEL all over again. That was the sticking point. Michelin was a proud company. Frank said, "They felt our asking for a guarantee of the investment was a bit of an insult to their integrity.

"So I went over from London to a meeting at the Michelin plant. They were selling $100 million a year to the Sears interests in New York, so the manager of their New York operations was there. And a New York lawyer, a Paris lawyer, Michelin's lawyer, and Bob Manuge and Bill Mingo." They all went to lunch at a private dining room in a nearby restaurant, and Frank sat next to François

Michelin. The sparring began. Frank: "He says, 'No one ever asked Michelin for a guarantee before. We have always looked after all our obligations.' So I said, 'Well, you have to understand the way politicians think. The Opposition will always try to embarrass the government over any of these deals.' "

He suspected the $18 million for the tire-making equipment was safe. "An American company would have been glad to grab it," and the Michelin empire had not built its reputation for super-secrecy by allowing competitors to snatch its machinery. Sure enough, François Michelin guaranteed over lunch that, if Michelin's Nova Scotian operations should fail, the mother company would buy back the equipment for the full $18 million. Minutes later, the Frenchman turned to the man from Stellarton and said, "What would you say if we were to guarantee sales of seventy-five per cent of the production [of the Nova Scotia plants] for seven years at New York prices, with no other mark-up or commission?" That did it. "I said I'd buy that," Frank said, "and that was all that was said. After lunch, the lawyers got busy. They drew up the contract that afternoon."

What with federal grants and assorted tax breaks, some calculated that $81 million in public money went into the campaign to get Michelin to settle in Nova Scotia. Whatever the exact amount, news of Michelin's decision left the Quebec government apoplectic. Jean-Paul Beaudry, minister of industry and commerce for Quebec, was quoted in the *Globe and Mail* (Aug. 2, 1969) as saying the move was "inexplicable . . . unthinkable, unwarranted and unaccountable. . . . We are competing with peewees." But the peewees had already won.

Quebec had thought it had the inside track. It had good financial backing, access to markets, a French-speaking population, and, for that matter, more English-speaking people than Nova Scotia. Moreover, no less a figure than Charles de Gaulle, the first president of the Fifth Republic, wanted Michelin to choose Quebec. But François Michelin was keen neither on the smell of labour militancy in Quebec, nor on de Gaulle. "After I signed the deal," Frank said, "I told him I'd been scared he'd go to Quebec. He

Frank and Irene Sobey celebrated their 44th anniversary at the Taj Mahal, November 24, 1968.

said, 'I'd never go to Quebec. General de Gaulle put a lot of pressure on me to go to Quebec. I never go anywhere for political reasons.'" Business and politics just didn't mix.

By 1979, Michelin employed 3,600 workers in Nova Scotia, its payroll nudged $60 million, and its annual payments to suppliers totalled $83 million. Moreover, Michelin was about to build a third plant, even bigger than the other two, at Waterville in the Annapolis Valley, decidedly not a hotbed of unionism. But some felt that the province had paid dearly to keep the giant happy; that the amount of public money spent to create each Michelin job had been exorbitant; and that Michelin's muscle had caused successive Nova Scotia governments to pass vicious anti-union laws. In southern Ontario, home of Michelin-threatened tire factories, the *Globe* sneered that the laws Nova Scotia passed to squelch union organization in Michelin's Pictou County plant suggested "Nova Scotia has a government that will turn cartwheels if the price is right. That reputation should make no one proud."

On the other hand, Gordon Archibald, chief of Maritime Telegraph and Telephone Company in the seventies, believed "Michelin is now much more important to Nova Scotia than the Sydney steel plant will ever be," and it was likely most bluenose businessmen agreed with him. Frank had no doubts at all. "There seems to be an opinion that IEL was too generous with Michelin but that's not correct," he said. "That was the last deal I signed before resigning from IEL, and it was without doubt the best deal we ever made." Moreover, it proved the value of IEL's record during the whole dozen years that he'd been its boss. "If IEL hadn't brought in all those other industries," he said, "Michelin would never have come."

Having announced the Michelin deal, Frank declared, "I've had the job twelve years now, and this is enough. . . . Now is the time for a younger man to take over." He'd been trying to quit IEL for years but had been trapped. When Stanfield entered federal politics in 1967 he begged him to stay on. After that, the Clairtone and heavy-water scandals erupted. Leaving then, the Cape Breton *Highlander* (Aug. 6, 1969) said, "would have been interpreted as quitting under fire, and Sobey would have none of that." The paper wasn't sure what it thought about IEL, but "As for Frank Sobey himself there is no question that he is an individual, than whom there is none ruggeder. The impact of his personality will be felt in Nova Scotia for generations to come." The *Chronicle-Herald* (Aug. 1, 1969) said, "Nova Scotia would be a much poorer province today without having had his services," and the New Glasgow *Evening News* (Oct. 18, 1969) was sure that "In Great Britain . . . he would be on the Queen's honour lists and would become Sir Frank, Baron Abercrombie, or the like." Frank was sixty-seven.

IEL soon became another kind of animal. The Liberals assumed power in 1970, and they owed their victory partly to Gerald Regan's having flayed IEL. As the new premier, he wanted to make it appear less like the conspicuous pet of prominent but sometimes bumbling businessmen and more like an anonymous, professionally run bureaucracy. IEL's flashiness was now out of favour. People wondered. Had it been wise to circle the globe in pursuit of inappropriate industries, to squander public money in naive dealings with shrewd multinational corporations? Wasn't small beautiful, and big ugly? Under Regan, IEL's image shrank while its staff multiplied. Its operating and promotional expenditures in 1969, Frank's last year there, were $302,763; nine years later, they were $1,103,007. Salaries alone had jumped from $139,926 to $612,353.

It had been Premier G. I. Smith, in his last months in office, who'd given IEL a paid president, Finlay MacDonald, who soon fell out with general manager Robert Manuge. The feud between MacDonald and Manuge was a staple of Halifax gossip in the early seventies. Soon, however, both left IEL for good. "IEL was never the same after Frank left," Manuge sadly recalled. "Something went out of it."

MacDonald was not reluctant to criticize the earlier management of IEL. "The old mistakes of industrial development corporations were made by people whose entire backgrounds had been financial," Geoffrey Stevens quoted him in *Stanfield*. "Just because you or I made seven million dollars because we inherited a buggy-whip business does not necessarily make us the kind of adjudicators you need as to the type of industrial development a province should have. Look, who can be conned faster than a big industrialist?" Other critics, notably the Atlantic Provinces Economic Council (APEC) in 1973, argued that the IEL investment, per job created, had been too high. APEC figured it averaged $21,000. The *Toronto Star* (Oct. 27, 1973) described provincial development agencies in the Atlantic provinces as "a weird blend of secrecy and taste for sensation, of caution and extravagance, of glamor and missionary zeal, of suspicion and naivety and, from time to time an apparent determination to prove that to err in a super way is superhuman."

What the critics forgot was how bleak Nova Scotia's prospects had been in 1957 when Frank first pleaded with Stanfield for an industrial park in Stellarton. If desperate problems require desperate solutions, the wonder is that IEL did not make more mistakes than it did. Mistakes were inevitable, which was why IEL's founders had abandoned their original plan to try to sell shares to the public. By 1971, fourteen IEL clients (not including Clairtone and Deuterium of Canada) had either collapsed or pulled out of Nova Scotia, but in nine of these cases new tenants had taken over the factories. Moreover, the successful clients totalled fifty-five, and provided direct employment to 4,352 workers. The Michelin plants were under construction. Egg-producer Donald Archibald, who sat on the IEL board throughout the Sobey years there, admitted later that "There were a lot of stupid little deals we got into," but he also thought the fact that Nova Scotia's unemployment rate was the lowest in the region was partly due to IEL. "In the sixties," he added, "it gave the province a certain drive." Stanfield thought that was IEL's finest achievement. "It changed the mood of Nova Scotia," he said. It weakened defeatism, strengthened confidence.

IEL might indeed have performed better than it did, Professor Roy E. George decided, but nevertheless "A careful, impartial observer can see much to admire in the first decade and a half [of IEL]. That it has benefited [Nova Scotia] seems beyond reasonable doubt, and the prospects are that industrial promotion of the type undertaken by IEL may well turn out to be the best approach that could have been taken to improve Nova Scotia's economic condition."

Frank Sobey hadn't a shadow of doubt. In the living room where he and his wife had once entertained industrialists from around the world, he puffed on his pipe, poked at a recalcitrant tape-recorder, talked about IEL. His elderly Clairtone colour TV, which he still loyally swore by, was mute. The black spheres of his once-fashionable Clairtone hi-fi, now seventeen years old, emitted soft music. The quality of sound was excellent. He did not believe the Clairtone misadventure had been his fault. He did believe IEL had been a resounding hit.

"Nova Scotia had very little manufacturing," he declared. "All it had was the steel company, and a few other old plants, and the fishing industry, and so forth. Industrial Estates changed all that. It changed the whole industrial make-up of Nova Scotia. You can go around now and find thirty-five, forty industries that Industrial Estates helped set up.[1] In fact, Nova Scotia today has a good industrial base, and more people are working in the industries that Industrial Estates established than in coal mining and the steel business put together." IEL had been his baby. At eighty, he was still a doer, and not about to sit still for an idle critic with foolish doubts. His years at IEL had been the most exhilarating, productive, and public-spirited of his life - even if they had cost his own business a million or two.

In a footnote to Frank's career at IEL, he came through for it more than three years after he'd quit. He could co-operate with Liberals as easily as with Tories, and now that Regan ran the province, Frank did the young fellow a favour or two. "He not only harboured no ill will [over the Liberals' earlier attacks on his beloved IEL]," Regan recalled, "he sought to be just as helpful with my government as he'd been with the previous government." No matter what Regan's public posture had been with respect to

[1]See Appendix D for a record of IEL businesses in Nova Scotia.

the ineptness of the Crown corporation Frank had headed, he had so much private regard for the aging supermarket tycoon that he appointed him a director of the provincially owned Sydney Steel Corporation. Moreover, Regan recalled, "Frank Sobey was genuinely dedicated to Nova Scotia, and I don't think he was the least bit interested in serving his own interests while serving the province's." (In this respect, Regan suggested, Frank was different from IEL's ex-chairman, J. C. MacKeen.)

It was for Yarmouth that Frank performed his last feat of industrial promotion. Cosmos Imperial Mills, Ltd., was the biggest employer in Yarmouth, providing more than five hundred jobs. It was crucial to the economic health of an entire county. But its management was weak, and its commitment to the textile business feeble. Its owners in Hamilton, Ont., were moving into other industries, and in Frank's opinion "bleeding" the Yarmouth operation. Cosmos Imperial went belly-up in 1972, and IEL began a frantic search for a new tenant. Regan consulted Frank, who suggested an approach to Canada's smartest, most enduring, and most aggressive textile company. He knew the virtues of Dominion Textile. He'd been buying its shares and cashing its dividends for sixteen years. He'd sat on its board for ten years, and, though he'd just resigned, his son David had promptly replaced him.

But Dominion Textile had shown little interest in Nova Scotia since 1917, when the Halifax explosion had wrecked a mill it had owned. Now, fifty-six years later, IEL's latest salaried president, D. W. Salsman, faced polite but impenetrable indifference at the company's head office in Montreal. Regan phoned Frank again. "So I asked Mr. Salsman who he'd been talking to up there, and he named somebody," Frank said. "I says, 'You weren't talking to Dominion Textile at all. The only man who's going to make a decision like that is Eddy King, or maybe Perowne.'" E. F. King was chairman of Dominion Textile and Ronald H. Perowne was president, but Salsman couldn't get to see either of them. This confirmed Frank's theory that big companies employ smoothies to keep visitors off the backs of the decision-makers. Now, once again, Frank opened a door for IEL.

He went to Montreal with Salsman, and lured King and Perowne to a lunch at the Mount Royal Club. Salsman was at last face to face with the top dogs at Dominion Textile, and, while Frank tossed in his practised pitch about the glories of Nova Scotia as a home for industry, Salsman laid out all that IEL could do for Canada's biggest textile manufacturer. King was hooked. He visited Nova Scotia, and negotiations began. On May 8, 1973, Dominion Textile officially opened its first mill in Nova Scotia since Frank was fifteen. He was now seventy-one.

"He was the catalyst when we went into Nova Scotia, and not only just then," Perowne said. Perowne had a taste for metaphor: "Frank had been needling the board about Nova Scotia for years, and when Cosmos Imperial went under, the call to arms came. Action stations were taken. We went into harness. The crowning point of his years with us was when we went into Yarmouth."

But the decision was not a crowning point for Dominion Textile. King had been a tough boss, but by 1982 he was a fragile man with a bony face, a gentle, flashing smile, and a diplomatic manner. He sat on a fragrant porch overlooking the Gulf of Mexico near Sarasota, and recalled horrendous labour problems at Yarmouth. He didn't want to make harsh generalizations but suggested Yarmouth workers lacked the dependability of the work force at Dominion Textile's gigantic Quebec operations. Moose-hunting, tending lobster traps, angling for salmon had all competed with production goals in Yarmouth, and work habits had been as variable as the weather.

"Not long after the lunch at the Mount Royal," Frank said cheerfully, "Eddy says to me, 'You bugger, you schemer, you cooked that up.' Well then, a couple of years later, he says, 'You sonofabitch, that was the worst decision I ever made in my life.'" And King recalled, "Frank was happy when we went into Yarmouth, and we were happy it made him feel good, but we didn't have that kind of money – just to make him feel good." In time, however, Dominion Textile cured its Yarmouth headaches. Perowne said in 1982 the deal had turned out well for the company, for the Sobeys as major shareholders, and for Frank as a Nova Scotian. "We employ 375 people down there," Perowne added. "The payroll is $3.5 million, and it goes up each year." Frank talked as though he'd known all along what would happen: "You see, it takes people like that [Dominion Textile's management team] to make things work, good operators who are also willing to hurt and bleed for a while."

"He really pushed hard for that deal and demonstrated his patriotism for the province," Regan concluded. "Dominion Textile has been a phenomenal success in stabilizing Yarmouth, and we were facing a disaster there." It was not every bluenose businessman who earned the unqualified gratitude of both Stanfield and Regan.

10

LOEB, PROVIGO, AND THE TAKEOVER WARS

IN JUNE 1977, when Frank was seventy-five, he and his sons tried to buy control of the Ottawa-based food-wholesaling empire M. Loeb, Ltd. They failed. But their reactions to their foes' moves in the struggle for M. Loeb earned them not only twenty-five per cent of an even bigger food industry – one that stretched from Quebec to California – but also tens of millions of dollars. Within their defeat lay another victory. At a hearing of the Ontario Securities Commission, they torpedoed a scheme by the gigantic Provigo food interests to squeeze them out of their M. Loeb holdings; and, among corporation lawyers, the OSC ruling in the Sobeys' favour was a landmark in takeover law. The story reveals much about the prickly relations between the food giants of Canada, and their craving to gobble rivals; and about the grade-school drop-out who was now the blunt patriarch of the biggest locally owned food chain in the Atlantic provinces.

M. Loeb, Ltd., had helped pioneer food distribution in Canada. Moses Loeb, a Russian Jew, bought a confectionery store in Ottawa before the First World War and, while his wife managed it, peddled candy from a horse-drawn wagon. The peddling business became M. Loeb, Ltd., wholesale distributors of tobacco and confectionery. Bertram Loeb, one of Moses' six sons, was elected president by his brothers in 1951. "My background was philosophy," Bertram said in 1982. "I was planning an academic career, but my father was dying of cancer of the colon, and he begged me to carry on with the firm." In 1952 M. Loeb got the franchise to supply stores of the Independent Grocers' Association (IGA) in eastern Ontario and western Quebec, and went on from there, "It had been a three-million-a-year candy outfit," the frustrated philosopher allowed, "and when I left in 1976, we were doing more than a billion a year."

By then, M. Loeb had an American subsidiary. Moreover, it owned 86.6 per cent of Horne and Pitfield Foods, Ltd., Edmonton, whose IGA outlets and Red Rooster convenience stores were bobbing along on the buoyancy of the Alberta economy. Horne and Pitfield owned big pieces of Alberta shopping centres, and its subsidiary, Market Wholesale Grocery Company, was a foothold in California. In sales and profits, 1976 was a record year for Horne and Pitfield; and, among M. Loeb holdings, it was the juiciest plum.

Frank knew all this. Years before, he'd considered making his own swoop on Horne and Pitfield shares. Now, in 1977, Sobeys Stores, Ltd., operated sixty-three supermarkets in the Atlantic provinces and Quebec, and numerous fast-food outlets and wholesaling arms that stretched all the way to southern Ontario. (Soon the Sobeys would suck up twenty-five per cent of the Hannaford Brothers supermarket and drugstore chain in New England, much to the horror of its American owners.) The Sobeys were also in the drugstore business, and so was M. Loeb, Ltd. Sobeys owned twenty drugstores in Nova Scotia, while M. Loeb controlled National Drug and Chemical, the country's biggest wholesaler of pharmaceuticals. It, too, would be among the spoils in the battle for M. Loeb.

M. Loeb looked specially inviting to Frank. He had once devoured books by Roger Ward Babson, a Massachusetts statistician who churned out advice, in sledge-hammer prose, on investment principles for the common man. A Babson rule: invest in a business in which you're already expert. No one who knew the Canadian supermarket industry doubted Frank was expert at selling groceries. So were two of his sons, Bill and David, now fifty and forty-six. Frank's third son, Donald, born in 1934, was more involved in expanding Sobey real estate and investment holdings, but with regard to M. Loeb he said that if they hadn't known the food business inside out, they'd never have sought the takeover.

Their move on M. Loeb was nevertheless like a mackerel attacking a cod. Not that the Sobeys were puny. They owned malls, office towers, auto dealerships, movie theatres, construction and insurance firms. Their Empire Company Ltd., which the financial press habitually called "the aptly named Empire Company", owned pieces of three chartered banks (Nova Scotia, Montreal, Toronto-Dominion), and of outfits that made construction equipment, textiles, paper, salt, and packaged fish. Empire's portfolio was worth millions. The Sobeys were mighty Maritimers, but compared to national food companies, they weren't big at all. Sales for Sobeys Stores, Ltd., amounted to $236,806,000 in 1977. Those of Horne and Pitfield alone totalled $367,189,000, and, as Bertram Loeb bragged, M. Loeb's surpassed a billion.

What made Frank think he could chew so massive a bite, and why was M. Loeb so vulnerable in June of '77?

Unlike Frank, the Loebs had sacrificed family control to finance expansion. Moreover, M. Loeb had suffered management problems, and, in the opinion of some, the most crucial of these was its mastermind, Bertram Loeb himself. "One retailing analyst said Loeb had been considered a problem for the company's management for some time," the Montreal *Gazette* (Dec. 11, 1976) reported. "He said Loeb 'didn't delegate authority effectively. He was never able to get a senior executive to work with him.' " Frank Warnock, who joined the firm as president (Bertram Loeb retained the chairmanship) in 1975, was diplomatic, but his careful words did not deny an image of Loeb as a know-it-all honcho who, after a quarter-century in the saddle, refused to relinquish a gram of authority: "As a rule, if an entrepreneur like Bert builds up his own business, he wants to go on running it. It's a classic business problem – and the Sobeys, by the way, are a great example of avoiding it. Don't get me wrong. Bert is brilliant. He's amazingly quick to grasp a situation, make the right decision, and move on it. But he tended to do things himself. The moment you have a billion-dollar business, it's just too large for any one man. We built a management team."

Warnock sold the company's Chicago division and, though the sale meant "an extraordinary one-time loss of $984,000", most M. Loeb directors were happy with it. But not Loeb. For him, Warnock said, "It was traumatic. The Chicago operation was something he was very keen on." The trouble was, "We were losing a million a year in Chicago. . . . That was the most competitive area in North America. It was a hotbed of price wars." The George Weston-Loblaw group had owned the National Tea chain there. "They pulled out, and stopped a haemorrhage," Warnock said. "Then A & P pulled out. Three local chains went bankrupt. Chicago was simply over-stored."

His decision, drastic as it was for M. Loeb, was small potatoes compared to the Weston-Loblaw group's surgery in Chicago. Of the 240 U.S. stores that Weston-Loblaw closed or sold in the mid-seventies, 140 were in its Chicago division. "The Chicago exit" came to stand for a brutal program of dumping unprofitable American stores, a program that Alexander Ross said in *Canadian Business* (March 1981) was central to "one of the classic corporate turnarounds in Canadian history". In the early seventies the Weston-Loblaw empire was "on the verge of collapsing under its own weight. . . . [But] after ten years of ruthless, painful reorganization . . . Galen Weston and his team have transformed the Weston-Loblaw group into a lean, profitable, progressive, rational, superbly managed company – a winner and a world leader in what is still a perilous, savagely competitive business." Getting lean in 1976 resulted in a loss for Loblaw Companies of $49.8 million. Analysts said Loblaw had acted courageously, but president Richard Currie argued it was no more courageous "than a doctor's decision to amputate a gangrenous arm".

Warnock felt the same way about M. Loeb's Chicago operation. The decision to unload it was easy for him, if not for Bertram Loeb. In December 1976, Loeb quit as chairman of the board. (His brothers voted to accept his resignation, and six years later

Frank Sobey visited Leningrad in 1966 as part of a delegation of prominent Canadian businessmen sponsored by Air Canada.

he said, "I still can't understand that part of it. I made them *rich*!") Troubled M. Loeb, Ltd., was becoming less troubled. "The improvement was no great secret," Warnock said. "You're showing your figures each month, and when you do something dramatic, like cutting the Chicago losses, and it's out there on the front page of the *Financial Post* . . . well, nobody needs a financial analysis. Everybody says, 'Hey, Loeb is at last taking some action!' " As early as December 20, 1976, the *Financial Times* of Canada suggested that M. Loeb, then trading for only $2.70 per share, was a prime takeover candidate. Six months passed. Then Frank and his sons secretly tried to buy up blocks of M. Loeb stock. They thereby triggered the skirmish that not only obliterated M. Loeb but also immensely fattened the voracious, Montreal-based Provigo Inc.

"I bled for a whole year," Bertram Loeb said.

What made M. Loeb a sitting duck was its ownership structure. The Caisse de Dépôt et Placement du Québec, a Crown corporation that invested funds from the Quebec pension plan, owned 25.3 per cent of the common shares; and, in Bertram Loeb's bitter opinion, what enabled Provigo, another Quebec outfit, to gulp his company was nothing less than "a diabolical conspiracy, all orchestrated by the Caisse de Dépôt." Loeb himself owned 14.1 per cent and, with the shares of associates, controlled 15.9 per cent. The only other significant block, 18.5 per cent, belonged to the Weston-Loblaw group, whose various holdings were so massive and intricate the *Financial Post* had once called it "a galactic empire". Weston-Loblaw measured its sales in billions. The Caisse de Dépôt measured its assets in billions. Smaller shareholders of M. Loeb, Ltd., were scattered about the continent, but the key to its control lay in the 43.8 per cent that, together, the Caisse de Dépôt and Weston-Loblaw owned. Anyone who wanted M. Loeb would have to reckon with these giants. Frank Sobey wanted M. Loeb, but his relationship with Weston-Loblaw was not cosy.

Rumours that Weston-Loblaw owned Sobeys Stores, Ltd., floated round the Maritimes for twenty years. Shoppers believed them. Maritimers knew that Upper Canadian enterprises had gobbled local industries, shut them down, or bullied them to death. They found it unlikely that a local boy's chain could not only trade blows with the likes of Dominion Stores but also, on occasion, send them reeling. Surely, then, Sobeys Stores were a Loblaw "front". The Sobeys, a close-mouthed pack, did not rush into print to correct the story. Ownership of their stores was nobody's business but their own. As long as their cash registers jingled, people could believe what they wanted. But the *Financial Post*'s (June 1979) description of Garfield Weston as Frank's "recently deceased friend and business associate" was too much. Frank told the *Post* that, although he'd admired Weston's parlaying a small bakery into one of the world's biggest food industries, "I have never had any correspondence nor any discussions with Mr. Weston in my life." That was true, just as it was true that never for a moment had Weston-Loblaw controlled Sobeys Stores, Ltd. Not that Weston's top man in Toronto hadn't tried every trick of persuasion he could concoct in order to get that control.

His name was George Metcalf, and in *Canadian Business* Ross called him "the Bible-thumping super-salesman who was Garfield Weston's North American lieutenant during the years of the company's greatest expansion. . . . Metcalf was ruthless, cunning, erratic and brilliant." Charles Burns, Toronto investment dealer, recalled that Metcalf was so haughtily secretive he once refused to give Burns information for a prospectus to raise money for Metcalf's own company. Burns found him insufferable, and so probably did the Loblaw shareholder who, having dared to ask Metcalf for precise information, got this reply: "The Good Book tells us we must be as meek as a lamb and as shrewd as an adder."

Metcalf's piety was not matched by modesty. He infected others with what he himself called his "inspired imagination", his urgings "to keep everlastingly at it, it can be done", and his upbeat faith that "The spirit, the drive, the courage to take giant steps sends a company soaring ahead to world leadership. I like this magic quality." He was also autocratic. "He was the kind of guy who'd walk in on the night before a store opening," Bill Sobey said, "and he'd say, 'I want that whole wall covered with mirrors by 9 a.m. tomorrow.'" Metcalf was Weston's chief devourer of companies in North America, and it was thanks to him that the Weston-Loblaw umbrella covered so many firms that not even his own senior men knew about all of them.

This was the man with whom Frank Sobey had found himself fencing in 1960. Metcalf had been blunt about his aim: to buy control of Sobeys Stores for Weston-Loblaw. Frank was less blunt about his goals: first, money for expansion and diversified investment; second, food-merchandising expertise from Loblaw; and a distant third, to sell Weston-Loblaw enough of Sobey Stores to discourage them from opening Loblaw outlets in his territory. What he did *not* want - and knew in his cunning heart he would never want - was to sell control of the chain that he and his father had nursed through the bloody heartbreak of the coal-mining days; through the cash droughts and the cheese-paring, price-slashing, two-bit competition of the grocery business in the Dirty Thirties; through the shortages, restraints, and meagreness of management of the Second World War.

Sobeys Stores, Ltd., was, as Nova Scotian historian James M. Cameron put it, "a merchandising achievement that has no parallel in this province", but it was scarcely an overnight achievement. Indeed, Frank had been a grandfather before "Sobeys" had meant "supermarket" to housewives across the Maritimes; and even in 1960, when Metcalf tried to twist his arm, the Sobey chain owned only twenty stores. Within six years Weston-Loblaw would have 1,850 and, through franchise arrangements, interests in another 1,500. Metcalf must have wondered, Why would this fifty-eight-year-old, small-town Nova Scotian want to resist such a tide of food-retailing destiny? But Frank had his reasons, and in all negotiations he was shrewd as an adder, if not meek as a lamb.

One reason was a corollary of "easy come, easy go"; hard to amass, hard to release. In 1924, while courting the curly-headed daughter of a New Glasgow church deacon, Frank had promised to build a food-store chain, invest its profits in the stock market, put together a business empire. In 1960 he knew he had made this dream come true, but, confronted by a Toronto man whose eagerness to possess his chain was as palpable as sweat, he also knew he had only begun. No one has ever accused Frank of having a deficient interest in money, but retiring at fifty-eight, with however many millions he could wring from Weston-Loblaw, simply didn't interest him. Retirement wouldn't interest him seventeen years later, when it would be his turn to try to buy something - shares of M. Loeb - from Weston-Loblaw. Retirement would never interest him.

There was something else: family. In ways less flashy than full Highland dress, there was a bit of the clan chieftain in Frank, and when he went up to Toronto to talk turkey with Metcalf he had many Sobeys to consider. His father had been dead for eleven years, and Frank had a birthright to protect. In his effort to enlarge it, he was bold, secretive, acquisitive. He enjoyed battle. He was careful to parcel out responsibilities to his sons. One day, he knew, their children would be rising in the clan business. He had his younger brother, Harold, to think about, too. Harold had struggled along with Frank to keep the stores going in hard old times. The obsession of the chief's whole life was to arrange the expansion of a clan kingdom. Metcalf didn't know it, but his chances of buying control of Sobeys Stores, Ltd., were infinitely worse than the Toronto Argonauts' chances of winning the Grey Cup. Dominion Stores had already tried, been rebuffed, backed off.

Frank took his sons to Toronto. The experience, he thought, might be good for them, and Metcalf would see flesh-and-blood proof that he was dealing not just with a man but with a dynasty. Bill, at thirty-three, was already a vice-president of Sobeys Stores. He'd opened several supermarkets himself and, ironically, had learned the basics of food merchandising while working as a youngster for a Loblaw groceteria. David, twenty-nine, was a director of Sobeys Stores. Donald, twenty-five, had barely begun the work that would turn the Empire Company into the investment treasury and corporate umbrella for myriad Sobey interests. J. N. Cole of the Montreal office of Wood, Gundy and Company, Ltd., rulers of the roost among Canadian investment dealers, joined the Sobey men in Toronto.

"I just went along to hold Frank's hand," Cole recalled. "Metcalf was the most prodigious talker. He talked all day. He wanted control, but Frank kept demurring." The Weston-Loblaw men were "so anxious", Frank remembered, "at one point they had it down to a deal where they'd get control if I died. I wouldn't agree to anything." Donald Sobey said, "They proposed all sorts of schedules and formulas. They even had it that they'd buy forty per cent then, and the other sixty per cent on some sort of schedule to give them control after the last of the three sons died. I remember that because I was the last of the three sons. . . . Anyway, Father wouldn't go along with any of these proposals. They were mad as hell, but Metcalf finally agreed to take forty per cent of the voting stock, without any strings."

"They didn't *want* to take just forty per cent," Frank recalled, "but they did. We gave them first refusal." This meant only that if the Sobeys ever decided to sell control, they'd give Weston-Loblaw first crack, but the concession was meaningless. The chief Sobey had cannily laid plans to protect Sobeys Stores from outside takeover, inside conflict, and succession duties on high. He'd tied up fifty-six per cent of the voting stock in a company called Sobeys Stores Holdings, with a voting trust among the three shareholders. "A third was owned by each of the boys," he explained. "If one wanted to sell, he'd have to sell to the other two. And my wife had special voting preferred shares. She could outvote the whole thing." In business matters, you may be sure, Mrs. Sobey listened to Mr. Sobey. Thus, the family owned one hundred per cent of a company that owned fifty-six per cent of the voting shares of Sobeys Stores, Ltd.

"I think Metcalf looked at us [the three sons]," David Sobey said, "and thought, 'I'll have that other sixty per cent in no time,' and if Father hadn't created Sobeys Stores Holdings, he might have been right. They might now be in control."

Though Weston-Loblaw paid nearly a million dollars for their forty per cent, Frank wanted more than money from them. Loblaw Companies were the top Canadian supermarket chain, and Frank wanted their expertise.

"He *always* wanted to know what the other fellow was up to," Harold Renouf said. A small, precise accountant who chose words as carefully as he handled numbers, Renouf in 1981 was chief of Ottawa's agency to monitor the petroleum industry, but as a younger man he'd worked closely with Frank for a dozen years. "He was highly personable," Renouf said. "He could extend friendships to the point where others didn't even see him as a competitor. At Loblaws, or Steinberg, or a chain down in the States, they'd invite him into their offices and talk to him as a friend about things he wanted to know. But a time came when he wanted information on a more-than-casual basis. He was also concerned about whether Loblaw was thinking of moving into the Maritimes. That's when he decided to sell them forty per cent."

"They [Weston-Loblaw] were going to give us technical assistance and advice," Frank remembered, "and they did – for a little while." The relationship quickly cooled. "We didn't ask for much," he said, "and they didn't want to give much." Indeed, they refused his offer of a seat on the board of Sobeys Stores. "After they bought the stock," J. N. Cole of Wood, Gundy said, "he scarcely heard from them. They were really no help to him whatsoever." Nor was he much help to them. The Sobeys were not famous for paying generous dividends. "By comparison with other businesses," said John Jodrey, son of Roy, "they have paid out only a very small portion of their earnings. They've put the money back in, and that's why they've grown so fast, but it hasn't been a very exciting stock." (Piling earnings back into the company, Frank explained, "paid off in the early eighties. The stock really moved." But by then the Sobeys had bought back the Weston-Loblaw share of their chain.)

Weston-Loblaw got meagre dividends, no influence, not a glimmer of hope they'd ever get control. Frank had the use of their money, but, as Renouf put it, "He didn't even consult them. He ran his own affairs just as if he owned one hundred per cent." Loeb said, "He never had any good things to say about them. There was no affection between him and the Weston group. Not even cordiality." But Frank denied there was ever serious friction between himself and Weston-Loblaw, and said, "We supported a lot of their products over the years." What's certain is that when the fight for M. Loeb began, Weston-Loblaw had been sitting on its boring investment in Sobeys Stores for seventeen years; and if relations between the two organizations were not hostile, neither were they warm.

Six years after Bertram Loeb quit the chairmanship of M. Loeb, Ltd., he said, "You wouldn't get me back into the food business today if you offered it to me for nothing." He was sixty-six. A stout, bald, bushy-browed, and very opinionated businessman, he described Frank Sobey as "a very opinionated businessman". Loeb had been a tough cookie in a tough business. Once out of it, he tried to be philosophical. He talked about the costs of building M. Loeb, Ltd.: a broken marriage; erosion of his health; time he'd failed to spend with his children; "the way my values got lopsided". Was it all worth it? "I'm not sure. You pay a high price for success. Winners have scars." But a young man "wants to make a mark, and one of the joys of life is hearing people tell you what can't be done, and then going out and doing it."

He saw nothing surprising in the idea that Frank might once have "harboured resentment" against Weston-Loblaw. "Reprisals prevail in the Canadian business community," he continued. "It's incredible. I've seen Tom McCormack [former president, Dominion Stores, Ltd.] and Sam Steinberg [Steinberg, Inc.] fight like two kids squabbling over a piece of candy." Speaking of Dominion and reprisals, Donald Sobey called its late chairman, John Angus McDougald, "a vicious competitor". Donald had just joined Canada's most exclusive businessmen's hangout, the Toronto Club. The man who'd made it exclusive had been McDougald, who'd have blackballed any Stellarton Sobey. "That's right," Donald said. "If McDougald were alive, I'd never have been accepted."

But the supermarket wars influenced more important matters than club memberships. Loeb said his firm had been the biggest Canadian customer for food that the Weston empire manufactured "simply because Dominion hated Loblaw's guts." Retail competition was the source of the hatred, and it was also why Steinberg, Inc., was sometimes loath to buy Weston products. M. Loeb, however, was primarily a wholesaling outfit and, "If we could get a better deal from anybody, we'd go get it. We went for the best deal." Things, however, weren't always that simple. "It is understood Weston and M. Loeb encountered a snag in their reciprocal supplier relationship," the *Financial Post* (Feb. 17, 1973) reported. "Industry sources say Bertram Loeb even ordered all M. Loeb operations to cease buying goods from Weston. At that point . . . Garfield Weston himself, chairman of George Weston Ltd., flew to Canada [from the United Kingdom] to try to smooth things over."

The friction had started in Chicago in 1972. "I needed volume there," Loeb said, "and I wasn't getting any from Loblaw. I went to see Ted Creber [G. E. Creber, then president of George Weston Ltd.] and I told him I wanted some of their Chicago business for Loeb." When Loeb left Creber, he thought that from then on Weston-Loblaw would indeed be buying from M. Loeb in Chicago. He was wrong. Outraged, he phoned Weston in England. The *Financial Post* said, "Creber . . . denies Weston came to Canada to patch up relations." Loeb, however, said later that Weston immediately flew to Toronto, and sent his private jet to Ottawa to pick him up. A Weston limousine whisked Loeb from the Toronto airport down to Loblaw head offices and there, before Garfield himself and his senior North American officers, "I told them my story. I held forth for two hours."

Weston, he recalled, was so impressed that he offered to absorb M. Loeb and guarantee Bertram Loeb a $7-million killing on his shares, "plus a ten-year management contract at $100,000 a year." Minority shareholders, however, would be out in the cold. "I have a conscience," Loeb said. He refused Weston's offer. "According to one source," the *Financial Post* reported, "Weston offered to buy out the Loeb family but they couldn't agree on price." Having failed to get M. Loeb from the Loebs, Weston-Loblaw wheeled on other shareholders. The *Post* said they made "a couple of large purchases from the Caisse de Dépôt and the University of Alberta". They also bought on the open market, and by early 1973 held twenty-four per cent of M. Loeb, Ltd. It had cost them $5.5 million. The *Post* speculated, "The year's epic stock-market battle may be under way between two of the country's largest food businesses - George Weston Ltd. and M. Loeb, Ltd."

But while Weston-Loblaw panted after M. Loeb, M. Loeb panted after the Alberta-based Horne and Pitfield Foods, Ltd. The Loeb firm and family already owned some of Horne and Pitfield, and Bertram was already its chairman. Now, however, he wanted it all. As business reporter Raoul Engel explained things,

"M. Loeb would, subject to directors' approval and no adverse acts of God, offer a share-for-share exchange of Loeb stock for the 1,833,000 Horne & Pitfield shares outstanding." Not only would this manoeuvre give M. Loeb control of an Alberta money-maker, but, since it would mean issuing new shares to trade for Horne and Pitfield's, it would also dilute the Weston-Loblaw portion of M. Loeb from twenty-four to eighteen per cent. And Bertram Loeb, market analyst David Chisholm speculated, "may feel agreeably that . . . control of the group will continue to rest in his family's hands."

To make Loeb feel even more agreeable, the Department of Consumer and Corporate Affairs galloped onto the scene. The government thought George Weston Ltd. already owned enough of the food industry, and that Weston control of M. Loeb would be bad news for shoppers. The result of a government inquiry was that in 1974 Weston-Loblaw agreed not only to cease buying M. Loeb shares but, when they could get a fair price, to sell those they owned. Bertram Loeb could breathe easily, but only for a while. Three years later, Weston-Loblaw would refuse to sell their M. Loeb shares to either the Sobeys or Loeb. Instead, they'd dispose of them in a way that would frustrate the Sobeys and enable Bertram Loeb's enemies to snatch the firm to which he had given thirty years of his life.

Within the M. Loeb camp, the Sobeys had a friend. He was Frank Warnock, the president. A compact man with a gravelly voice, trim, wavy grey hair, and a ruddy, slightly battered face, Warnock looked like an ex-hockey player who'd remained fit. He'd arrived in Toronto from Scotland in 1947, worked as a floor-sweeper, joined the Toronto staff of a British manufacturer of worsted yarns, bounced from there to a fourteen-year career with Scott Paper. For Scott Paper he worked out of Halifax for two and a half years; and as their Montreal-based manager for Quebec and the Maritimes in 1965-68, he regularly returned to Sobey country. Scott Paper sold to Sobeys Stores the usual line of paper towels, napkins, toilet paper, etc. Indeed, Sobeys Stores was Warnock's biggest Maritime customer, and though he usually dealt with Bill or David, he met Frank, too. Warnock was so confident he could get along with the Sobeys that he actually wanted them to gain control of the company of which he was president. That, he said later, would have been preferable to invasion by Provigo Inc. of Montreal.

Few had noticed what an acquisitive and burgeoning outfit Provigo was. Typically, however, Frank had his eye on it. He liked its management. He and his sons liked its efficient pushiness and its justified cockiness. The fact was that, thanks partly to English-Canadian contempt for French-Canadian business, its market price was below its real value. "The guys in Toronto don't want to buy it [Provigo stock]," the *Financial Post* said (Feb. 21, 1976). But the guys in Stellarton would.

Provigo's chairman, chief executive, and father was Antoine Turmel. A dapper, owlish, quizzical-looking man with straight hair, rimless glasses, wide lapels, and a taste for Oriental art, he was a business genius. He was so formal that John Saunders of the Montreal *Gazette* said his idea "of getting casual in his own living room is to unbutton his suit jacket." He was not blatantly egocentric, but neither was he troubled by false modesty. He described himself to a business reporter as "naturally optimistic, determined and, above all, patient".

If anyone told Turmel he was lucky, the *Montreal Star* (Dec. 19, 1977) reported, he replied, "There is no such thing as luck in business. Some people know when to grab an opportunity. . . ." There was, however, such a thing as hard work: "I worked seven days a week, and sometimes on Sunday I'd work from morning until well after midnight. It wasn't easy. It took a lot of sacrifice." Turmel liked to tell journalists about the courage that had enabled him to convert misfortune into success. He was one of seven children of a Coca-Cola bottler in Sherbrooke, Quebec. The crash of '29 ruined the bottler. He lost his house, Buick, bottling plant, and all hope of sending Antoine to medical school. He wangled the boy a job with a grocery wholesaler. At night, Antoine sweated over mail-order courses in business practice because "I always wanted to own a business." The words might have been taken right out of Frank Sobey's mouth.

At twenty-seven, he bought into a doomed toy factory and lost his life savings of three thousand dollars, a mistake he never forgot. Soon, however, he owned a share of a tobacco and confectionery wholesaler in Sherbrooke, and for twenty years he worked like a dog to expand this into a grocery-distribution network. "I bought this small company with two associates who sold out in later years," he recalled for *Executive* (September 1980), "and I ran it from, initially, $200,000 a year to $50 million in 1969. Then we merged with two other [food wholesalers], one running at $50 million a year, and the other at $80 million to $85 million." Thus Provigo was born, and its boss was the man who conceived it. He had dreamed up the merger, he claimed, while recovering from an automobile accident that had laid him up for six months.

His confidence was so monumental that some wondered if he were rational. Provigo was only a year old when he told a sceptical investment community that within six years its sales would double and its profits triple. He turned out to be right. Moreover, he had the nerve to proclaim sunny five-year plans for his company, a habit that could leave gobs of egg on one's face. But not Turmel's. "No company," the *Financial Post* (June 6, 1981) decided, "is more committed to growth than Provigo, where Turmel each five years goes public with astounding objectives – which since 1970 the company has achieved."

He believed the reason Anglo institutions refused to invest in Provigo was anti-French bigotry, but even a French-Canadian investment analyst admitted to the *Globe and Mail* (Dec. 22, 1979) that Turmel's massive ambition was unnerving: "He speaks so calmly and so rationally that it's easy to believe he has it all under control. But when you really listen to all his plans for restaurants, shopping centres, rationalization here, expansion there, you start to wonder if things shouldn't slow down." But when Frank tried to swoop on M. Loeb, Provigo was speeding up. Its sales in 1977 stood at $512,220,000, more than twice those of Sobey Stores. It owned 11 food warehouses, and supplied nealy 1,300 affiliated grocers. More than 700 of these used Provigo house names: Provigain (supermarkets), Provibec (middle-sized stores), Provipop (corner stores). Moreover, the new Provi-Soir outlets, a franchise operation under Provigo control, were popping up at Quebec gas stations like mushrooms in a rain forest. Provigo also owned 33 supermarkets and 17 discount stores. Turmel and a young management team – headed by president Pierre Lessard, a Harvard-educated native of Quebec City – had fashioned this many-tentacled food-distributing machine with what the *Globe* called "the precision of a master strategist".

"Swallowing Loeb," the *Financial Times* (July 4, 1977) thought, "would be a large mouthful for a company that has existed . . . only since 1969 and is still evolving its strategy even in Quebec. But rapid growth, much of it by acquisition, has been Provigo's hallmark." Moreover, if Provigo were to meet Turmel's publicized objective – a billion dollars in sales by 1980 – it would have to capture a food business outside Quebec.

"Nobody ever knew," Turmel told *Executive*, "but we had tried to buy [M. Loeb, Ltd.] two years before [in 1975]. . . . We decided to postpone it because of some legal problems." Bertram Loeb said that M. Loeb's biggest shareholder, Caisse de Dépôt – which also happened to be Provigo's biggest shareholder – had been trying "for three or four years to get Provigo and ourselves to merge voluntarily." Pierre Arbour, who was both a director of Loeb and senior corporate adviser to Caisse de Dépôt, had urged the merger. "I asked him, 'Who will be the emerging company or, rather, who's to be the *surviving* company?' " Loeb said. " 'Whose name will be on the trucks?' He'd say, 'That's something you'd have to work out for yourselves.' . . . Well, you know, Arbour is a tough, hard-nosed, independent businessman, and I'm even worse." If Loeb could not see himself working for Weston, he certainly could not see himself working "for a guy like Turmel. He's not an operator, he's an accountant, a financial man. . . . So I told Arbour, 'If Turmel wants to sell, he knows where I am.' " Indeed he did. He also knew where the shares of M. Loeb were.

Meanwhile, in early 1977, M. Loeb was still the furthest thing from the Sobeys' minds. Their investment preoccupation wasn't buying, it was selling. They owned thirty-seven per cent of National

Sea Products Ltd., which, with sales of $127 million in 1976, was the biggest fishing and fish-processing company on the east coast. They were not overjoyed by the investment. "The directors of National Sea resented us buying these shares," Frank said. "We offered to work with them, but they refused." The Sobeys wanted to unload the stock but they were stuck with it.

National Sea's profits capsized in 1974 after several years of impressive growth. Price of the stock soared to $18 in 1973, plummeted to $5 in 1974. "We knew the fish business was cyclical," Donald Sobey said, "but we never knew it was *that* cyclical." In 1974 he was lunching at the Halifax Club, the Victorian haunt for bluenose business grandees, when an acquaintance told him National Sea had just announced it had quit paying dividends. The Sobeys had sunk millions into National Sea, and they counted on its dividends to finance other ventures. Moreover, the announcement would send the share price of National Sea into a tailspin. "When he told me," Donald said, "I was almost physically sick." The Sobeys had already tried and failed to sell their National Sea shares to another Maritime-based, food-based, family-owned business empire, the McCain brothers of Florenceville, N.B. "Once National Sea cut its dividends," Donald said, "we were stuck. . . . But when it collapsed from about $17 to $6, we bought again." By the summer of 1977, the shares had partly recovered. They were selling at $11.50. What's more, H. B. Nickerson and Sons, Ltd., a fish-processing outfit in North Sydney, N.S., wanted control of National Sea. The time for a deal had ripened.

Meanwhile, David Sobey bought a thousand shares of M. Loeb, Ltd., for himself. He'd been watching it since Warnock had become its president. David bought his shares through Stellarton broker Richard Giles, and Warnock immediately phoned him from Ottawa to find out why a "Mr. Gillis" of Stellarton had suddenly bought a small chunk of his company. "Oh, that's Dick Giles," David said. "He was buying for me." Warnock's keeping such close watch on the stock suggested he was both able and fearful.

Frank Sobey was at his winter house in Bermuda. "I phoned him," David said, "and told him I'd talked with Warnock and bought some shares. I thought I might go up to see Warnock." His father said, "Stick to your own business. Don't go into new business." But Frank's 75-year-old nose for a good thing warned him not to forget M. Loeb and, since he was in Toronto in mid-June, he flew to Ottawa to see what he could worm out of Warnock. It was enough to set him on a course that would earn for the Sobeys a massive investment killing.

There's a blunt Frank Sobey and a persuasive Frank Sobey. Warnock heard the persuasive one. (The blunt one, after surveying a lavish new supermarket in Halifax, growled at his sons, "You fellows keep building stores for *show*. I want stores for *dough*.") Sobey was so persuasive that Warnock served him as a consultant on how to take over M. Loeb. Warnock could think of no majority shareholder in M. Loeb that he'd rather have than the Sobeys, and he knew his management team would agree. Frank, for his part, decided Warnock "could run this business and run it successfully. I'd never have gone for it [a takeover of M. Loeb] if I hadn't thought it had good management."

They soon got down to the nuts and bolts of who owned how much of M. Loeb, and what it would cost the Sobeys to buy it. Warnock had talked to Weston-Loblaw, and "it was my understanding that $6.00 or even $6.25 a share might not secure [Weston-Loblaw's 18.5 per cent]." But he had also visited Marcel Cazavan, president of the Caisse de Dépôt - the outfit that owned 25.3 per cent of M. Loeb - to introduce a potential buyer of its block. "He was trying to get it for under $5.00 a share," Warnock said. That wasn't good enough, but Warnock now knew what was. He told Frank the Caisse de Dépôt would sell its shares for $5.00 (they were trading publicly for $4.20), but that the buyer would have to take the entire block. "This," Warnock recalled, "appeared to fit nicely into Mr. Sobey's evaluation."

Warnock had also learned from Cazavan that two other "interested parties", neither of them in the grocery business, hoped to get the Caisse de Dépôt's chunk of M. Loeb. He knew, too, that Ray Wolfe of Oshawa Group Ltd., a big Ontario-based food-distributor, wanted to take over M. Loeb. (Wolfe later told the

Frank Sobey receives the 1965 Award for Distinguished Contribution to the Industrial Development of Canada from Gérard Lévesque, Quebec's Minister of Industry, on behalf of all of Canada's provincial departments of trade and industry.

Montreal *Gazette* that Turmel had outfoxed him. Turmel, he said, "was smarter than us. While I was talking to the directors, he moved.") What Warnock still did not know, though Bertram Loeb did, was that the real threat to M. Loeb was Provigo. What neither the business press, nor the Caisse de Dépôt, nor Weston-Loblaw knew was that Frank had dealt himself into the game. "His interest was most timely," Warnock recalled. "Stocks [of M. Loeb] were still at a depressed level, but our financial results were improving. Management had settled down. The company was poised for a brighter future. The worst was behind it." He urged Frank to move fast.

By the time Frank headed home to Pictou County, he'd sensed a gorgeous opportunity. He had always had an eye for the main chance, and now M. Loeb looked like the biggest chance of all: a chance at an investment bargain; a chance to reap benefits from the buying power and high-volume rebates of a huge wholesaler; a chance for his sons to command an outfit whose sales were four times those of their own chain; a chance to expand the family empire across the continent. The Sobeys, he thought, could take over M. Loeb.

Speed counted. Gregor Fraser, a Halifax accountant, said Frank was "the fastest, smartest businessman I ever met. If you're talking about a financing concept and trying to figure out where you're going to end up, he's twenty paces ahead of everyone else in the room." He was invariably the first to see the famous "bottom line". The source of this swiftness was a mystery to Fraser, as it has been to Sobey allies and enemies in business wars over half a century. Certainly he did not pick it up at the Harvard School of Business Administration. In grade school he was a mother's despair, a teacher's curse. As a youth, he itched to be in business. As an old man, he was asked to identify qualities that made some businessmen more successful than others. Irritation flickered on his face, as though he thought the question stupid. Then he said, "You've got to *think* business, and you've got to think business all the time. Some men think about sports or whatever, but you've got to think business." When you leave school, he continued, "you know how to read and figure, and from then on you use these tools to keep on learning."

Thinking business on June 17, 1977, he calculated that the price of the Caisse de Dépôt's 1,147,400 shares of M. Loeb, at $5 per share, would be nearly $6 million. He and his sons instantly moved on the block. When the Sobeys wanted something, they wanted it so fast some Halifax lawyers refused to work for them. But as Fraser put it, "Speed is the essential difference between government at its worst and private enterprise at its best. The Sobeys go full steam ahead. They don't wait for studies, reports, research, analysis of the research, and so on. They sniff an opportunity, and they want things done, and they want them done right away, *right now*. That's different from government."

After a council of war, the Sobey clan sicked the Montreal office of Wood, Gundy, Ltd., onto Caisse de Dépôt's block of M. Loeb. Headquarters for Caisse de Dépôt were in Montreal, but there were other reasons for choosing Wood, Gundy, and Wood, Gundy alone. However many brokers the Sobeys might use in sporadic market buying, it made tactical sense to use only one during a raid on so substantial a chunk of one company. Halifax broker David Hennigar, a frequent Sobey ally, explained that "In the early stages of any takeover, you can't have two or more agents possibly working at cross-purposes. If there's more than one guy wandering through the garden it creates problems. You don't want to tip your hand. You don't want to arouse the kind of excitement that raises the market price of the stock. You especially don't want to give some other outfit a chance to make a move on what you're after." Walls have ears, the Street has tongues.

Whom do you choose for a mission of such delicacy and swiftness? "Well," Hennigar continued, "the Sobeys would have wanted someone who knew all the motives and the, uh, possible vulnerabilities of those who held the blocks, someone who knew the *nuances* of the deal. Or at least someone who had the connections and willingness to get on the phone to find out." Wood, Gundy filled the bill. It was not only the discreet lion in the Canadian jungle of investment dealers, it was also an outfit whose services to the Sobeys stretched back two decades.

What happened next happened within hours. On the very day that Frank met Warnock in Ottawa – Friday, June 17 – Wood, Gundy, acting on Sobey instructions, offered the Caisse $5 for each of its 1,147,400 Loeb shares. Wood, Gundy went to the top, of course, to chairman Marcel Cazavan. But the Caisse had investments not only in Loeb but also in Provigo and now – having already urged Provigo to try to grab Loeb, and realizing that the Wood, Gundy offer meant non-Quebecers might snap it up first – the Caisse tipped off Provigo president Antoine Turmel and said, in effect, "It's now or never." Donald Sobey: "I haven't the slightest doubt that's what happened. In fact, Turmel told us later Cazavan had got in touch with him." Loeb saw the fine hand of Pierre Arbour in Provigo's swoop. Arbour, remember, was both a director of M. Loeb and adviser to the Caisse. Talking about him and Turmel, Loeb said, "When you have two men of the same ancestral background, and Quebec trying to make a name for itself in the business community, and they're meeting for cocktails . . . Well?" In any event, Turmel proved to be at least as hawk-like as the Sobeys. "Those Loeb shares," Donald Sobey said, "went to Provigo over the weekend." A letter by Warnock, confirming the gist of his Friday morning talk with Frank, was still on its way from Ottawa to Stellarton.

The Sobeys had moved on the Caisse's block within hours, if not minutes, of Frank's session with Warnock, but nevertheless he cursed himself for having been too slow. Respected for decisiveness, he was privately a worrier-after-the-fact, a self-torturing second-guesser. "Suppose you and Frank decided to drive to Charlottetown," a friend said. "Well, all the way down the highway and on the ferry, he'd be saying, 'Maybe we made a mistake. Maybe we should have gone to Halifax.' " Bill Mingo, the lawyer who worked closely with Frank at IEL, said, "Before a negotiating meeting, we'd agree that we might get this, but might have to give that, and should hold the line on something else. Suppose we then got everything we'd hoped to get, and gave away nothing we hadn't wanted to give, *but the other guys seemed happy*. Well, that bothered Frank. He'd complain later that 'Those fellows looked *pleased*. I guess we weren't tough enough.' "

Now, having failed to get what he wanted from the Caisse, Frank fretted. If only he'd gone directly to the Caisse's office in Montreal the moment he'd left Warnock in Ottawa, if only he'd bearded that "fine gentleman" Marcel Cazavan that very day, Friday, June 17, 1977, and slapped a cheque down on Cazavan's desk. "I should have gone right down to see him," he recalled. "Instead, I fooled around."

By Thursday, rumours of Provigo's takeover ambition had already caused the market price of M. Loeb to spurt from $4.30 to $4.45, and the Montreal and Toronto exchanges suspended trading in the shares. Now Provigo announced not only that it had paid $5 a share to get the Caisse's block of M. Loeb but also that it was out to get all the other Loeb shares and would pay the same amount till August 1. "The first quarter results [for M. Loeb], which showed an increase of fourteen cents a share in profit, may have sparked renewed efforts on the part of Provigo, long considered a suitor for M. Loeb," the *Globe and Mail* (June 24, 1977) speculated. The real spark that had got Provigo off the pot, however, had come from a calculating Loeb suitor in a Nova Scotia town that most central Canadians scarcely knew existed. Frank was playing with the big boys. As the fight continued, he proved he knew how to keep his chin tucked into his chest and his elbows up. And how to hang tough.

To gobble all of M. Loeb at $5 a share would cost Provigo almost $23 million, but few believed Turmel would succeed. Warnock had recently told the press he doubted anyone was plotting a takeover bid, "and certainly not Provigo." The *Globe* reported, "Any major amalgamation that might result from a takeover would probably need approval from the federal government, Mr. Warnock said." Since the feds had saved M. Loeb from Weston-Loblaw, surely they would save it from Provigo. Warnock feared, "If we reduce the food industry through mergers, we will be regulated like the telephone industry." Loeb, who had violently disagreed with Warnock on other matters, was with him on this one. He predicted the feds would foil Provigo because its control of Loeb "would substantially lessen competition, particularly in Quebec."

But leaving aside the possibility that the feds might stop Provigo (they didn't), many agreed with Toronto investment analyst William Chisholm that "They're dreaming if they think they can get one hundred per cent at $5." The book value of M. Loeb, based on current earnings, was $6.50 a share; and therefore, as Chisholm put it, the Provigo offer was "not a particularly generous one." Loeb was characteristically forceful in his contempt for the offer. It "sounded ludicrous." He said, "There is no way in the world that I will tender my shares at this price." Provigo would "never get mine for anywhere near $6." Indeed, by Tuesday, June 28, his anger had reached such a boil that he said Provigo would never get his Loeb shares at *any* price. "It's a free country," said Provigo executive René Provost. "He's free to do what he wants with his property." But Frank would remember Loeb's defiant promise, and exploit it.

"Bertram Loeb," Donald Sobey said, "was bitter, and he had a right to be bitter. At $5, it was a steal." Nor was Weston-Loblaw ecstatic. The government had ordered them to unload their 18.5 per cent of M. Loeb, but not at a loss. Weston-Loblaw could keep the stock till the price rose. "Weston paid $6.03 a share initially," the *Globe* said, "and wants at least $6.40." William Sloan, vice-president of finance for Weston, said $5 was "not the price we had hoped to receive. . . . We don't have any specific price but it certainly wouldn't be any lower than $6.03. We think the shares are worth more than that." Yes, he repeated, $6.03 was the "rock-bottom price" that Weston would accept. Warnock, Frank Sobey, Loeb, everyone who failed to stop Provigo – and indeed even tax sleuths from National Revenue – would later recall Sloan's statements.

On Monday, June 25, Frank and his sons hotfooted it up to Galen Weston's office. "The brushed aluminum doors fit flush with the brushed aluminum walls, and shut so silently and tightly that you can hardly tell they're doors at all," Alexander Ross wrote (*Canadian Business*) while describing Weston's office. "The visitor feels as if he's blundered into the interior of an enormous Japanese stereo receiver." The Sobeys, whose offices in a fixed-up warehouse beside railway tracks were so modest that Frank and Bill discussed business by shouting through a wall, sat down in this environment of "relentless modernity" to negotiate with the 37-year-old, polo-playing tough guy who'd led the Weston-Loblaw turnaround. If they could get their hands on the 18.5 per cent of M. Loeb stock that Weston-Loblaw owned, they might still beat Provigo in the race for the wholesaling company. Frank first proposed that, after the Sobeys had a chunk of Loeb, which they were now buying on the open market, "we put yours together with ours." He described the lucrative Sobey partnership with Famous Players theatres, but, in David's memory, Galen Weston bluntly replied, "We're not interested in just investing. We buy you out, or you buy us out." David added, "They weren't interested in partnerships, only in control." And, indeed, they weren't keen on their seventeen-year-old partnership with Sobeys Stores either.

Did resentment over that investment colour the Weston-Loblaw attitude? "I think some of the old antagonism came into play there," Donald said. "Anyway, Galen Weston wasn't anxious to sell at all." The Sobeys would have paid more than Sloan's "rock-bottom" $6.03. Indeed, they were already considering throwing a spanner into Provigo's works by making a public offer of $6.25 or $6.50. But in Weston's office, Donald said, "The nuts and bolts of it was that in no way were they going to sell to us. They said, 'Maybe, but you'll have to pay a lot.' We said, 'Set your price.' They said, 'We'll let you know,' but they never did."

Meanwhile, the Sobeys and speculators were buying M. Loeb so briskly its market price surged to $5.50. Traffic between Stellarton and central Canada was increasing, too. Still ignorant of what Weston-Loblaw would do, Frank and Donald Sobey secretly met Turmel in a Montreal hotel room. "We discussed what might happen if we just made a public offer of $6.50," Donald said. "He tried to discourage us. He said that would just make the takeover more expensive for Provigo." Turmel talked as though Loeb was already in the bag, and Frank emerged from the meeting with the hunch that Provigo had somehow lined up the Weston-Loblaw block. If he was right, the Sobeys had lost all hope of capturing M. Loeb. But he had a second hunch, and it was like the one he'd felt twenty years earlier after meeting D. G. (Bud) Willmot in another Montreal hotel room. "I sized up Turmel as a real top businessman and manager," he said. "That was the most important asset Provigo had. I remember I said to Donald right then, 'That's a smart fellow. Why not buy Provigo?' "

By now, Wood, Gundy men were popping in and out of Stellarton as the Sobeys prepared their general offer; and Bertram Loeb, forming an axis of necessity with the Sobeys, also arrived in Nova Scotia. Together, they hatched a plot: First, Loeb would pool his and his family's shares and sell them to the Sobeys' Empire Company at $6.25; second, Loeb would buy the Weston-Loblaw block, also at $6.25, and sell that, too, to Empire; and third, Empire would make sure its public offer was so much more attractive than Provigo's (still $5), that the Sobeys would end up with at least fifty-one per cent of M. Loeb. Loeb had arranged to borrow $6 million from the Bank of Montreal, and believed he had a promise from Galen Weston to sell him the Weston-Loblaw block. He talked with both Donald and David Sobey, but "I felt Frank was calling the shots." Frank was calling the shots more than Loeb knew. The key to the plan was Loeb's ability to get the Weston-Loblaw shares. Frank, however, was certain Turmel already had these signed up. Loeb, he recalled, "had no chance of getting them. I knew that. That's why I deliberately left the agreement [between Bertram Loeb and Empire Company] fuzzy."

They signed the agreement on Tuesday, July 12. Two days later, astounding news hit the papers: "PROVIGO BUYS WESTON SHARE OF M. LOEB. . . . LOEB CONTROL MOVES CLOSER FOR PROVIGO. . . . PROVIGO TAKES CONTROL OF LOEB. . . . I'M STILL NOT SELLING, BERTRAM LOEB SAYS." The moment he heard Weston-Loblaw had sold out to Provigo, Loeb phoned Frank, who said, "I'm not surprised." Donald and the Wood, Gundy men were in his Stellarton office when the news came rattling over the Dow Jones ticker. "Well, that's it," Donald said, and the Wood, Gundy men went home to Montreal. Added to the Caisse block and other shares Provigo had picked up, the Weston-Loblaw lump gave Provigo forty-seven per cent of M. Loeb. "We were just at the starting gate," David Sobey said, "but Provigo was already way down the road."

What would buzz round the food industry for months, what Warnock and Loeb would unhappily remember years later, was that Weston-Loblaw agreed to accept from Provigo only $5 a share. Not three weeks had passed since they had flatly stated they wanted not less than $6.03, and preferably $6.40. Now the difference between $5 and $6.40, multiplied by 837,005 shares, is $1,171,807. Why had they given that up? The answer lay in a side-deal. The *Globe and Mail* (July 14, 1977) said, "The sweetener appears to be [Weston-Loblaw's] sale to Provigo of nine food supermarkets operated by Dionne Ltee., a wholly owned subsidiary of Loblaw Cos. Ltd., now eighty-seven percent controlled by Weston." The Dionne chain, a loser by rumour, was mostly in Montreal, and "It

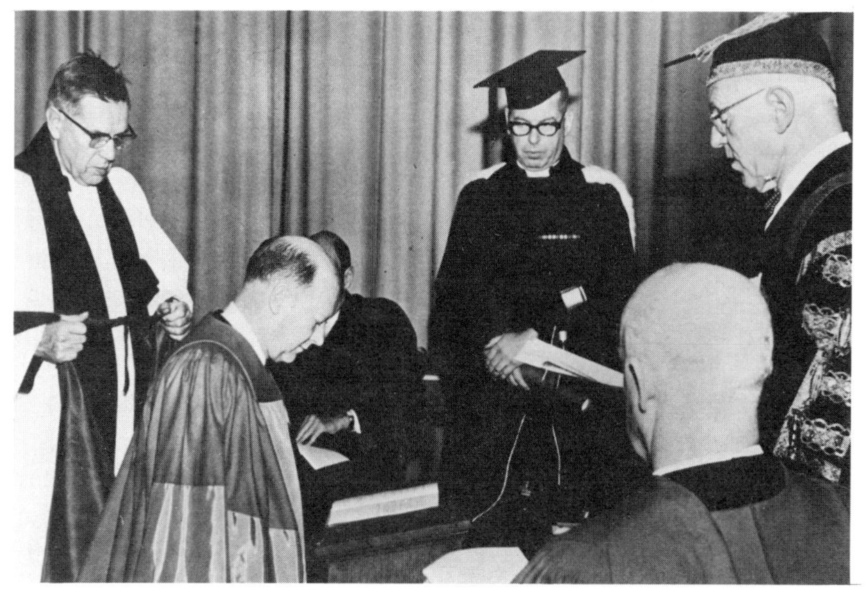

Frank Sobey receiving an honorary Doctor of Laws degree from King's College, Halifax, 1964.

augured well for Weston to unload it to a capable operator such as Provigo, which has a thorough knowledge of the Quebec market, and get $5 a share anyway." Turmel said Provigo had been looking at the Dionne chain "for some time, and we thought we could close two deals at once."

"The two deals were synchronized perfectly," Warnock said. "That's why some figure Weston got their $6.50, after all. They got a sweet deal on the sale of the Dionne stores." Loeb went further: "There were so many sweetheart deals [involving the Dionne stores], they really got more like $10." Four years later, National Revenue investigators, still smelling something fishy, raided the Sobey offices, demanded statements, grabbed files. James Gogan, a Sobey executive, reported to Frank and his sons: "They warned me . . . that I should be aware they have already seized documents and had statements from Bert Loeb and others transacting in Loeb shares. . . . They volunteered on leaving that they are concerned as to why Westons sold their Loeb shares to Provigo for $5 when

. . . Westons could have obtained a higher price from at least two other sources. Apparently they feel the sale of some Dionne stores in a separate transaction, and possibly considerations of entrance to a buying group, may have represented additional considerations for the sale, and on which no capital gains tax was levied." By now, Weston-Loblaw had doubtless had its fill of government. First one department told them to quit buying M. Loeb shares, and sell what they had. Then, when they did sell, another department tried to nail them for tax evasion.

Provigo's victories made it major news in English-speaking Canada for the first time. "There has been much talk on the Street – and some bitterness, too – about the jockeying for position that has been going on," the *Financial Post* (July 23, 1977) said. "Quite obviously, it was something of a poker game. Naturally, Bertram Loeb did not want to see the company, started by his forebear, Moses Loeb, taken over by an organization in another province and with another faith." The *Financial Times* (July 5, 1977) said that if Provigo's "audacious bid" were to succeed, "Provigo will have blossomed from a strictly Quebec-based, francophone food distributor into a diversified food company implanted in much of Canada and large sections of the U.S." Indeed, its sales would zoom to $1.8 billion, making it Canada's fourth-biggest food company, behind only Weston-Loblaw, Dominion Stores, and Canada Safeway. Some saw even larger implications. The Provigo move on M. Loeb, Amy Booth wrote in the *Financial Post* (July 9, 1977), "shows returning market confidence in Quebec stocks. As one analyst put it, 'The market is saying there is zero possibility Quebec will separate.' This is a clear turnaround from November when the Parti Québécois was elected and stocks with a Quebec content took a beating." The business press talked a lot about "aggressive and acquisitive Provigo Inc.".

But what was the aggressive and acquisitive Frank Sobey thinking in Stellarton? Not since he had triggered Provigo's raid on M. Loeb a month earlier had the Sobey name appeared in the press. Outside of the players the Sobeys had approached, no one knew about their role in the affair. Nor did anyone know that after Frank and Donald had emerged from their Montreal meeting with Turmel, the Sobeys had decided to bite off pieces of the very outfit that had defeated them. Provigo's steam-rolling progress toward absorption of M. Loeb only confirmed that it knew what it was doing; and the Sobeys figured that if Turmel's team had looked good without Loeb, it would look three times as good with Loeb. "You see, we knew what a tremendous buy they'd made [in paying only $5 a share for M. Loeb stock]," David Sobey said, "because we'd have paid more." Donald added, "It was a steal, and that's why we went after Provigo."

Frank Warnock, who quit the M. Loeb presidency four years after Provigo took over, glumly recalled the steal. By September 1977, Provigo had paid $18 million to get eighty per cent of M. Loeb, and in Warnock's opinion "That was peanuts. It was a real coup. You had to admire them for it, even if you didn't like it. We could have sold just Horne and Pitfield for that amount. I always figured Provigo ended up buying Horne and Pitfield, and the rest of M. Loeb was just thrown in for nothing. We had Horne and Pitfield running well. We had our western U.S. operations running well. We had M. Loeb *recovering*. From a timing point of view, Provigo could not have done better. Incidentally, if you're talking to Turmel, you'd be smart not to mention my name. I sent a letter to Loeb shareholders to say $5 was not enough, and he'd have taken strong exception to that."

"The important factor" in the Sobeys' raid on Provigo shares, Donald said, "was Father's encouragement and aggression." Now Turmel, like Loeb before him, would know how it felt to have strangers tear off hunks of the company he'd spent so much of his life building. First, however, the Sobeys would need millions of dollars. "We used a $12-million bank credit to buy Provigo," Frank said. They also sold their wedge of National Sea to H. B. Nickerson and Sons for roughly $10 million, and that, Donald said later, "loosened us up to go after Provigo. We had such a slug of National Sea. We were concerned. We thought we should lighten up, but then, with Provigo, we got in heavy all over again."

Nobody who read stories about the Sobeys' selling their National Sea shares in the summer of 1977 would connect them to a Montreal *Gazette* headline that said, "Provigo Now Holds 70% of M. Loeb Ltd." Nor would anyone who pondered Donald's public statements suspect the Sobeys were already pursuing Provigo stock. "We are looking around for investment opportunities," he told the *Globe and Mail*. "We have nothing in mind right now." But, of course, they did. This time the Sobeys used not Wood, Gundy but David Hennigar, manager of the Halifax office of Burns Fry Ltd., stockbrokers and investment counsellors. They knew him well. When Nova Scotians talked about families that dominated bluenose business life they inevitably coupled Jodreys and Sobeys, and Hennigar was already known as a large chip off his grandfather Roy Jodrey's block.

Through Hennigar and a cohort in the Montreal office of Burns Fry, the Sobeys now bought lumps of Provigo from the Sun Life Assurance company and the pension plans of Bell Telephone and Air Canada. To prevent Provigo allies from moving in with higher offers, or from applying what Hennigar called "other pressures", both speed and secrecy were once again crucial. Hennigar's manner was avuncular, jovial, open. He was heavy-set, as his grandfather had been, and appeared neither fast nor furtive. But the moment he knew what the Sobeys wanted in August of 1977, he phoned his man in Montreal. "He got up from his desk and went to work," Hennigar recalled. "To enable him to move quickly, I gave him considerable bargaining freedom." At this stage, not even the Toronto office of Burns Fry knew what its Halifax man was cooking up in Montreal.

"You go and talk to the institutional shareholders to see if you can buy their blocks," Hennigar said. "The way the game works is you go around and you ask them, if you were to offer to trade at, say, two points above the market before a certain deadline, would they sell? You line things up, put it through, and at the last minute maybe others want in on it. The panicky stragglers come in." In the case of Sun Life, the Sobeys paid $14 per Provigo share, which was $1.50 above the market price, but Sun Life insisted on an unusual provision: if, within two years, the Sobeys were to offer a higher price while trying to take over Provigo, they would then pay Sun Life the difference between $14 and the higher amount.

The Sobeys had no intention of taking over Provigo. They only wanted a juicy segment of it, and, as early as the first week in September, Sobeys Stores, Ltd., already owned 470,000 Provigo shares, or 12.5 per cent. Those figures popped up so often in the press that they seemed to represent the total Sobey investment in Provigo. What was not so widely known was that the family, through other companies,owned another 200,000-odd shares; and that, in total, the Sobeys held 18 per cent of Provigo. They were already its second-biggest shareholder, next only to Caisse de Dépôt with 23 per cent.

The Sobeys' buying fuelled rumours of a takeover attempt, and drove the stock to record levels, from $8 to $14 in six weeks. Donald Sobey had little admiration for the investment savvy of the institutions that had sold their Provigo stock to his family. "These outfits," he said, "always have poor timing. They have no investment instinct. It's investment by committee." But a dealer told the *Financial Post* that, once the Sobeys had driven Provigo to $14, "Institutions simply [had] to take another look at their holdings. Where else in this market can you make that kind of capital gain? Holders would be crazy not to think of taking some profit." Now that the Sobeys had an 18-per-cent wedge of Provigo, they wanted even more, and they'd get it in a way that Turmel would neither expect nor relish.

Would it be accurate to say that in September 1977 Provigo feared a Sobey takeover attempt? David Hennigar, who had helped round up roughly 400,000 Provigo shares for the Sobeys, laughed and said, "That would be an understatement." The Sobeys assured Turmel they wanted only "a substantial investment position", and not control; but after 700,000 Provigo shares traded on the Montreal and Toronto exchanges in only eight days, he began to look over his shoulder. On September 17, the *Globe and Mail* reported he'd ordered Provigo's transfer agents to provide an up-to-date list of all shareholders. (As a general rule, Turmel believed, "It's part of a chairman's responsibility to see where the blocks of stock are going. Otherwise you are the target of a takeover, and then you look stupid.")

Provigo executive René Provost said, "We are looking at these transactions very carefully and attempting to find out who is buying and selling our stock. Right now this is the major task of the company's executives. We *have* to know where the shares are going." Not many more would go anywhere for a while. Turmel had been buying Provigo for himself all summer and now owned 9.5 per cent. On September 23, he said that his shares, plus those of other management and of "friendly financial institutions" in Quebec, guaranteed that control still rested "firmly in the hands of management".

Remembering the summer of '77 in 1980, Turmel suggested that the Sobeys, by investing heavily in Provigo, proved they were both more shrewd and less bigoted than the Anglophone investment houses and institutions that had ignored the stock. He had reason to resent the Sobeys in 1980. They had beaten him in a hearing of the Ontario Securities Commission, and had horse-traded their victory into an even bigger share of Provigo for themselves than they'd had in '77. But looking back, he conceded, "They were very smart. . . . They – and I – were the only ones who bought Provigo stock then. Everybody else was selling. Not having been able to purchase Loeb, the Sobeys started buying Provigo and they're now very close to being our largest shareholder, with roughly twenty-five per cent. They've done very well out of it. . . .

"Quite a few large institutions in Montreal – including the pension fund of Air Canada, the pension funds of CNR, Bell Canada, a lot of pension funds, Sun Life – held some of our stock, and all of these sold at $12 or $14. In 1977, the Dow Jones and the Montreal and Toronto exchanges were going down, so I assume that portfolio managers got jittery. They almost all bailed out. The Sobeys were the bidder. Now the stock is at $33, and I think the Sobeys paid an average of no more than $15 for it. So they've made a fairly good killing.

"They were smart people," Turmel continued. "They looked at what Loeb would do to Provigo when the two were joined together. Now my point is, 'Why can't the institutions do the same thing?' There were thousands of institutions that could have looked at it. Portfolio managers tend to take as few chances as possible. They wanted to see what Provigo would do with Loeb before they got involved." The institutions waited. The Sobeys moved. Bertram Loeb sat.

Throughout late 1977 and early 1978 he sat on the last big chunk of M. Loeb, Ltd., that Provigo had failed to get. In April 1978, the *Ottawa Citizen* reported, "He said the scars from the Provigo takeover had healed, and he was going through an emotional rebirth." He said, "I bear no malice toward anyone and do not carry grudges to the grave." His scars may indeed have healed, but nevertheless he'd sworn never to sell his conspicuous wedge of M. Loeb to Provigo, and Provigo needed it. His malice may indeed have melted in Ottawa's spring thaw, but nevertheless in June he launched a class-action suit against M. Loeb and Provigo for discontinuing quarterly dividends. (The Supreme Court of Ontario turned him down.) His grudges may indeed have dissolved during his "year of mourning", but nevertheless, in July, when he finally did sell all that he still owned of the firm his father had founded, he sold to people he knew had enough gristle to stand up to Provigo: Frank Sobey and his sons. In view of Loeb's "emotional rebirth", it would be wrong to suggest he sold to the Sobeys to get revenge against Provigo. But in view of the use to which the Sobeys put the stock he'd sold them, he might be forgiven a last, secret chuckle at Provigo's expense. Within three months Provigo would have reason to resent his selling to the Sobeys.

"It was Father's idea to buy the block from Bert Loeb," Donald Sobey recalled. "He said, 'Why don't we get those shares? Some day they may be valuable.' " Some day Provigo might have to pay through the nose for them. For Provigo's ownership of eighty per cent of M. Loeb did not mean it could do whatever it wanted with the wholesaling giant. It could appoint directors to M. Loeb and run M. Loeb, but not solely for its own benefit. It could not override the interests of the pesky minority that owned twenty per cent. "In borrowing and financing," a Toronto corporation lawyer explained, "you can't just strip the assets of a subsidiary to support the parent, and there might also be tricky decisions on the location of supermarkets, the closing of warehouses. There's a whole raft of conflicting interests in running two similar businesses through two public companies. If you get one hundred per cent, you eliminate the conflicts." Donald said, "We knew Turmel had to get the whole thing. He had to get his hands on Loeb's treasury, and since there were still quite a few minority shareholders, he couldn't just move money around. He needed the treasury." Again it was Hennigar whom the Sobeys fingered for a mission. He had an old, if slight, acquaintanceship with Bertram Loeb, and he flew to Ottawa to see him. "In this case," Hennigar said, "all I did was act as an agent in a private transaction."

"There was no real market-place haggling," Loeb said. Then he described the market-place haggling: "I said I wanted $7.50 a share. Mr. Hennigar said $6.50. I said $7.25. Mr. Hennigar said $6.75. I said, 'I'll tell you what. I want $7.00, and I want it next week.' Mr. Hennigar said, 'Done.' I had the cheque in a few days." Since he'd sold more than 550,000 shares, the cheque was for almost $4 million. Though this was $1.1 million more than he'd have collected if he'd meekly accepted Provigo's $5 offer, it was several millions fewer than he'd have reaped if he'd held onto his shares and used them as the Sobeys soon did. But he no longer had the heart for such manoeuvring. He was sick of the food business and had loans to pay. He wrote to Hennigar to say their agreement had been quick, clean, and satisfying.

"I sold to Sobeys simply because I got the price I was looking for," Loeb said. "I wanted $7.00 a share, and I didn't care who the buyer was [as long as it was not Provigo]. I wanted to retire bank debt. I wanted $7, and I told Mr. Hennigar, 'I hope it goes to $14.' I was happy to sell it. I was happy to get my price. I was happy to sell to Frank Sobey, and I was happy the Sobeys were ultimately able to use those shares to increase their position in

Provigo. . . . I keep a hundred shares of Provigo, just to stay in touch with my former business. They send me the annual reports."

Nine weeks after the Sobeys paid $7 for each of 550,000-odd shares of M. Loeb, Ltd., Provigo tried to force them to sell those same shares to Provigo for $8 each. Now a $550,000 gain during one summer might smell tantalizing to some, but not to the Sobeys. "We wanted shares, not cash," Frank said tersely. "If we took cash, we had the capital gains tax." Moreover, as Donald put it, "We just didn't want to be forced out. We had bought a position in the grocery industry of Canada, and that's very hard to get. We didn't *want* cash."

Press accounts referred not to a squeeze-out but to "a proposed amalgamation" or "a consolidation". The *Toronto Star* (Sept. 26, 1978) said, "The directors of Ottawa-based M. Loeb Ltd. and of Edmonton-based Horne and Pitfield Foods Ltd. have agreed in principle to amalgamate with Provigo, creating a corporate giant with projected sales of almost $2 billion. . . . Loeb will become a wholly owned subsidiary of Provigo, and Horne and Pitfield a wholly owned subsidiary of Loeb." Since M. Loeb owned 86.6 per cent of the common shares of Horne and Pitfield, and Provigo owned 80.3 per cent of M. Loeb, it did not take a detective to determine who was calling the shots. Provigo, in the jargon of investment people, was "going private" with M. Loeb by eliminating the minority shareholders.

Turmel's squeeze play began on September 22 when Provigo transferred its own M. Loeb shares to a company called "Holdings". Holdings was a shell, a squeeze-out tool. The idea was that M. Loeb and Holdings would amalgamate, and all shares of Holdings would be converted into common shares of the amalgamated company. Provigo would own one hundred per cent of the new outfit, and would simply cancel the 80.3 per cent of M. Loeb that it had transferred to Holdings. Owners of the remaining M. Loeb stock (19.7 per cent) would get one preference share of the amalgamated company, immediately redeemable at $8, for each of their M. Loeb shares. Provigo, in short, would become M. Loeb's sole shareholder. All this was to come to pass at a special meeting of M. Loeb shareholders on November 3. Then, presto! Provigo would have what it wanted. The minority shareholders, instead of getting the $5 per share that Provigo had offered in 1977, would now get $8, and everyone would live happily ever after.

But Frank did not see it that way at all. As his lawyers argued later, "The effects of the proposed transaction are (a) to permit Provigo to acquire compulsorily the balance of the Loeb common shares with Loeb's assets and (b) to force each holder of a Loeb common share (other than Holdings) to sell his Loeb common share for $8 per share cash, whether or not he wishes to sell at this time, and whether or not he wishes to sell at [this price.]" The Sobeys did not want to sell either at that time or at that price; and when push came to shove, Frank, despite his loathing for legal costs, had never been reluctant to call a lawyer. Corporation lawyers are the mercenaries of the business world, and the Sobeys wanted the best. Naturally, they went to Henry Rhude.

Rhude, at fifty-four, was a discreet star among the three dozen lawyers at the venerable Halifax firm of Stewart, MacKeen & Covert, and seemed likely to inherit the unofficial title of Mr. Corporation Lawyer in Nova Scotia. Moreover, Rhude had helped mould the Sobey empire, and Frank valued his advice. Rhude's advice was to hire H. Garfield Emerson of the Toronto firm Davies, Ward & Beck. Emerson's office was on the forty-seventh floor of Commerce Court West in the high-rise heart of the Big Business neighbourhood. Emerson was a neatly tailored, neatly barbered, bespectacled man with a cherubic face. He was actually thirty-eight, but if he hadn't been so confident and articulate one might have suspected his pipe was a prop to make him look mature.

His task was to persuade the Ontario Securities Commission to confirm one of its own policies, and apply it. A spate of squeeze-outs, force-outs, and ruthless amalgamations had inspired the OSC to outline "the majority-of-the-minority test". This required "that a squeeze-out element of a going-private transaction should not be carried out *unless approved by a majority of the minority shareholders affected.*" The OSC had distributed the test on July 14,

1978. On July 21 the Ottawa *Citizen* announced that Bertram Loeb had sold out to the Sobeys. Now they had 11.7 per cent of M. Loeb. That made them the majority of the minority, which was bad news for Turmel.

On the face of it, Provigo could not squeeze out the Sobeys against their will. "But a policy of the Ontario Securities Commission is not a *law*," Emerson explained. "It's therefore subject to change." Moreover, the test itself had not been tested. The OSC's majority-of-the-minority policy was untried, and its future fascinated corporation lawyers. That was why it was that, on October 23, 1978 – when Frank and Donald Sobey arrived in Toronto from Stellarton to attend a hearing of the OSC, and Turmel arrived from Montreal for the same showdown – they found a buzzing audience of expensively tailored men. "The place was jammed," Donald said. "It looked like practically every lawyer in Toronto was in the room."

They were there, Emerson recalled, partly because "this was a classic squeeze-out attempt." Provigo's timing had been typically sharp. M. Loeb "had been turned around," but before the market had reflected the improvement Provigo tried to mop up its stock. "So the shares of M. Loeb were undervalued," he said. That was interesting, but not so interesting as the matter of Sobey toughness. "In all these squeeze-out things," Emerson continued, "you need a leader." Minority shareholders were often weak, ill-informed, and scattered, but Frank was not an easy man to confuse or bulldoze. "Here you had a large and resolute minority shareholder," Emerson said, "one that was prepared to defend its rights. The Sobeys knew the company. They knew its shares were worth more than $8. They knew the deal they were getting was unfair, and they had the determination to hire us to fight for them. . . . That ended up benefiting the other minority shareholders as well."

Provigo lawyers urged the OSC not to let the Sobeys exploit the new policy in order to twist Provigo's large arm on their own behalf. The Sobeys, they argued, wanted to use their M. Loeb block simply to increase their fat (now nineteen per cent) share of Provigo or, failing that, to pry out of Provigo more than $8 for their Loeb

J. W. Sinclair, a director of Empire Company Limited.

shares. Moreover, Provigo insisted, $8 was *fair*. The stock had peaked at $7.50 in September. Nesbitt Thomson Securities, Ltd., had evaluated it at $6.75. The Sobeys themselves had paid the knowledgeable Bertram Loeb only $7. On top of all this, the Sobeys could always resort to the so-called "appraisal remedy". This meant that the squeezed-out could appeal to a court to set a higher price. "Their argument," Emerson explained, "was that the minority shareholders are already protected because they can always go to court to seek their price. So what's the fuss?" The fuss was that the Sobeys said no.

"We didn't object to Provigo's wanting the hundred per cent," Emerson said. "It was the *manner* of the squeeze-out the Sobeys opposed. They didn't want to be forced out for cash. . . . We argued that the shares weren't currency, they were property. This is my desk, right? It's a piece of property. No one can take it away from me, *even if the price is fair*. . . . Now in this case, the Sobeys were saying, 'These are our shares. We don't think others should have the power to force us to sell if we don't want to sell. Not at *any* price.'"

"It was argued [by the Sobeys] that a share is personal property," the OSC reported, "and any particular shareholder may have his own sufficient reasons for wishing to retain that property. . . . Empire . . . does not want cash when its holdings in Loeb and Provigo provide the only available means for it to participate in the grocery business on a nation-wide basis, and to a lesser extent in the United States. No dollars can compensate for those holdings when no other equivalent holdings are available."

The OSC's decision was sweet news for the Sobeys, the other minority shareholders, and Emerson: "It is fairness that [the majority-of-the-minority policy] is directed to, and it is not for the majority to tell the minority what is fair or what is in its best interest. It is for the minority to make that decision by a majority vote. . . . It is that Policy that we insist on being adhered to in this transaction, and in issuing a cease-trading order to prevent the squeeze-out proposed."

"We'll be in the law books," Emerson exulted. Donald Sobey, who was less thrilled about that than about having Provigo over a barrel, said later, "So far as Canadian takeovers go, I guess it was a revolutionary ruling." On December 5, 1978, *Toronto Star* financial editor Robertson Cochrane called it "a landmark decision". Emerson happily recalled, "Everyone wanted copies of our brief," and the OSC sent it off to provincial securities commissions across the country. (It is a tribute to the Toronto Stock Exchange's domination of the Canadian investment scene, incidentally, that Montreal and Nova Scotian grocery tycoons could not settle their differences without appearing before an Ontario business tribunal.) Emerson, who'd been a history student at college, felt, "The real significance of the decision lay in the deals that, from then on, would never even be attempted."

As the hearing broke up, Donald remembered, "Father and I went up to Turmel and said, 'Any time you want to talk . . .' But he was decidedly cool." Within two months, however, Turmel warmed a bit. Holding a grudge against the Sobeys would not get him one hundred per cent of Loeb. Dealing with them might. Just before Christmas, Turmel phoned Donald and they met to discuss what the Sobeys had wanted all along: an exchange of their M. Loeb stock for Provigo stock. On April 24, 1979, Provigo and M. Loeb announced a plan to amalgamate Loeb with a wholly-owned Provigo subsidiary, and at the same time to give the M. Loeb minority shareholders one common share of Provigo for each two common shares of Loeb. "Mr. Turmel," the news release continued, "also said that this proposal values the Loeb common shares at about $12 per share, based on the current market price of Provigo common shares." For 1,800 shareholders who had stubbornly clung to their stock, M. Loeb had come a long way in the twenty-two months since Provigo had begun to corral it at $5 per share. They could thank the Sobeys for that.

Provigo soon absorbed M. Loeb in an "Amalgamated Corporation to save expenses associated with being a public corporation and to have greater flexibility in financing operations and pursuing new business objectives, and to eliminate certain potential conflicts of interest." M. Loeb, in short, had "gone private", which meant it had gone. Provigo had finally gulped all of it, but gulping that last 19.7 per cent had been costly. Perhaps the cost Turmel disliked most was the 277,750 shares of Provigo he'd handed over to the Sobeys in order to get their block of M. Loeb. Pierre Lessard, the president of Provigo and a man forty years Frank's junior, told him later that buying Bertram Loeb's shares was "the smartest deal you ever made".

"We ended up with a total of about a million shares," Donald said. That was twenty-five per cent of the hottest food-merchandising corporation in Canada, an outfit whose sales in 1979 would reach $2.3 billion. By November of '79 Provigo stock, which had sold for as little as $7 only three years before, had reached a record high of $29 on the Toronto Stock Exchange. Moreover the best was yet to come.

A year later, after Dominion Stores and a consortium of Quebec government co-ops had dickered for months over the sale of all of Dominion's Quebec supermarkets to the co-ops, Provigo barged into the negotiations, shouldered aside the consortium, and made Dominion an offer it couldn't refuse. What gave Provigo its chance was that the co-ops were dithering and gossipy. Provigo, in a style the Sobeys doubtless applauded, was quick and quiet. Only Turmel, Lessard, and one other executive had a hand in Provigo's negotiations. Allen Jackson, Dominion's president, said the bargaining occurred during only two telephone calls and three short meetings. Conrad Black, who, along with Montegu Black, controlled Dominion Stores through Hollinger Argus Ltd., said, "We told Provigo we were close to a deal already so that we couldn't give them a significant amount of information. But Provigo took a flamboyant view and came in with a substantially better offer in cash terms."

Provigo offered $105 million, roughly $10 million more than the co-op. For that, it got eighty-seven supermarkets, seventy of them in and around Montreal, and six warehouses. "This is a way to increase our market share in the Montreal area in one swoop," Lessard said. Provigo's 1980 sales, he predicted, would reach $3 billion; but in 1981 the acquisition of Dominion's Quebec division would add a further $500 million. Now, said the Montreal *Gazette* (Dec. 19, 1980), Provigo was "Canada's second-largest food retailer". Only Loblaw was bigger. On the Toronto Stock Exchange the price of Provigo, which had been $28 earlier in the year, closed 1980 at $56.50; and in Stellarton, Frank and his sons, who had bought a million shares at an average price of $12 or $13, had massive paper profits to celebrate the New Year.

The stock soon rose to $65, and the market value of the Sobeys' share of it hovered around $65 million. On this one adventure alone then, Frank's family, led by him in his late seventies, achieved a paper gain of more than $50 million in four years. "Their judgment was excellent on that," said John Jodrey, uncle of David Hennigar, and president of Canadian Keyes Fibre, Hantsport, N.S. A Jodrey company had bought some Provigo, but, he said ruefully, "We should have bought more. We make Provigo's egg cartons. Of course, we also make Loblaw's egg cartons, and Dominion's egg cartons, and the Sobeys' egg cartons."

The story of the Sobeys and Provigo was not over.

Shortly after the Sobeys' victory at the Ontario Securities Commission, their eighteen-year relationship with Weston-Loblaw came to a nasty head. Sobeys Stores, Ltd., called a special shareholders' meeting on December 1, 1978, to get authority to raise $10 million in equity financing. Sobeys stock was attractive, the time was ripe. "When people want something and are ready to pay for it," Donald Sobey said later, "that's when you give it to them." Trouble was, Loblaw Companies Ltd. still owned forty per cent of the voting stock, and according to Nova Scotia law that was more than enough to squelch the proposed financing. Loblaw now chose to do exactly that. It sent Halifax lawyer George B. Robertson to Stellarton as its proxy, and he refused to vote the Loblaw shares in favour of the special financing resolution. Having acted as the Loblaw agent in the frustration of major Sobey plans, he now returned to Halifax; and Loblaw doubtless assumed the matter was settled for a while.

But on December 11, only ten days after that seemingly decisive meeting, Sobeys Stores, Ltd., held *another* shareholders' meeting. No one at Loblaw knew about this one till it was all over, which was wonderfully convenient for Sobeys. With no Loblaw representative to gum up the works, shareholders now passed the crucial financing resolution and agreed to hold the required "confirmatory meeting" on December 27. Loblaw, a Halifax lawyer recalled, was "absolutely livid", and immediately sought a court injunction against the holding of the confirmatory meeting. Loblaw believed its ignorance of the December 11 session had been no accident.

The date on the notice of this second (and in Loblaw's opinion, clandestine) gathering was December 1, which suggested Sobeys Stores had decided to call it the moment Robertson was out the door. He later swore he talked with Bill Sobey by phone on December 5, and advised him to phone Loblaw president Richard Currie about certain operational matters. Bill, however, did not tell Robertson about the shareholders' meeting that was now only six days away, and he did not phone Currie. Notice of the meeting reached Loblaw headquarters on the eleventh, the day it was held, and landed on Currie's desk on the twelfth. Some Stellarton guys, Loblaw decided, had just pulled a fast one.

While applying for an injunction to undo what Sobeys Stores had done, Loblaw lawyers argued that some directors had bet "on the exigencies of the mails, particularly in a pre-Christmas time," to enable them to exclude Loblaw from the shareholders' meeting: "The intent of what was done was to improperly and in bad faith deprive Loblaw of [its] right to receive timely notice, instruct a proxy, attend at the meeting, speak on the Resolution and vote its shares." *Improperly and in bad faith.* That was tough talk. Faced with the injunction threat, Sobeys Stores, in the third week of December, called off the confirmatory meeting of the twenty-seventh.

But why had Loblaw blocked the refinancing plan in the first place? "Extortion" was too harsh a word to apply, but the veto did demonstrate that, if the Sobeys wanted to run their chain in their own way, then they'd really have to buy back that forty per cent, wouldn't they? And if their need was great, the price might also be great, mightn't it? It took them and Loblaw another two years to come to terms. "Loblaw bought those shares twenty years ago with an obvious eye toward purchasing the rest at a later date," Frank told the press in November 1980. "That did not happen, and wasn't about to happen, so we reached an agreement with them to buy the interest back. With the purchase of the Loblaw interest we now control almost one hundred per cent of the voting shares in Sobeys Stores, Ltd. We had about fifty-eight per cent before, and this leaves very few around." The shares were back where they belonged, in his family's hands.

Currie was also pleased. For two decades Loblaw had sat on this passive investment, reaping only modest dividends. Now it would have fresh millions to pump into operations. In 1960 Loblaw had paid under $1 million for the stock, and in 1980 it got roughly $5 million, considerably above market value. Ironically, the Sobeys were partly paying the price of their own shrewdness: thanks to their Provigo machinations, the trading price of the Sobeys stock they bought back from Loblaw was higher than ever before.

New machinations began in January 1982. Empire and the Caisse de Dépôt flirtatiously circled each other, and to those unaware of Sobey pragmatism the subsequent alliance would seem improbable. Only five years had passed since the Caisse had helped Provigo beat the Sobeys for M. Loeb. Moreover, many national corporations now feared that the Caisse, a Crown corporation, was an instrument of Quebec nationalism and would buy enough shares of their companies to influence their direction.

"As manager of employee pension funds worth $14 billion, including the Quebec Pension Plan," the *Globe and Mail* said in March 1982, "it holds the country's largest portfolio of Canadian stocks and bonds. Its tentacles are everywhere. . . . Yet the Caisse is not required to file an insider trading report with the Ontario Securities Commission. . . . As long as huge bodies like the Caisse are free to pop up like wild cards in the middle of the stock exchange, other investors will be playing against a stacked deck."

Frank detested government intrusion in the marketplace, but he was also the eternal pragmatist. With respect to the Caisse's controversial acquisitions, he said, "It's bad when government gets into these things, but there they are. You can't fight city hall." The Sobeys wanted money. The Caisse was rolling in it. On January 5, 1982, as Empire was preparing to issue shares to the public for the first time, Donald went to Montreal to see Jean Campeau, chairman and general manager of the Caisse. His ostensible purpose was to intrigue the Caisse with the new Empire stock. "I also wanted to talk about Provigo," he recalled, "but I didn't want to walk in and just start right in by talking Provigo." So they talked about Empire until it became clear that what Campeau really wanted was some of the Sobeys' Provigo stock. With his brother David, Donald next met Campeau and other Caisse officials over lunch in a private room at a Montreal hotel.

Sobey companies and the Caisse together owned well over forty per cent of Provigo. But Turmel preferred to run things his own way, and he'd invited to his board neither his allies at Caisse during the struggle for Loeb, nor his antagonists at Empire. Caisse had asked for Provigo directorships, and Turmel had said no. "The Caisse was furious," Donald said. "No, let's just say the Caisse didn't like this at all. They felt that, with their stake in Provigo, they should be involved in policy discussions at the board level."

The Sobeys were happy with Provigo management, and had

not asked for directorships, but, as Donald put it, "When you have that much money in a company it's important to be able to watch it closely." Moreover, the Sobeys' stake in Provigo was so substantial, and the political climate of Quebec so tricky, that they felt vulnerable. No national chain would dare buck the mood of Quebec, not to mention anti-combines sentiment in Ottawa, to try to take over Provigo. Moreover, law restricted the Caisse from ever owning more than thirty per cent of Provigo's voting stock, and the Caisse already had twenty-two per cent. "So we had four million shares of Provigo," Donald said, "but if we ever wanted to sell them, who would we sell them *to*? We were concerned that some day we might get left out in the cold." It was Campeau who suggested the Sobeys and the Caisse strike a deal not only on the sale of Provigo shares but also on working together to force Turmel to give them directorships and thereby reduce the chances of being left out in the cold.

"I put it right up front at the beginning," Donald said. "I said, 'We want some liquidity, and we want you fellows to be the bankers. And we also want to be on the board.' " Bill Sobey joined his brothers for heavy dickering with the Caisse on February 11. "Those were very tiring negotiations," Donald said. "You had to be on your toes." Provigo stock (which had split, four for one) was trading at 9¾, but the Sobeys wanted a premium for their block, and they hung tough till they got it. The haggling was also intense over their demanding the right to repurchase in future the shares they were now selling. They got that, too.

By Friday, March 12, the deal was final. The Sobeys sold 1,444,427 common shares of Provigo to the Caisse for $15,888,697, or $11 per share. "Bill, Donald, and I met in the Caisse boardroom [in the Montreal Stock Exchange building]," David said, "and, with a couple of concessions, we tendered the shares." Sobey lawyer Robert Dexter rushed the cheque to the nearest Bank of Nova Scotia, which transferred the funds to the Stellarton branch just in time to draw interest over the upcoming weekend, a little matter of roughly $20,000. Now Caisse owned thirty per cent of Provigo, its legal limit, while the Sobey holding was reduced to thirteen per cent. Out of the deal, however, arose a Sobey-Caisse axis, an agreement to use the combined clout of their forty-three per cent to wrest directorships from Provigo.

"When we finished the deal," Donald said, "we left it to the Caisse to tell Turmel what had happened." It had seemed wiser to let the French Canadians discuss the ticklish development in their own language. "Jean Campeau [president of the Caisse] told me later Turmel wasn't happy at all. In fact, he was furious." But there was little he could do. By summer, four new directors were popping up at board meetings of Canada's second-biggest food-distributor. Two were from the Caisse. The others were Donald and David Sobey.

Finally, the sales agreement specified the Sobeys could buy back their Provigo shares, over nine years, at a price guaranteeing the Caisse a twenty-per-cent gain. In short, the Sobeys could get them back at a fair price if Provigo zoomed on the stock market. The buy-back clause would prove to be worth millions to the Sobeys.

"How'd you get such a good deal?" Frank asked at an Empire directors' meeting.

"They [the Caisse] were so anxious for that vote," Donald said. "They really wanted to get someone on that board."

11

THE MAN, THE EMPIRE, THE DYNASTY

FRANK, on occasion, was tough enough to chew spikes. He was tough about investment decisions, tough in real-estate transactions, tough on anyone he felt had betrayed him, tough on organized labour. But since Frank had none of the snootiness of some arch-capitalists, he got along well with certain labour leaders. He was a straight talker, a fine fellow for a working man to sit down with over a beer, a guy who'd known miners all his life and worked alongside them at the Stellarton town council. Stephen Dolhanty of Florence, N.S., an officer of the United Mine Workers, sat with Frank on the Atlantic Development Board, and they enjoyed having a drink together. But Dolhanty was not trying to start a union in a Sobeys store or warehouse, and that's why Frank found him such a decent bloke.

Leo McKay had a vivid memory of just how tough a younger Frank Sobey could get with a union. Born in Stellarton himself, McKay was executive secretary of the Nova Scotia Federation of Labour in 1983, but a quarter-century earlier he'd been an employee at the car works in Trenton. He was also a part-time labour organizer, "and I organized the Sobey warehouse. I signed them all up. Then they were certified as Local 1015, the Retail, Wholesale and Department Store Union." John Lynk (chairman of the Workers' Compensation Board in 1983) "did the negotiating, he negotiated an agreement. It went to the conciliation board, and we went through the whole dance. You know what? Frank flatly refused to sign it." (Frank says today that the union failed to sign up a majority of the workers.)

"Not only that, he told the employees they could strike if they wanted to, as a matter of free choice, but that if they did, he'd just go around them. He wouldn't use the warehouse. He could still deliver by truck to all his stores. I knew he could do that, and I advised them not to strike. They couldn't have won. He was too big, and they were too small. It was a fight that lay dormant for twenty years.

"Then when the Sobeys opened their big new warehouse in Stellarton, the union dusted off its old certification and reactivated it, and this time they got a contract. Later, they switched to United Food and Commercial Workers and [after a company lock-out] struck for a better contract. That was a bitter one. People were fired and never taken back again. They were black-balled. . . . Sobeys Stores still have people on staff to keep the unions out."

"You want to know how we keep the unions out?" Frank said. He explained that although fewer than five per cent of the stores are unionized, the company gives employees in all the stores the same benefits that those under contract have won. Then there was the pension and profit-sharing plan. It was so successful it had enabled some employees to retire on higher incomes than they'd earned as workers. "The plan had become very attractive to our employees," he said. "I think it's the best pension plan in eastern Canada." Union members are eligible for other benefits, but not for the profit-sharing part of the plan.

Distasteful as unions were to Frank, he was too practical to pretend the chain could avoid dealing with them. You couldn't stop the world from changing. You could only adjust your ground, and go on from there to make the best possible deal for yourself. The chain survived fierce strikes in the seventies, particularly in Saint John and Sydney. While the Stellarton warehouse walk-out loomed in 1981, the 79-year-old honorary chairman told his sons and the rest of his management team, "I often wonder what it would cost us *not* to have a strike." Some looked confused. During negotiations, he continued, it might be smart to "sweeten things early" to get a long-term contract: "If you can get a three-year contract, it might pay to put on a little front-end load."

The Sobeys Stores annual report for 1962 said, "The company's largest supermarket is being readied for an early fall opening in the Webb and Knapp Halifax Shopping Centre," but behind that flat statement lay a story about Frank's speed, bravado, and tenacity. His ally in toughness was Henry B. Rhude.

J. G. DeWolf, Frank's real-estate eyes in Halifax and "a good Catholic", tipped him off that a church institution was about to sell a tantalizing tract. Not only that, DeWolf said, the T. Eaton department-store empire was going to bid on it. Frank went straight to Toronto to see William Park, vice-president and secretary-treasurer of most Eaton's companies. Frank knew he couldn't afford the land, but he tried a bluff. "Why bid against each other?" he said. "We'll only drive the price up." He returned to Stellarton with a verbal deal, confirmed only with a handshake. Eaton's would buy the land, but Sobeys Stores would get a prime supermarket location. Better still, the Sobeys would get a piece of the equity in the entire development, and its size would depend on the proportion of the mall the supermarket occupied. "If the whole thing was 100,000 square feet and our store was 5,000 feet," he explained, "then we'd get five per cent of the equity."

Eaton's, however, soon arranged to turn all the land over to Webb and Knapp (Canada) for development, on the understanding the department store would be the major tenant. Top dog at Webb and Knapp was the legendary New York developer William Zeckendorf, the man behind the $105-million Place Ville Marie. With more rental space than the Empire State Building, Place Ville Marie would soon change the face and character of downtown Montreal; and Webb and Knapp, a predecessor of the Trizec Corporation, was among the mightiest development firms in the world. A promise by Eaton's to a fellow named Sobey meant little to them.

"Webb and Knapp didn't want any partners," Rhude recalled, "so here was Frank, apparently pushed out in the cold, with no written agreement. Eaton's told them about the obligation to him, but they didn't take it too seriously at first. I think they thought that here was a little guy who was rumoured to have five per cent, and the hell with him."

"They tried every way they could think of to get Eaton's to break this verbal deal with me," Frank said. "I heard they even threatened to pull out entirely unless Eaton's agreed to cut me out, but Eaton's kept its word. . . . So Webb and Knapp finally came to me and said I'd have to put up $5 for every $100 they put up. I'd get five per cent of it, after all, but they told me I'd have to put up five per cent of the money. I said I would, but I knew I wouldn't have to. I knew I'd never have to put up a dollar because I knew they wouldn't either. They'd just borrow it all.

"Well, then they wanted to sell fifty per cent to an English company, and here I was, sitting in the middle with five per cent. I knew they had to have it." At the showdown in Montreal, Rhude and Frank squared off against Webb and Knapp lawyers and executives, including James A. Soden, the next president of the company and later the chairman of Trizec. The Nova Scotians hung tough.

"They thought they had us over a barrel," Frank said, "but I knew we had them over a barrel, and Harry's a tough negotiator." Rhude picked up the story: "We knew they had a time problem regarding their commitments, and we threatened to get an injunction to prevent them mortgaging the property. We'd actually have had a hard job getting that, but we talked big. That's the only way to talk in these circumstances. We came up with this outrageous figure, a big figure for this five-per-cent interest. A very big figure." Frank sold his "interest" to Webb and Knapp for $185,000, and put the money into Empire Company. Aside from travel and legal expenses, he hadn't put up a nickel.

Nor was the $185,000 all he got. In his usual style, he'd phoned a crony, Loblaw general manager George Huffman, to discover that Webb and Knapp was charging Loblaw $1.85 per square foot at a West Coast mall. He used this information during his haggling with the development giant, and when the Halifax Shopping Centre opened in 1962, its supermarket anchor was a Sobeys store paying $1.87 per square foot on a twenty-year term, with three renewal clauses. Just how good a deal this was may be seen in the fact that by 1980 some Nova Scotian supermarkets were paying as much as $10 a square foot.

"Eaton's was very, very reliable," Frank concluded. "With all these larger companies, I have found that their word was as good as their bond."

But that was not how he ultimately felt about his friend Charles MacCulloch. MacCulloch came from Kennetcook in the forests between Windsor and Truro and, in *Maclean's* words, was "an empire builder in the best Maritimes rags-to-riches tradition of Lord Beaverbrook and Sir James Dunn," not to mention Roy Jodrey and Frank Sobey. MacCulloch, Jodrey, and Frank were the conspicuous self-made millionaires from the boondocks among the directors of Halifax Developments Ltd., which built the $60-million Scotia Square on a former slum in the heart of Halifax. Scotia Square was partly the result of a remarkable alliance of families: Sobeys, Jodreys, MacCullochs, and the Oland brewing family. One director was Malcolm H. D. McAlpine of the British family whose Canadian construction firm, Robert McAlpine Ltd., got the contract to build Scotia Square.

The Canadian director of the firm, another Robert McAlpine (a kinsman of the British family but not a close relative), recalled, "I was in on the very inception of Scotia Square, and I don't know of any similar venture in Canada that was ever created by a group of families getting together like that. . . . I knew that if Malcolm McAlpine died, his sons would complete it. I knew that if Frank Sobey died, *his* sons would complete it. Frank brought up the most amazing family. Without them, there were times it [Scotia Square] would have died." The McAlpine firm built huge malls for both the Sobeys and MacCulloch. "Frank and Charlie were great friends," McAlpine said, "but there was also great rivalry between

Robert Manuge, former general manager of IEL and a current director of Empire Company Limited.

them." He liked both men, and would wonder where he stood when their feud erupted in a way that both horrified and titillated the close-knit bluenose business community.

Frank and MacCulloch were sufficiently close in the late sixties that MacCulloch was a director of a Sobey company. He was also on the board of Frank's beloved IEL. When Halifax Developments Ltd. faced financial collapse in 1967, it was MacCulloch who negotiated a $16-million mortgage from Metropolitan Life in New York, and his friends therefore saw him as the saviour of Scotia Square. But Frank never bought that theory. "Anybody could have got that [mortgage]," he snorted. "The president of Metropolitan Life in Ottawa told me that any time we wanted more we could have it. It was the property that got that mortgage, plus the names on the board. You don't get a mortgage on the strength of your face. You get it on the value of your property."

The HDL board nevertheless named MacCulloch president. Moreover, he succeeded Frank as chairman of IEL in 1970, and, at the Micmac Mall in Dartmouth, plunged into the development adventure of his life. MacCulloch's roller-coaster career was hurtling towards its highest peak.

He was aggressive, daring, hard-headed, well-tailored, well-built. He'd once been a rowing champion. He wore a mustache, and his cocky, virile charm reminded some of movie star Clark Gable. The comparison did not displease him. He impressed women, and owned an entire resort island in the West Indies. Beside other blue-nose tycoons he was flashy and, even by their standards, a shade too acquisitive. A convivial man, he was also a bit of a loner. It was sometimes said of him that, "If you're into something good with Charlie, he wants you out. If it's bad, he wants you in." E. G. Odette, president of Eastern Construction Company Ltd., recalled that when his firm was helping build Scotia Square, "MacCulloch saw all our cement coming in, and he says to my ready-mix man, 'Hey, I want you to come and manage my ready-mix cement firm.' Well, my man says, 'But you haven't even got a ready-mix firm,' and MacCulloch says, 'No, but I'm sure as hell going to have one soon.' "

By the time HDL had the major financing for Scotia Square, Robert McAlpine Ltd., the general contractors, had already spent a million dollars, mostly on installing the footings and foundation. "Well, Charlie was prepared to let us hold that bag, and lose that money," Robert McAlpine said. "Frank didn't think that was fair. I remember his chilly blue eyes while he assessed the situation. Charlie had this tendency to ride on other people's money. He really didn't see anything wrong with that [letting the McAlpine firm absorb the million]. He simply thought it was good business." It was a measure of MacCulloch's personality and ability that, despite such tendencies, men like McAlpine, Roy Jodrey, and Frank continued to like him. Thus it was with more affection than rancour that Jodrey, upon hearing of MacCulloch's heart trouble, drily remarked, "I didn't know Charlie *had* a heart."

MacCulloch and Frank were as hard-boiled as any businessmen in the province. They could be mulish when pushed, dangerous when crossed. They were demanding, and sometimes suspicious. They were rumour-sniffers, and a seething swarm of rumours that someone was plotting to snatch control of HDL lay behind their sensational rift in the winter of 1971-72. So did unhappiness in the Sobey-Jodrey camp over MacCulloch's high-handed, trouble-making management style at the complex. But the fight really started when MacCulloch broke a promise to invite a Sobeys supermarket into the Micmac Mall. "MacCulloch promised me that," Frank said in 1982. "We had a rental agreement all set up."

MacCulloch's lieutenant in the engineering of what Frank would later see as a perfidious double-cross was William B. Hardman. "You see," Hardman said a dozen years later, "it was Frank who got me down here from Calgary in the first place." Hardman had established twenty Woolco stores in western Canada for the Woolworth organization; and in 1963, after the Sobeys had acquired land for the Avalon Mall, St. John's, Nfld., Woolworth sent him there to meet Frank. Hardman, already a young hotshot in the mall business, impressed Frank. Soon the Sobeys and a company Hardman formed, Hardman, Bryson and Associates, entered a fifty-fifty partnership in the ownership of the Avalon Mall. To exploit subsequent tax legislation, however, the Sobeys needed a hundred per cent, and bought out Hardman, Bryson. "Frank was a tough, tough negotiator," Hardman recalled. "The terms of our contract meant he had to write us a cheque for $250,000 and another for $300,000. I'll tell you, he squealed."

He may have squealed but he did not lose his respect for Hardman's ability. Hardman, Bryson and Associates soon developed Highfield Square, Moncton, for the Sobeys, and, thanks to Frank's influence, became the general managers of Scotia Square. That meant that, on a daily basis, the man to whom Hardman answered was HDL president Charles MacCulloch. Hardman, a compact and seemingly candid man who liked to work in his shirt-sleeves, exuded sureness and management ability. By 1970, Hardman, Bryson was working for MacCulloch not only at Scotia Square but also at the Micmac Mall across the harbour in Dartmouth.

He had come a long way during his seven years in Atlantic Canada. He was now at the heart of the two newest and mightiest mall developments in Halifax-Dartmouth. He enjoyed the contracts and confidence of both Frank Sobey and Charles MacCulloch but, in the case of the Micmac Mall, he was MacCulloch's man. Control of the development, he said, broke down as "roughly a third for Charlie, and a third each for Eaton's and Simpsons". Frank figured Sobeys Stores would be a shoo-in at the mall. Not only did he know Hardman as a friend, he figured Hardman owed

John Robert Sobey, a director of Empire Company Limited and vice-president, retail operations, Sobeys Stores Limited.

him markers he had a right to call in. Not only did he know MacCulloch as a friend, he had MacCulloch's word that the Micmac Mall would boast a Sobey supermarket. As Frank understood things, they would arrive at the square-footage price after MacCulloch had talked with Eaton's and Simpsons.

Bill Sobey recalled that, along with Rhude, he met Hardman in the Hotel Nova Scotian, "and we negotiated a deal with Hardman to pay a minimum rent of $5 per square foot. . . . After this, we three shook hands, all of us agreeing that that was the deal. Bill Hardman left [for] the MacCulloch development office [in Scotia Square], and Harry Rhude [went] to his office to draft the formal letter of agreement or intent."

It was never signed.

Eaton's and Simpsons, it turned out, wanted MacCulloch to give Dominion Stores a crack at the site, and Dominion was putting heat of its own on him, as well. Within hours of negotiating with Bill Sobey and Rhude, Hardman found himself negotiating with Dominion Stores. He liked what he heard, and so did MacCulloch. Dominion would pay $8 per square foot. "Hardman phoned me," Bill Sobey said, "and he said, 'You're going to be very upset about this, but we have made a deal with Dominion Stores. The price was considerably higher than the amount *we* discussed.' I reiterated that we had made a firm deal, and that we expected Hardman and MacCulloch to hold to that. He said, 'You'd have had to match the price and I didn't think you could afford it.' "

Hardman later insisted Dominion was so wary of Frank's inside track that it gave MacCulloch only minutes to think; that Tom Bolton, president of Dominion, phoned Hardman at home at 11.30 one night to announce that MacCulloch had till exactly midnight to decide on the $8 offer. Take it or leave it. MacCulloch took it, and nothing he could have done was more certain to enrage Frank. "When you come right down to it," a Halifax accountant said, summarizing the opinion of Frank's allies, "Charlie went for money instead of friends."

Dominion had been Sobeys Stores' roughest competition ever since the fifties, and had recently launched a price-cutting war so vicious it threatened to demolish smaller chains. Frank and MacCulloch were friends, business partners, and fellow Nova Scotians. Now, as Frank saw the situation, MacCulloch had double-crossed him in favour of a Toronto-based supermarket mammoth. This was the ultimate villainy.

"He was absolutely livid," Arthur Crockett said. Crockett had been deputy chairman of the Bank of Nova Scotia, and he recalled that the poison between Frank and MacCulloch split the business community so fiercely that Premier Gerald Regan feared its effect on Nova Scotia's image. "He phoned my Toronto office from Halifax," Crockett said, "and he told me, 'Look, you've got to make peace between those two guys.' "

Had MacCulloch really promised Frank the location? Even Hardman said, "In a sense, he probably did. Charlie was like that. He'd say one thing one day, and the opposite thing the next day. He used the funnel method of decision-making. You pop something in the top of the funnel, it bounces off one side, hits the other side, rattles around the cone, finally shoots out the bottom, and there's your decision." MacCulloch said yes to Frank, later said no to himself, and still later pushed his promise entirely out of his mind.

Frank nursed his fury, awaited his chance. It was not long coming. Though MacCulloch was too cocksure to worry about it, he'd lost favour among certain HDL directors. He regarded some as inconsequential, and let this opinion show. Among partners who were not his fans were Russell Harrington, the president of Nova Scotia Light and Power; elderly financier J. C. MacKeen; the shrewd and gentle Jodreys; and now, of course, the Sobeys. Even before Dominion won the Micmac Mall site, the Sobeys were jaundiced about MacCulloch's posture as president of HDL, and the Jodreys were even less happy about it.

MacCulloch behaved as though he were the only one with the vigour and ability to run Scotia Square. "He started all kinds of conflicts," Frank said. "He had a company of his own, and he wanted to make a deal with Halifax Developments for $60,000 a year, plus expenses. This company would run Halifax Developments, and he tried to tell us no one else could run it." Thus, at the time MacCulloch infuriated Frank by accepting the Dominion Stores offer, some HDL directors already felt it wouldn't be a bad thing to see him cut down to size.

Meanwhile, like animals sniffing danger, several directors sensed someone was orchestrating a takeover of their company, and they were sure the villain was MacCulloch. HDL was not yet a money-maker, and in more amiable times he and other directors had discussed a financial reorganization and a change in the ownership structure. "Charlie had talked to Frank about the two of them getting together to buy out the other shareholders," Hardman said, "and the Jodreys were interested, too." Now, however, Charlie and Frank weren't talking to each other about anything, and something fishy was happening on the stock market. "Suddenly there was a day," Hardman recalled, "when about 100,000 shares of HDL traded on the market."

"When the fun began," Halifax broker David Hennigar said, "there were two million shares outstanding. The Jodreys had 12.5 per cent, the Sobeys about 10 per cent, and MacCulloch about 10 per cent." Hennigar was a grandson of Roy Jodrey and nephew of John Jodrey. The Sobey-Jodrey camp feared that MacCulloch (or he and an ally) was scheming to get 40 per cent, buy more shares by paying a premium to certain directors, and thereby take control for himself. But why was MacCulloch the prime suspect?

"Well, they [Sobeys, Jodreys, and friends] would be dealing with a whole lot of brokers," Hennigar explained. "The first firm clue would be that sudden increase in the volume of trading on a daily basis. In a small community, there just aren't that many potential players. . . . So the next thing is, people begin to talk. Someone says, 'What do you think of that?' The other fellow says, 'I don't think much of it at all.' So the first fellow says, 'I think maybe we should do something.' And it follows from that that something was done. One option was to spend some money, to buy some shares. It's rather like an election. If you consider negative net counting, every vote that *you* get is two the other guy doesn't get."

The "something" that was done was a stock-market swoop by Frank Sobey on HDL shares and rights to HDL shares. He wanted not only to thwart MacCulloch's takeover attempt but also to settle a score, and his campaign was boundless and swift. It took only three days, drove the share price from $1.25 to $3.00, created such pandemonium that the Toronto Stock Exchange halted trading in the stock. "Halifax Developments had put out more shares," Frank said, "and I just started buying them. I kept buying and buying. I tried to reach John [Jodrey], but he was out of town. Anyway, I ran the price up to three dollars. John comes back, and he says, 'You paid an awful high price.' I says, 'I know, but do you want half?' and John says, 'Oh yes, we'll take them.' "

Between them, the Jodreys and the Sobeys now owned almost seventy per cent of HDL; and MacCulloch, as a force in the affairs of Scotia Square, was washed up. Only a few weeks had passed since he'd chosen Dominion over Sobeys Stores at the Micmac Mall. McAlpine dismissed vengeance as Frank's motive for ousting MacCulloch from HDL: "Charlie was going to gobble the whole thing up, and Frank saw that. Frank outfoxed him, that's all."

Hardman disagreed. He said that MacCulloch never sought control of HDL and that, while Frank thought MacCulloch was the buyer of that first big lump of shares that traded during one day and triggered the suspicions, MacCulloch thought it was Frank. A tempting theory is that it was actually an incredibly sly third party, someone who knew about the MacCulloch-Sobey rift, bet on the outcome of his suddenly buying a whack of HDL, and, when Frank drove the price to three dollars, reaped a windfall. In any event, Hardman believed that if what Frank had wanted was control of HDL for Sobeys and Jodreys, he might have found a cheaper way to get it than a raid on the stock market.

MacCulloch knew the raid had doomed him at HDL. "At the annual meeting in early May, I was elected president," Donald Sobey recalled, "and Charles resigned. He remained a shareholder and director for six months longer. Then the Jodreys and ourselves bought him out when he convinced us that he was going to sell his stock to someone else. At that time, he resigned as a director." The self-styled saviour of HDL went on to other things. He'd suffered the indignity of defeat and exile from HDL, but he had not suffered financially. "Charlie bought at one dollar and sold at three," HDL director Robert McAlpine said. "That's a three-hundred-per-cent profit in only a few years."

With Donald Sobey as the new president, David Hennigar joined the board. So did J.T. MacQuarrie, a partner in Stewart, MacKeen & Covert, who also happened to be a son of Frank's old friend, politician J. H. MacQuarrie. Henry B. Rhude soon joined the board, and by April 1980, eight years after the ousting of MacCulloch, all these men were still directors of HDL. So were John Jodrey and Frank. The Sobeys and Jodreys together owned more than 3,000,000 of the 4,463,705 outstanding shares, and they were getting along just fine. Frank was seventy-eight, and MacCulloch had been dead for six months. (During a cruise in the South Pacific with his second wife – a young blonde from Britain with a theatrical background – he had died of a massive heart attack. He was sixty-eight.)

Hardman had paid for his failure to help Sobeys Stores beat out Dominion at the Micmac Mall. He recalled that after MacCulloch's defeat, "Everyone said, 'Oh my God, let's call a halt.' So they agreed to stop fighting, but they weren't going to forgive. Frank was mad at me. He thought he'd sponsored me in the region, and he had. He felt I'd turned on him." Hardman's lucrative consulting contract with the Sobeys "was terminated. My work for them stopped for eight years." By the eighties, however, he was running Hardman Group Ltd. from a rambling, renovated house in downtown Halifax, and was once again taking on jobs for the Sobey empire. He was still useful, and the bile of 1972 had finally dissolved in the currents of business necessity.

Had something so unsavoury as revenge caused Frank to force MacCulloch out of HDL? Ten years after the event, his friends said no, that was impossible, it wasn't in his nature, he hadn't a vengeful bone in his body, he'd only wanted to stop a MacCulloch takeover and guarantee proper management. All this was a tribute to the loyalty Frank could inspire, but he himself, at eighty, saw nothing embarrassing in the truth about himself. Sipping a sweating glass of beer on a screened porch at his Florida condominium, he said he'd never known for sure that MacCulloch was trying to amass control of HDL. He cheerfully allowed that if MacCulloch had not broken his pledge to rent supermarket space to Sobeys Stores at the Micmac Mall, "I wouldn't have bought the shares and made the changes at Halifax Developments." Reflecting on his son's performance as president there, he added, "But it's a good thing I did." That, however, wasn't the point. The point was: "If Charlie hadn't done that to me, I wouldn't have done that to him." Charlie had crossed the wrong guy.

The widow Creighton knew a Frank Sobey that MacCulloch would never have recognized. "Now I'm going to tell you something I've never told anyone," she said. Lois Creighton's father-in-law, J. J. Creighton, was a cousin of Frank's mother, and Mrs. J. J. Creighton was a cousin of Frank's wife, but that was not the secret. That was just Pictou County bloodlines. Lois Creighton, in 1936-42, worked at Number One as Frank's secretary, bookkeeper, and payroll clerk; and the secret, forty years later, was simply his bottomless loyalty to a pioneer employee. "My husband, Ian, drowned eighteen years ago," she said, "and Frank immediately offered me a job at his head office. I just went in on Mondays for two or three years. But you know, every single Christmas since Ian died, Frank has come out here personally with a gift. He's never missed. In eighteen years. He'd stay for a while, have some coffee, and return to his family. One Christmas Eve, he left a big party to get here, and then went back to the party." The round trip between the Sobey home in Abercrombie and Lois Creighton's brick doll's house in Tatamagouche is more than sixty miles.

"Anyone who's worked for Sobeys Stores for twenty years is never fired," author James M. Cameron said, "unless he's stolen." In retirement as well, those who'd worked for Frank benefited from his enlightened paternalism. As early as 1950, he founded the company pension plan. By 1984, more than 2,100 employees of Sobey companies were in the plan, and its portfolio totalled $32 million. Company and employees had put up roughly $20 million of this, but the rest represented unrealized gain from smart investing and profit-sharing. Frank was proud of the fund. "It's actually been doing better than Empire," he said, "because it's not so speculative. All this money is invested in industry and bonds, and that's helping create jobs in Canada. Starting this fund was perhaps the best thing I ever did. I was always interested in seeing our employees have something to look forward to in their retirement. These are the people who built our business. They deserve a share in the profits." Retired meat man Cecil McLaren said that when the chain introduced the fund, some older workers either wouldn't or couldn't invest enough to guarantee themselves a comfortable old age, "so Frank paid for them out of his own pocket."

"He was always a man who thought of his friends," New Glasgow paint manufacturer Bob Tibbetts said. "I don't think he ever betrayed a friend." Decades after Andy Murray helped Frank break into a building in Trenton to install the Bank of Nova Scotia's sign in a front window, Murray suffered a heart attack. Frank phoned him from Bermuda every day. Later still, as Murray lay dying, Frank made daily visits to his bedside.

Frank's loyalty also embraced cronies in Halifax, Montreal, and

Toronto. Once you were on his side, he was on your side. "I can only say good things about that guy," Jean-Claude Hébert said. A handsome, soft-spoken man, approaching seventy but appearing fifty, he leaned back in his chair at Place Ville Marie and sang the virtues of Frank Sobey. They'd been fellow directors of Dominion Textile and in 1969, when Hébert quit his job at the Canadian International Development Agency to take on the presidency of Warnock Hersey International Ltd., he was relieved to find Frank on this board, too.

The Warnock Hersey conglomerate owned everything from billboard companies to steel plants, hotels to furniture factories. It enjoyed annual sales of $120 million, and the new president was nervous: "You come in on a company like that, well, it's very diversified. It takes time to learn. Frank was a great help to me. He's the kind of guy you can ask to stick around and chew the fat with after a board meeting. I could talk over problems with him. He'd been on the board a long time." Both men eventually left the Warnock Hersey board, but whenever Frank visited Montreal he still dropped in on Hébert. "We'd always have a chat, and if I'd listened to him, I'd be rich today," Hébert said. "He had a real flair for investment. Of course, he'd pick your brain clean in about two minutes, too. If he was out at the airport he'd phone. He'd say, 'Hey, Claude, how you doing? How are things going anyway?' I was thinking of buying a company three years ago, and right on the spot he offered to come in with a substantial sum. He said, 'How much you want?' I named a big figure. Frank said, 'No problem, Claude.' "

Frank was loyal to institutions, as well as to people. He yearned for years to join Roy Jodrey on the board of the Bank of Nova Scotia, and many bluenose businessmen wondered why Horace Enman failed to get him a directorship. Frank's friend W. R. Monteith toiled for the bank most of his life, but not even he understood what kept Frank off the board. "I used to push Enman on it myself," Monteith said, "but he'd just say, 'We'll see.' " When Enman died, Frank still had no bank directorship. "We have no titles in this country," Halifax lawyer Bill Mingo said. "No House of Lords, no knighthoods. So for a businessman, specially one of Frank's generation, the best thing to be on was the board of a national bank. That was the mark of distinction." (Mingo, himself, was by now a director of the Bank of Canada.) "Being on a bank board," Donald Sobey said, "is belonging to one of the best clubs in the world. You not only get exposure to all the other directors, you get a very good lunch."

Frank finally got his invitation in February 1964, but it didn't come from the Bank of Nova Scotia. It was not from the Royal Bank either, his second choice. Nor was it from the venerable Bank of Montreal. The canny offer came, instead, from the Toronto-Dominion Bank, which, with only eight branches in the Maritimes, was a puny presence in Frank's territory. Allen T. Lambert, chairman and president of TD in 1964, said that when he asked Frank to join his board, "He was very direct. He said, 'Your bank hasn't much by way of representation down here. Is this much of a compliment to me?' " Lambert replied that that was exactly why TD needed him, to help it expand down east.

Frank, who was sixty-one, said yes. But before TD publicized its catch, the Bank of Montreal offered him a seat on its board. A TD directorship carried far less prestige than a Bank of Montreal directorship. Frank could still renege on his TD commitment without public embarrassment but he stuck by his private word to Lambert. TD had honoured him first. He already owed it his loyalty. His decision struck Mingo as "almost uncharacteristic. He usually managed to pursue his own naked self-interest."

Despite Frank's ancient relationship with the Royal Bank and particularly with the Bank of Nova Scotia (which, Lambert happily recalled, was "internally concerned" about TD's capturing him), the man from Stellarton performed well for his new friends at TD. Lambert said, "We relied on his knowledge of retail industries, textile manufacturing, and, after we got into the venture-capital business, about junior industries in Atlantic Canada that needed assistance to expand." Moreover, he not only needled TD to open branches down east, but also suggested sites. Sam T. Paton, the bank's chief general manager in the sixties, once responded defensively to the needling: "I said, 'Look you have to balance regional representation with the bottom line. Here in Toronto, you can put a branch in any one of these highrises, and you're making money in the second year.'" You couldn't do that in Maritime towns, "but Frank would argue right back that the banks had a larger responsibility. He'd say, 'That wasn't the purpose of the banks in this country,' and he was right, of course."

The Bank of Montreal, having failed to net Frank, later appointed his oldest son, Bill, to its board. When Frank retired from the TD board, his friend Gordon Archibald, head of Maritime Tel & Tel, replaced him there; and when Archibald retired, his successor was none other than Frank's youngest son, Donald. Between 1964 and 1981 the number of TD branches in the Atlantic provinces quadrupled. The needle had worked.

"If you go to a party at Frank's house," Robert Manuge of Halifax said, "you'll find the same friends he's had for thirty or forty years." Manuge felt the reason he was on the Empire board was simply Frank's loyalty to the man who'd run beside him at Industrial Estates Limited. Friends who were out of Frank's sight were not out of his mind. "This was one of the few years we didn't get down to Ingonish to see Mrs. Enman," he said sadly in 1982. Horace Enman had been dead for two decades.

When W. R. Monteith arrived in New Glasgow as an accountant with the Bank of Nova Scotia in 1935, the Sobeys invited the Monteiths to a New Year's Eve ball in an upstairs hall, and that was the beginning of a friendship that outlasted Guy Lombardo. The Monteiths lived in Saint John in 1982. They'd left New Glasgow some forty years before, but now the two elderly couples drove to Moncton, N.B., from opposite directions just to get together again for a weekend. They'd been chums for forty-seven years, and had spent New Years after New Years together at the Sobeys' winter home in Bermuda. "It is wonderful," Mrs. Monteith said, "that Frank and Rene still hold hands."

Frank's boyishness, even at eighty, continued to amaze his friends. "He has such a damned youthful approach to everything," New

Glasgow lawyer R. B. MacDonald said. Mrs. Robert Manuge asked, "Can you imagine a man of his age standing on his head for a while every day for his health's sake? Well, he does." While dining at home with his wife and a visitor, Frank suddenly put down his cutlery, jumped to his feet, and, without a trace of self-consciousness, jogged around the table three times. "I do this every morning when I get up," he explained. "I run around upstairs. I count five hundred steps, and by the time I've finished [the Sobeys' maid] has put my kippers on."

He ate a lot of fresh fish, cooked to perfection, and liked top-quality steak, properly aged, properly cooked, and unadorned. While carefully spooning the melted butter off the surface of his seafood chowder one noon-hour at the Abercrombie Country Club, he asked, "Why do they do such stupid things to food? You know, they even put pats of butter on steak these days." To the old butcher, nothing seemed more absurd. He said he preferred hotdogs to hamburgers because hotdogs came from reputable packing houses, and "you never know what's in hamburger."

Frank was a near-fanatical sports fisherman. Even in his late seventies, Walter Miller said, "he thought nothing of hiking a mile or two through the bush, over a rough trail." Miller, the lanky, slow-talking, American-born president of Scott Maritimes, Ltd., had made several springtime treks with Frank to a lake in Guysborough County where "an old bachelor had an old camp on the shore." They'd take sandwiches and breakfast food with them. The lake bottom was rock. The speckled trout were firm, deep red, and, in Miller's words, "the best eating trout I've ever had." In August 1981, when Frank was seventy-nine, he and a friend plunged into Guysborough County wilderness with a guide, and ended up struggling through three miles of dense bush. Frank boasted that the guide, a woodsman he'd known for years, later confided that "He wouldn't normally have put a man of fifty through that. I felt fine."

The Halifax *Chronicle-Herald* (June 16, 1982) reported that Frank's wife and sons accepted an award for him because "Mr. Sobey was unable to attend." That was wrong. He'd simply gone fishing. The Canadian Food Brokers Association had wanted to give him its Industry Award for Excellence, but only days before the ceremony he'd written to explain that something more important had come up: "For years, when I was a director of – and since I have retired from – Fraser Companies, I have been invited to go fishing with the directors every year on the Kedgwick River [in northern New Brunswick], and [now that] I have reached my eightieth birthday, I am loath to miss this year's fishing party. . . . Last year, I was able to land four salmon, two weighing twenty-two pounds, and two weighing eighteen pounds." The food brokers understood. They sent him a recording of all the compliments he'd received during a banquet at a hotel in Halifax while he'd been fly-fishing at a lodge in New Brunswick.

"He's always game for anything," construction magnate Robert McAlpine said. "As soon as he arrives in Florida, he phones everyone he knows, and says, 'I'm here, what's going on?' " The Sobeys, the McAlpines, and some Nova Scotian friends owned condominiums at Seven Lakes Leisure Village, Fort Myers. No one under forty could buy a unit there, and, according to McAlpine, a village policy was, "If you're old, you gotta be busy. The action appeals to Frank. He likes nothing better than belting out golf balls on a driving range." He also enjoyed "scrambles", which was golf as a blind date. Two men and two women, all strangers, played in a foursome. Whenever a man shot a birdie he could claim kisses from the women. "He'll sashay along with anybody who promises fun," McAlpine said. "You know, so many others become sterile and bent over, because they never walk a beach. Not Frank."

Beaches at Sanibel Island, carpeted with billions of seashells, were a choice picnic site for the Nova Scotians at Fort Myers. They'd pack folding chairs, parasols, chicken, white wine and coolers, and, during the obligatory group photo, Frank would hang a Sobeys Stores shopping bag from a conspicuous limb of a tropical tree in the background. To get to Sanibel, they crossed a causeway in a fleet of six cars. He insisted Mrs. McAlpine ride in the lead car to sweet-talk the toll-collector. It normally cost three dollars per car to visit the island, but a local friend could get her books of twelve one-dollar tickets. These were really for the use of only one auto, but Mrs. McAlpine invariably cajoled the uniformed official into accepting one for each car in her party. Thus, the little gang of wealthy bluenosers saved twelve American dollars every time they went to Sanibel Island. The game delighted Frank. "That's a good deal," he'd chortle, as though he'd just walked out of a Montreal hotel room with $185,000 from Webb and Knapp.

Striking a good deal, no matter how small, was like snagging a salmon: one of the pleasures that life offered. Businessman H. R. Murphy, who'd known Frank since selling him Lever Brothers products in the thirties, recalled finding himself and his wife seated beside Frank and his wife in the first-class section of a Toronto-Halifax flight on a Friday night. After drinks before dinner and wine with dinner, the stewardess offered liqueur. "Rene said, 'Oh no, thank you,' " Murphy laughed, "but Frank said, 'Yes she will, she'll take two Drambuies, and I'll have two Drambuies, too.' He drank his, and put Rene's in his pocket. They came in those tiny bottles and, of course, in first class they were free." But they weren't really free, and Frank knew it. If circumstances forced him to pay first-class air fares, he was going to get what he could for his money.

In a Bermuda grocery store, Mrs. Monteith said, Frank overheard a woman exulting over the low price of wax paper, "and he bought Rene the most massive roll I've ever seen. She asked, 'How many years do you suppose it'll take to use that up?' but Frank just said he couldn't pass up such a good deal." A golf course surrounded "Nova Haven", the Sobeys' home in Bermuda, and since their friend and neighbour Dr. Gordon Black kept dogs that terrified any golfer who approached the houses to retrieve a ball, Frank harvested basketfuls of golfballs and carried them home to Nova Scotia. Every morning in Florida, Frank drove to a restaurant that served a good, cheap breakfast, bought the Toronto *Globe and Mail* and the *Wall Street Journal*, read them, and then later loaned them to the McAlpines, to save them buying the papers themselves.

But on his overseas jaunts Frank was a big spender. He believed in economizing on business trips but living it up on pleasure trips. He'd sometimes fly economy class to London because he didn't want Nova Scotians to see him pampering himself in the first-class compartment, but once in Europe he ate, slept, and moved in luxury. He and Irene were travel addicts. They circled the globe in both directions. Usually with friends – New Brunswick industrialist Ralph Brenan and his wife, Edna, were among their favourite travelling companions – they explored Britain, France, Monaco, Italy, the Vatican, Bavaria, Switzerland, Hawaii, Hong Kong, South Africa, and Australia.

They swam in the Pacific at Pango Pango, caught trout in New Zealand, went fishing at the Hampshire manor of Sir Thomas Sopwith, a pioneer of the British aircraft industry. They attended a wedding in Japan, caroused at a lavish wedding in Bombay, celebrated one of their own wedding anniversaries at the Taj Mahal. Once, bound for England, they and the Brenans had the best suite of staterooms the *Empress of Britain* could offer. They toured France in a seven-passenger Cadillac, complete with an expert chauffeur-guide. They hired a Citroën on one trip to the French Riviera, then picked up a Mercedes-Benz in Switzerland. When Frank rhymes off the places where he and Irene stayed, he sounds as though he's reading from a guide to the world's finest (and most expensive) hotels.

The pleasure Frank derived from expensive travel and small bargains, from his attention to his diet and physique, the joys of golf, fishing, and reuniting with friends may all have contributed to his vigour at eighty. But there was something more important. It was that he'd never retired, and never willingly would. He was still the businessman that, as a boy, he'd dreamed of becoming; and his businessman's compulsions kept rejuvenation flowing in his being. One had only to hear him in Florida to know that.

Driving a persistent visitor around Seven Lakes Leisure Village, he explained that the developer bought the land, built the apartments, and then got himself clear by selling them to the residents, who ran the place, set the rules, calculated and levied maintenance costs. The set-up intrigued Frank, who'd been reading a book about the success of Canadian developers in the United States; and, as he drove, he multiplied the number of units per

The Sobey clan in the late 1960s. Seated, left to right: Elizabeth (Mrs. Donald) Sobey, Frank Sobey, Irene Sobey, Bill Sobey, Diane Sobey. Standing, left to right: Faye (Mrs. David) Sobey, Donald Sobey, Doris (Mrs. Bill) Sobey, David Sobey.

floor by the number of floors, added up the buildings, multiplied again, considered the average cost per condominium. He seemed to be trying to reckon the developer's profit. That sort of mental arithmetic was not every Canadian's idea of how to have a diverting time in sunny Florida, but Frank was not your average snowbird.

Out on a nearby highway, he pointed to a tract of land. "I could have had that for a million dollars a few years ago," he said. "It's probably worth ten million now." The moment he and the visitor seated themselves for oysters at a "raw bar", Frank cased the joint. "It's busy here, and there's not much overhead," he said. "I bet this place makes money. Not a *lot* of money, but a little money." To make idle conversation, the visitor reported rumours among lawyers that West Germans were buying commercial properties in central Halifax. Frank did not say, "Oh, that's interesting." He looked up from his oysters, and snapped, "Which properties? Do you know? What streets?" The day was sweatbox hot and, for rare moments only an hour before, it had oppressed him and made him look his eighty years. Now, while firing questions to nail down real-estate gossip, he was suddenly a tough sixty-year-old, and it did not seem possible that he'd been alive since before the incorporation of Fort Myers in 1905.

"How many family companies survive three generations in Canada?" George C. Hitchman challenged in 1982. He'd joined the Bank of Nova Scotia fifty-one years earlier, and been in the national business community long enough to know the unspoken answer was, "Damn few." But, "I have never heard anything about the Sobey family going down." When a wilful man struggles all his life to erect a successful business, his sons may either blow the chance to keep it growing or, wanting no part of the old man's creation, let it pass into outsiders' hands. "What you often find," said J. William Ritchie, president, Scotia Bond Company, Ltd., Halifax, "is that one son's a drunk, another's in jail, and the third guy's off in Tanzania or somewhere."

"That's the biggest thing that's impressed me about Frank Sobey," A. Garnet Brown said. "It's the way he's been able to bring those generations along." Brown, a former provincial cabinet minister and one of modern Nova Scotia's most eccentric and colourful Grits, was a food broker, like his father before him. "Frank encouraged and developed his boys," Brown continued. "He allowed them to advance. That's not an empire where Frank's God Almighty. You know, I've seen so many families deteriorate because they couldn't get along, but I've never seen the Sobeys argue. If they have dirty linen, they don't wash it in public."

But the division of power in the Sobey businesses inevitably meant the Sobeys did have differences, particularly over the use of money. As president of Empire Company, Donald had a powerful interest in such stock-market triumphs as the Provigo adventure. But meanwhile David, as president of Sobeys Stores, Ltd., spent "ninety-five per cent of my time" doing right by the supermarket chain. While gobs of money flowed into the stock market, "I was thoroughly convinced that for Sobeys Stores to survive we had to restructure our market position to match Dominion. We'd survived the price wars of the early seventies, and I felt we had to go back and spend a lot to upgrade what we had, to get higher productivity and more equipment." It did not make David any more comfortable to know that his father, as ever, wanted new stores at new locations.

"Dividends came in tax-free to a public company like Sobeys Stores, and their interest costs were deductible," Donald explained, "so that was a good place to have Provigo stock. But then it became so important to the stores that the operating people thought, 'Hey, let's get out of that, and put it all into operations.' So I'd say, 'Yeah, but you wouldn't *have* so many millions for this or that if it hadn't been for the Provigo investment.' " By March 1982, interest rates had reached such brutal heights that the Sobeys sold $16 million worth of Provigo shares, partly to reduce bank debts and to increase the liquidity of the supermarket chain.

Since every business must decide what to do with its resources and how to adjust to meet changing conditions, boardroom tension was scarcely unique to the Sobey companies. People, however, somehow expect brothers in the same business to be specially argumentative, and since the bluenose business community was as gossip-ridden as any village beauty parlour, a buzz of speculation arose after the *Financial Post* (June 16, 1979) suggested Donald was the "heir apparent" to his father. "While William and David spend much of their time at the Sobeys' head office in Stellarton," the *Post* said, "Donald travels Canada and the world, seeking new investments, controlling the family investment portfolio and generally representing the Sobey name in the world of high finance." What people wondered, would Bill and David think of *that*?

If they thought anything of it at all, these amiable, close-mouthed, publicity-shunning men weren't giving outsiders the satisfaction of knowing what it was. If there were cracks in Sobey solidarity, the press never found them. The few non-Sobeys on Sobey boards said that, even in the extreme privacy of directors' meetings, father and sons invariably settled disagreements with a blunt cordiality that left no residue of bitterness.

"Frank doesn't say too much," Bill Ritchie of Scotia Bond said in April 1981, remembering Sobeys Stores directors' meetings. "But he could raise hell and really make it stick." Scotia Bond, in the previous five years, had raised close to $40 million for Sobey enterprises. "If the board was discussing construction of an office tower," Ritchie continued, "Frank might say, 'Never mind about the bloody new building for now. Let's look at these receivables. . . . These expenses seem to be going up awfully fast.' "

"I don't know whether it's worth putting out such a fancy statement," Frank complained at a Sobeys Stores board meeting in August 1981. He was considering the company's annual report, which included sixteen colour photographs and had cost all of $15,000 to produce and distribute. "I've commended you before for the cleanliness, efficiency, and competitiveness of the stores," he told his sons and other senior executives, "but you fellows still don't see what's under your own noses. Your head office expenses are too high. I go over your telephone expenses and see a thirty-five-per-cent increase. . . . You walk into your offices and go to work, but you don't see what's under your own noses."

The atmosphere was not electric with tension behind the closed door of the Sobey boardroom that morning, but there was a degree of squirming. Frank was seventy-nine, and still keeping a hawkish eye on details. (Ronald Perowne, chairman of Dominion Textile, recalled sharing a cab with David Sobey before a Montreal-Toronto flight: "David said, 'I guess I won't be sitting with you. My ticket's economy.' I said, 'At Dominion Textile, we all travel economy, too,' and you know what David's answer was? He said, 'Good, Father will be pleased to hear that.' ")

Frank's boardroom behaviour, however, was not just a matter of carping over spending. He wanted to jerk the reality out of numbers that others set before him. Elaborate projections of company performance aroused his suspicion. He wondered aloud if his executives didn't adjust projections as circumstances changed to make the figures look more prophetic than they were. He wanted the original projections preserved, because "I'd like to see the target you were aiming for, and how far you're off it." He expressed similar wariness when a Sobey Stores vice-president said he'd based his interest-rate predictions on analysis by "Wood Gundy Ltd. and other financial experts." Frank retorted, "What's that worth? Right now I'd like to see what they predicted this time last year." He suspected, too, that accountants wasted time on constructing complicated budgets. He liked simple budgetary discussions that made two things clear: "What did we do last year? And let's do better next year."

Frank was a goad. "When something's got to be done," he told the directors of Empire on December 13, 1982, "I like to see it done. . . . Somebody's dragging his feet." He was wearing a midnight-blue business suit and didn't bother removing his galoshes all morning. During a discussion over the right moment to close down a small, unprofitable shopping centre in Prince Edward Island, he said shortly, "Just remember, every day you delay is costing you money." He asked vice-president William H. Richardson, "What are you doing? What have you got coming up?" It was Richardson's job to run Empire's drugstores, and when he said the chain would soon rent space from a non-Sobey developer to open a new store, Frank cracked, "If you don't get a better deal than you get from Sobeys, you're not doing very good." His ultimate compliment was "That's a pretty good statement."

By the summer of 1983 Frank, at eighty-one, was still chairman of Empire and honorary chairman of Sobeys Stores, Ltd. Other Empire directors included its president, Donald Sobey; Bill Sobey, a vice-president, also chairman of Sobeys Stores; David Sobey, the treasurer, also deputy chairman and chief executive officer of Sobeys; John R. Sobey, vice-president, retail operations, for Sobeys, and son of Frank's late brother, Harold; and J. William Sinclair, a forestry technician, and son of Frank's sister, Edith. The only other Empire directors were J. Skiffington Murchie, the first non-Sobey to serve as president of the supermarket chain; James W. Gogan, Empire's top non-Sobey; J. William Ritchie, the president of Scotia Bond; and three friends with whom Frank had worked for decades. These were Halifax art-gallery proprietor Robert Manuge, once Frank's top man at Industrial Estates Limited; lawyer Henry B. Rhude, now chairman of Central Trust Company; and Arthur H. Crockett, a Pictou County man who'd spent his life with the Bank of Nova Scotia and had just retired as its deputy chairman.

Meanwhile, younger Sobeys were advancing in Empire subsidiaries. As vice-president, retail operations, Frank's nephew John R. Sobey was already part of senior management at Sobeys Stores. Grandsons, too, were moving up company ladders. "Both of Bill's boys are in the business," David said. "I have one son and he's in the business, and Donald's kids aren't old enough yet." David's son Paul, a chartered accountant - and, incidentally, a ringer for his great-great-grandfather, Sergeant William Sobey - was vice-president, finance, and secretary of Atlantic Shopping Centres. Frank C. Sobey, son of Bill, ran the real-estate management division of Atlantic Shopping Centres, and was also on the ASC board. Karl Sobey, other son of Bill, was district supervisor, central Nova Scotia, for Sobeys Stores.

But as proof of Frank's determination to establish a house of Sobey in the business world of Canada, the ownership of Empire was even more telling than the rise of Sobey men in the operating companies. When Empire "went public" for the first time in April 1982, the stock it issued was non-voting. Through investment companies of their own, Donald and David each owned 17.3 per cent of the *voting* shares, and Bill had 15.9 per cent. The three sons, in short, had a total of 50.5 per cent. Meanwhile, Central Trust held 28.3 per cent in trust for Frank's eleven grandchildren, and a further 1.4 per cent in trust for the late Harold Sobey's children. Since Central Trust sent the proxies for the shares it held to management, Empire Company with its thirty subsidiaries was essentially a collection of businesses and investments that older Sobeys oversaw till younger Sobeys matured enough to take over.

All of this was as Frank had designed it to be. It was precisely what he'd had in mind when he'd pumped his own investments into Empire, and taken in return only notes that bore no interest. He was so satisfied to see this family-run machine not only humming and growing, but also showing every sign of perpetuating itself as a Sobey force indefinitely into the future, that his personal stake in it scarcely mattered to him. When the New England supermarket chain Hannaford Brothers took legal action to limit Sobey buying of its shares, U.S. lawyer Robert A. Moore asked Frank, "What percentage of the voting stock in Empire Company do you own or control?" Frank said, "I don't know, to tell you the truth." Moore's next question suggested he found that unbelievable. "You don't know?" he asked. Frank obligingly replied, "No. Empire Company stock was split. I haven't got a very big holding. My wife has half of what I have. . . . I gave her half what I had. Half of everything." Then, just for laughs, he added, "I can't afford to divorce her now." Moore, at times, seems to have found the elderly architect of the Sobey empire a baffling man to interrogate.

If family counted more in Nova Scotia than in other parts of Canada, it counted more in Pictou County than in other parts of Nova Scotia, and it counted more in Frank Sobey's mind and creation than even in other parts of Pictou County.

Frank's idea of family encompassed more than his own wife and children. When both his father and his sister Edith's husband died in late 1949, Edith Sobey Sinclair replaced the late J. W. Sobey on the Empire board, though her business experience was limited. Moreover, Frank immediately took a fatherly interest in her young son, Bill. "He was very kind to me," Bill recalled. "I was growing up in a house with only women [his mother and his grandmother, Eliza Creighton Sobey], and he used to take me out to hunt and fish, things on an outdoorsy note. He'd take me down the St. Mary's River in his black '55 Chrysler. It had those old soft, plushy seats, and it stunk. There's no other word for it. It smelled of *cee-gars*, and gas. I used to enjoy it. My gracious, I enjoyed it." Without a father, Bill was reluctant to attend Boy Scout father-son banquets. Frank more than once offered to accompany him.

Edith Sinclair remained a director of Empire for thirty years, and the man who replaced her in 1980 was her son Bill. Harold

Sobey, though he chose to drift away from the grocery business in his middle age, remained on the boards of both Sobeys Stores and Empire till he died at sixty-four of cancer in July 1976. The turnout at Harold's funeral proved just how popular he'd been. "An amazing variety of people came," his daughter Karen Simoneau recalled, "and they came from all walks of life. There were whites, blacks, people he'd just picked up hitchhiking, and old army friends he'd been in Italy with, everybody you could think of. [Frank] hadn't known that Dad knew all these people. He was moved. His younger brother dead. I remember him holding me." In an earlier time, she'd often visited Frank and Irene, and "I'm sure he disapproved of things I did and said, and rightly so, because I went through a rather stormy adolescence crisis, but he never made me feel I was being judged, and I always felt welcome. . . . I really got to know him better after my father died."

Following the funeral, "He wrote me a letter. We exchanged books by mail, and kept up this correspondence. It was very important to me." She was bilingual and lived at Luceville, Quebec, near Rimouski, where she taught psychology. She was in love with another teacher, Pierre Simoneau, and Frank urged her to marry him. "One summer I came home," she recalled, "and he said, 'I thought I told you to get married.' There were practically tears in his eyes. It was important to him, and it was important to me that it was important to him. I said I'd only get married if he'd promise to come to my wedding."

The wedding party occurred on January 7, 1978. "We had this little house with a little kitchen table," she said. "We thought we could get nine English in, and nine French. But the English couldn't speak French, and the French were mostly separatists. We had no idea how it would turn out." Sobeys, ever loyal to their own, showed up in force. Karen's sister Susan, with husband, came from London, Ontario. Her mother, her brother and his wife, and her aunt Edith all came up from Pictou County. Frank flew from Bermuda to Montreal, sat around the cold CN terminal there for a couple of hours, caught a train that chugged its way eastward through the Quebec winter, disembarked more than three hundred miles downriver from Montreal, and showed up right on time at Luceville. He was seventy-five but he'd given his word, and he wanted to see his brother's daughter properly married. Cultural barriers melted in talk and singing. "He enjoyed himself immensely," Karen said, but around midnight he caught another train and vanished as quickly as he'd appeared.

The Sobeys' big brick waterfront house at Abercrombie had quarters for two servants; a tigerskin rug under a spiral staircase in the front hall; golden swan-shaped taps in the downstairs powder room; wallspace for his valuable collection of traditional Canadian paintings; and an outdoor pool that's mostly used for family swimming parties. ("I used to keep the pool heated," the thrifty senior Sobey said, "but that cost more than heating the house did, so I don't any more.") Irene Sobey took a strong hand in the design of Crombie. The large dining-room windows overlook the inner waters of Pictou Harbour. The living room boasts a cavernous fireplace, a screened-in extension for breezy comfort on hot afternoons, and a sunny wing for the enjoyment of Clairtone stereo and television.

Crombie fascinated Pictou County. In the supermarket age, Frank had succeeded ancient giants of shipbuilding, mining, and steel-making as the most important man in the East River towns. Surely his new mansion would be worth seeing. It seemed to Irene that people from all over the county came up their driveway to rubberneck, but Frank refused to erect a "No Trespassing" sign. He did not want anyone to think he was snooty, inaccessible, or, as the saying goes, full of himself. His name was on his letterbox. His number was in the book. His life had been lived among the people of these towns and hills. To older folk, he was not Dr. Sobey, or even Mr. Sobey. He was just Frank, as he'd been when he'd lugged turnips and beef to the Ora Hotel for his father.

The Sobey men give no cause for anyone in Pictou County to call them fools or snobs. They are totally unlike the spendthrift, faddish, gonzo, quick-buck artists of western Canada, as described by Peter C. Newman in *The Acquisitors*: "[men who] seem to be perpetually just shy of forty years old, the most outrageous of them sporting dyed beards and tousled curls. If they decide to wear diamond pinky-rings, order new Cadillac Eldorados every April or, like Vancouver's Nelson Skalbania, paper a bedroom ceiling with $100,000 worth of gold leaf, who in the hell is going to tell them it's not *bon ton*?" In Pictou County, where Frank and all his sons have chosen to spend their lives, such tastes would mark a man as pretentious, risible, and stupid enough to deserve to lose his money. Frank had raised peacocks for his own amusement but, like his neighbours, he's never wanted either to look like one, or be seen with a woman who looks like one.

The way the Sobey families live is a balance between affluence and not putting on the dog. "The boys" are like any small-town, middle-class businessmen whose idea of luxury is a second car for the wife and a second home for the family in summer. Donald and David own roomy but unspectacular houses within a few minutes' drive of Sobey headquarters, and summer places at Chance Harbour. Donald had his cottage built at a spot he'd loved since childhood, and David's once belonged to his aunt Edith. Bill Sobey owned a house in town and his parents' old place at Chance Harbour, but eventually saw no point in maintaining two houses and built a new, year-round home along the shore at King's Head.

The salt-water beaches of Pictou County are close to New Glasgow, and in summer it's doubtful if any businessmen in Canada lead pleasanter, more convenient lives than those with family houses along that warm shore, offices along the East River, and, if they like golf, memberships in the Abercrombie Country Club. David owned a cruising sloop for a while, but he sold her, because he was no longer using her enough to justify maintenance costs. David's idea of a good time is to go camping with his wife – and speaking of wives, the Sobey men do not trade them in as fashions change. Each remains married to the first woman he married.

You sometimes hear it said of a successful man that "he never forgot his roots," but the Sobeys had no chance to forget theirs because they never cut them. Frank would not leave Pictou County, and he would not pull Sobeys Stores, Ltd., out of Stellarton.

Rumour occasionally had it that the Sobeys thought Moncton made better sense than Stellarton as a distribution centre, or that Halifax was the logical headquarters for Empire. "Those boys have so many directorships up here," a Montreal investment dealer said, "it'd probably make more sense for them to move to Montreal or Toronto." As it was, they had to drive for ninety minutes just to reach the Halifax airport. (They eventually hired a chauffeur - one driver for four Sobey men - so they could at least use the travelling time to plan, read, concentrate on business.) But no matter how inconvenient Stellarton sometimes seemed, Frank insisted the business stay put, and retired meat man Cecil McLaren knew exactly why: "He felt it was the people around him that made him, the people around here that was buying his stuff all those years. If he'd moved Sobeys Stores out, it wouldn't have looked too good."

No matter how exalted or exotic the circles in which Frank found himself, he never shook the dust of Stellarton from his feet. At a wedding in Bombay, at Sir Thomas Sopwith's manor in Hampshire, England, aboard an Air Canada junket to Moscow with the biggest of Canada's big businessmen, or sipping tea with the Queen at Heathrow, he remained an unpretentious, plain-spoken Stellarton businessman, a fellow who knew he'd soon be back at his desk in the former warehouse on King Street.

No matter where business takes Frank's sons, they too remain men of the East River. Thus, Bill Sobey, while wearing his hat as mayor, wrestled with the question of whether or not Stellarton really needed its first set of traffic lights, but, while wearing his hat as a Bank of Montreal director, met regularly with the likes of Charles Bronfman, head of the House of Seagram Ltd., David Kinnear, then chairman of T. Eaton Company, H. R. Crabtree of Wabasso Ltd., and Senator Hartland de Montarville Molson of Molson Industries, Ltd. Bill is the most dedicated promoter of good causes among the Sobey men - though all of them do their bit - but here, too, he is both a national man and inescapably a county man. If he's been a director of the Canadian Council for Christians and Jews, and the World Wildlife Fund of Canada, he's also twisted local arms for money to renovate a tumbledown summer camp for boys, and served on the Top Level Gifts Committee of the Pictou County YMCA. If he's been chairman of the Dalhousie Medical Research Foundation in Halifax, he's also been chairman of the Pictou County Heart Fund.

David's corporate obligations may take him to Montreal one day and to Portland, Maine, the next, but his community obligations have enmeshed him in the presidency of the West Side Community Club, New Glasgow, and in running United Appeal for the county. Donald may find himself discussing Krieghoff paintings with fellow-collector Lord Thomson of Fleet at a banquet in Toronto, but he knows he'll soon be back in Sharon St. John's United Church, where a stained-glass window commemorates that most community-minded of men, his grandfather J. W. Sobey. Empire Company donated it when Donald, now Empire's president, was fifteen.

The Sobey men dress, talk, and spend in a way that lets neither their wealth nor their power distance them from others. The style is not calculated. It's the result of their absorption of a relentless principle of small-town life: if you can't get along with neighbours and customers, you are deficient in character and should fail. Frank was among the first Canadians to be accepted as participants in the world's most prestigious insurance group, Lloyd's of London; but, decades before that, the New Glasgow Gyros had already accepted him. It's unusual in Canada to find small-town boosters who are also big-time financiers. It's rarer still to find an entire family of them.

While she was still alive, Frank and his wife had four residences for their own use, but they didn't live as lavishly as that fact suggests. Their house in Bermuda was indeed a luxury, but that's not because it was sumptuous. It's because owning just about any house in Bermuda was a luxury. Their two-bedroom condominium near Fort Myers, Florida, was a pleasant spot for elderly golfers, but it's not on the expensive ocean front. Then there's the cabin in Guysborough County. It's five miles north of Sherbrooke and sits on the west bank of the dark, gurgling, ocean-bound St. Mary's River.

Irene Sobey accepting the Canadian Food Brokers industry award for excellence on behalf of her husband, June 1982. With her, left to right: Bill Sobey; Ian Kennedy, President, CFBA; David Sobey; and Frank Leach, Chairman, CFBA (Wamboldt-Waterfield Photo)

This was the place that cost Frank the least and that he loves the most.

He discovered how fine it was to be near the St. Mary's River in the mid-twenties, but it was not till 1945 that he made up his mind to build the cabin. The decisive factor was one of those miraculous warm spells that July occasionally awards to January. The day was so strangely summery he took his family out for a mid-winter picnic, and they ended up cooking hotdogs on a grassy shelf of the riverbank near a salmon pool. This, he decided, was the perfect spot for a more-or-less-secret retreat. His friend the Attorney General, J. H. MacQuarrie, told him not to worry about the spot's being Crown land; and his friends at Eastern Woodworkers Ltd., New Glasgow, built him a cabin for a bargain price.

On the long weekend of May 24, 1945 – Frank's birthday, as well as Queen Victoria's – he and Rene and their four children, aged five to seventeen, opened the cabin for the first time. The war in Europe had been over for two weeks. "We all love it here," Rene wrote in the first entry of a logbook that, almost four decades later, would still be in the cottage. "Had grand weather and caught about seventy trout. My Dad came down Friday night and stayed until Saturday." Billy Jamieson, who'd killed lambs with Frank a quarter-century before, showed up on Sunday with one Marian MacFadden. Three weeks later, Billy and Marian returned. "Had glorious time for four days," Rene wrote. "Frank and Bill caught a grand catch of salmon on Wednesday. Bill caught five, Frank three. Bill and Marian left for Marie Joseph [doubtless for Belle Baker's renowned seaside hangout]. Frank caught four more salmon. Went down to Marie Joseph the next day and had good feed. . . ."

The postwar years at the cabin on the St. Mary's River followed the happy pattern of '45: good fishing, good eating, good jokes, good friends and family. In the spring of '51, Frank and Irene put an addition on the cottage and installed inside plumbing. By the mid-sixties their grandchildren were using the place. Frank Sobey, son of Bill Sobey, left evidence of his visit on June 5, 1965, by announcing in Rene's book, "Had to set out mousetraps."

Seventeen years later, on June 5, 1982, Frank, and sometimes Rene – who is frail and uncertain – sit with a visitor in a sunroom that overlooks the southward-sliding river and was once an open, cottage-wide porch. Now it's an extension of the cabin's main room, which is lined with knotty pine, gleams with varnish, and houses a grab-bag of furniture, bric-à-brac, and souvenirs that may not belong at Crombie but do belong in the lives of Frank and Rene Sobey. A sign in the cramped kitchen displays a cartoon skunk and asks, "Why be disagreeable when, with a little effort, you could be a real stinker?" Another sign suggests, "Keep your temper. No one else wants it." Ceramic ducks wing their way across one wall of the dining space between the kitchen and the living room. Framed, glossy photos hang there, too; and they're personally signed by Dennis Morgan, Ginger Rogers, Wendy Barrie. Things have a way of surviving in a hideout that a man knows he'll never sell.

Above the sunroom windows that overlook the river hangs a tinted photo, almost sixty years old, of Frank and Rene sitting in a field near Truro just before they married; and an enlarged snapshot of him showing off the 28.5-lb. salmon he caught in the Margaree River, Cape Breton Island, in 1940. Then there are photos, taken a couple of decades after *that*, of the Sobeys on pleasure trips in Europe with New Brunswick industrialist Ralph Brenan and Mrs. Brenan. The cottage is also the repository for photo albums, a slide projector, and hundreds of colour transparencies of Sobeys and friends standing before castles, canals and cafés, palaces, museums and mountains. The Sobeys have had some of the best times of their lives here at the cabin, but they've also turned it into an informal museum of their happiest adventures in other places.

The visitor notices seven rocking chairs, most of them leatherette, a four-foot-long cribbage board, and a couple of bunk beds. Making those bunk beds is one of the few cottage chores Rene has always disliked. An ash tray declares the golden anniversary of Kraft Foods Company in 1963, and beside it there's a package of Amphora Regular pipe tobacco. China statues of wild turkeys sit on the mantel over the stone fireplace, and above them softly glows a schmaltzy painting of a young blonde with long hair, huge eyes, Bardot lips, and a blue, breast-revealing shirt. The visitor suspects somebody gave the painting to the cottage as a joke, but Frank does not care what the visitor suspects. This is his place, and he likes it the way it is.

Here, he is almost forthcoming. While discussing the film business, he says he abides by the old show-biz rule, "Never put a hat on a bed." Later, he offers, "You know there's no difference between a government and a big family on a farm. If some want to loaf, bum around, and spend money, then the others, the ones who work, they're the ones who end up looking after them. If there's fewer working, the others have to carry the load. Another thing, in the old days the young people would take over the farm and look after the old people. Nowadays, they say, 'The hell with you. Let the government look after you.' "

Then, as the visitor leaves, Frank says something uncharacteristic. It is the only thing the visitor will ever hear him say to suggest he's occasionally experienced even the faintest twinge of self-doubt, and it is also the same thought that has probably comforted a million Canadian cottage-owners. "You know," he says, "Rene and I always thought that if anything ever went wrong, we could come down here to live."

The visitor joins Frank for breakfast at Crombie. Frank eats oatmeal porridge, sprinkled with lecithin, and a kipper. He and his guest sit in the dining room, but not at the big showpiece table. Frank has chosen the smaller one by the window. The trees swing in the wind, yellow leaves dance over the cold pool and scuttle across the grass, the harbour beyond ceaselessly glitters and moves, and the cutlery and linen are so hefty they remind the visitor of the railway dining cars of his childhood. Frank startles him by saying he likes to eat here "because it reminds me of a dining car on a train, except that you never pull into the station." Pulling into stations does not interest the old man. He's in one of his restless moods.

They sit in the living room after breakfast while Frank explains how Stellarton got a movie theatre in 1967: "I called up Rube Bolstad [president of the Famous Players chain], and I said I'd like to build a theatre in New Glasgow. I said, 'What about those old fifty-fifty deals?' He says, 'Frank, they're gone, long ago.' So we talked for a few minutes, and he says, 'Maybe I could resurrect one.' He sent down a plan, and I called him up and I says, 'This plan's pretty rich, and we've trimmed it a bit.' He says, 'As long as you think it's all right,' and then I told him I wanted to build the theatre in Stellarton. He says, 'Is Stellarton bigger than New Glasgow?' and I told him it was only half as big. He says, 'So why would you build it in Stellarton?'

" 'Well,' I says, 'I was mayor of Stellarton for twenty-two years, and it *needs* a theatre.' Rube says, 'Boy, I never heard of that one before. Can we make any money?' I says, 'I don't think so. Do you want to check the progress payments?' He says, 'No. Just build the theatre and send me a bill.' So I did." A year later, "I got an assessment from the town for the land under the theatre, and I'd forgotten to put that in the deal. It was about $10,000, so I called up Rube and he laughed. He said, 'I guess you're stuck now,' but it wasn't long before I got a cheque for $5,000 from Famous Players. They were great people to do business with." George Destounis succeeded Bolstad as head of Famous Players, and when he first saw the spiffy but financially unpromising theatre on the main street of Frank's favourite town, he dubbed it "The Frank Sobey screening room".

By Frank's standards, the anecdote is long. Has he volunteered it as advance compensation for the fact that he's about to cut the interview short and report to his office? The phone rings. James Gogan, executive vice-president of Empire, is on the line, and the stock market's making him jittery. "You fellows didn't go through 1929," Frank tells him. "We may go through that again. Interest rates shot up just before the crash in '29, too. . . . He's too optimistic, you know. He never went through a bad market, either. . . . Always sell on the good news, and buy on the bad news . . . I would just kind of sit a little today, and see what happens. This'll last perhaps two or three days. We're in pretty good shape in Empire, aren't we? Did you notice that Wajax held? . . . No, I'm busy here for the moment."

He hangs up, and immediately offers to show the visitor around Stellarton. Each drives his own car to the parking lot at Sobey headquarters on King Street, the visitor jumps into Frank's Mercedes-Benz, and the tour begins. Coming upriver from Crombie, they've already passed the first shopping plaza Frank ever built; Sobeys Stores' vast, turquoise distribution centre; the Sobey-owned Eastern Sign Print Company; the railway-red coal-washing plant that's all that's left of the cursed Allan Shaft that J. W. Sobey helped build in 1905-07; the ramshackle stone tower that's all that's left of the equally cursed Foord Pit, down which Frank dropped peb-

Frank Sobey and his "boys", Bill, Donald, and David, in 1982.

bles in his boyhood; and the tarpaper-swathed bus depot that was once headquarters for the longest street railway in Nova Scotia. Many's the night the "Lovers' Special" brought him home from New Glasgow.

Now Frank cruises through Brown Row and Bunker Hill. There's an old saying that "A miner never paints his house," and he recalls that when he used to bring a horse and wagon in here to deliver groceries, "there wasn't a bit of paint on these houses. They were all bare, but now they're all painted. The doors were all on the other side. They faced the lanes in those days." Red Row was all painted red, but "There wasn't a tree on it." He follows a road past the ancient Albion and MacGregor mines to the notorious Bull Pen, and in a few minutes noses the car past the industrial park that was once the Bear Brook amusement centre. "I got that industry there," he says. "I put that one in when I was with IEL.

. . . An Italian ran that place [a textile factory] for a while. He was one of the early ones. Simpsons-Sears is in that Clairtone building. I think they got 150 people working there, so that turned out all right."

He enters a high neighbourhood of ample bungalows, and manicured lawns and shrubs. Sobey companies built these houses. Donald Sobey and John Robert Sobey both live up here somewhere, and Frank thinks it's pretty funny that for a while he's lost. Back in older Stellarton, he shows off the town ballpark. Hills behind the foul lines made it a natural amphitheatre, so the stands were easy to build, and "We had great ball teams here." Old houses slumber in summer shade. "These trees were just saplings when we put them in while I was mayor," he says. "Just look how big they are now!" But if his pride in what's here is strong, so is his memory of what's gone: "There used to be woods and a pond up there where that school is now. We used to skate there, and fool around." The school where Sylvia Keith strapped him with industrial belting has disappeared, but he knows precisely where it stood, just as he knows that "A brook went across right there. There was a swampy place there, and a brook."

Near the top of Allan Avenue, he points out a small house that his father built and sold three-quarters of a century ago, and, coming down the hill, he slows the car before the plain white wooden house where he and Rene raised all their children, and endured the Depression, the Second World War, and the hectic, expansionary fifties. Lower still, at the corner of Allan and Foord, he indicates the house where he grew up, the last of the several homes of J. W. and Eliza Sobey. Foord is the main drag and now, at Royal Visit pace, the blue Mercedes-Benz follows it south. Except as a greeting, Stellarton people are disinclined to honk their horns at Frank Sobey.

Here, on our right, we have Stellarton Quik-Pik, a variety store where once stood Number One, and beside that looms an unusually tall Stedman's five-and-dime. Did showgirls once flash their thighs here? Did Alice Faye entrance hundreds of miners, not to mention the young grocer next door, in this very building? Did a small boy crawl through its innards with electric tape in a time before the shot heard round the world, and did he grow up to own the joint? Yes, it's the old Jubilee theatre. And on our left, please observe the Foord theatre, which Famous Players said should be in New Glasgow but Frank said should be in Stellarton.

Back on our right, we present the town hall, where, for twenty-two years without ever having to face an election, Frank held the mayoralty. And here's the little old wooden building that is now home to Harry's Barber Shop and Jim's Taxi, but was once headquarters for the Angus Rankin meat business. J. W. Sobey bought that trade shortly after a Chicago cartoonist depicted a dachshund inside a bun and thereby made the "hot dog" immortal. At Foord Street and Acadia Avenue, Frank turns east and passes between a Bank of Nova Scotia, which occupies land the Sobeys sold to the bank, and a Sobeys supermarket, which occupies land that was once headquarters for the town's economic master, the Acadia Coal Company.

Only now does it dawn on the visitor that since passing Frank's old house on Allan Avenue, the Mercedes-Benz has followed the route that Frank and one of his black Labs took on foot virtually every weekday morning throughout the fifties. The destination was always the same. Now Frank is driving north on King Street, moving downriver parallel to his previous upriver passage on Foord, and the railway tracks are on the right and, sure enough, he wheels right into the parking lot at Sobey headquarters. The visitor's car awaits him.

The Stellarton tour has taken all of fifteen minutes. "You got everything you need?" Frank asks. Courteously but firmly, and perhaps only for the valuable time being, Frank is dumping the visitor. After all, it's 11.30 in the morning, and the office has been open for three hours. Frank Sobey is merely in the eighth decade of his life. He's still got work to do.

EPILOGUE

ALZHEIMER'S DISEASE afflicted Irene Sobey in her late seventies, and she grew tentative in her speech and gestures. Her good nature rarely flagged, but she had difficulty finding the words she wanted to utter. Once, referring to Frank, she told Willard and Helen Monteith, "I'm just like a lost puppy without him." The Sobeys and the Monteiths had maintained their friendship since the time of marathon dancing and Shirley Temple. As they all grew old, the continuing affection between Frank and Irene pleased and touched the Monteiths. On the weekend of August 12-14, 1983, the Monteiths celebrated their fiftieth wedding anniversary, and the Sobeys drove to Saint John, N.B., to see them once again. Irene, who'd always enjoyed shopping while travelling, had a chance to explore the boutiques in the city's impressively renovated waterfront area.

On Monday, back at Crombie, Irene McDonald Sobey "took a turn", as they say in Pictou County; and early on Tuesday morning, August 16, she died of a stroke. She was seventy-nine, and she'd been Frank's wife for fifty-eight years.

"She was with me wherever I went all those years," he said later. "Even when I went fishing somewhere, she'd be out in the boat with me. Or sometimes she'd sit in the car and read till I finished fishing. She was a great companion. . . . During the war, we both worked very hard. Men were scarce. Most of my good men were

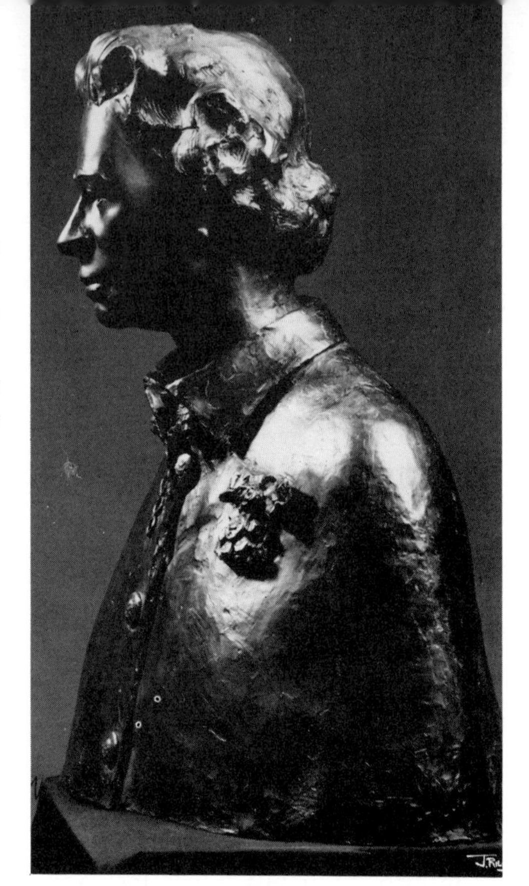

The bust of Queen Elizabeth by J. M. Reynolds donated to Confederation Centre, Charlottetown, by Frank Sobey in memory of his wife.

headed overseas, and we were running our stores with girls. One day my wife drove this large delivery truck for us. Our meat man, who couldn't drive, went along with her to deliver the orders.

"Rene could jump in and do anything. I suppose I caused her some headaches at times, but she was a wonderful girl to live with. She never nagged. We had a very happy life together."

Together, he and Irene had met Queen Elizabeth at the Confederation Centre of the Arts in Charlottetown in 1964. That was one of the best years of their lives. Frank was a founding director of the centre, and "Rene took a great interest in it. She always came to the Island with me when I attended the meetings." Moreover, "We were both very interested in royalty. We were loyal subjects." So now, twenty years later, in the season of his grief, this elderly grandson of a British soldier donated to the centre an elegant bronze bust of Her Majesty, in memory of his wife. The work was by Canadian sculptor John (Mac) Reynolds, who completed it after going to England for sittings with Queen Elizabeth.

Since the opening of the centre in 1964 with *Anne of Green Gables*, the show had played to packed houses every single summer, and now, in 1984, after the curtain had fallen on the thousandth showing of *Anne*, an audience of 1,200 witnessed the unveiling of the bust on stage. The Sobey family was out in force, along with friends from Pictou County and Halifax. "I know Rene would be very proud of this bust," Frank said later. "It will sit in the Confederation Room in the centre, I hope, indefinitely."

Following Irene's death, Frank drew comfort from lifelong friends in Pictou County, from his sons, and particularly from his daughter Diane. But his blood pressure was high, his ability to read declining, his fatigue increasing. "He has slowed down a lot," Donald said, "but, you know, he still enjoys getting into a business meeting. That's the one thing that revives him." He continued to attend all the directors' meetings of not only the Stellarton-based family companies but also Halifax Developments and the Sydney Steel Corporation.

Meanwhile, the empire he'd spent his life building relentlessly rolled ahead on all fronts. For the year that ended April 30, 1984, the consolidated revenues for Empire Company totalled $755 million, up almost $130 million from the figure for the same period in '83. Empire's equity had a book value of $71 million. Moreover, there was an unrealized capital gain on its publicly listed investments of $65 million above cost.

Empire and Sobey Leased Properties owned 36.8 per cent of the outstanding common shares of Halifax Developments Ltd. and, along with the Jodrey interests, controlled it. HDL's chief asset was the Scotia Square complex in the heart of Halifax, but it also owned half of Durham Leaseholds Limited. In March 1984 it bought the other half from the Toronto-based Oxford Development Group, and this meant that the Sobey and Jodrey interests now controlled the company (HDL) that owned not only Scotia Square but also, through Durham Leaseholds, the nearby Royal Bank building, the Canadian Imperial Bank of Commerce building, and the Delta Barrington hotel. "If you add it all up," Donald Sobey said, "it amounts to five large office towers, two hotels, three residential towers, and one of the largest downtown shopping malls in Canada. Scotia Square has almost three times as much shopping space as the Toronto-Dominion Centre in Toronto." By early 1984, HDL was carrying out major renovations in the mall.

"Those guys virtually *own* downtown Halifax!" a journalist marvelled after HDL bought out Oxford Development Group. He was talking about the Sobey and Jodrey families, and if his statement was an exaggeration, it was an understandable one. Nor was real estate all that HDL was up to. Through a subsidiary, it had begun to nibble and then gulp at Nova Scotia Savings and Loan Company, and by March 22, 1984, it was the beneficial owner of 36.4 per cent of the issued and outstanding common shares of NSSL. (Litigation over the ownership of some NSSL shares was pending.)

By the spring of '84, the Sobeys were negotiating with the Odeon theatre chain to buy still more movie theatres in the Maritimes. They were also launching a £5 million insurance business in London. Moreover, before the year was out Empire's subsidiary, Atlantic Shopping Centres Ltd., had purchased about $65 million worth of shopping centre assets throughout the Maritime provinces, increasing its size by over fifty per cent.

Meanwhile, Donald Sobey had led Empire into an investment to help save National Sea Products Ltd. from tumbling into government hands. National Sea, one of the world's biggest fishing companies, employed 7,000 workers in thirteen plants. It had assets of $300 million, but it also had debts of roughly $220 million. Among the debts were $75 million in loans from the Bank of Nova Scotia; and the bank, in the jargon of business, was threatening to "pull the plug".

While bankruptcy loomed, governments, banks, and private interests frantically tried to negotiate a restructuring of National Sea. Foremost among the private interests was Halifax broker David Hennigar, grandson of the late Roy Jodrey, who spoke for his family's Scotia Investments Ltd. "In December [1983], I was talking to Hennigar," Donald Sobey recalled, "and I said we might be interested in joining their effort to privatize National Sea. I said

Donald Sobey, President of Empire Company Limited, between meetings with National Sea Products Limited during the company's restructuring in early 1984.
(Canapress photo)

maybe we can get Empire to take some [shares], and we might put some in Halifax Developments." Donald now expressed the central fear of the Sobeys, the Jodreys, and much of the bluenose business community: "We simply felt it would be a disaster for Nova Scotia to have National Sea in government hands."

The Sobey support, he continued, gave Hennigar "additional impetus to put it across to the public and banks that this was a serious proposal, and from then on we co-operated on the deal." Donald was not only president of Empire but also a director of the Toronto-Dominion Bank, and he got the bank together with Hennigar. In the complicated restructuring that finally came about in February, the Toronto-Dominion played a crucial part. It agreed to buy $75 million of "financial difficulty" term preferred shares from a National Sea subsidiary, and this money went to pay off the Bank of Nova Scotia. That left Toronto-Dominion and the Royal Bank as the main bankers behind the restructured company.

The deal was so complicated, the *Globe and Mail* (Feb. 7, 1984) reported, that Hennigar said it had taken sixty-eight minutes simply to explain it to National Sea's restructuring committee. Basically, however, it involved the Toronto-Dominion purchase, purchases of preferred shares by the federal and provincial governments, and purchases by private interests – notably the Sobey-

Jodrey alliance – of some $15 million in common shares. "We are now in the process of offering that to the employees, and then to various suppliers and friends," Donald said in April. "We'll place in our own accounts what's left over."

Those sales, however, would not alter the fact that the new boss of National Sea was David Hennigar, chairman. For Scotia Investments now had 47 per cent of the company's common shares, and first rights to buy the federal government's interest. The Sobeys had owned a massive chunk of National Sea in the seventies, but the company had never offered them a directorship. They'd sold the stock during their assault on shares of Provigo, but now, seven years later, they again had a sizeable piece of the fish-packing giant. This time round they had a man on the board. It was, of course, Donald Sobey.

Two distinctions came to Frank Sobey in 1984, the year he turned eighty-two. Dalhousie University gave this grade-school drop-out an LL.D., his third honorary degree; and the Canadian Business Leadership Conference, established in 1979 by Junior Achievement of Canada, bestowed on him the greatest honour of his life. The conference named him a laureate of the Canadian Business Hall of Fame. He thus joined such giants of Canadian business history as Timothy Eaton, Sir Joseph Flavelle, Sir Herbert Holt, Hart Massey, Henry Birks, Samuel Bronfman, and Lord Thomson of Fleet. Laureates from the food industry include Sam Steinberg, W. Garfield Weston, and now Frank Sobey. Laureates from the Maritimes include Izaak Walton Killam, K. C. Irving, and now Frank Sobey.

Only a handful of the three dozen members of the Business Hall of Fame are still alive, and at the black-tie banquet in the Winnipeg Convention Centre on April 26, 1984, Frank was the only living man among those inducted. Close to a thousand guests paid $170 per plate to be there that night, and Knowlton Nash was the narrator for a kind of this-is-your-life slide show about Frank and his family.

In nominating Frank, New Brunswick industrialist Harrison

Frank Sobey with George Richardson and Royal Bank Chairman Rowland Frazee at his induction into the Canadian Business Hall of Fame, April 26, 1984.

McCain had written, "I can think of no other Maritimer, or, for that matter, Canadian, who is more deserving of this distinction." Now a horde of prominent Maritimers showed up in Winnipeg to prove they agreed. They included Robert Manuge, Dr. George Whitman, David Hennigar, Arthur Crockett, A. Garnet Brown, J. Gregor Fraser, and others from Pictou County, Halifax, and New Brunswick. Sobey executives James W. Gogan and William H. Richardson were there, and so, of course, was a platoon of Sobeys.

It's unlikely that a Canadian Business Hall of Fame banquet has ever witnessed such a display of family solidarity. The Sobey delegation included Frank's sister, his children, many of his children's children, a nephew, a niece, a whole passel of in-laws. Eighteen in all. "There were so many of us," his grandson Frank said, "that every time you phoned the hotel and asked for a Sobey, the operator started giggling."

At the end of a long evening, Frank told the crowd he was lucky to have been born at the start of an exciting century. He said he'd experienced the horse-and-buggy age, the automobile age, two world wars, the Great Depression, and the postwar boom. He'd lived on into the computer age and the space age - "and even into the age of deficit financing". Once again he expressed his lifelong conviction about the importance of good management, and then he mentioned all the Sobeys who were there that night to share with him another good moment in his life.

There could be no more impressive, living proof of the durability of the Sobey dynasty.

APPENDIX A

CORPORATE STRUCTURE OF EMPIRE COMPANY LIMITED

The following chart includes the names of the principal subsidiaries of Empire, their respective jurisdictions of incorporation, and the percentages of voting securities in such subsidiaries owned by Empire.

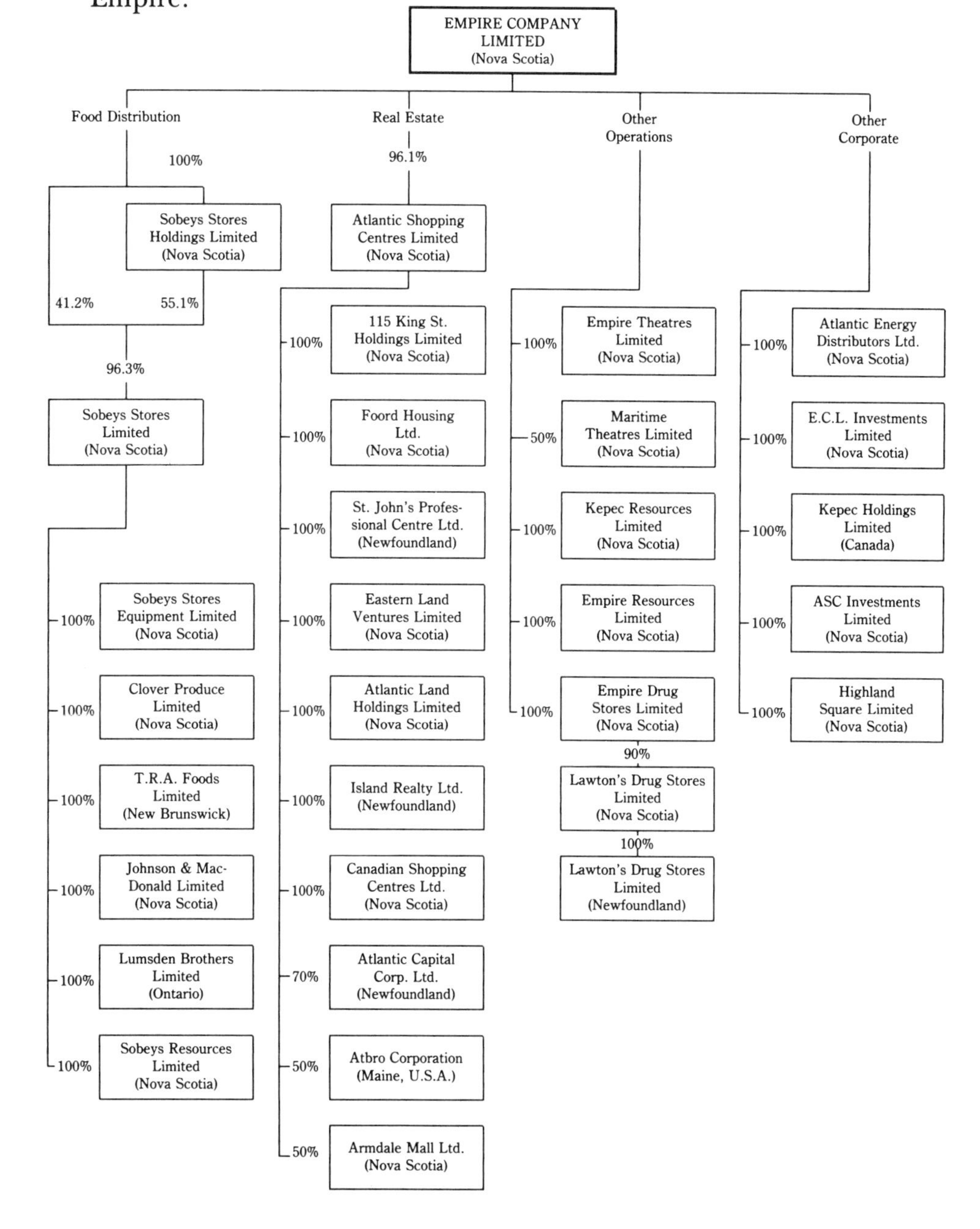

APPENDIX B

DIRECTORS AND OFFICERS OF EMPIRE COMPANY LIMITED

The name, municipality of residence, and *principal occupation* of each of the directors and officers of Empire are as follows:

Arthur Holmes Crockett
Toronto, Ontario
Director
Corporate Director

James Wilson Gogan
New Glasgow, Nova Scotia
Director, Executive Vice-President and Secretary
Executive Vice-President, Empire Company Limited

Robert William Manuge
Halifax, Nova Scotia
Director
Chairman, Manuge Galleries Limited

James Skiffington Murchie
New Glasgow, Nova Scotia
Director
President, Sobeys Stores Limited

Henry Burton Rhude
Halifax, Nova Scotia
Director
Chairman and Chief Executive Officer, Central Trust Company

John William Ritchie
Halifax, Nova Scotia
Director
President, Scotia Bond Company Limited

John William Sinclair
Pictou County, Nova Scotia
Director
Forestry Resources Technician, Province of Nova Scotia

David Frank Sobey
New Glasgow, Nova Scotia
Director and Treasurer
Deputy Chairman and Chief Executive Officer, Sobeys Stores Limited

Donald Rae Sobey
Stellarton, Nova Scotia
Director and President
President, Empire Company Limited

Frank Hoyse Sobey
Pictou County, Nova Scotia
Director and Chairman
Chairman, Empire Company Limited

John Robert Sobey
Stellarton, Nova Scotia
Director
Vice-President, Retail Operations, Sobeys Stores Limited

William MacDonald Sobey
Pictou County, Nova Scotia
Director and Vice-President
Chairman, Sobeys Stores Limited

William Herbert Richardson
Bedford, Nova Scotia
Vice-President
President and Chief Executive Officer, Lawton's Drug Stores Limited

APPENDIX C

DIRECTORS AND OFFICERS OF SOBEYS STORES LIMITED

Directors

Merritt G. Crawford
New Glasgow, Nova Scotia
Chairman
Atlantic Shopping Centres Limited

James W. Gogan
New Glasgow, Nova Scotia
Executive Vice-President
Empire Company Limited

William G. Lumsden
Burlington, Ontario
President and Chief Executive Officer
Lumsden Brothers Limited

Arthur R. Lundrigan
Corner Brook, Newfoundland
President
Lundrigans Limited

James L. Moody, Jr.
South Portland, Maine
Chairman and Chief Executive Officer
Hannaford Bros. Co.

James S. Murchie
New Glasgow, Nova Scotia
President
Sobeys Stores Limited

Henry B. Rhude
Halifax, Nova Scotia
President and Chief Executive Officer
Central Trust Company

J. William Ritchie
Halifax, Nova Scotia
President
Scotia Bond Company Limited

David F. Sobey
New Glasgow, Nova Scotia
Deputy Chairman and Chief Executive Officer
Sobeys Stores Limited

Donald R. Sobey
Stellarton, Nova Scotia
President
Empire Company Limited

Frank H. Sobey
Pictou County, Nova Scotia
Honorary Chairman
Sobeys Stores Limited

John R. Sobey
Stellarton, Nova Scotia
Vice-President, Retail Operations
Sobey Stores Limited

William M. Sobey
Pictou County, Nova Scotia
Chairman
Sobeys Stores Limited

Officers

Frank H. Sobey
Honorary Chairman

William M. Sobey
Chairman

David F. Sobey
Deputy Chairman and Chief Executive Officer

James S. Murchie
President

Donald F. Arsenault
Vice-President Retail Operations Newfoundland

Nigel F. Byars
Vice-President Finance, Treasurer, and Assistant Secretary

James F. Fitzpatrick
Vice-President Distribution

Frank J. Hickey
Vice-President Merchandising

John K. Lynn
Vice-President Personnel

Darrell M. Rushton
Vice-President Wholesale Operations

Gilbert J. Vienneau
Vice-President Corporate Marketing

Robert P. Dexter
Secretary

APPENDIX D

IN LATE 1970, Nova Scotia's new Liberal government undertook an extensive review of Industrial Estates Limited's record during the dozen years that Frank Sobey had headed it for Progressive Conservative governments. The results appeared in the Halifax *Chronicle-Herald* on January 7, 1971. IEL had approved $106,136,178 in assistance for the twenty-five outside firms that it had lured to the province; $4,352,200 for nine new Nova Scotia-owned operations; and a further $12,515,950 for expansions at twenty going concerns. The total was $123,004,328. In direct employment, the money had already created 3,586 new jobs and, thanks mostly to the recent agreement with Michelin Tire, this figure would shortly surpass 5,000. In the lists below, the bold type indicates companies that were still in business in 1983.

FIRMS FROM OUTSIDE NOVA SCOTIA (AND THEIR IEL FINANCING):

Anil (Canada) Limited ($15,916,866); **Atlantic Cans Limited** ($2,298,780); Bonda Meal and Oil Limited ($235,000); Buckingham Mills Limited ($1,056,000); **Canada Cement Company Ltd.** ($8,000,000); **Canada Envelope Company** ($129,548); Canadian Motor Industries Ltd., ($1,400,000); Canso Chemicals Limited ($6,167,084); **Chester Plastics Limited** ($489,400); **Crossley Karastan Carpet Mills Ltd.** ($4,427,000); Donato Faini & Figli (Canada) Ltd. ($400,000); **Dover Mills Limited** ($1,900,000); General Instrument of Canada Ltd. ($2,900,000); **Genu Products (Canada) Ltd.** ($140,800); **Huyck Canada Limited** ($1,500,000); **C. M. McLean Limited** ($549,500); **Michelin Tires Mfg. Co. of Can. Ltd.** ($50,000,000); **Phillips Cables Limited** ($1,510,000); **Polymer International (N.S.) Ltd.** ($1,835,000) ; Pyrominerals Limited ($3,300,000); **Simmons Limited** ($100,000); **Surrette Battery Company** ($666,000); **Swift Canadian Company Limited** ($115,000); **Volvo (Canada) Ltd.** ($1,000,200); **Zenith Electroplating Limited** ($100,000).

NEW NOVA SCOTIA PLANTS (AND THEIR IEL FINANCING):

Atlantic Galvanizers Limited, Amherst ($205,000); Atlantic Wood Products Limited, Weymouth ($175,000); Fristamat Limited, Canning ($52,000); **Industrial Marine Products Ltd.**, Dartmouth ($449,000); K. & W. Enterprises Limited, Liverpool ($271,400); **Mic Mac Egg Processors Limited**, Port Williams ($172,800); **Oland's Brewers Limited**, Halifax ($250,000); Producers Milk Products Ltd., Halifax ($177,000); Yarmouth Industrial Fabrics Ltd., Yarmouth ($2,600,000).

EXPANDED NOVA SCOTIA PLANTS (AND THEIR IEL FINANCING):

Angel Manufacturing & Supply, North Sydney ($66,000); **Atlantic Bridge Company**, Lunenburg ($1,381,750); **Eastech Limited**, Windsor ($140,000); Eastern Manufacturing Co. Ltd., New Glasgow ($354,000); **Federal Products Limited**, Truro ($236,000); **Glasgow Metals Limited**, New Glasgow ($65,000); **M. W. Graves Limited**, Berwick ($644,000); **Guildford's Limited**, Dartmouth ($558,000); Hermes Electronics Limited, Dartmouth ($1,157,000); Industrial Shipping Company, Mahone Bay; **Lunenburg Sea Products Limited**, Lunenburg ($3,476,000); **Marden Wild of Canada Limited**, Amherst ($250,000); **Marine Colloids Limited**, Toney River ($31,000); **Maritime Paper Products Limited**, Burnside ($2,177,000); Rolph-Clark-Stone Eastern Ltd., Halifax ($449,000); **W. H. Schwartz & Sons Limited**, Halifax ($850,000); Springhill Homes Limited, Springhill ($73,000); **Stanfield's Limited**, Truro ($200,000); **Tibbett's Paints Company**, Trenton ($210,000); Wilson's Truck Body Shop, Truro ($198,200).

Some clients came back to IEL for further financing for plant expansions. Notable among these companies were Volvo Canada, Anil Canada, Crossley Karastan Carpet Mills, National Sea Products, and Maritime Cans (later, Atlantic Cans).

By 1970, a year after Frank Sobey retired from IEL, a total of sixteen companies had ceased to operate in plants IEL had helped to finance. This, however, did not mean sixteen "failures". Though the Nova Scotia government had taken over the two most expensive disappointments - Clairtone and Deuterium of Canada - other companies had moved into most of the plants that the original clients had abandoned.

BIBLIOGRAPHY

BOOKS

Beck, J. Murray. *The Government of Nova Scotia*. Toronto, University of Toronto Press, 1957.

Beckman, Theodore N., and Herman C. Nolen. *The Chain Store Problem*. New York, McGraw-Hill Book Company, Inc., 1938.

Bergman, Andrew. *We're in the Money*. New York, New York University Press, 1971.

Bird, Isabella Lucy. *The Englishwoman in America*. London, John Murray, 1856.

Bird, Will R. *These Are the Maritimes*. Toronto, Ryerson Press, 1959.

Brand, Dr. Norman. *Modern Supermarket Operation*. New York, Fairchild Publications, 1963.

Broadfoot, Barry. *Ten Lost years: 1929–1939*. Toronto, Doubleday Canada, 1973.

Brooks, John. *The Autobiography of American Business*. New York, Doubleday, 1974.

Bruce, Harry. *RA: The Story of Roy Jodrey, Entrepreneur*. Toronto, McClelland and Stewart, 1979.

Burton, C. L. *A Sense of Urgency*. Toronto, Clarke Irwin, 1952.

Cameron, James M. *Industrial History of the New Glasgow District*. New Glasgow, N.S., Hector Publishing Co., 1960.

——. *Political Pictonians, 1767–1967*. Published by the author, 1966.

——. *Pictonians in Arms*. Published by the author, with the University of New Brunswick, 1968, 1969.

——. *Pictou County's History*. Printed by Kentville Publishing, Kentville, N.S.; published by Pictou County Historical Society, N.S., 1972.

——. *More About New Glasgow*. Printed by Kentville Publishing Co., Kentville, N.S., 1974.

——. *The Pictonian Colliers*. Halifax, Nova Scotia Museum, 1974.

——. *About Pictonians*. Hantsport, Lancelot Press, N.S., undated.

Campbell, D., and R. A. MacLean. *Beyond the Atlantic Roar: A Study of the Nova Scotia Scots*. Toronto, McClelland and Stewart, 1974.

Carson, Gerald. *The Old Country Store*. New York, Oxford University Press, 1954.

Crane, David. *A Dictionary of Canadian Economics*. Edmonton, Hurtig Publishers, 1980.

Cross, Jennifer. *The Supermarket Trap*. Bloomington, Indiana University Press, 1971.

Dennis, Clara. *More About Nova Scotia*. Toronto, Ryerson Press, 1937.

Dorrington, Aubrey. *Stellarton*. Publisher unidentified, undated.

Dunn, Charles W. *Highland Settler: A Portrait of the Scottish Gael in Nova Scotia*. Toronto, University of Toronto Press, 1953.

George, Roy E. *The Life and Times of Industrial Estates Limited*. Halifax, Institute of Public Affairs, 1974.

Grant, Reverend Robert. *East River Worthies*. New Glasgow, Scotia Printers, Ltd., undated.

Halliwell, Leslie. *Halliwell's Film Guide: A Survey of 8,000 English-Language Movies*. London, Granada Pub., 1977.

——. *Halliwell's Filmgoer's Companion*. London, Granada Pub., 1977.

Hawkins, Marjorie, Hector L. MacKenzie, and John MacQuarrie. *Gairloch, Pictou County, N.S.* Publisher unidentified, 1977.

Hayward, Walter S., and Percival White. *Chain Stores: Their Management and Operation*. New York, McGraw-Hill Book Co., Inc., 1928.

Hopkins, Garth. *The Rise and Fall of a Business Empire: Clairtone*. Toronto, McClelland and Stewart, 1978.

Horn, Michiel. *The Dirty Thirties: Canadians in The Great Depression*. Toronto, Copp Clark, 1972.

Kuhns, William. *Movies in America*. Publisher unidentified, 1972.

Lebhar, Godfrey. *Chain Stores in America*. New York, Chain Store Publishing Corporation, 1963.

Logan, John Daniel. *Pictou Poets: A Treasury of Verse in Gaelic and English . . .* Pictou, N.S., Pictou Advocate, 1923.

Lucas, Rex A. *Men in Crisis: A Study of a Mine Disaster*. New York, Basic Books, Inc., 1969.

MacDonald, H. M., ed. *The Clarsach: An Anthology of Scottish Verse*. Toronto, Copp Clark Co., 1955.

MacLaren, George. *The Pictou Book: Stories of Our Past*. New Glasgow, N.S., The Hector Publishing Co., Ltd., 1954.

Maclean, Reverend Alexander. *The Story of the Kirk in Nova Scotia*. Pictou, N.S., Pictou Advocate, 1911.

MacPhie, Reverend J. P. *Pictonians at Home and Abroad*. Boston, Pinkham Press, 1914.

MacQuarrie, John R. *Malagash Salt*. Published under auspices of The North Cumberland Historical Society, N.S., 1975, 1981.

Mahoney, Tom, and Leonard Sloane. *The Great Merchants*. New York, Harper & Row, 1966.

Markin, Rom J. *The Supermarket: An Analysis of Growth, Development and Change*. Pullman, Washington State University Press, 1968.

Mast, Gerald. *A Short History of the Movies*. New York, Pegasus, 1971.

Newman, Peter C. *Flame of Power*. Toronto, McClelland and Stewart, 1959.

——. *The Canadian Establishment, Volume One*. Toronto, McClelland and Stewart, 1975.

——. *The Acquisitors*. Toronto, McClelland and Stewart, 1981.

Nova Scotia Relief Map Directory, 1931.

Orwell, George. *The Road to Wigan Pier*. London, Secker & Warburg, 1959 (c1937).

Patterson, Frank H. *John Patterson, the Founder of Pictou Town*. Truro, N.S., Truro Printing & Publishing, 1955.

Patterson, Reverend George. *A History of the County of Pictou, Nova Scotia*. Montreal, Dawson Brothers, 1877.

Rose, Clifford. *Four Years With the Demon Rum, 1925-1929*. Fredericton, Acadiensis Press, N.B., 1980.

Roy, James A. *The Scot and Canada*. Toronto, McClelland and Stewart, 1947.

Sherwood, Roland H. *Pictou Parade*. Sackville, N.B., Tribune Press, 1945.

——. *Pictou Pioneers*. Hantsport, Lancelot Press, N.S., 1973.

Spedon, Andrew Learmont. *Rambles Among the Blue-Noses*. Montreal, John Lovell, 1863.

Stevens, Geoffrey. *Stanfield*. Toronto, McClelland and Stewart, 1973.

Stewart, Walter. *Hard to Swallow*. Toronto, Macmillan of Canada, 1974.

Thorp, Margaret Farrand. *America at the Movies*. New Haven, Yale University Press, 1939.

MEMOIRS

Rutherford, Jane MacKay. *I Came from Pictou County*. Ottawa, unpublished, 1975.

PAMPHLETS

Cameron, James M. *Tram Cars in East Pictou*. Kentville, N.S., Printed by Kentville Publishing, 1973.

Logan, John Daniel. *Canada's Champion Regimental Band*. Pictou, N.S., Pictou Advocate Printing Co., 1916.

Williams, Lawson. *A Brief History of Stellarton*. Prepared for the Diamond Jubilee Committee of the town, 1964.

Historic Pictou County, circa 1968.

Industrial Opportunity in the East River Valley, County of Pictou, Nova Scotia, Canada. New Glasgow Board of Trade, 1948.

Journal of Education. Semi-annual supplement to report of the Superintendent of Education for Nova Scotia, October 1917.

Letters of Reverend Norman McLeod, 1835-51. Bulletin of the Public Archives of Nova Scotia, Vol. II, No. 1, 1939.

"Marching-On" Through Time with the Soldier. Halifax, The Army Museum, Halifax Citadel, undated.

Nova Scotia for Beauty and Business. Publisher unidentified. Introduction by Beatrice M. Hay Shaw, 1923.

Nova Scotia's Industrial Centre, New Glasgow, Stellarton, Westville, Trenton. Issued under approval of councils of New Glasgow, Stellarton, Westville, Trenton, 1916.

Nova Scotia, The Land of Evangeline and the Tourist's Paradise. Yarmouth Steamship Company, 1893.

Where to Stay in Nova Scotia. Halifax, Government of Nova Scotia, 1938.

REPORTS

Cann, D. B., and R. E. Wickland. *Soil Survey of Pictou County*. Truro, N.S., Canada Department of Agriculture, 1950.

Cheasley, Clifford Henry. *The Chain Store Movement in Canada*. Montreal, McGill University Economic Studies, No. 17, circa 1930.

Graham, John F. *Provincial Municipal Fiscal Relations and Economic Development in a Low-Income Province: Nova Scotia*. Thesis for Ph.D., Columbia University, 1959.

Palmer, John R. *The Role of the Federal Deficit in the Economic Growth of Depressed Regions: A Case Study of Nova Scotia, 1950-1965*. Halifax, Institute of Public Affairs.

Wood, K. S., and J. Palmer. *Natural Resources of Northeastern Nova Scotia*. Halifax, Institute of Public Affairs, 1970.

Annual reports, R. B. Seeton & Co., Ltd., food wholesalers. Halifax, 1938, 1939.

An Industrial Survey of Pictou County. Canadian National Railways, August 1958, revised July 1962.

Report of the Royal Commission on Price Spreads of Food Products. Ottawa, 1959.

ARTICLES

Beattie, Earle. "Barnum of the Supermarkets." *Maclean's*, Aug. 6, 1955.

Bodsworth, Fred C. "Store With a Million Salesmen." *Maclean's*, Nov. 1, 1948.

——. "He Knows His Groceries." *Maclean's*, Nov. 15, 1948.

Bradfield, Michael. "Michelin in Nova Scotia." *Canadian Forum*, December/January, 1981.

Bruce, Harry. "The Collector: Fine Art for Fun and Profit." *Axiom*, March 1976.

Campbell, George S. "Business Conditions in Nova Scotia." *Journal of Commerce*, September 1977.

Foster, Elizabeth MacDonald. "The Backwoods of America." *Dalhousie Review*, April 1948.

French, C. V., and Ralph Allen. "How I sell pretty nearly everything." *Maclean's*, Nov. 21, 1959.

Gray, F. W. "Evolution of St. Lawrence Market." *Journal of Commerce*, September 1927.

Gray, Francis William. "The Saga of a Coalfield." *Dalhousie Review*, April 1944.

Innes, Col. Robert. "Various, Rich, Abundant, Her Resources." *Journal of Commerce*, September 1927.

Kimber, Stephen. "Michelin Tire Rolls On." *Financial Post Magazine*, April 26, 1980.

——. "The Selling of Nova Scotia." *Financial Post Magazine*, Nov. 8, 1980.

MacGregor, Hon. A. "First Things in Pictou County." Publisher unidentified, 1920.

Morris, Jan. "Dover's Soul." *The Guardian*, Aug. 9, 1981.

Ross, Alexander. "Salvation by Surgery." *Canadian Business*, March 1981.

Walker, Dean. Interview with Antoine Turmel. *Executive*, September 1980.

——. Interview with Donald Sobey, *Executive*, February 1984.

"Nova Scotia's Opportunities." *Journal of Commerce*, September 1927.

"100 Years of Coal Mining in Nova Scotia." *Journal of Commerce*, September 1927.

To spare readers from wrestling with footnotes, I named and dated my printed sources in the body of the text. But under "Articles", above, I singled out only those that were specially useful. I saw no point in listing here the dozens of periodicals and newspapers (ranging from the *Presbyterian Witness* to the Hollywood *Citizen News*, from *Progressive Grocer* to the *New York Times*) that the text had already identified. Nor did I feel it necessary to list the annual reports of Sobey companies I pored over, or each prospectus for a stock or bond issue that I examined.

HARRY BRUCE

INDEX